THE BIBLE
IN THE
BALANCE

Books by the author . . .

The Battle for the Bible
The Harper Study Bible
When You Pray
The World, the Flesh and the Devil
Handbook of Christian Truth
Missionary Principles and Practice
The Bible in the Balance

THE BIBLE IN THE BALANCE

Harold Lindsell

ZONDERVAN
PUBLISHING HOUSE
OF THE ZONDERVAN CORPORATION | GRAND RAPIDS, MICHIGAN 49506

THE BIBLE IN THE BALANCE
Copyright © 1979 by The Zondervan Corporation
Grand Rapids, Michigan

Library of Congress Cataloging in Publication Data

Lindsell, Harold, 1913-
  The Bible in the balance.

  Includes index.
  1. Lindsell, Harold, 1913-   The battle for the
Bible.   2. Bible—Inspiration.   3. Bible—Evidences,
authority, etc.   I. Title.
BS480.L553L56   220.1'3   79-4350
ISBN 0-310-27690-X

Printed in the United States of America

Contents

THE BIBLE
IN THE
BALANCE

1

The Introduction:
Reviewing the Past

The Battle for the Bible appeared in print in the spring of 1976. *Time* magazine featured it in the religion section shortly thereafter. In a few months' time the book elicited national and international responses which ranged from enthusiastic approval to intense opposition.

The book was reviewed in major journals and periodicals. In them the opponents of biblical inerrancy voiced their objections vigorously. The journals of the Southern Baptist Seminary in Louisville, Kentucky, and Southwestern Baptist Seminary in Fort Worth, Texas, for example, carried critical appraisals, and dissent was registered in other periodicals.

This writer has published fifteen books through the years, but no other work has drawn such a response through the mails. More letters concerning this book were received than for all of the other published works combined. The mail was supportive, encouraging, and appreciative, except for two or three letters at most. Those who reacted negatively chose to make their opinions known in other ways.

A number of interesting chain reactions occurred following the release of the book. Some denominations and institutions changed their doctrinal statements because they were imprecise with regard to inerrancy. They strengthened them considerably to offset the possibility of misunderstanding as to their institutional posture and image. The National Association of Evangelicals made biblical trustworthiness the theme of its annual meeting in 1977. The *Wall Street Journal,* a business daily newspaper which normally limits its coverage to financial and business matters, ran a feature story on its editorial page relative to the question.

Fuller Theological Seminary responded in a number of ways. Dr. Hubbard gave a speech. One issue of the seminary's *Theology, News and Notes* was devoted fully to the issue. Word Books published a paperback volume titled *Biblical Authority* in 1977 which was edited by Jack Rogers of the Fuller faculty and had in it essays by him, David Hubbard, Paul Rees, Bernard Ramm, Berkeley Mickelsen, Clark Pinnock, and others. This was responded to by other evangelicals in a book titled *The Foundation of Biblical Authority* which was published in paperback by Zondervan.

The International Council on Biblical Inerrancy was organized (This writer had no direct part in its creation although he now serves on the Advisory Board). The council includes scholars like James M. Boice, Francis A. Schaeffer, James I. Packer, Kenneth Kantzer, John Gerstner, Edmund P. Clowney, Robert D. Preus, Gleason L. Archer, and Robert C. Sproul. The Advisory Board roster includes Hudson Armerding, John W. Alexander, Henri A. G. Blocher, W. A. Criswell, Elisabeth Elliot, James Kennedy, Charles Feinberg, Fred H. Klooster, Roger Nicole, Harold John Ockenga, Raymond Ortlund, Lorne Sanny, G. Aiken Taylor, Larry L. Walker, and John F. Walvoord among others. Its stated purpose is "to take a united stand in elucidating, vindicating and applying the truth of Biblical inerrancy as an integral element in the authority of Scripture."

The *Christian Century* carried a critical article against biblical inerrancy written by Donald Dayton of the North Park Theological Seminary. The Union Theological Seminary, the New York City-based liberal standard-bearer for neoorthodoxy when Reinhold Niebuhr, John Bennett, and Henry Pitney Van Dusen were there, devoted the Winter 1977 issue of its *Union Seminary Quarterly Review* to evangelicals. Of particular note was an article titled "Biblical Hermeneutics: The Academic Language of Evangelical Identity," which was written by Gerald T. Sheppard, a graduate of Fuller Seminary. This will be referred to later. More recently, the Westminster Press published a volume titled *The Debate about the Bible* by Stephen T. Davis, associate professor of philosophy and religion at Claremont (California) Men's College. In this book he took issue with Francis Schaeffer and myself, arguing for infallibility in matters of faith and practice but not in other matters. The introduction was written by Clark Pinnock. At the end of his book Dr. Davis said that for evangelicals "our task is to convince people not that the Bible is inerrant but that it is the only infallible rule of faith and practice." And of this book and of the difference between infallibility and inerrancy more will be said later.

This brief summary of the developments indicates the great interest in the subject of biblical inerrancy. Later on more details of reader response to *The Battle for the Bible* will be considered and specific rejoinders given to the questions and objections which have surfaced. In the meantime I must repeat what I think to be the basic questions under consideration.

The Major Thrust of *The Battle for the Bible*

The Battle for the Bible asked two fundamental or foundational questions: (1) What is the source of our religious knowledge; i.e., from where do we get answers to life's important questions— such as Where did I come from? Who am I? What is the purpose of life? and What happens to me when I die? (2) Is the source from which I get the answers to my basic questions reliable—i.e., does the source tell me the truth?

The replies to these two questions were as follows. First, the foundation for the Christian faith lies in the two Words of God, the Word of God incarnate which is Jesus Christ who is very God of very God (as stated in the Chalcedon creed), and the Word of God written, which is the Bible. The only Jesus the church can know is the Jesus of the Word of God written. Without the Bible there can be no knowledge of the Son of God and the Savior of the world. Therefore the written Word of God is foundational to the Christian faith.

The second response was that the written Word of God is trustworthy in all its parts. The Bible is authoritative, and as the authoritative Word of God it is revelatory. God has made known to men that which they could not discover any other way. God has revealed Himself in nature but man cannot find Him through nature. If God is to be known, He must reveal Himself. He has done this through special revelation, which consists in the incarnation of the Son of God and the revelation of that Son through the written Word. The written Word is inspired, i.e., it was composed by chosen men through whom the Holy Spirit worked to get written what God wanted written. And this inspired Word of God is inerrant because the prophets and apostles labored under the inspiration of the Holy Spirit who kept them from making errors even as He commanded their gifts and abilities. The Bible is the Word of God and the word of men. But as the New Hampshire Confession of Faith says, "it has God for its author." It is thus the Word of God.

If the Bible contains both truth and error, it differs from no other book in the world. And if truth is mixed with error, who is to decide which parts are true and which parts are not true? The presuppositions of *The Battle for the Bible* thus were twofold: the Bible is the source of man's religious knowledge, and the source of this knowledge is trustworthy in all its parts. But why do we believe this latter presupposition?

Basic Theses

1. *The Bible Teaches Inerrancy*

The Battle for the Bible asserted that the doctrine of biblical inerrancy is taught in Scripture. Just as justification by faith, the vicarious atonement, the deity of Christ, and other doctrines are derived from the Bible, so the doctrine of biblical inerrancy comes from the teaching of the Word of God.

Those who object to biblical inerrancy have sought to distinguish between infallibility and inerrancy. In the book I stated that these words are synonymous. Professor Davis, in his recent book, *The Debate about the Bible,* states the position this way: Infallibility consists in the truthfulness of Scripture about matters of faith and practice; inerrancy includes all the phenomena of Scripture, not just matters of faith and practice. Therefore Dr. Davis believes the Bible is infallible but not inerrant. This raises the question about the teaching of Scripture concerning its own truthfulness. *The Battle for the Bible* asserted that Scripture teaches inerrancy. Paul in Timothy says that *all* Scripture is God-breathed. No Scripture is excluded from this definition. All Scripture is *profitable.* Error cannot be profitable. Thus all Scripture must be true.

Peter says that the prophetic word came as "men moved by

the Holy Spirit spoke from God" (2 Peter 1:21). Holy men and the Holy Spirit were conjoined together to write the Word of God. Holy men can err, but the Holy Spirit cannot. It is His work that guarantees the truthfulness of what holy men wrote.

Jesus said that "scripture cannot be broken" (John 10:35), and in that statement He certainly excluded nothing from the Old Testament to which He was bearing witness. His word that Scripture is unbreakable teaches us that inerrancy is true. He also said that before a jot or tittle could be removed from the law or the prophets heaven and earth must first pass away (Matt. 5:17, 18). This strong statement can be understood to mean that Scripture is trustworthy in all its parts. Of course, there are many other places in the Bible where similar claims for trustworthiness are made.

2. *The Church Has Believed Inerrancy Through the Centuries*

I propounded a second thesis: The church through the ages has believed and taught that the Bible is inerrant. This has been true of the Orthodox churches, the Roman Catholic Church, and the Protestant churches. One must ask, of course, whether the churches through the ages could have been mistaken about this matter. Since the New Testament states that the Holy Spirit leads God's people, it appears highly improbable that inerrancy would have been the consistent testimony of the church through the ages if this view is false. Just as trinitarianism, the deity of Christ, the virgin birth, and the bodily resurrection of Jesus from the dead have been and still are taught, so we can conclude that the view of the Bible entertained by the church for two millennia is likewise true. Later in this book, this issue will be probed from the perspective of objections which have been raised.

3. *The Changing Scene*

My third thesis was that biblical inerrancy has become the focal point for defection in the modern church. Just as the christological controversies stirred the early church, and as justification by faith alone lay at the heart of the Protestant Reformation, so the trustworthiness of the Bible lies at the center of the theological struggle today. This is not to say there were no opponents of biblical inerrancy for the first eighteen centuries of the Christian era. But it does mean that opponents of inerrancy constituted a small minority and the issue itself was not the centerpiece of any great controversy.

I alleged that the churches have been infiltrated in the last two centuries by a growing number of people who claim the Bible is errant. This is indisputable, if for no other reason than that theological liberalism and neoorthodoxy of the past century have openly and unequivocally torn Scripture asunder. But I did more than this. I claimed that present-day evangelicalism is now being infiltrated by those who hold to an errant Bible. I pinpointed instances where this is true. I spoke of individuals, institutions, and denominations established on a base of biblical inerrancy who now have in their midst those who disavow biblical inerrancy.

I even went further than that. I claimed that once anyone departs from a commitment to biblical inerrancy he opens the door to a disavowal either in principle or in practice of other important doctrines of the Christian faith. In other words, it is virtually impossible for anyone who, in the beginning, limits biblical inerrancy or infallibility to matters of faith and practice, to hold this view consistently or persistently over a period of time. I presented evidence from the writings of some who later abrogated their commitment to infallibility in matters of faith and practice after first having departed from a commitment to biblical inerrancy. I did not then, and I do not now, claim it is impossible for an occasional individual to remain theologically faithful to the basic corpus of Christian truth except for inerrancy. But I must make it clear that anyone who denies biblical inerrancy by that decision has already fallen into a christological error. Since Jesus taught that Scripture cannot be broken, whoever denies what Jesus taught has a defective Christology. In other words, it is impossible to deny inerrancy without immediately and automatically falling into a christological error as well.

I went still further and prophesied that once inerrancy is abandoned it inevitably results in further concessions and points in the direction of apostasy. I gave as a specific example the case of the Unitarian Universalist Association which is apostate. It is not a Christian church, and cannot be a Christian church. That is one reason why even the National Council of Churches and the World Council of Churches do not number the Unitarian Universalist Association among their member churches. Two points must be made in this connection.

I recognize how difficult it is for a Baptist, a Presbyterian, a Lutheran, a Methodist, or an Episcopalian to admit the possibility that his church could become apostate. I can only point out that it has happened, and I can only specify the signs which suggest it is happening among some of the denominations around the world today. It is difficult to say when a particular church has become apostate. But even as Israel apostatized and as New England Congregationalism apostatized so can churches apostatize today.

The second point is that there still may be true believers in churches which are defective or even apostate. I would not wish to say that no member of an apostate church can be saved. I must assert, however, that whoever believes what an apostate denomination professes and teaches cannot be saved, just as Muslims and Buddhists cannot be saved. But there may be some among them who believe differently from what the denomination professes. They would be inconsistent, of course. There would be no credible reason for them to remain within the fellowship of such a church. If a person who trusts Christ, inconsistent though he or she may be, is a member of an apostate body, that person is saved despite membership in the apostate body.

4. Who Is an Evangelical?

Perhaps the most complex and perplexing question I addressed deals with the definition of who is and who is not an evangelical. This particular discussion brought forth loud dissent and raised the hackles of some who wish to be called evangelical despite their denial of inerrancy. I will postpone further discussion of this question until later, but I will not avoid it. Suffice it to say for the moment that it is an important item on the agenda and requires further elaboration in response to the negative reactions occasioned by the intimation that those who deny inerrancy cannot really be evangelical. I will discuss the issue fully.

Objections to *The Battle for the Bible*

Here I will speak only of general objections to my book. Later I will speak specifically about objections raised by particular individuals and will indicate what their objections are. But at the outset it is important to say an explanatory word about some of them. The list must include what the critics failed to do and say as well as what they did do and say. I need not address myself to the people who agreed with the theses I adduced, but I will speak of certain nonreactions which are significant.

1) No one has produced evidence to show that my basic claim, that the evangelical camp has been infiltrated with the noninerrancy viewpoint, is untrue. Indeed the opposite has happened. A number of people who claim to be evangelicals have openly affirmed an inerrancy or infallibility limited to matters of faith and practice.

2) My book did not show how deep or how pervasive the shift against inerrancy really is among evangelicals. The responses to the book indicate that my basic claim was conservative. There are more evidences of departure from inerrancy than I was aware of.

3) There are those who say that to raise the issue of inerrancy is wrong in principle and perverse in intention. Some have intimated that spite rather than conviction lies at the root of the matter. This, of course, is a judgment on the heart for which there is no answer. God and God alone at last must judge the intentions of the heart.

4) It has been said that to raise the issue of inerrancy is to be divisive. This requires some sort of response. The first and most obvious response is that I did not create the problem; I only drew attention to its existence. Those who hold to a viewpoint which contradicts the historic position of Christendom, and their denominational doctrinal statements as well as those of their educational institutions, are the ones who have brought about the new reality. On the other hand, I do not run away from the fact that there is a sense in which raising the issue *is* divisive. If to stand for the truth of Scripture is divisive, then I am divisive. So be it. And if a Christian must

choose between theological compromise, which will hurt both the faith and believers who are subverted by error, or silence, inaction, and consent to error, then the answer is plain enough.

What I have done, even though in good conscience, is wrong if it can be shown that (a) evangelicalism has never insisted on inerrancy (which is patently untrue), or that (b) it is wrong to divide evangelicals even though heresy lies at the root of the division. I think the conclusion is clear.

5) A number of people have been embarrassed by the book. I called attention to their deviations. Embarrassment was inevitable. I suspect I might be angry myself, given similar circumstances. No one likes being brought before the tribunal of truth, even when the intention is remedial and the hope is entertained that the surfacing of truth will produce reformation and renewal. It involves the necessity of facing the situation openly and honestly. If the truth of my allegations is acknowledged, certain inevitable consequences flow from the acknowledgment. It may cost the recipient the loss of support, confidence, and rapport with his constituency. It usually requires an explanation and some sort of response to offset the negative reactions. I do not see how embarrassment can be avoided, except by unpardonable silence.

6) The assertion has been made that unity will be fractured by my book. It raises the old question of the peace and the purity of the church. This usually comes down to the question of whether a Christian group, be it a denomination, an institution, or a parachurch operation should ever have its peace fractured. The answer depends upon one's opinion about the body as an inclusivist organism. In other words, is there anything in the Christian faith of such magnitude that its denial is a cause for division? For example, can a church include in its fellowship theists and atheists? I can only say that when the purity of the church or group is the issue, then peace must play a secondary role. Peace at the expense of theological purity means a denial of what is foundational to the existence of the body.

Certainly the peace of the body should not be disturbed by differences of opinion about inconsequential items. But if the issue is of signal importance, there is no choice. One must defend the purity of the body even though the peace of the body will be disturbed as a consequence. When the physician discovers an incurable cancer in the patient's body, he must disturb the peace of the body by radical surgery to remove the cancer. This figure is apt with regard to the Christian body when it has been infected with theological or spiritual cancer.

7) The charge has been leveled that my book was written lovelessly; that it was polemical. If I was or am lacking in love, I can only apologize and hope to do better in this volume. But when it comes to the question of irenics and polemics another picture emerges. I tried to be irenic. I may have been polemic. In either case there is room for both the irenical and the polemical in church history. And when the battle wages hot, charges and countercharges often become the common coin of the day. I will show that those who object to the viewpoint I adhere to have themselves said some rather bitter things. I realize how offensive my allegations must be to them. And I can appreciate how sanctification can be challenged when responding to allegations we dislike.

The other side of the coin with respect to love must be presented. We are commanded to love our enemies. And if this be true, we are surely to love those who are not our enemies, but with whom we are in disagreement. Love, however, is not the only attribute of God. He is holy, just, and righteous as well. The love of God cannot annul His other attributes. All of them are coordinate with each other. None cancels out the others, and all of them together function without disagreement or confusion. One of the attributes of God has to do with divine anger. Jonathan Edwards preached his famous sermon, "Sinners in the Hands of an Angry God." He was biblical when he did this. It is the spurning of the love of God that produces the anger of God. God so loved the world that He gave His only Son. But when the gracious offer in Jesus is spurned, then the offender experiences the wrath of God rather than the love of God. The wrath of God is a subject often slighted by some who have a rather unbiblical view of the love of God.

The apostle Paul was not loveless when he took issue with Peter over the question of circumcision. He says: "But when Peter came to Antioch, I opposed him to his face, because he stood condemned" (Gal. 2:11). Obviously Peter was wrong about circumcision, and clearly even an apostle could be wrong when he was not writing Scripture. Paul pronounced judgment on his fellow apostle and went so far as to say that "Barnabas was carried away by their insincerity" (Gal. 2:13). These are hard words, but it would be imprudent to suggest that Paul who spoke so harshly did not love Peter. Indeed, he manifested the deepest love when he provided the correction Peter needed. Love demanded that something be done to counter Peter's error.

Toward the end of his life Paul stood before Ananias the high priest, although he did not know that he was the high priest. When Ananias commanded that Paul be struck the apostle said to him: "God shall strike you, you whitewashed wall! Are you sitting to judge me according to the law, and yet contrary to the law you order me to be struck?" (Acts 23:3). Did this mean that Paul was defective in his love?

Jesus called the Pharisees hypocrites, fools, blind, serpents, generations of vipers, murderers, and persecutors (Matt. 23:1-39). Surely speaking the truth is not in itself loveless. Did not the Savior's heart bleed for these people and did He not die to redeem them too? Saul of Tarsus in his opposition to Jesus was one of those Pharisees who later consented to Stephen's death. And Jesus died for him and saved him. Jude spoke some hard words about those who apostatized. Paul likewise spoke hard words when he described what some people will be like in the last days. Moreover in the case of Alexander the coppersmith he said: "(he) did me great harm; the Lord will requite him for his deeds" (2 Tim. 4:14).

One of the most telling words of Paul in Scripture comes from the passage in Timothy on biblical inspiration. All Scripture is profitable "for reproof, for correction" (2 Tim. 3:16). Sometimes reproof and correction should be sweet; sometimes it should be stern; and still other times it must include a word of judgment. Again and again the apostle Paul made a defense for himself and for his actions. If he was called upon to defend himself, how much more should we be willing not only to defend ourselves, but also to defend the written Word of God against attack and disbelief.

The Present Need

I am not unhappy that *The Battle for the Bible* has produced a fallout. Far more attention has been directed to it and to the viewpoint it expounds than I anticipated. There is deep interest in the question and there is need for ongoing dialogue. The International Council on Biblical Inerrancy is planning the production of a rather extensive literature on inerrancy. This program is slated to take a decade. Some who are involved are older and some younger members of the evangelical community. But they see the need for such a literature and manifest a willingness to devote their time and energies to this program. In the meantime what can I add to the current discussion?

I have taken the fallout from my book seriously. I wish to address myself to the objections raised by those who disagree with me. I am also interested in the questions they have asked. Moreover, I wish to add to the case I presented in the first book, so that even the most obdurate will have to admit there is a problem with noninerrancy in regard to the trustworthiness of Scripture, not only as to matters having to do with history, science, and the cosmos, but also as to theological matters having to do with faith and practice, both directly and indirectly.

There is one group of evangelicals to whom some attention must be given for another reason. I speak now of those who claim they believe in full biblical inerrancy, but who object to the surfacing of this issue among evangelicals. I have in mind men like Clark Pinnock and Carl F. H. Henry, who think inerrancy is important, but not important enough to make an issue of it. I feel they are mistaken in this, and the reasons why they are must be made known to them and to those who are influenced by them. The above named individuals happen to be included in the book *The Debate about the Bible* written by Stephen T. Davis. Mr. Davis asked Professor Pinnock to write the Foreword, a Foreword which is most difficult to understand in view of Clark Pinnock's assertion that he believes in inerrancy. Second, in a footnote (no. 44, page 144), Dr. Davis says: "Henry is a believer in inerrancy, but I would like to say that I admire and appreciate his attitude toward the current debate." I hope to make plain how unfortunate it is that men like Drs. Pinnock and Henry come to the aid and abet disbelievers who use the present attitude of Messrs. Pinnock and Henry as an excuse to justify their erroneous positions and to support their claim that the matter is of secondary concern. I say this particularly since Clark Pinnock himself, at one time, thought the issue sufficiently serious to write a rather full opus entitled *Biblical Revelation,* published by Moody Press, and Dr. Henry has published or will shortly publish two volumes (in a projected four-volume opus) which will deal with biblical inerrancy. It is hard to understand why he would devote a full-scale treatise to this subject if it is so unimportant that he does not wish to challenge those who deny it.

So we ask the question: How goes the battle?

2

Reactions of the Critics:
A Response to Their Questions

The Battle for the Bible produced its own fallout on different levels. Some of the book reviews were written by critics having a special relationship to certain denominations. For example, the Southern Baptist Theological Seminary of Louisville registered its complaints through its President, Duke McCall, and through the *Review and Expositor.* Fuller Seminary expressed its reactions through a variety of means which we will discuss in this work. Reactors of this type are being addressed in connection with the organizations or institutions they represent. Some key critics cannot be said to represent this sort of constituency; yet, their comments are influential, and some of their remarks have received wide circulation.

I have in mind such people as Timothy L. Smith of Johns Hopkins University, Clark Pinnock of McMaster, Carl F. H. Henry of World Vision, Bernard Ramm, formerly of Eastern Baptist Theological Seminary, and a few others. Their observations, their questions, and their criticism of *The Battle for the Bible* call for a response. A substantial number of favorable reviews have appeared; in number they outweigh the critical ones. But the continuing dialogue will not be served best by enumerating the favorable reviews. It is far more important to interact with those who have been critical. To this end I propose to respond to some of the major critics, beginning with Professor Smith.

Timothy L. Smith of Johns Hopkins University

The November 10, 1976, issue of the *Christian Century* carried an article titled " 'The Battle for the Bible:' Renewing the Inerrancy Debate." It was written by Donald Dayton of the North Park Theological Seminary, who is a strong opponent of biblical inerrancy. Professor Smith, himself a Nazarene minister and faculty member at Johns Hopkins University, addressed a letter to the *Century*, commenting on Donald Dayton's essay. In the letter he made it plain that he does not accept biblical inerrancy and he challenged several of the theses contained in *The Battle for the Bible*.

Professor Smith took exception to Donald Dayton's assertion that "evangelicals who reject the verbal inerrancy of the Scriptures on matters of history and cosmology are taking their cues from modern biblical scholarship."[1] He also asserted that "those of us who come from Wesleyan, Lutheran, or Calvinistic backgrounds draw upon the writings of the Reformers themselves to affirm our conviction that the meanings, not the words, of biblical passages are authoritative, and that understanding these meanings requires close and critical study of the texts, rather than incantation of supposedly inerrant words."[2]

The response to this first objection of Dr. Smith is to agree with Donald Dayton that modern critical scholarship in truth lies at the center of the rejection of biblical inerrancy among evangelicals today. He later introduces the notion that nineteenth-century evangelicalism was committed "on all sides" "to the authority of the Bible in matters of faith and doctrine, not history and cosmology."[3] He is incorrect in this as we shall see shortly, but let us suppose for a moment that this observation were to be considered correct. It would not alter the facts of the situation in the twentieth century. Evangelicals in this century have adhered to biblical inerrancy. Some of them now have departed from that commitment, and they have been influenced to do this by the acceptance of the historical-critical method. If the denial of biblical inerrancy is a recovery of an evangelical heritage as Dr. Smith would seem to say, then that recovery came via the use of the historical-critical method. This, in turn, leads to the question raised by Dr. Smith's assertion whether indeed nineteenth-century Christianity limited infallibility or inerrancy to matters of faith and doctrine.

Surely Dr. Smith must know that Luther, Calvin, and the Reformers generally believed in an inerrant Scripture. That has been documented by both those who hold to, and those who deny, biblical inerrancy. Even in the case of John Wesley, who was not a Reformer, it has been established that he held to complete biblical trustworthiness. In the American colonial period one would have to search hard before finding clerics or scholars who denied inerrancy. Prior to the Civil War conservative Congregationalist, Baptist, and Presbyterian evangelicals, as well as Wesleyan, Pietist, and Mennonite, or Anabaptist traditions in the nineteenth century held to inerrancy. One need only look at the two major Baptist confessions, the Philadelphia and the New Hampshire. Moreover, the non-Unitarian Congregationalists were generally adherents of the Westminster Confession.

Dr. Smith's thesis falls apart when he talks about the Presbyterians. He makes the statement that the Warfield-Hodge axis was responsible, after the Civil War, for making verbal inerrancy the touchstone of orthodoxy. Even Jack Rogers in his book *Biblical Authority* acknowledged that every Presbyterian student before Warfield and Hodge's days studied François Turretin. And he left behind the impression that the Bible may have been written by dictation. The only thing Drs. Hodge and Warfield can be held accountable for is that they continued what they themselves and all others who preceded them had been taught at Princeton via the work of Turretin.

Professor Smith goes on to state that Warfield and Hodge "were either rejected or ignored by such religious leaders as Dwight Moody, William Booth, Adoniram J. Gordon, the Methodist preachers in charge of the National Holiness Association, and the faculty of the Southern Baptist Seminary at Louisville."[4] If there is any truth in that assertion it simply means that non-Presbyterians were not interacting with Presbyterian scholarship. And one would hardly suppose that Methodist Arminians then would pay too much attention to Calvinistic Presbyterians. But the real question which must be asked is whether the people and groups Dr. Smith refers to, did or did not hold to biblical inerrancy. Dr. Smith leaves one with the impression that they did not. And this is hardly correct.

Dwight Lyman Moody

Dwight L. Moody did invite to Northfield some who did not hold to biblical inerrancy, but it must be remembered that Mr. Moody was not trained in theology and did not understand the implications of a departure from inerrancy. Mr. Moody himself adhered to inerrancy. In James F. Findlay, Jr.'s biography *Dwight L. Moody* he makes this statement:

> One of the keys to Moody's power as a preacher was that he seemed to express so frequently the full intensity of the spirit evangelicals felt when contemplating the Bible. Shortly after his death one of his close friends summarized his general attitude toward the written Word. "The plenary authority of the Bible was the fulcrum of his work. . . . On his platform it was not subject to dispute or debate, though it always was strongly defended as well as affirmed. . . . He knew that there were difficulties to be accounted for in Scripture as we have it. . . . [But] he believed that the Bible not only claims a Divine authority for all of its teachings, but vindicates its own claims." In a practical sense, too, the Bible was of overriding importance to him. It was the only book that he read and reread constantly. His personal copies of the Scriptures were dog-eared and heavily thumbed, and they contained innumerable marginal notes in the owner's sprawling handwriting.[5]

William R. Moody, son of the evangelist, wrote a biography of his father. In it he talked about his father's belief in the Bible. One could not expect a man of Moody's limited education to understand the implications of German rationalistic criticism in his day. Time had not yet shown how this form of unbelief would empty the German churches and destroy the faith of many. But Mr. Moody himself held strongly to an inerrant Scripture. His son said of his father:

> "I believe," said Mr. Moody, "that there are a good many scholars in these days, as there were when Paul lived, 'who, professing themselves to be wise, have become fools'; but I don't think they are those who hold to the inspiration of the Bible. I have said that ministers of the Gospel who are cutting up the Bible in this way, denying Moses to-day and Isaiah to-morrow, and Daniel the next day and Jonah the next, are doing great injury to the church; and I stand by what I have said. I don't say that they are bad men. They may be good men, but that makes the results of their work all the worse. Do they think they will recommend the

Bible to the finite and fallen reason of men by taking the supernatural out of it? They are doing just the opposite. They are emptying the churches and driving the young men of this generation
into infidelity . . . ."

He often told this experience:

" 'Mr. Moody, what do you do with that?'

" 'I do not do anything with it.'

" 'How do you understand it?'

" 'I do not understand it.'

" 'How do you explain it?'

" 'I do not explain it.'

" 'What do you do with it?'

" 'I do not do anything with it.'

" 'You do not believe it, do you?'

" 'Oh, yes, I believe it.'

" 'Well, you don't accept anything you can't understand, do
you?'

" 'Yes, I certainly do. There are lots of things I do not understand, but I believe them. I do not know anything about higher
mathematics, but I believe in them. I do not understand astronomy, but I believe in astronomy. Can you tell me why the
same kind of food turns into flesh, fish, hair, feathers, or hoofs,
according as it is eaten by one animal or another? A man told me a
while ago he would not believe a thing he had never seen, and I
asked him if he had ever seen his own brain? Did you ever notice
that the things at which men cavil most are the very things on
which Christ has set His seal?' "

When a liberal preacher declared that the story of Jonah and
the whale was a myth, reporters asked Mr. Moody his opinion of
the question. His reply, contained in four words, was telegraphed
far and wide: "I stand by Jonah." [6]

Richard Ellsworth Day had his own word to say about Mr.
Moody and his attitude toward the Word of God. In *Bush
Aglow* he wrote:

> Moody's words on the Bible at this point are as timely as if
> uttered to a moribund church over this afternoon's national
> hook-up:
>
> "Thirty years ago people did not question the gospel. They
> believed that the Lord Jesus Christ, by dying on the cross, had
> done something for them. . . . And my work was to bring them to
> a decision to do what they already knew they ought to do.
>
> "But all is different now.
>
> "The question-mark is raised everywhere. There is need for

teachers who shall begin at the beginning and show the people what the gospel is.

"WHAT WE NEED TODAY IS MEN WHO BELIEVE IN THE BIBLE FROM THE CROWN OF THEIR HEADS TO THE SOLES OF THEIR FEET: WHO BELIEVE IN THE WHOLE OF IT, THE THINGS THEY UNDERSTAND, AND THE THINGS THEY DO NOT UNDERSTAND!"[7]

In still another biography of Dwight L. Moody the author repeats what other biographers had discovered in their research. In this instance, as in the others, comment is made about Mr. Moody's associations with those who did not hold to the same view of the Bible that he did. Here is one statement concerning George Adam Smith:

Although Moody's views of the Bible were regarded by many scholars as exceedingly narrow, the most radical of the modern critics could find no fault with the treatment which they received at his hands. For the higher criticism he had little use, but for many of the higher critics he exhibited the warmest regard. "We met at Yale," says Prof. George Adam Smith in *British Weekly*, "where I discovered for the first time what a hold Moody had on the respectful attention, I think I can say admiration, of American students. He asked me to speak at the commencement exercises of the Northfield schools, and at the American students' conference there. I hesitated, pleading on how many points I differed from the Northfield teaching about Scripture. His answer was, 'Come, and say what you like,' and I felt at once the inspiration of his trust. At Northfield we had several conversations on O. T. criticism, some alone, some with others.

"I shall never forget," continues Professor Smith, "his patience, the openness of his mind, his desire to get at the real facts of criticism, or the shrewdness and humor with which he combated them. It was then that he finished one talk with the words, 'Look here, what's the use of telling the people there's two Isaiahs when most of them don't know that there's one?' But most beautiful was his anxiety about the effect of criticism upon piety and preaching. He had on his heart not only some congregations which had suffered many things from criticism in the pulpit, but the divisions in the churches which were due to critical views. But he was very fair, and said that these divisions were probably not due only to the new opinions about Scripture, but to the temper in which they had been met by the other side."[8]

This same biographer repeated one statement by Dwight

Moody that could be misinterpreted. When talking about higher criticism Mr. Moody said: "It is not the authorship of the book that matters, but the contents."[9] So far as I know this was spoken within the context of a conversation about the authorship of Isaiah. I suppose that it related to Isaiah 40–66 and the notion that because those chapters do not offer direct evidence which supports Isaiah's authorship as do earlier chapters that the authorship is of no moment. First, it is a generally true statement that the contents of a book are more important than the authorship. Certainly it is equally fair to assume that Mr. Moody could simply have meant that since many people authored books that make up the canon of Scripture what is important is what they said rather than who wrote them. However, Mr. Moody never offered any criticism of Isaiah 40–66 as to its messianic claims, nor did he ever suggest that its prophecies were written after the events took place. No liberal scholar, to my knowledge, claims that Second Isaiah, as they call it, could have been written in Isaiah's day even if it were not written by the prophet himself. What these scholars refuse to believe, really, is predictive prophecy, especially as it refers to Cyrus.

Any study of Moody's life makes it impossible to believe that he would have had any patience with the view that Paul did not write Ephesians and the pastorals, or that Peter did not write the two epistles ascribed to him. Since he accepted the historicity of Jonah it would require a great leap of imagination to suppose he would at any point deny what the Scripture so clearly affirmed.

Adoniram J. Gordon

Timothy Smith also used A. J. Gordon as an example of those who rejected or ignored inerrancy as a touchstone of orthodoxy. If A. J. Gordon did not hold to inerrancy it is more than strange, it is highly unlikely, that Gordon College and Gordon-Conwell Theological Seminary which came from the Bible school he started would have committed themselves to an inerrant Bible.

Ernest B. Gordon wrote a biography of his father. He also wrote a book titled *The Leaven of the Sadducees* in which he exposed those who had departed from the fundamentals of the faith—including inerrancy. It is hardly to be supposed that Ernest Gordon's views marked a departure from those of his father as though the senior Gordon did not believe in an inerrant Bible. He did, indeed.

Chapter 13 of Ernest Gordon's biography of his father is titled "Errant Man and the Inerrant Book." The title alone tells its own story, but the author expanded on the title and spoke clearly to the issue. It is obvious that A. J. Gordon did not wage a battle on the subject of inerrancy, but that did not mean he did not hold to inerrancy or that he thought it inconsequential. Once again we must remember that higher criticism had not reached the flood stage in his day. Moreover, he appeared to have only a marginal interest in the whole matter, something not unusual in that day or this. There were literally thousands of clergymen who held to biblical inerrancy whose names never made the newspapers and would be unknown to most of us today. There are tens of thousands of clergymen right now who are so busily engaged in the work of ministering to men and women in local congregations that they spend little or no time studying or combatting the conclusions of the higher critics. I know this, for I have talked with hundreds of clergymen myself who are simply unaware of the implications of redaction, form, and source criticism.

Ernest Gordon did have this to say about his father and the Bible:

> As to modern Old Testament criticism, he doubtless felt, as do many others, that though it may be as scientific as paleontology, it is also as lifeless and as dry . . . . The time is short. Speculation soon dies out if not fed with the oil of controversy. Fruitfulness is more important than an abstract accuracy . . . . He shut the door behind him, therefore, leaving the sanhedrin of critics and conservatives to wrangle and bicker, and passed out into the world of the needy and the sorrowing.
>
> And again: "Upon the much-mooted question of 'inerrancy' we do not presume to enter. But we do express the wish that our higher critics were as ready to test their own inerrancy by Scripture as to test the Scripture's inerrancy by their own.
>
> "And as to our personal use of Scripture, is it not better that we use the Bible as a search-light for illuminating our understanding than to use our understanding as a search warrant for discovering whether some error or contradiction may not be hiding in the

nooks and crannies of its history or chronology?

"An errant Bible is exactly what is demanded by errant youth. To a 'man beholding his natural face in the glass' of Scripture it is a vast relief to be assured, on scientific authority, that the glass is perchance considerably convexed, so that the sinful self seen therein, which has often been so troublesome, after all, may have been greatly exaggerated. Our plea is not, however, for war on the critics, but for watch over ourselves—that we let no day pass in the new year in which we do not turn the light of Scripture upon our lives, subject our hearts to its searching inquisition, and rejoice to be found out by it concerning those sins of which we have been willingly ignorant."

This reverential regard for the Bible pervaded his whole teaching and gave to his theological opinions an anchorage in days of drift and uncertainty.[10]

The Southern Baptist Seminary at Louisville

Dr. Smith's observation about Southern Baptist Seminary happens to be inaccurate. I need only refer to the chapter on the Southern Baptists in this present work and point the readers to the statements made by Basil Manly, James Petigru Boyce, and John R. Sampey. They held to inerrancy; they recognized the threat liberalism posed to orthodoxy; and they realized that the problem sprang from rationalistic criticism. It was Dr. Sampey, the Old Testament scholar, who was especially cognizant of the dangers inherent in the liberalism of higher criticism.

Basil Manly, as I have shown, did know about B. B. Warfield and Charles Hodge, and it was he who quoted from President Patton of Princeton who reflected in his book on inspiration the viewpoint of Hodge and Warfield. Dr. Patton certainly regarded biblical inerrancy as a watershed and said so. Professor Manly neither rejected nor ignored the Princeton divines. He agreed with them and manifested that agreement in his own book on inspiration.

Other Illustrations

I have made no effort to check William Booth or the Methodist preachers in charge of the National Holiness Association. I rather suspect that the evidences would show in those instances that Professor Smith is wrong again. But, perhaps, the worst allegation advanced by Dr. Smith has to do with Paul and Jesus. He stated:

> The efforts of Francis Schaeffer and Harold Lindsell, then repre-
> sent a third round in that long struggle to impose upon modern
> evangelicals a view of Scripture which Jesus and Paul renounced
> in rabbinical Judaism.[11]

It is patently untrue to say that the biblical inerrancy advocated by Francis Schaeffer and myself is one that "Jesus and
Paul renounced in rabbinical Judaism." It is precisely the
commitment of both Jesus and Paul to biblical inerrancy which
underlies my viewpoint and, I think, the viewpoint of Dr.
Schaeffer. Let me make it plain that the Bible teaches a doctrine of inspiration. And let it be added that inspiration has
little value if all it does is guarantee us the Bible has in it both
truth and error. If the doctrine of inspiration taught in Scripture was renounced and denied by Jesus and Paul, then
evangelicals are off base. But the doctrine of inspiration and
the testimony of Jesus and Paul are coordinate. The one com-
plements the other. There is no disjunction or disharmony in
those witnesses. If Jesus or Paul taught that Scripture can and
does err then the teaching of biblical inerrancy falls to the
ground.

It is true that many who reject inerrancy have argued in
favor of a limited inerrancy (which is a contradiction in terms)
or what some of them who dislike the word *inerrancy* speak of
as "infallibility in matters of faith and practice." When those
who hold to this are asked why they believe in infallibility for
matters of faith and practice, they too must resort to Scripture
and to the words of Jesus and Paul. Unfortunately for them the
data they use do not allow for the limitations they wish to
impose, so their case falls apart.

But enough for the objections presented by Dr. Smith. I now
turn to Carl. F. H. Henry and his observations.

Carl F. H. Henry

I have known Carl F. H. Henry for many years. We were
classmates in college, we served on two faculties together, I
was associate editor of *Christianity Today* when he was editor,
and I was best man at his wedding. I succeeded him as editor
of *Christianity Today*.

Upon the appearance of *The Battle for the Bible*, Dr. Henry was provided with a platform for visibility based on assuming an adversary role in connection with the book. It began with his remarks in *Time* magazine and extended to reviews and interviews which appeared in several publications. From the beginning he acknowledged that he held to biblical inerrancy himself. He made it apparent that giving visibility to the defection from inerrancy among evangelicals was bad strategy, and it offended him in his own drive to forge a larger evangelical grouping for a massive offensive such as he had described in several of his own books.

Dr. Henry feels that evangelicals are not getting through to opinion-makers because "our evangelical leaders shifted the public reception of the evangelical movement from its role as a dynamic life-growing force to a cult squabbling over inerrancy."[12] This can only mean that Dr. Henry does not think the issue of inerrancy is really worth "squabbling" about. If it is not, then what *is* worth squabbling about? Is the bodily resurrection worth squabbling about? Is the vicarious atonement worth it? Is the deity of Christ worth it? If any of these is worth squabbling about, we must remember that the views concerning these are derived from the Scriptures. If the Scriptures cannot be trusted, then we cannot be sure concerning these doctrines either. But Dr. Henry is sure to reply that he is talking about the scrapping of inerrancy as it pertains to matters of history, science, and the cosmos. Apparently he wishes to maintain inerrancy as it relates to matters of faith and practice. Yet he has spent valuable time and energy on the third and fourth volumes of his four-part work, which are designed to reinforce biblical inerrancy. It must have sufficient importance for him to write two volumes about it.

If inerrancy is not all that important, why then should he object to a change of stance by institutions such as Fuller Theological Seminary? And how could he say that "I think Lindsell's domino theory is far closer to the truth when applied to institutions rather than to individuals, but I don't think he carefully makes that distinction"?[13] If my domino theory is close to the truth, then a battle for inerrancy should be high on the agenda if for no other reason than once you forsake it other unfortunate consequences follow.

Dr. Henry has stated: "I think it highly unfortunate that the *primary* thing that should now be said about men like F. F. Bruce and Berkouwer, men who have made significant contributions to the conservative position—even though we might have hoped for somewhat more from them—is that they are not evangelicals because of their position at this one point."[14] I did ask whether those who deny inerrancy are entitled to the use of the term evangelical. And I must say that in my judgment the best one can say of anyone who denies inerrancy is that he is an inconsistent evangelical. But even here Dr. Henry missed the point.

Dr. Berkouwer has gone beyond denial of biblical inerrancy. He doubts the historicity of Adam and Eve. Moreover, I have in my files information that in his classroom teaching he has denied the existence of hell. In Professor Bruce's case, he wrote about Paul King Jewett's book *Man as Male and Female* in the *Evangelical Quarterly*. This is the book in which Dr. Jewett says that the teaching of the apostle Paul in Ephesians about a wife obeying her husband is rabbinic in origin and in error. He contrasts Paul's teaching in Ephesians with Galatians 3:28 that there is neither male nor female in Christ and says that Paul is wrong in Ephesians. Dr. Bruce said:

> Dr. Jewett's survey of the biblical evidence and its interpretation over the centuries has the advantage of not being influenced by current fashions in opinion . . . . To all readers may be recommended especially his exegesis of the relevant Pauline passages. . . . Dr. Jewett interprets Paul with the respect which his apostolic authority requires, but in doing so he vindicates Paul's title to be acknowledged as the patron saint not only of Christian liberty in general but specifically of women's liberty.[15]

This statement by Professor Bruce must be seen in the context of Dr. Henry's evaluation of Professor Jewett:

> One of the finest sections in Dr. Lindsell's book is its survey of Fuller Theological Seminary, where the faculty has been unable to keep faith with two successive statements of its view of Scripture. Until recently, after revising the original statement, they held the line at least in respect to faith and morals; but with Dr. Jewett's contention that the Apostle Paul erred on the issue of the subordination of women, there is a breaching of the inerrancy of Scripture also at the level of Christian practice, or ethics.[16]

Two observations are worth making. First: Dr. Bruce, like Dr.

Jewett, has gone beyond simple errancy to errancy in a matter of faith and practice. And if Dr. Henry thinks it right to criticize Dr. Jewett at this point, why is it wrong for me to criticize Dr. Bruce at the same point? Both Dr. Jewett and Dr. Bruce do not believe that the Bible is free from error in matters of faith and practice, nor is it free from errors in matters of history, science, etc. Second, Dr. Henry says the Fuller Seminary faculty "has been unable to keep faith with two successive statements of its view of Scripture." But this is also true of Drs. Bruce and Berkouwer, and it is excellent evidence in support of my thesis that once you drop inerrancy, it opens the door wide to further departures about matters of faith and practice. And this is what has happened in the cases of Professors Bruce and Berkouwer as well as in the case of Paul King Jewett.

Carl Henry was especially critical of several sentences at the end of *The Battle for the Bible*. He did agree that early in my book I said it should not be inferred that because someone holds the opinion that the Bible contains incidental errors, he cannot therefore be a Christian. But near the end of the volume he had second thoughts. He implied that I think that all who accept scriptural errancy are destined to damnation and hell. He told a Washington *Star* reporter in the November 26, 1977, issue of the newspaper:

> Particularly unfortunate, Henry said, is Lindsell's "unjustifiable" emphasis that those who balk at the inerrancy of the Bible are "false evangelicals" even if they subscribe to all other Christian doctrines.
>
> "Such people are doubtless 'inconsistent' evangelicals," Henry said, "but to imply that they will be numbered with the tares in Christ's judgment is unjustifiable."

Dr. Henry, of course, is familiar with the analogy of faith by which one interprets an unclear statement by a clear statement. I thought the statement about the wheat and tares was clear enough and had nothing more in it than the biblical observation that there are wheat and tares awaiting the harvest. I did not have in mind as tares those whose only transgression is a denial of inerrancy. I had in mind the denial of the major doctrines of the Christian faith. I gladly clear up any misunderstanding and would offer reassurance to Dr.

Henry what my intention was. In any event none of us determines who is in the kingdom and who is not. That belongs to God who is the true judge of the human heart. And lest Dr. Henry and others think I said the number of those who believe in inerrancy is few, let me remind him and all others of one statement in *The Battle for the Bible* about Southern Baptists: "At this moment in history the great bulk of the Southern Baptists are theologically orthodox and do believe that the Word of God is inerrant" (p. 104).[17] Southern Baptists number more than thirteen million and "the great bulk" of them alone would be sizable.

A last remaining point concerning the views of Dr. Henry should be made. In the article syndicated by the Evangelical Press Association Dr. Henry said that inerrancy is not explicitly taught in Scripture. He said this in the following statement: "I would say that inerrancy is clearly implied, logically deduced from, and a necessary correlative of inspiration, though not *explicitly* taught." Dr. Henry stated that I agreed with Warfield that inerrancy is taught in Scripture "but at least Warfield gives the passages which he affirms to teach the doctrine, Dr. Lindsell gives none." Dr. Henry is wrong in saying I gave no Scripture to support the position I advocated. He certainly could say, if he wished to, that he was not satisfied with the number of Scripture quotations, but, after all, it only takes one clear statement of Scripture to support a theological position. The virgin birth is reported in only two of the four Gospels. Paul never mentions it. But this does not invalidate the virgin birth nor does it reduce the likelihood of its being true.

On a lecture trip months later Dr. Henry spoke at the China Evangelical Seminary in Taipei, Taiwan. This is the seminary presided over by the great-grandson of J. Hudson Taylor. In its *News Bulletin*, the seminary reported Dr. Henry's lecture series and said of them:

> Dr. Henry has a high view of the Bible, believing that the autographs were inerrant, and that the copies are trustworthy. He argued that inerrancy is taught in the Scripture, and that this was the view of Jesus. He does not agree with those who assert that anyone who compromises inerrancy is apostate. He considers this criterion of apostasy as more appropriate for institutions than for individuals.

In his syndicated article Dr. Henry said inerrancy is implied and logically deduced, but not explicitly taught. At the Taiwan seminary, according to the article in the *News Bulletin*, he said it *is* taught (and that can only mean it is explicit) and that inerrancy is the view of Jesus. Now if it is the view of Jesus, then it must have been taught by Jesus or affirmed by Him. Once anyone says inerrancy was the view of Jesus, that should be sufficient to drop the notion of its being implicit, and to come out for explicit inerrancy. In any case, Dr. Henry is inconsistent, for the two statements are not in agreement with each other. Of course it may be that he has given up his earlier view and this would be all to the good.

Clark Pinnock

Aside from Carl F. H. Henry perhaps no one else has put more words on paper about the current debate on inerrancy than Clark Pinnock. Any study of Pinnock's writings brings with it the judgment that his pilgrimage has been inexplicable. There has been a noticeable shift from right to left. He recently left the halls of Regent College in Vancouver for the liberal corridors of McMaster Divinity College in Hamilton, Ontario.

In 1968 Dr. Pinnock was a member of the faculty of the New Orleans Baptist Theological Seminary in Louisiana. In that year a booklet titled *A Challenge to Southern Baptists* appeared in print. Professor Pinnock appeared like a tiger stalking his prey. His words were strong medicine. In his first article in this booklet, "The Evangelical Imperative," he stated:

> Charles Haddon Spurgeon saw the Baptist Union of his day drifting slowly but relentlessly toward a compromise with false teaching and ambiguity of faith . . . .
> Peace and tranquility are wonderful blessings in a church. It is difficult to accomplish things for God without them. But peace at any price is not good. Peace that involves us in compromise is sinful. Paul was a militant in this matter. . . . Truth mattered to him. Our unwillingness to identify and act against false doctrine does not spring from our supposed charity, but from our spinelessness and lack of principle. . . . James Stalker put it precisely. 'Excessive aversion to controversy may be an indication that a Church has no keen sense of possessing truth which is of any great worth, and that it has lost appreciation for the infinite difference in value between truth and error.' . . .

There are, however, some troubling signs even in our own church (The Southern Baptist Convention). We discover a certain reluctance to question sub-biblical teachings in our pulpits and institutions. . . . A few years ago it was common to find error confronted and opposed, but now it is not so, and the state of affairs springs more from cowardice than from tolerance. Furthermore, there is a conspiracy of silence, almost an amnesia, over our traditional conservative theology still held by so large a number of our pastors. . . . Our theological decline, while serious enough, is at a relatively early stage, and can yet be checked. The cancer is not yet malignant (unfortunately a cancer is always malignant—my note).[18]

In his second chapter titled *"Sola Scriptura"* Dr. Pinnock spoke even more boldly. Here are some of the extracts of what he said:

The Bible in providing a verbally inspired divine revelation is the epistemological foundation of Christianity. . . . Jesus taught, 'The Scripture cannot be broken.' . . . The majority of theologians in all branches of the Christian Church have held to a high view of the Bible since the time of Christ whose example they followed in this respect. The Southern Baptist Convention has been no exception until recently. Even today the majority of her pastors have the highest regard for the absolute trustworthiness of Scripture. They believe it is the very Word of God, true in its every utterance, and binding in its divine authority. They make no artificial dichotomy between the Bible's historical facts, its ethical judgments, and its spiritual truths. All alike are received as from the mouth of God. In no other large denomination does belief in the inerrancy of Scripture receive such a warm welcome as in our own. . . .
. . . among men teaching in our seminaries and colleges . . . some have found it expedient to jettison the historic high view of Scripture, and accept a scaled down version. . . . The Convention in Kansas City sensed the difficulty when it called upon our institutions to uphold the high view of Scripture 'as the authoritative, authentic, infallible Word of God.' . . . For while reform was called for, little reform took place. Professors did not resign, lectures were not rewritten. . . . Even today students report that in many places of Baptist higher education the doctrine of Biblical infallibility is either completely ignored or openly held up to scorn. . . . To affirm Christ and reject infallibility is an act of intellectual impenitence and schizophrenia. . . . In the past a professor trembled to contradict God's Word; now he trembles to go against the current liberal consensus. Do not misunderstand. Scholarship

is the gift of God. But scholars have erred time and time again, while Scripture has never erred. . . . We have tried resolutions and they have not worked. It is time for action, before it comes too late to act. It takes but a few rebels to overthrow a government, and a few rioters to burn a city. Our Church could be destroyed if we do not take steps to ensure that the integrity of the gospel is preserved.[19]

These words of Dr. Pinnock are strong words indeed. Enough of them have been cited to show what his viewpoint was in 1968. It had not changed in 1971 when his volume *Biblical Revelation* was published by Moody Press. Moody Press has been noted for its constant fidelity to biblical inerrancy and its books have always asserted it. This was no exception.

Biblical Revelation was reviewed in the January, 1972, issue of *The Bookstore Journal.* The reviewer said that Dr. Pinnock's capable and orthodox work concluded with the assertion that "to cast doubt on the complete veracity and authority of Scripture is a criminal act creating a crisis of immense importance for theology and faith."[20] It was Dr. Pinnock at this stage of his pilgrimage who said that "if inspiration cannot guarantee the integrity of what is actually set down in Scripture, what can it guarantee?" He was the one who took issue with Dr. Daniel Fuller, the former dean of Fuller Seminary, who said that the Bible has both revelational and nonrevelational parts. Revelational parts are absolutely trustworthy; nonrevelational parts have errors in them. Dr. Pinnock said of Dr. Fuller's position: "The claim that Scripture does *not* err in those places where it may not be tested is meaningless if it *does* err in those places where it can. . . . The factual assertions of Scripture are bound up with the theological assertions (e.g. Mt. 12:41). The theological truth is discredited to the extent that the factual material is erroneous. Fuller has only made it harder to defend Scripture. Futhermore, Fuller's (and Dewey M. Beegle's) point that the Bible does not claim for itself complete inerrancy, is false."[21]

The Battle for the Bible came out in 1976. And Dr. Pinnock's pen became active. This time it was used to strike down the very things he himself had said in the earlier writings to which I have just referred. I do not see any difference between my view and his view of an earlier date. He called for more extreme action than even I did. He concluded that to deny inerrancy opens the door wide to further defection. Then came his review of my book in *Eternity* magazine. Instead of the attacking tiger (he had observed in his earlier publication: "Observe how quickly a wild tiger committed to a zoo becomes docile") he had become a muzzled tiger. He now played the role of reconciler calling for amity and peace.

In his paper "The Inerrancy Debate among the Evangelicals" he deplored my book, which he said, "threatens to create a new wave of bitterness and controversy on account of its militant tone and sweeping attacks."[22] He argued that the "category 'inerrancy' should not occasion controversy." "Surely," he said, "James Orr had a point when he said that an obsession with the accuracy of minor details in the Bible put the Christian apologist in a foolish, even suicidal position."[23] This was strange doctrine far removed from Professor Pinnock's observations when he was on the faculty of the New Orleans Baptist Seminary. It is also strange because James Orr, who was no believer in inerrancy, declared in his 1897 Elliott lectures at Western Theological Seminary: "Christian faith in every age must be a battle. That battle will have to be fought, if I mistake not in the first instance, round the fortress of the worth and authority of Holy Scripture" (*The Progress of Dogma* [Grand Rapids: Eerdmans, 1952], p. 352).

Dr. Pinnock also defined inerrancy in a different fashion from his earlier works. When applied to Scripture "inerrancy . . . is relative to the scope, purpose, and genre of each passage." Then he went on to speak of how

> . . . the biblical writer pictures the natural world in the modes of expression common in his day, scientifically precise references neither being intended nor made; where the degree of historical precision correlates with the author's intention—in confusing the facts of the Abraham story in Acts 7 we fault neither Stephen for citing the facts as he recalled them nor Luke for recording what he believed Stephen said; where Job cites the errant opinions of liars; where the Chronicler recounts figures quite different from those in parallel passages, his intention being only to set forth the record as he found it in the public archives; where the *ipsissima verba* of Jesus are handled with a certain freedom depending on the purpose of the redactor Evangelist, or where Paul cites the Old Testament in line with some concept he wishes to teach us. . . . I

doubt whether the upholders of inerrancy have reflected sufficiently on the implications of this qualification, according to which
one could fairly say that the Bible *contains* errors but *teaches*
none, or that inerrancy refers to the *subjects* rather than to all the
terms of Scripture or to the *teaching* rather than to all the compo-
nents utilized in its formulation. . . . But let it be plainly stated that
according to this understanding of inerrancy, the Bible is not free
of all 'errors' in its whole extent, but free of errors when its intended teachings are concerned.[24]

It should be understood in this connection that the latter part
of this paragraph was written against the backdrop of a remark
by B. B. Warfield to the effect that we must take into account
the "professed or implied purpose of the writer." But the two
points here are: first, Dr. Warfield also stated that a single error
would invalidate his case. Second, Dr. Pinnock has now lowered his own view of inerrancy.

Dr. Pinnock also published an article in *The Church Herald* of
the Reformed Church in America titled: "Why Is There a Battle
for the Bible?" His new posture is evident here also, but he
made some strange statements for a professed believer in inerrancy. Speaking of Professor Berkouwer who denies inerrancy
Dr. Pinnock says something that might possibly be attributed
to Dr. Berkouwer but seems to be either Pinnock's own view
or at least his agreement with a view that Dr. Berkouwer asserts:

There is a lowliness and frailty which characterizes the Bible, as it
did also Jesus, and which, though it may offend the cultivated, will
not deceive the pure in heart. It is simply further eloquent proof of
the gracious condescension of God who gives us his Word in
weakness, though it is the power of God.[25]

One word used is "frailty" which according to Webster means
"morally weak; easily led astray or into evil; an inadequacy, a
fault or a sin resulting from weakness." When such a word is
applied to the Bible and to Jesus, it leaves one under the impression that both Christology and Bibliology have been seriously assaulted and breached.

Professor Pinnock also published an article in *Theology
Today* under the larger heading "Theological Table-Talk." His
particular piece is listed as "Evangelicals and Inerrancy: The
Current Debate." One section of it is particularly important

because Dr. Pinnock now says there are three categories of evangelicals in relation to inerrancy. Here is the complete section of that article:

We can distinguish at least three positions being taken at present within the evangelical coalition. First, there are the militant advocates of unqualified biblical inerrancy, who continue in the tradition of Warfield and the fundamentalists. They equate the Princeton doctrine of the perfect errorlessness of the original autographs of Scripture with the historic view of the church, and they do not anticipate further doctrinal development on this subject. For them the inerrancy assumption is an essential component of true evangelicalism, if not true Christianity, and objections to it are handled defensively. A great deal of evangelical literature, as James Barr has recently shown, is impregnated with this presupposition, and a great deal of effort is expended in its defense and vindication (*Fundamentalism*, 3, 5). Harold Lindsell's book [The] *Battle for the Bible* articulates this strict position, and he probably speaks for a large majority of evangelical people.

Second, there are advocates of a modified definition of biblical inerrancy. These are often evangelicals who have been exposed to biblical studies and have come to realize that if inerrancy is to be held, as they believe, it must be broadened and nuanced so as to accommodate certain biblical phenomena, such as the presence in Scripture of a Semitic cosmology, variants in the synoptic gospels, peculiarities in genealogical lists, and the like. In speaking of "inerrant in all it affirms" *(Lausanne Covenant),* it is possible to liberalize the concept of inerrancy and give it a more general sense. Needless to say, there is a close parallel in Roman Catholic struggles with such terms as inerrancy and infallibility as they relate both to Scripture and the Magisterium.

These advocates of modified inerrancy (see my own book *Biblical Revelation,* 1971) find themselves under attack from two directions. The militant advocates suspect them of watering down the inerrancy conviction close to meaninglessness, and left wing Protestants like James Barr ridicule the effort to be critically honest and still retain biblical inerrancy in any form. From both sides it seems that this moderate position is unstably tottering between inerrancy and non-inerrancy and likely to come down eventually on the non-inerrancy side. While it is still too early to say, I think the prediction may be quite probable, especially if the militants gain control of evangelical institutions and societies as they may well do.

Third, there are the evangelical opponents of biblical inerrancy.

Though a distinct minority, they happen to include some of the best known and most capable of the scholars evangelicalism has produced: F. F. Bruce, G. C. Berkouwer, David A. Hubbard, G. E. Ladd, and others. Because it is controversial, their theology of biblical inspiration has been slow in surfacing, but the outlines of it are becoming quite clear now. Their study of the Bible and theology has convinced them that the assumption of scientific precision and accuracy, such as the term inerrancy connotes, is inappropriate when it comes to biblical realities. Not only do the critical phenomena discredit it, but the Bible itself does not place high value on precision but often subordinates it to other ends. In addition, these evangelicals have come to question what the Bible claims for itself. Contesting Warfield's theory of the perfect errorlessness of the original biblical autographs, they feel the biblical inspiration is a much less formal and more practical affair. It relates to the sufficiency of Scripture through the Spirit of God to nourish and instruct the church for its faith and life, and not to an abstract perfection. A new evangelical doctrine of biblical inspiration is emerging, and just because it calls the time-honored inerrancy assumption into question it has come under heavy criticism from the militant side. It is now a question of whether this group of evangelicals is going to be able to develop a strong and affirmative concept of biblical authority (it is not enough to be against inerrancy) such as can gain the consent and support of the evangelical constituency long used to stricter formulations.[26]

Now Dr. Pinnock places himself in the second category of "modified inerrancy." This is markedly different from his position when at New Orleans and when his book *Biblical Revelation* was published. If he then held to a modified inerrancy, it did not come through to the reader. He does say something very important: "From both sides it seems that this moderate position is unstably tottering between inerrancy and non-inerrancy and likely to come down eventually on the non-inerrancy side. While it is still too early to say, I think the prediction quite probable, especially if the militants gain control of evangelical institutions and societies as they may well do."

What is very significant is the third category which he denominates "the evangelical opponents of biblical inerrancy." He includes in it F. F. Bruce, G. C. Berkouwer, David A. Hubbard, G. E. Ladd, and others. He agrees that "their theology of biblical inspiration has been slow in surfacing, but the outlines of it are becoming quite clear now." Dr. Pinnock is acknowledging that my allegation that these men and Fuller Theological Seminary have departed from inerrancy to non-inerrancy is correct. And why should my listing them as non-believers in inerrancy be such a horrendous deed, especially since he lists men like myself and Dr. Schaeffer as "militant advocates of unqualified biblical inerrancy"?

Toward the end of this article Dr. Pinnock states: "I cannot accept the morality which allows believers so closely united on the great biblical and creedal affirmations to attack the integrity and authenticity of one another's faith and person."[27] Actually, I did not attack the *persons* of those who deny inerrancy. All I did was to show they had done so. If this constitutes an attack on personhood, then no dialogue is possible on any of these matters, including Dr. Pinnock's own dialogue, for he attacks the militant advocates of unqualified inerrancy with some vigor and also questions their morality.

At the end of his paper Dr. Pinnock hopes that "evangelicalism will find room for diversity of human opinion on the nature of biblical inspiration and discover rich and productive theological renewal as a result."[28] This of course cannot be, unless inerrantists change their minds about the importance of inerrancy. This appears to be unlikely for the very reasons Dr. Pinnock stated in his own early writings on the subject.

Many of us who are committed to biblical inerrancy had counted on Dr. Pinnock to play an important role in the present discussion by reinforcing what we have to say. Alas, this is not to be. He is free to defect from his earlier position as he has done. We wish him well. And we hope he goes no further than limiting inerrancy to matters of faith and practice. But his uneven track record leaves some of us with an uneasy thought that additional damaging concessions may be on the way.

Bernard Ramm

Bernard Ramm is a name to be reckoned with. He has written a number of books, some of which have been published by recognized evangelical publishers. He has taught at Biola, Baylor, the Southern California Baptist Theological Seminary, Bethel Seminary, and Eastern Baptist Theological Seminary.

His book *The Christian View of Science and Scripture* has been widely read and is well known in theological and scientific circles. Dr. Ramm reviewed *The Battle for the Bible* in *The Reformed Journal*. This magazine is owned and published by Eerdmans Publishing Company. It stands to the left of the Christian Reformed Church's *Banner* and is the sounding board for those in the Christian Reformed tradition who are left of center. Among the editors of *The Reformed Journal* are two Fuller Seminary professors, James Daane, and Lewis B. Smedes. The magazine on whose masthead their names appear provides the *avant garde* leadership for their denomination. This background is essential to understand why Dr. Ramm was selected as a reviewer and what the general orientation of the magazine is.

Dr. Ramm was unhappy with my book for a number of reasons. He does not think that biblical inerrancy is a watershed for evangelicals. He concluded that I think those who do not hold to inerrancy are "to be found in the goat's corner at the Second Coming." He added that "to disagree with Lindsell is to be caught in the devil's corner already."[29] I am happy to reflect on statements like this.

Indeed it is true that whoever disavows that which the Scripture teaches is "in the devil's corner." The doctrine of inerrancy is just as true and binding a doctrine as any other which is taught in Scripture. He who realizes that Christ believed in the inerrancy of the Old Testament and yet refuses to believe it, has in effect rejected the authority of Christ, and therefore also the sovereignty, the lordship of Christ.

Whoever rejects what is clearly taught in Scripture, then, at that point is in the devil's corner. That leaves open the question whether one who does not accept inerrancy and thus is in the devil's corner is a regenerated person. I cannot answer that question because it depends on the person's heart attitude toward the Scriptures. If he or she thinks inerrancy is not taught in Scripture perhaps this puts that one in the same category as those who differ about premillennialism and amillennialism or pedo- and anti-pedo baptism. If, on the other hand, the person voluntarily and deliberately rejects a doctrine known to be taught by Scripture the issue would be different.

I will leave that issue with God who knows the hearts of all men. What I did do and will continue to do is ask the question whether anyone who rejects inerrancy is entitled to be called an evangelical. And if such a person is an evangelical, he or she at best is an inconsistent evangelical. What other basic doctrines and how many of them one can deny and still be numbered among true believers unto salvation is another matter. But I certainly will make a stab at that one later.

In this connection, let us take the case of William Barclay, whose New Testament commentaries have sold hundreds of thousands of copies and have helped many pastors in preparation for their preaching. I do not think William Barclay was a Christian. In his autobiography he clearly stated that he was not a Trinitarian, he did not believe Jesus is God, he denied the doctrine of the vicarious atonement and also the virgin birth of Christ, and his view of the Holy Spirit fits no discernible orthodox definition in the history of the Christian church. Needless to say, he did not believe in the inerrancy of the Bible. Had he done so he would have believed the above mentioned doctrines because they are taught in Scripture. A word of caution must be added. Thus, I feel that William Barclay was not a Christian because by no reasonable understanding of the Bible could he be called one. It is the Bible which makes it impossible to claim this man as a fellow believer without emptying Christianity of its basic content.

Dr. Ramm, who is surely knowledgeable, went far out on a limb and made a strange generalization. He said that

> to reduce the issue of the faith down to Lindsell's [sic] view of inerrancy . . . is all too neat, all too simple, all too precise. . . . Furthermore, it leads to oddities. By having a *sufficient* reason for the inspiration of Scripture but not a *necessary* reason Lindsell makes all sectarians and cultists into evangelicals in that they too believe in the inerrancy of Scripture. And that isn't all! Such stalwarts as Kornelis H. Miskotte, Helmut Thielicke, Otto Weber, and Helmut Gollwitzer, who have fought liberalism, existentialism, and Bultmannianism on the continent, are suspect because they do not believe in inerrancy, but some eschatological fanatic who believes in inerrancy is theologically safe![30]

The phrase "Lindsell makes all sectarians and cultists into evangelicals" is obviously wide of the truth. Any reading of recent church history will show that evangelicals have been the leading opponents of the cults. Neither I nor any other evangelical I know of has ever said that inerrancy in and of itself is the whole story. Evangelical faith comprises a cluster of foundational truths, a series of propositions concerning fundamental doctrines of the faith. Inerrancy is *one* of them. Dr. Ramm supposes that Dr. Schaeffer and I are in effect saying that inerrancy is a doctrinal watershed, and is therefore [in and of itself] the only pole on which the Christian flag can be mounted. It is true that inerrancy *is* the crucial question, the watershed question of this age, just as Christology was the watershed question for the early church. During the Reformation the watershed question was justification by faith alone. If the battle for biblical inerrancy is won, we can be sure that some other major question will be raised to vex the Christian church. It may be that the new unitarian challenge will be the coming watershed in the days ahead.

Of course there are people who claim to believe in the inerrancy of the Bible and then proceed to deny other basic doctrines of the faith. In that event, their belief in inerrancy has no saving effect whatever. Inerrancy is compatible with orthodoxy in its totality, not when divorced from the other foundational truths of the Bible. But inerrancy does play an important role in all of this. No one can deny *any* essential doctrine of the faith without also impugning biblical authority, biblical inspiration, *and* biblical inerrancy. We also need to remember that biblical inspiration precedes inerrancy and has a dynamic relationship to it. We do not believe the Bible is inspired because it is inerrant. We believe it is inerrant because it is inspired—inspired by the God of all truth. But today's problem is that some who claim to believe in the inspiration of the Bible refuse to believe in its inerrancy. Dr. Ramm appears to be one of these, and this is the reason why he and other scholars of like mind have been and will continue to be unhappy about *The Battle for the Bible.* They will be even more unhappy about this second volume, and about that stream of new books in favor of inerrancy which are projected for publication during the next decade.

Dr. Ramm was of the opinion that I am fighting the wrong battle. He called my book the "misplaced battle line." This is his statement about the real problem as he saw it:

> The contemporary battle for the Bible asks whether most of bibli-
> cal history is credible, or whether all we have of the true words
> and deeds of Jesus is a demitasse full of shreds, or whether the
> Prison Epistles and the Pastoral Epistles are Pauline, or whether
> the Revelation is anything more than a weird book of Christian
> apocalypticism.[31]

I am delighted that Dr. Ramm has made this statement. It puts
his problem and the case for inerrancy in proper perspective.
Let me illustrate what I mean. The prison Epistles include
Ephesians, Philippians, Colossians, and Philemon. The pas-
toral Epistles include 1 and 2 Timothy and Titus. Dr. Ramm
says the contemporary battle is whether these books were
written by the apostle Paul. The very asking of such a question
has to do with the whole biblical doctrine of inspiration and
inerrancy. In each of these letters the claim is made that Paul
was the author. If Paul did not write these letters, then the
Bible is not telling us the truth about their authorship. To say
that Paul did not write these books is to deny what the Bible
itself affirms. And whoever brings extra-biblical evidence to
bear on the question of authorship, and on that basis refuses
to believe what the Bible teaches, has automatically put something above the Bible in the matter of final authority. The only
way in which the authorship of these books purported to be by
Paul can be part of the contemporary battle is for an individual
to start with the ungrounded assumption that they were probably not written by Paul. This introduces a hostile bias from
the start which makes it impossible to handle the evidence
fairly.

Whoever believes the Bible to be inerrant accepts without
question the claims of these letters that they were written by
Paul. This does not mean the evangelical should not concern
himself about their Pauline authorship. He certainly will do
so, but from an entirely different perspective. He will examine
the claims of those who deny Pauline authorship and he will
build a case to elucidate the reasons why such unbelief is
unjustified. This sort of question would be no problem for Dr.
Ramm *if* he started with the belief that the Bible is true in all
its parts. But apparently he cannot bring himself to accept the
concept of an inerrant Scripture. All that his review does is

show that my allegation in *The Battle for the Bible* is correct: the evangelical camp, and Dr. Ramm, who has been numbered among those in that camp, have been infected by those who hold an aberrant view of the Bible.

Dr. Ramm's own hesitancy about inerrancy was expressed in this review. Here is his own analysis:

> Further, we are not home free if we claim there are no errors in Scripture. Anybody who has lived with biblical criticism through the years knows the cluster of problems we face *on every page of Scripture* (my italics). If we told a logician that there are no errors in Scripture but a thousand problems (not an exaggeration in view of the huge books on Old and New Testament introduction) he would die laughing. We must not have a view of Holy Scripture which—to use a current philosophical phrase—dies the death of a thousand qualifications.[32]

At the end of his review Dr. Ramm did agree that "we can never surrender *sola Scriptura*. In evangelical theology the Holy Scripture is the supreme and final authority in matters of faith and conduct. Further, the concept of evangelical is not indefinitely extensible."[33] From this it will be seen quickly that Dr. Ramm has given himself some severe problems which may be greater that those he said the inerrantist must face. He said he believes that we cannot surrender "the Bible only" principle. But he limits the Bible-only principle to matters of faith and conduct. However, he also says that every page of the Bible is crowded with a cluster of problems. And he argues that a logician would laugh if you told him the Bible has no errors but a thousand qualifications. Now if there are a thousand qualifications and every page of the Bible is crammed with problems Dr. Ramm has a mighty tough problem of his own: Which parts of the Bible can be trusted and which parts have errors in them? He has another problem: He is backed into the old liberal dilemma of either having to say inspiration does no more than guarantee both truth and error or he must find the Word of God in the Bible, i.e., the canon in the canon. And this is impossible to do except on a highly subjective basis devoid of logical validity.

Dr. Ramm's posture is not without other problems. Carl F. H. Henry made mention of some of them in his two-volume work *God, Revelation and Authority*. This is what Dr. Henry had to say about Dr. Ramm and his views:

> Bernard Ramm has recently proposed an evangelical redefinition
> and relocation of the concept of myth. He firmly disapproves
> Bultmann's notion that biblical supernaturalism needs to be de-
> mythologized and understoood existentially, and laments the fact
> that Strauss and Bultmann have given the concept of myth a bad
> name in the theological arena (*The Evangelical Heritage*, p. 164).
> But he approves the view of Brunner and Niebuhr that myth is the
> essential character of theological language, and endorses
> Ricoeur's contention that myth is the only way that the universal
> and transhistorical character of religious experience can be ex-
> pressed. Ramm notes that "myths in Holy Scripture presented no
> offense to such evangelical literary geniuses as C. S. Lewis and T.
> S. Eliot" but in their view, "enhanced the power of Scripture to
> communicate" (p. 165). He concludes that "evangelicals must
> come to terms with modern linguistics, modern theories of com-
> munication, and contemporary linguistic or analytic philosophy"
> (p. 166), and thinks that computer science will force them "to
> rethink the entire problem of the authenticity of Scripture (the
> power of Scripture as a written document to function as the Word
> of God)" (p. 166).
> These remarks are in some respects nebulous and ambiguous,
> since to rethink need not mean to revise. Ramm shuns "a capitu-
> lation to modern mentality" but seeks "a restatement or reformu-
> lation or reconceptualization of the biblical message . . . which
> does not surrender the uniqueness of the scriptural revelation and
> at the same time remains in real communication" with one's own
> generation (ibid., pp. 168f.). It could be that Ramm's openness to
> myth in Scripture reflects an extension of his earlier position about
> the nature of the revelatory Word. In *The Christian View of Sci-
> ence and Scripture,* his exposition of the Genesis account subor-
> dinates the creative work of the Logos of God ("and God said
> . . . and it was so") into a pictorial representation. But he insisted
> that "the writers of the Bible are free of the grotesque, the
> mythological, and the absurd" (p. 71). Ramm nonetheless con-
> siders propositional revelation too narrow a concept to be
> theologically normative for the Bible.[34]

I conclude my observations about Dr. Ramm's review of my
book by relating one of his remarks concerning the two-
volume work of Carl F. H. Henry just quoted. Dr. Ramm observed: "I don't think Lindsell has any idea how thoroughly he
will turn off those evangelical scholars who know that the bat-

tle and the issues are elsewhere and must be elsewhere." Indeed, if I did not know this, I know it now from Dr. Ramm's review. He makes it clear that he has been turned off. The same thing was said about Dr. Henry's massive and able work. The Princeton Theological Seminary journal *Theology Today* gave it a bad review. The writer argued that Dr. Henry was talking about outmoded matters and that his case was virtually worthless. He regarded it as anachronistic. He was completely turned off. Dr. Ramm said that "there is no essential difference between the theses of this article (the famous article by A. A. Hodge and B. B. Warfield—'Inspiration,' in *The Presbyterian Review* for April 1881) and Lindsell's book." In other words, my book is "old hat." Let's get on with modernity, as the *Theology Today* reviewer said about Dr. Henry's book. In any event, we should not forget the real question, which is not whether it is "old hat" but whether it is true.

I expected my book would turn off those who have never held to or who have surrendered biblical inerrancy. The book has also made clearer who they are who do not hold to biblical inerrancy.

Stephen T. Davis:
The Debate about the Bible:
Inerrancy versus Infallibility.

Stephen T. Davis is associate professor of Philosophy and Religion at the Claremont Men's College, in Claremont, California. His book *The Debate about the Bible* was published by Westminster Press and appeared in print in 1977. Dr. Davis studied at Fuller Seminary for a season and acknowledged his indebtedness to some of the faculty members. His book was written as a tract for the times in support of Fuller Seminary and in opposition to *The Battle for the Bible*. The Foreword was written by Clark Pinnock whose uneven pilgrimage has just been surveyed. The question arises naturally why Dr. Pinnock was selected to write the Foreword and why he agreed to do it.

Dr. Pinnock writes from the vantage point of an uneasy conscience for he opens his Foreword with a question showing this. "Why," he says, "should I, an evangelical theologian committed to the position of Biblical inerrancy which Dr. Davis is endeavoring to overturn, find it fitting to write the

Foreword on its behalf, encouraging others to consider his thesis and arguments?" His response to his own question is intriguing. He says:

> First, it is because I believe that there are many more ways than one to defend a high view of the Biblical inspiration and authority, and that all of them should be tried. This is especially true in a climate in which some vocal evangelicals are suggesting that Warfield's perfect errorlessness is the only sound position, and the alternative to it is liberalism and apostasy. This I consider divisive sectarianism. Therefore I am pleased rather than disconcerted when a work such as this appears. We need to listen to Dr. Davis, who strives to present a sturdy concept of Biblical authority without employing the category of inerrancy in it. The evangelical public needs to consider this thesis and to judge whether it is successful.[35]

Fortunately Dr. Pinnock could not swallow all that Dr. Davis wrote and was forced to include a disclaimer. The disclaimer is important for two reasons. But, first the disclaimer itself:

> The fact that I believe that people ought to give Dr. Davis a hearing does not mean I feel no uneasiness and see no dangers in his proposal. . . . However, I cannot look out over the theological landscape today and feel content for evangelicals to leave themselves so vulnerable and unguarded in their convictions about the Bible. I feel much happier myself with the strong but flexible wording of the Lausanne Covenant, "inerrant in all that it affirms."[36]

This Foreword was written before Dr. Pinnock's article appeared in the April 1978 issue of *Theology Today*. In this latest discussion he shows that he has defected from his preliminary statement that he is a believer in biblical inerrancy. In *Theology Today* he now has the three categories I have spoken about and he lists himself in category two—a modified inerrantist. Second, he has recorded his opposition to the Warfieldian viewpoint, but while doing so he wrongly suggests that this is the stand which characterizes hard-line believers in inerrancy today. Let it be shouted from the housetops and from Dan to Beersheba that the view called Warfieldian is the view of the Bible itself, the view of St. Augustine, the view of Calvin and Luther, the view of the historic Catholic Church up to the present century, and certainly the view of most of the Protestant churches through the ages. Professor Warfield's view and that of Professor Hodge was not original with either of them. It predated them from the days of the Old Testament and from the beginning of the New Testament as well.

But the other observation connected with this second point has to do with his assertion that the statement in the Lausanne Covenant appeals to him—"inerrant in all that it affirms." The phrase "in all that it affirms" has become a catchword and a loophole through which some people have delivered themselves from a commitment to biblical inerrancy. For when they find what seems to them to be an error or something hard to accept, they simply deny that this part of the Bible "affirms" anything. But let us look to Dr. Davis's own approach to inerrancy.

At the heart of Dr. Davis's book is the assertion that he wants to distinguish between the words "inerrancy" and "infallibility." We must grasp this point first of all and see what he means. By infallibility he means those matters in Scripture which have to do with faith and practice. By inerrancy he means going beyond matters of faith and practice, i.e., to matters relating to historical accuracy, scientific truth, and the like. Dr. Davis expressed himself very clearly as he wrote:

> But the specific highly technical claim that the Bible is inerrant is one that in all humility I cannot affirm. Let us say that a book is "inerrant" if and only if it makes no false or misleading statements. Thus, to claim that the Bible is inerrant is to claim much more than that it is "the only infallible rule of faith and practice." It is to claim that the Bible contains *no errors at all*—none in history, geography, botany, astronomy, sociology, psychiatry, economics, geology, logic, mathematics, or any area whatsoever.
>
> It is true that in most contexts of English usage the terms "infallible" and "inerrant" are synonymous. Nevertheless I believe that each term has come to have its own distinctive theological connotation.[37]

Dr. Davis opens the formal section of his book by making the following statement:

> The Bible is *inerrant* if and only if it makes no false or misleading statements on any topic whatsoever. The Bible is *infallible* if and only if it makes no false or misleading statements on any matter of faith and practice. In these senses, I personally hold that the Bible is infallible but not inerrant.[38]

Since Professor Davis classes himself as a believer in infallibility but not in inerrancy, I am willing to discuss his case on the basis of his own definitions. We must find out how he handles the data of Scripture as he commits himself to infallibility in matters of faith and practice.

I note first that Dr. Davis says the Bible *is* the Word of God.[39] Second, he says "that the Bible teaches that it is inspired, authoritative, and trustworthy."[40] Then he adds: "But it neither teaches, implies, nor presupposes that it is inerrant." These two statements have an Alice-in-Wonderland quality about them. If the Bible, all of it, is the Word of God and nevertheless contains error, then either God is the God of error or He has allowed error to slip into the Bible. Whatever is of error cannot be the Word of God, however. So it is impossible for Dr. Davis to say that the whole Bible with all of its errors is the Word of God without making nonsense. Second, if the Bible is inspired in all its parts and contains errors, then all inspiration does is give us a book which has error and truth in it. If so, then who can tell for certain which parts are true and which parts are false? And who can distinguish clearly between that which is a matter of faith and practice and that which is not? And who determines which one of the two is correct when one argues for one viewpoint and the other for the opposite viewpoint? How then can the Bible be authoritative unless it is authoritative for both? How can opposing viewpoints both be correct?

On such a basis as this it is impossible for Dr. Davis to affirm any longer that the Bible is authoritative and trustworthy. The most that he can say is that it is trustworthy and authoritative only when it treats matters of faith and practice. What he ends up with is a limited authority and a limited trustworthiness, for this brand of "inspiration" seems to guarantee error as well as truth. This is a most confused concept of the Bible. The reason is clear. At no time can Dr. Davis or anyone who holds this view ever tell men that all the Bible is infallible. He cannot say all of the Bible is authoritative. He cannot say all of the Bible is trustworthy. He must, of necessity, qualify all these statements by saying they pertain only to certain parts of the Bible, not to all of it. This makes for an infallible or inerrant human judge to determine which parts of

Scripture are true (and therefore binding upon our souls) and which are false.

When I examine the thesis of Dr. Davis further I find that he has no assurance even about matters of faith and practice. Here is what he writes:

> . . . there are historical and scientific errors in the Bible, but I have found none on matters of faith and practice. I do not claim *a priori* that the Bible is or must be infallible, just that I have found it to be so. Perhaps someday it will be found that the Bible is not infallible.[41]

With these words the last objective safeguard is gone, for Dr. Davis is uncertain even about infallibility. The most he can say is that he is presently of the opinion that the Bible is infallible but it may not turn out to be the case. If it fails to be infallible, its authority is called in question. He waits for the next disclosure from learned biblical scholars who may convince him that the infallibility he holds is no longer tenable.

But Dr. Davis goes even beyond this as he undercuts and renders useless his own foundation. Here are his words:

> I believe that the Bible is or ought to be authoritative for every Christian in all that it says on any subject unless and until he encounters a passage which after careful study and for good reasons he cannot accept.[42]

Given this statement Professor Davis opens a door so wide that everything can pass through. The Trinity, the deity of Christ, the virgin birth, and the bodily resurrection of Jesus from the dead can be easily dispensed with. Right now there are a number of scholars who have what seems to them to be perfectly valid reasons to say Jesus is not God. Dr. Davis in chapter 4 of his book speaks to the issue of the slippery slide. He laughs at the notion that once a man gives up inerrancy he sits on a slope and moves downhill, not uphill. Yet no better vindication for this can be found than in Dr. Davis' own book. His own arguments illustrate the very process he claims to be unnecessary. How slippery his slide is we shall see.

After Dr. Davis departs from his own infallibility stance he shows a tendency to water down one point after another. Thus he can write:

> Nevertheless, I admit that I am unable to stipulate a clear and

infallible criterion to distinguish Biblical passages that are *crucially* (my italics) relevant to faith and practice from those that are not. . . .

I should reiterate that my affirmation of Biblical infallibility means simply that I find no errors in the Bible that are crucially relevant to Christian faith and practice. It does not necessarily mean that I find no *theological error* in the Bible as opposed, say, to scientific or historical error. For example, as we have seen, the Bible claims that the slaughter of Canaanite innocents was the will of God, and I claim this could not have been God's will. Is this, then, a theological or a historical error in the Bible? "Theological" is a hard word to define, but even if it is indeed a theological error, it will not refute my notion of Biblical infallibility. For I see nothing here that is crucially relevant to Christian faith and practice. As I do exegesis and theology, no point of Christian faith and practice seems to me to hinge on the Bible's being correct at this point.[43]

We now discover that Dr. Davis thinks infallibility in matters of faith and practice is limited to *crucially* relevant items. In other words, some matters of faith and practice are not crucially relevant and thus can be erroneous. In addition, he admits he cannot determine which matters are crucially relevant and which are not. From there Professor Davis adduces the case of the slayings of the Canaanite civilians in Joshua and renders an astonishing and important judgment. He says:

I speak for no one except myself, but I believe that killing innocent people is morally wrong. And killing Canaanite civilians is to be sharply distinguished from killing Canaanite soldiers in the battles that were necessary for the Israelites to conquer the land that God had promised them. I frankly find it difficult to believe that it was God's will that every Canaanite—man, woman, and child—be slaughtered. Since the Bible clearly says that this was God's will, I must conclude that the Biblical writers (not to mention, of course, those who actually performed the slaughter) in this case were mistaken.[44]

I suppose no one would object to the assertion that killing innocent people is morally wrong. But some mention should be made that even this statement is true only because it has been revealed to us in Scripture. When Dr. Davis then concludes the women and children of the Canaanites were innocent, that is mere opinion which does not necessarily follow from the biblical record. Indeed who is there of whom it can be said that he or she is truly innocent? Moreover, since this case definitely involved a matter of "practice," it is obviously important, for Dr. Davis claims to believe the Bible is infallible in matters of faith and practice. But this turns out to be a passage which is not "crucially relevant." Also, Dr. Davis says the biblical writers were mistaken. What does this do to the doctrine of inspiration? If the writers of Scripture were wrong on one matter of practice, why might they not be wrong on other matters having to do with practice? And where was the Holy Spirit, the author of inspiration, when He allowed the writers of Scripture to speak errantly on a matter of practice in which they are supposed to be infallible? The more one reads how Dr. Davis develops his thesis the more incredible it becomes. It is exceedingly difficult to believe that Fuller Seminary in whose defense he has written will accept this.

Dr. Davis is committed to the use of the historical-critical method and from this as well as from many other remarks we can see that he has fallen into the "Semler Syndrome" of which more will be said later. This syndrome starts with the presupposition that the Bible and the Word of God are not synonymous. Thus, we must find the Word of God in the Bible. This is the old "canon in the canon" problem and does great violence to all objective teaching authority in the Bible.

Toward the end of his work Dr. Davis talks about the implications which follow from what he has said. He opens chapter 7 with this observation concerning the different classes of evangelicals:

> Let me introduce a distinction between two sorts of people who believe in inerrancy. There are those whom I call "divisive inerrantists" and those whom I will call "non-divisive inerrantists." Divisive inerrantists are those who (1) believe in inerrancy and (2) believe that a person cannot be considered an evangelical Christian unless he believes in inerrancy. Non-divisive inerrantists are those of whom 1 but not 2 is true. I have no particular quarrel with non-divisive inerrantists. I disagree with their doctrine but applaud their attitude.[45]

Then Dr. Davis states the real reason for opposing what he calls "divisive inerrantists." He expressed it in these words:

> Suppose the divisive inerrantists win out and people like me can no longer be considered evangelicals—what will this mean prag-

matically? Will it mean that non-inerrantist professors can no longer be hired by certain undergraduate and theological faculties? Will it mean that non-inerrantist editors will be fired from editorial boards of religious publications? Will it mean that non-inerrantist missionaries will be asked by their home agencies to give up their work and return home? Will it mean that non-inerrantist seminary graduates will be refused ordination? Will it mean that non-inerrantist ministers will be tried for heresy? I do not know the answers to these questions; I am not sure precisely what the divisive inerrantists mean to suggest. But the prospects are horrifying.

. . . let me counter with a dire prediction of my own. I say that truly alarming results will follow if divisive inerrancy gains wide acceptance in evangelical ranks. For it is plainly the case that many evangelical organizations—denominations, educational institutions, missionary groups, evangelistic enterprises, publishing houses, and religious periodicals—have both believers and nonbelievers in inerrancy in their employ.[46]

Thus Professor Davis eloquently expresses his concern for what might happen if those who believe in inerrancy gain control of certain Christian organizations. First, let it be stated plainly that there are many evangelical organizations which have and always have had doctrinal commitments in the form of confessions of faith. For the most part their confessions opt for inerrancy. This can be illustrated by denominations like the Christian and Missionary Alliance, The Baptist General Conference, and the Evangelical Free Church; by institutions like Wheaton College, Westmont College, Moody Bible Institute, Bethel College and Seminary, Gordon-Conwell Theological Seminary, Westminster Seminary and a host of others; para-church organizations like InterVarsity Christian Fellowship, all of the faith mission boards, *Moody Monthly* and *Christianity Today*. Larger denominations like the Lutheran Church-Missouri Synod, the Wisconsin Evangelical Synod, and the Southern Baptist Convention all have confessions which opt for inerrancy. Some Southern Baptist seminaries like Southwestern have doctrinal statements which also opt for inerrancy.

Dr. Davis seems to be asking in connection with institutions like these the following question: Will those who deny inerrancy be separated from their jobs? I note first that Dr. Davis is in agreement with my contention in *The Battle for the Bible* that evangelical groups which have traditionally stood for inerrancy have been infiltrated by those who do not so believe. The pragmatic question is what to do with those who no longer believe what these institutions were brought into being to uphold. The answer is relatively simple. They must either enforce their doctrinal commitments or change them. But those who sign doctrinal statements saying they believe in inerrancy when they don't, should be ethical enough to leave and seek employment elsewhere. If they are not ethically sensitive and they are found to be noninerrantists, they should in all honesty be separated from the group or organization. I will take the Moody Bible Institute by way of illustration. That school has always stood for biblical inerrancy. (So does the *Moody Monthly* and the Moody Press.) Therefore no honest person should be working for M.B.I if he is a noninerrantist. Any noninerrantist should be relieved of his job on the grounds that he no longer subscribes to the organization's principle. Why should the Institute hire those who do not assent to the Moody statement of faith? But there is another side to the issue.

Dr. Davis may also have had in mind denominations and organizations which do not have a commitment to biblical inerrancy and have on their staffs some who believe in it and some who don't. What would happen if the believers in inerrancy should gain political control of these groups? This question can be looked at from two perspectives: first, in the case of organizations which once stood for inerrancy but no longer do so; and second, organizations which never stood for inerrancy in the first place.

Fuller Seminary falls in the first category; it once believed in inerrancy but no longer does so. Yet, the answer should be clear enough. If the institution could defect from inerrancy, it could also reverse that decision and return to its original stand. In that event it would make no sense if it were to continue in its employment those who are noninerrantists. The second category is somewhat different, i.e., organizations which never did commit themselves to inerrancy. What if inerrancy advocates gained control of these organizations? Practically speaking, it is doubtful indeed that such a thing could ever happen. But if inerrantists infiltrated groups which either opposed the view or were neutral toward it, the ethical implications still control. I do not see how it would be proper for me as an inerrantist to join such a group, change its doctrinal commitment, and then fire those who did not hold the same view. There are enough places to serve God where inerrancy is involved in the orginal commitment, that there would be no need to find a place of service among those groups which opposed inerrancy from the start, or were neutral toward it. Dr. Davis in my judgment is tilting against windmills on this matter.

Dr. Davis concludes his book by referring to men like Francis Schaeffer and myself. He does so with respect to Dr. Schaeffer's opinion that those who trouble Israel today are the noninerrantists who have departed from the faith of the fathers. Dr. Davis does not believe that inerrancy was the historical view of the church. If he refuses to accept the evidences, he is not apt to be convinced by my repeating them. But he wants Francis Schaeffer and myself to accept the onus or the blame for taking what he terms a divisive stand. That is not the real question. The real question is whether the view Dr. Schaeffer and I have opted for is true or false. If it is a false view, then we are indeed guilty of divisiveness. But if it is a true view of the Bible, then we would be faithless servants of Christ if we did not press for the acceptance of it. To press for truth cannot fairly be condemned as divisive, nor can it be labelled as narrowminded sectarianism. The same sort of argument is commonly advanced to justify leaving men attached to non-Christian religions in their error. Men have the right to believe anything they wish to believe. But the true believer must, of necessity and in faithfulness to Christ, warn those who entertain error of the consequences they must face if they spurn the truth. I think Dr. Davis should heed this warning, and in love I urge him to reconsider his ways.

I strongly recommend that all inerrantists read Dr. Davis's book with great care. It is a splendid refutation of Fuller Seminary's position which he has pushed to its logical extreme. Moreover, as he spells out the implications, he undercuts his own viewpoint so effectively that he is left altogether vulnerable in *The Debate about the Bible!*

The Mennonite Brethren

The Mennonite Brethren denomination has schools in Manitoba, Canada, Hillsboro, Kansas, and the Pacific College and the Mennonite Brethren Biblical Seminary in Fresno, California. The schools of the denomination have a quarterly publication *Direction*. The April 1977 issue was almost completely devoted to a discussion of inerrancy and particularly *The Battle for the Bible*. The quarterly makes it apparent that the infiltration of an aberrant view of the Bible is to be found in depth in that denomination's institution.

The review of my book by David Ewert calls for a response on my part to his criticisms in several areas. Another essay titled "Biblical Infallibility: An Examination of Lindsell's Thesis" by Howard Loewen was the major article in this issue of *Direction* and certainly requires a rejoinder. In ancillary fashion the revealing story of the academic and spiritual pilgrimage of Devon Wiens is worthy of comment as well.

Howard Loewen

Dr. Loewen seeks to do two things generally in his article criticizing my thesis. First he states that the basis for my acceptance of inerrancy lies in two passages of Scripture: 2 Timothy 3:16, 17, and 2 Peter 1:21. Then he chooses to concentrate on the passage in Timothy. Unfortunately, Professor Loewen missed or overlooked my discussion of the view and teaching of Jesus on the subject of inerrancy (pp. 43-45). I did say that 2 Timothy is a major passage for inerrancy, but I also made reference to such other Scriptures as 1 Thessalonians 2:13 and 1 Corinthians 14:37. Since the book was only intended to be a survey, nowhere did I treat the subject of inerrancy in depth from the full biblical perspective. It has been treated by B. B. Warfield, Charles Hodge, and the faculty members of Westminster and Trinity Evangelical seminaries who are more capable than myself to advance the case. The second effort of Dr. Loewen centers around Martin Luther who Loewen says did not really hold to inerrancy. Even if Dr. Loewen makes a case against my thesis by correctly exegeting 2 Timothy 3:16, 17 differently and referring to Martin Luther in a way which would negate my thesis, he still will not have been home safe. There is the witness and testimony of countless others in the church, and the Bible is filled with direct and indirect evidences of its truthfulness in all its parts. Let's take a look at Dr. Loewen's essay.

Dr. Loewen treats the Timothy passage as follows: (1) "The Scripture itself has the *ability, the power*, to be useful for Timothy's faith;" (2) "Scripture's power lies in the fact that it is able to make us wise unto salvation. This, in a nutshell, constitutes the efficacy of Scripture;" (3) "The source and means by which the power within Scripture becomes effective for us is the *faith in Jesus Christ*. . . . Therefore it is incorrect to speak of the authority of Scripture apart from faith in the living reality of Christ."[47] Dr. Loewen concludes that "unless 2 Timothy 3:13-17 is understood in this light its essential message is bypassed." Now no one would counter what Dr. Loewen says here about God's intention to use Scripture for the salvation of men. That question is not the one around which the discussion centers. The question is whether the Scripture which God has given for our salvation is only partially trustworthy or whether it may be fully relied on.

From his treatment of the passage in Timothy Dr. Loewen goes on to discuss Martin Luther and his use of the terms "the incarnate Word," "the written Word," and the "spoken Word." All of this is interesting, but hardly relevant to the issue of inerrancy. What Dr. Loewen tries to do is to break down my assertion that Martin Luther held to an inerrant Bible. But he himself makes this statement: "This, of course, does not prevent Luther from asserting the infallibility of Scripture itself from time to time. Indeed, he explicitly states that the Scriptures are true and do not lie."[48] And that is what I said about Luther. He did not believe the Scriptures lie, and thus he believed in an inerrant Bible. Of course, New Testament proclamation preceded the writing of the canon itself. But all we know of New Testament proclamation we get from the written Scripture now. Let no man come along with a proclamation he claims to be apostolic unless he can show it derives from the written Word of God as we have it. Dr. Loewen should have checked out some of the Lutheran writings about the great Reformer. The standard Lutheran Encyclopedia has this to say:

The main thing for Luther was that Scripture is the Word of God, the absolute authority of which is above every subsequent decision of the church, and that this Word speaks strongly, challengingly, and comfortingly, as Law and Gospel to the generation today.

The Lutheran Confessions show a similar attitude. They presuppose the inspiration of Scripture.

In the Lutheran area the doctrine of inspiration was first elaborated and emphasized by the dogmaticians of the 17th century. . . . Inspiration guarantees certain properties of Scripture, such as inerrancy, authority, clarity and efficacy. Inerrancy applies not only to matters of Christian doctrine, but to everything else in Scripture as well, history, chronology, astronomy, genealogy, onomastics, etc."

The same conception of inspiration and most of its characteristic marks can be found in the scholastics of the Middle Ages.[49]

Despite what Dr. Loewen says, this Lutheran Encyclopedia gainsays his statement and provides a better appreciation and understanding of Martin Luther and the Lutheran tradition than he does. I will stick with the encyclopedia. Now back to Dr. Loewen's exegesis of Timothy.

From his exegesis of Timothy Dr. Loewen concludes that "the authority of God's Word is essentially a confession of our faith regarding its ability to accomplish its purpose, not a definition of the accuracy of the biblical text itself." Then he adds: "The authority of Scripture pertains solely to its redemptive purpose: making us knowledgeable in salvation." He further says: "The nature of biblical authority is such that it can never be satisfactorily formulated by an assertion regarding the accuracy of textual details," and he then draws his final conclusion that "the belief that the Bible is infallible is an integral part of the basic affirmation that Scripture is the church's essential authority for faith and life."[50] In other words Dr. Loewen is saying that the infallibility of the Bible is limited to that which has to do with matters of salvation but does not extend beyond that point.

Professor Loewen makes any number of statements to which exception must be taken. Among them are the following. He says, "the Word of God does not come to us apart from Scripture. It must be sought *in* (my italics) and through the Scripture."[51] Martin Luther accepted and all orthodox believers have embraced the principle that all of the Bible *is* the Word of God. We do not try to find the Word of God *in* Scripture. This is the error of the Semler approach (of which more will be said later).

Secondly Dr. Loewen says: "We cannot begin to speak about the nature of the incarnate, written or spoken Word on the one hand, nor the function of the Word in terms of its authority, receptivity and efficacy on the other, unless we have first concretely appropriated that Word for our lives."[52] This is hardly true. Dr. Loewen seems to be saying that the Word of God becomes the Word of God only in experience; it is not the objective revelation of God whether one understands and appropriates it or not. I have made reference to William Barclay, who denied some of the major doctrines of the Christian faith. I cannot believe he was a Christian in the New Testament sense of the term. Yet he certainly understood the Word of God better in many ways than Dr. Loewen does who professes to be a Christian.

Dr. Loewen does not like the idea of tying any doctrine of Scripture to 2 Timothy 3:15-16. He exegetes it differently from B. B. Warfield and he certainly fails to do justice to the word *theopneustos*. But what is really significant is this: The Mennonite Brethren Biblical Seminary in Fresno, California, has a doctrinal statement, and this is what it says:

> That the whole Bible is the inspired and infallible Word of God, and is the supreme and final authority in all matters of faith and conduct. 2 Peter 1:21; 2 Timothy 3:16.[53]

I note first the confession of his own denomination affirms that the whole Bible is the infallible Word of God. This Dr. Loewen does not say and cannot agree with. Neither here nor elsewhere in the doctrinal platform of the confession does it say anything or allude to anything that Dr. Loewen makes central to his thesis. He is the one who claims that the authority of Scripture pertains solely to its redemptive purpose. But the Fresno statement says nothing of this supposedly vital conclusion. Second, the Fresno statement uses 2 Timothy 3:16 as an anchor for its view that the whole Bible "is the inspired and infallible Word of God." But Dr. Loewen has in effect nullified this view in his exegesis of the verse. The doctrinal statement also includes 2 Peter 1:21 which Dr. Loewen never considers. To be sure, the doctrinal statement (perhaps for reasons of brevity) omits mention of the teaching of Jesus on this point. But neither does Dr. Loewen pay any attention to what Jesus said about Scripture. Why not? A last word on Professor Loewen. He states:

> For the real infallibility of the Word of God can never be established unless the message of Scripture has in fact transformed heart and mind, thought and deed.[54]

This observation should be considered in the light of Dr. Loewen's concentration on Martin Luther. The Mennonites and the Lutherans are poles apart on so many aspects of the Christian faith that it is hard to know where to start or where to stop. Among them are questions of believer's baptism, infant baptism, the real presence of Christ in the sacrament of the supper, ecclesiology, law and gospel, and many others. Beyond question, both Mennonites and Lutherans are members of the body of Christ if they hold to the full authority of Scripture. Yet it should be recognized that while they both believe in the real infallibility of the Word this does not necessarily mean there is agreement on denominational distinctives. They agree that a true member of Christ's body believes in justification by faith alone. However, Dr. Loewen's "transformed heart and mind" does not necessarily bring about agreement over certain theological questions about which Christians have honestly differed over the centuries. Surely the Holy Spirit cannot lead some to believe in the real presence of Christ in the Lord's Supper and others to take the opposite tack. Somebody must be wrong. Dr. Loewen's subjective existentialism suggests to me that he overlooked the objective nature of the Bible which can be intellectually understood and rightly interpreted by those who are strangers to grace. Unredeemed scholars can know what it says and still not believe it. James says that even the demons of hell believe and tremble, for they know who Jesus Christ is and they know that God is one (James 2:19).

Devon Wiens

In the same issue of *Direction* Dr. Devon Wiens contributed an essay titled "Hearing the Word: To understand what I

read—the Pilgrimage of a Bible Scholar." He made the following observation:

> In seminary, where I experienced personal renaissance both spir-
> itually and intellectually, some old myths that had never worn
> very well anyway, such as the exegetical methods of fundamen-
> talism and dispensationalism, were shattered. In a more positive
> vein, what I imbibed there was a sense of the propriety (indeed,
> the necessity) of becoming conversant with critical modes of in-
> quiry, but also of the need to engage these *critically.*
>
> In the doctoral program, I gained considerable appreciation for
> Bultmannian theology and hermeneutics. Since those days, how-
> ever, I have become somewhat less enamoured of this existen-
> tialist thrust (one comes sooner or later to realize that Barth,
> Bultmann and Tillich were only human after all!) and have settled
> an urgent need to "remythologize" it in accordance with a "mod-
> ern" scientific *Geist.*
>
> My present perspective has, I suppose, been largely informed
> by a reaction to opposing tendencies in today's evangelical world.
>
> In response to a traditionalist ham-stringing of the Word with its
> carefully-structured, predictable ways and with "old fashioned"
> ethical mores and doctrinal stances remaining inviolate, the Ref-
> ormation anabaptist stress upon allowing the Spirit to break forth
> new meanings from his Word has taken on significantly new di-
> mensions for me. The contemporary charismatic renewal has also
> spoken effectively to this point.[55]

Dr. Wiens writes neither in the language nor the thought pattern of historic orthodoxy, as these quotations indicate. No
one would imagine for a moment that he stands in the evangelical orbit or that he has any interest in doing so. When one
reads his words over against the doctrinal platform of the
Mennonite Brethren Biblical Seminary it is easy to see that the
confession is antiquated, according to Dr. Wiens' standards,
and that his viewpoint is quite at variance with it. For him to
affirm a belief in inerrancy would be difficult to imagine.

David Ewert

Of greater interest is the review of *The Battle for the Bible* by
Dr. David Ewert, professor of New Testament at the Fresno
seminary. He said: "Lindsell makes inerrancy—that is, as he
understands inerrancy—the watershed between the faithful
evangelicals and those who have no right to use that name."
He went on to add: "Our Mennonite Brethren confession of

faith is content with using biblical phraseology: 'We believe that all Scripture is inspired by God as men of God were moved by the Holy Spirit' (2 Tim. 3:16 and 2 Peter 1:21)."[56] Perhaps Professor Ewert should take another look at the confession of the institution in which he is a teacher. It says: "the whole Bible is the inspired and infallible Word of God. . . ." This is quite different from what he asserted to be the position of his denomination.

Perhaps this is the place to make a very important observation. Apologists for partial errancy of Scripture speak of "Lindsell's understanding of inerrancy" as though the viewpoint I put forth is something which I invented. But this is wide of the truth. Inerrancy is not something I dreamed up, nor do I profess to have been its originator. I simply have followed in the tradition of the Scripture and also in that of the innumerable company of the saints who went before me. I am the recipient of the Christian tradition, not the formulator of it. It has been handed down to me, as to every other believer, in Holy Scripture, in the great creeds, in the statements of faith adopted by post-Reformation denominations, as well as in the writings of the fathers of the church through the ages. Some opponents of inerrancy have argued that it has not been the view of the church through the ages, but such a denial only shows a refusal to face the facts.

Dr. Ewert goes on to say that once I had decided upon my view of inerrancy, I then went on to set myself up "as a judge over other Christian denominations and institutions. . . . The saddest chapter is the one in which he writes devastatingly of that fine evangelical institution, Fuller Theological Seminary (where he himself taught at one time)."[57] Apparently it is all right for Professor Ewert to criticize me and set himself up as a judge over what I have written, but it is wrong for me to do that with respect to anyone else. He misses the point of it all in his remarks about Fuller Seminary. He should have asked himself the question whether what I said was true or false. All I alleged in *The Battle for the Bible* was that Fuller Seminary at one time believed in an inerrant Scripture and that it no longer does. Since Fuller Seminary has had at least two years since 1976 to correct that statement and point out wherein I have been wrong, one would expect they would have done so by this time. All that Fuller Seminary has done by way of rebuttal only serves to validate the allegation I made. Since the publication of my first book Fuller Seminary has never said that it holds to inerrancy as an institution in the way in which it formerly did.

All that the April, 1977, issue of *Direction* does is make known to the Christian public that the Mennonite Brethren have also been infiltrated with a view of Scripture which impugns inerrancy, contradicts the doctrinal platform of their seminary in Fresno, and in effect limits the trustworthiness of the Bible to salvific or redemptive matters, and lays down the dictum that "the nature of biblical authority is such that it can never be satisfactorily formulated by an assertion regarding the accuracy of textual details."[58] And whoever accepts this proposition either becomes an agnostic about inerrancy (and thus cannot justifiably denounce those who do believe in inerrancy), or he is making a dogmatic statement that no one can make a credible statement that the Bible is free from error in textual details.

NOTES

[1]*The Christian Century*, November 10, 1976, "'The Battle for the Bible:' Renewing the Inerrancy Debate," p. 977.

[2]Ibid., March 2, 1977, "Readers Response," p. 198.

[3]Ibid.

[4]Ibid.

[5]James F. Findlay, Jr., *Dwight L. Moody* (Chicago: U. of Chicago Press, 1969), pp. 256, 257.

[6]William R. Moody, *The Life of Dwight L. Moody* (New York: Fleming H. Revell Company, 1900), pp. 495, 496.

[7]Richard Ellsworth Day, *Bush Aglow* (Philadelphia: Judson Press, 1936), p. 210.

[8]Edward Leight Pell, *Dwight L. Moody* (Richmond, Va.: B. F. Johnson Publishing Co., 1900), pp. 97, 98.

[9]Ibid., p. 98.

[10]Earnest B. Gordon, *Adoniram Judson Gordon* (New York: Fleming H. Revell Company, 1896), pp. 299-301.

[11]"Readers Response," p. 198.

[12]*Evangelical Newsletter*, Vol. 4, No. 25, December 16, 1977.

[13]Carl F. H. Henry, *Whose Battle for the Bible?* (Evangelical Press Association: syndicated article, n.d.), p. 4.

[14]Ibid.

[15] *The Reformed Journal*, July-August 1976, p. 24.

[16] Carl F. H. Henry, p. 5.

[17] Harold Lindsell, *The Battle for the Bible* (Grand Rapids: Zondervan, 1976), p. 104.

[18] Clark Pinnock, *A New Reformation* (Tigerville, S.C.: Jewel Books, 1968), pp. 2-5.

[19] Ibid., pp. 6-10.

[20] *The Bookstore Journal*, January 1972, p. 131.

[22] Clark Pinnock, *Biblical Revelation* (Chicago: Moody Press, 1971), pp. 78-80.

[22] Clark Pinnock, *The Inerrancy Debate among the Evangelicals* (Mimeographed paper, May 1976), p. 1.

[23] Ibid., p. 4.

[24] Ibid., pp. 6-8.

[25] *The Church Herald*, September 17, 1976, p. 16.

[26] Clark Pinnock, "Evangelicals and Inerrancy: The Current Debate" in *Theology Today*, April 1978, p. 66, 67.

[27] Ibid., p. 68.

[28] Ibid., p. 69.

[29] Bernard Ramm, "Misplaced Battle Lines" in *The Reformed Journal*, July-August 1976, p. 37.

[30] Ibid., pp. 37, 38.

[31] Ibid., p. 38.

[32] Ibid., p. 37.

[33] Ibid.

[34] Carl F. H. Henry, *God, Revelation and Authority* (Waco: Word Books, 1976), Vol. I, pp. 66, 67.

[35] Stephen T. Davis, *The Debate about the Bible: Inerrancy versus Infallibility* (Philadelphia: Westminster, 1977), p. 11.

[36] Ibid., p. 13.

[37] Ibid., p. 16.

[38] Ibid., p. 23.

[39] Ibid., p. 115.

[40] Ibid., p. 65.

[41] Ibid., pp. 114, 115.

[42] Ibid., p. 116.

[43] Ibid., p. 118.

[44] Ibid., pp. 96, 97.

[45] Ibid., p. 130.

[46] Ibid., pp. 130, 131.

[47] Howard Loewen, "Biblical Infallibility: An Examination of Lindsell's Thesis," in *Direction*, Volume VI, No. 2, April 1977, pp. 6, 7.

[48] Ibid., p. 10.

[49] Julius Bodensieck, editor, *The Encyclopedia of the Lutheran Church* (Minneapolis: Augsburg, 1965), Vol. 1, p. 236.

[50] Loewen, Ibid., pp. 13, 14.

[51] Ibid., p. 12.

[52] Ibid., p. 13.

[53]1975-1977 Catalog, Mennonite Brethren Biblical Seminary, Fresno, California, p. 8.

[54]Loewen, p. 15.

[55]Devon Wiens, "Hearing the Word" in *Direction*, Volume VI, No. 2, April 1977, pp. 36, 37.

[56]David Ewert, "Book Reviews" in *Direction*, Volume VI, No. 2, April 1977, p. 39.

[57]Ibid.

[58]Loewen, p. 13.

3
The Smaller Groups:
The Updated Story

Size is not the sole criterion for determining whether a church or Christian organization will be infiltrated by the errancy virus. Normally one would suppose that the smaller the group the less likelihood there would be for the infection to strike. It is true, of course, that a large denomination is more likely to develop the infection if, like the Southern Baptist Convention, it has more than twelve million members. But its size does not mean it will have an equal number of errancy advocates proportionately. The United Methodist Church has a greater number of errancy advocates than does the Southern Baptist Convention. The Lutheran Church-Missouri Synod has far fewer errancy supporters than does the United Church of Christ, the Lutheran Church in America, or the Protestant Episcopal Church. Denominations numbering fewer than a million members can easily have in them strong coalitions of errancy advocates. Moreover it can happen that the smaller the group the greater the influence of a vocal albeit tiny segment of opponents of inerrancy especially if they hold teaching positions in their denominational schools.

So far as Christian colleges are concerned it does not seem to make too much difference whether the school has eight hundred or three thousand students. With the exception of a few institutions most Christian colleges have been infected with the virus and are committed to the use of the historical-critical method, which is the surest guarantee that the schools will move leftward and away from inerrancy. Parachurch groups do not conform to a single pattern. Young Life has been subjected to more infiltration than the Inter-

Varsity Christian Fellowship. And, in turn, InterVarsity has experienced more problems than has Campus Crusade for Christ which appears to have been curiously preserved against the virus.

The Bible Colleges seem to be less likely subjects for errancy invasion than the liberal arts colleges. The reason for this probably is that the liberal arts colleges offer many majors and most of the professors have taken graduate work in secular universities where they have been conditioned against theological orthodoxy directly or indirectly. In addition, the Bible Colleges have been staffed in greater numbers by graduates of theological institutions steeped in historic orthodoxy. A substantial number of Bible Colleges are committed to dispensational theology and have employed a large number of Dallas Seminary graduates who have taken their postcollegiate master's and doctoral work at the same institution.

Missionary organizations, especially those of the faith type and those of the smaller denominations, have been shielded from incursion by the errancy viewpoint. The Interdenominational Foreign Mission Association has in it most of the faith missionary agencies. These mission boards have been kept from serious attack for a variety of reasons. Many of their candidates are Bible institute and Bible college graduates. Those who come from theological seminaries are carefully screened. Many of these boards fall within the dispensational tradition. On the other hand, the Evangelical Foreign Missions Association of Evangelicals includes in its roster faith missions and missionary agencies of smaller denominations. Its independent missionary boards are generally like those of the IFMA. Their denominational agencies usually reflect the pattern of the particular denomination. If the denomination has been infected with the errancy virus, it would tend to make its presence felt sooner or later in the mission board as well as the denomination's institutions.

This chapter will deal with smaller evangelical groups generally, but with particular attention to the National Association of Evangelicals. Since it contains several of the smaller denominations and also local congregations of larger communions, it seems logical to deal with it first and then go on to other small denominations outside of NAE and various parachurch groups.

The National Association of Evangelicals

The National Association of Evangelicals came into being in 1942. Harold John Ockenga was one of the founding fathers and its first president. It was established as a counterbalance to the Federal Council of the Churches of Christ in the United States of America, now known as the National Council of Churches. At the time of the founding of the NAE it was hoped that men like Carl McIntire would be part of the new organization. However, he and others of like mind established the American Council of Christian Churches. Dr. McIntire himself established and still publishes *The Christian Beacon*.

The NAE put together a statement of faith, the first article of which dealt with Scripture, and reads as follows:

> We believe the Bible to be the inspired, the only infallible authoritative Word of God.[1]

The NAE said that the Bible is inspired, that it is infallible, and that it is authoritative. There was no limitation on the Bible's infallibility. The statement said nothing about infallibility being limited to matters of faith and practice. The formulation was understood without difficulty in that day. Today it is possible to make something of the fact that the NAE used the word "infallible" rather than "inerrant." Dr. Hubbard said this: "It is worth noting that the National Association of Evangelicals chose the word 'infallibility' rather than 'inerrancy' for its statement."[2] But his observation carries little or no weight, because back in 1942 "infallible" and "inerrant" were used interchangeably. Moreover, Dr. Hubbard needs to remember that one of his own colleagues at Fuller Seminary, who is also associated with him on the "Joyful Sound" radio broadcast, namely Daniel Fuller, has stated that these two words are synonymous. Moreover, in the "Joyful Sound" paper, *Today's Christian*, Dr. Fuller says he has always believed in an inerrant Scripture. Dr. Hubbard also knows that Fuller Seminary's statement says that the Bible is "the infallible rule of faith and practice." One supposes that the word "infallible" in Fuller's statement means that everything having to do with faith and practice must be truthful. We can substitute the same idea for the NAE formulation, except that it includes all of the Bible, not just some of the Bible, as in the case of Fuller Seminary.

It would not be unexpected for the NAE to be infiltrated by some who do not accept inerrancy. After all, the organization has in it denominations which have been influenced by that approach, so that the infection in any of the member groups would sooner or later reflect itself into the NAE as well. For example, Dr. Fred P. Thompson, Jr., is the president of Emmanuel School of Religion in Johnson City, Tennessee. He has been a regular contributor to the NAE magazine *United Evangelical Action.* His institution, which is connected with the Disciples of Christ, is more liberal than the Cincinnati Bible College, which is unabashedly conservative. When *The Battle for the Bible* was published, Dr. Thompson devoted one of his *At Issue* columns to it. He entitled it "The Wrong War." In the course of his discussion he made it plain that he does not believe in biblical inerrancy.

Dr. Thompson went on record as saying:

> I state herewith categorically my confidence in Holy Scripture as the Word of God written, the infallible rule of faith and practice for the people of God. I believe it to be inspired by the Holy Spirit and thus profitable for the instruction, correction and admonition of the church.[3]

It will be seen immediately that Dr. Thompson is saying something different from the NAE statement of faith. He believes the Bible to be "the infallible rule of faith and practice." But the NAE statement says that the Bible is "the inspired, the only infallible Word of God." The latter statement is unlimited; Dr. Thompson's statement is limited. Dr. Thompson goes on to say: "I do not regard the doctrine of inerrancy helpful or relevant." Later he said: "Historical criticism is therefore an indispensable method for scholarly work in the study of the Bible. Dr. Lindsell repudiates this method with the judgment, 'Orthodoxy and the historical-critical method are deadly enemies that are antithetical and cannot be reconciled without the destruction of one or the other.' " Then he adds: "The alternative to historical criticism is an unhistorical and uncritical approach to Scripture, an alternative which, as Carl F. H. Henry says, 'Will be rejected outright by most evangelical scholars' (*The New Review of Books and Religion,* September, 1976.*''*[4] Several observations are in order.

In *The Battle for the Bible* the term "the historical-critical method" was used deliberately. This term has specific content and meaning. It must be said again and again that this specific and well-known methodology is the Bible's greatest enemy, and a later chapter in this book will enlarge on that thesis. But Dr. Thompson is wrong when he states that the alternative to this methodology is "an unhistorical and uncritical approach to Scripture," and he drags in a comment from Carl F. H. Henry. The Bible is a historical book even though it is not a textbook of history *per se.* Of course Bible students must look at the Bible from a historical perspective, but they do this from an entirely different frame of reference from those who use the historical-critical methodology, technically so called. Believers in inerrancy accept what the Bible says, so that if there are secular or pagan materials which disagree with what the Bible states to be true, they accept the Bible over against nonbiblical sources. The Babylonian "Enuma elish" gives an account about creation. But it contains many differences from the biblical account of creation for example, and implies that primeval matter existed before the creation of the gods. Inerrantists do not for one moment think Moses got his information from the Babylonian Epic or that the Babylonian Epic can sit in judgment on Scripture. Rather Scripture sits in judgment on the Babylonian Epic, which must be understood and interpreted from within the Bible context rather than the Bible in its context.

Moreover, Dr. Thompson fails to make clear that which is intrinsic to the historical-critical method. It distinguishes between *heilsgeschichte* (that is, salvation history) and *historie* (that is, straight history, the facts or the nuts and bolts). The traditional historical-critical approach thinks that the salvatory message gets through even though the facts in which the message is couched may be untrue. Thus this kind of critic can deny the supernatural, including the virgin birth, and the bodily resurrection of Jesus, and also the deity of Jesus and still have some sort of salvatory idea. No evangelical ever says that the alternative to the historical-critical methodology is "an unhistorical and uncritical approach to Scripture." Rather, he

starts with the presupposition that Scripture is factually historical, so that when it says Jonah was swallowed by a great fish
for three days and three nights and emerged unscathed it is
true. It is true (that is, it is historic) that Jesus died on the cross
and rose in the body from the dead. And what Jesus is purported to have said by the evangelists in the Gospels He really
said. The evangelical critical approach to Scripture is quite
different from that of the advocate of historical criticism. The
evangelical starts with the basis of faith and trust. He is critical
in the sense that he wants to find out by careful objective study
exactly what the Scripture says. The historical-critical advocate
however starts out with quite a different approach. He does
not believe what Scripture says until he has convinced himself
that there is good reason to believe it. If it does not suit his
categories of probability or appeal to his sense of reason, then
he does not believe it. The evangelical believes the Bible re-
gardless of how it goes counter to his personal preferences or
criteria of probability.

In the aforesaid article Dr Thompson makes the significant
statement that "Lindsell contends further that the Bible claims
to be inerrant. If this contention can be demonstrated I will
concede the battle."[5] Note immediately what Dr. Thompson
says. He says he believes the Bible is not inerrant. However,
he is willing to change his mind, *if* inerrancy can be proved.
No Bible student should refuse to engage in dialogue with Dr.
Thompson about whether the claim that the Bible is inerrant is
true or false. But he has not seen what the issue really is. It is
this: The NAE statement of faith says that the Bible in all its
parts is infallible. Dr. Thompson signs that statement of faith.
Yet Dr. Thompson does not presently believe that the Bible is
infallible in all its parts. What right, then, does Dr. Thompson
have to remain in the NAE when he does not believe the basis
the NAE has set up for membership? What right does he have
to use *United Evangelical Action* magazine to discount and tear
down what the NAE stands for? This is an ethical question,
not simply a matter of scholarship or theological theory. No
one wants Dr. Thompson to say he believes something he
disbelieves in his heart. But members of the NAE have every
right to expect him to honor the NAE statement of faith either
by having it changed, as Fuller Seminary finally did, to en-

compass his current view or else leave the NAE.
No one should quarrel with Dr. Thompson if he rejects the
notion that one proved error in Scripture invalidates the
whole. Nor is it a key issue whether he thinks the Bible was
written by men apart from the Holy Spirit, or by the Holy
Spirit apart from men, or a combination of both. Nor should
we concern ourselves at this moment with his question
whether the Holy Spirit "guaranteed that their essays (that is
the books written by the human authors of the Bible) would
never contain a single mistake." What is important is this:
wholly apart from the question whether the Bible has a single
provable error in it or not, the NAE has adopted a platform in
which it says that the entire Bible is the infallible Word of God.
Let us concede for the sake of discussion that the NAE and
inerrantists may be wrong. That doesn't change the facts in the
case. And Dr. Thompson is out of bounds because he signs
what he doesn't believe whether it is right or wrong. Honesty
should move him to stop writing for *Action* and to demit the
NAE because he does not believe what the NAE is committed
to—whether it happens to be right or wrong. It is not that any
inerrantist thinks the NAE statement to be wrong. They can
concur with it and believe it in full.

Toward the end of his essay Dr. Thompson says that "the
doctrine of inerrancy directs our attention away from the supreme focus of faith—Jesus Christ as the Word of God made
flesh. It comes perilously close to making an end out of what is
clearly an instrument. It easily hardens into a creedal and sectarian attitude which draws lines between 'real' Christians and
not-so-real ones."[6] Dr. Thompson could not be more wrong.
Inerrancy draws men closer to Jesus, the incarnate Word of
God, who said the Scripture cannot be broken. Those who
believe what Jesus said about Scripture are not by that belief
drawn farther away from Him but nearer to Him. Moreover,
the statement about hardening into "a creedal and sectarian
attitude which draws lines" is not true. The NAE statement of
faith was formulated to draw lines. That's what statements of
faith are intended to do. Statements of faith bind people of like
mind together. They also have circumferences outside of
which stand those who cannot in good conscience agree with a
particular statement of faith. Let Dr. Thompson set up an or-

ganization comparable to the NAE. Let him construct his own statement of faith. Let him frame a doctrine of Scripture which limits infallibility to matters of faith and practice. But he should not sit where he now sits when he cannot honestly agree with a statement of faith he has put his name to. Dr. Gleason L. Archer of Trinity Evangelical Divinity School responded to Dr. Thompon's essay in the Spring 1977 issue of *United Evangelical Action*.[7] His remarks appear in the Appendix for the benefit of the reader who is interested.

The NAE picture becomes murkier when one looks at its thirty-fifth anniversary celebration in 1977. The educational arm of the NAE presided over by Carl Lundquist of Bethel College and Seminary invited David Hubbard and Bernard Ramm to be the speakers for the occasion. It is especially ironic since the major theme of the convention had to do with a trustworthy Bible.

When the 1978 NAE convention came around, Timothy Smith of Johns Hopkins was one of the major speakers. He is the one who wrote a letter to *Christian Century* in which he denied any belief in inerrancy and challenged inerrantists to show that their position is true in the light of his observations about Dwight L. Moody, A. J. Gordon, and the Southern Baptist Seminary of Louisville, among others. This we did in this volume.

The NAE does have in its midst those who do not believe in inerrancy. It remains to be seen what it will do and how it will deal with men like Dr. Thompson who is out of line so far as the NAE statement of faith is involved. It is surely not the function of the NAE to take action against individual members of denominations which are related to it. That's the business of each denomination. So long as the denomination has a theological posture which is in accord with that of the NAE there is no problem. But the NAE also has individual memberships in which those who so relate themselves to the NAE must sign the doctrinal statement. Thus the NAE has the obligation to take action with respect to anyone who is an individual member of the NAE and who signs a statement he disavows elsewhere. It also has the responsibility to see that its editors and continuing contributors to its *United Evangelical Action* believe and speak in accord with the NAE statement of faith. This is not true of Dr. Thompson. And the NAE should direct its attention to this.

The Christian Reformed Church

In *The Battle for the Bible* the Christian Reformed Church was discussed, but mostly in connection with the Free University at Amsterdam. In particular the names of Professors Berkouwer and Kuitert were mentioned, along with their changing stance on theological matters pertaining to biblical inerrancy. Subsequent to the publication of *The Battle* considerable tremors were felt in the Christian Reformed Church. Numbers of the lay people as well as three publications related to the church one way or another got into the act. The church's own paper, *The Banner*, got involved as did *The Outlook* which is independent and committed to inerrancy. *The Reformed Journal* was the third publication which involved itself deeply in the ongoing discussion. Its editors represent the avant garde intellectuals who are generally left of center in the denomination. Two of them, James Daane and Lewis Smedes, are on the Fuller Seminary faculty.

Lester De Koster

It all started when Lester De Koster, editor of *The Banner*, broke into print with a series of editorials dealing with inerrancy. The issue had surfaced in the denomination earlier when the synod dealt with it in connection with the Reverend Doctors Edwin Walhout and Allen Verhey. Dr. De Koster joined together the discussion of the synod and *The Battle for the Bible*. He termed the book "a highly incompetent work, at most a reservoir of unseemly gossip. Unfortunately it has secured some hasty endorsement by Reformed writers who, on reflection, will have occasion to reconsider, I think, their enthusiasm. . . . The closer you look, the worse this book looks, as we shall see together sometime soon."[28] Thus the good editor damned the book to the readers of the magazine before they knew what it contained, and he did so in such a fashion that no one would suppose his future editorials would be objective.

Dr. De Koster opened his discussion in the following issue of *The Banner* appropriately with the background of the Christian Reformed Church's confession. The Belgic Confession, which dates from 1561, is the theological cornerstone of the church. In its statement about the Bible the confession says: "We receive all these books, and these only, as holy and canonical, for the regulation, foundation, and confirmation of our faith; *believing without any doubt all things contained in them* . . . because the Holy Spirit witnesses in our hearts that they are from God."[9] The statement is plain enough about the Bible. Men are to believe without any doubt; they are to believe *all things* contained in the Bible. And the Holy Spirit witnesses to them that the Holy Scriptures are from God.

Moreover, Dr. De Koster used some accurate and telling statements from John Calvin about the Bible: Through the Bible "God opens His own most hallowed lips"; so that His "truth should abide forever in the world"; and the Scriptures "are the very school of God's children." They "obtain full authority among believers only when we regard them as having sprung from heaven, as if there the living word of God were heard." And certainty about the Bible "is not established until we are persuaded beyond doubt that God is its Author."[10] These are strong words indeed! What then was Dr. De Koster's problem? All *The Battle for the Bible* said was that the Christian Reformed Church had in it those who neither believe the Belgic Confession about Scripture nor what John Calvin taught. So two points should be made with regard to Dr. De Koster's editorials.

The first has to do with the witness of the Holy Spirit "that the Bible is God's Word." If there is anything the Holy Spirit cannot do it is to witness out of both sides of the divine mouth at the same time. That is, the Holy Spirit cannot witness to some of God's people that the Bible is free from all error in the whole and in the part and then to others that the Bible has errors in it. The *News Bulletin*, published by the Association of Christian Reformed Laymen, had this to say about Dr. De Koster's arguments:

Lester De Koster is touting a centuries-old argument in his "defense" of Scripture. The opponents of the Bible and the enemies of the Church have called his argument the "Achilles-heel" of the Reformation. Dr. H. J. Scholten, modernist in the extreme, the teacher of Dr. Abraham Kuyper, used it as the cornerstone of his teachings in the dogmatics. Strauss, one of the early 19th century proponents of what is known today as the "historical-critical" method of Bible study, took a particular delight in challenging his Bible-believing opponents with that argument. Look, he said, the Spirit witnesses one thing in your heart, and something else in the heart of your fellowman, and again something else in the heart of a Catholic, or Methodist, or Lutheran. By what *standard* are we to judge what "the Spirit" witnesses in the hearts of all these people? And he mercilessly chastised them for getting bogged down in a quagmire of subjectivism. If that is the Reformed Confession of Scripture, he said, what makes you so sure that you are not believing your own spirit instead of the Holy Spirit? De Koster has no answer to Strauss, Scholten, the Catholic church, and others who have tried to nail the true believer down with that piece of circular reasoning. On the contrary, by presenting it as a true "Calvinist doctrine" he only provided more ammunition for his opponents. If the trustworthiness of Scripture depends on the inner witness of "the Spirit" in De Koster's heart, then the ground of the authority of Scripture is replaced from the text of Scripture into the heart of De Koster, the Pope, the people of the "inner Word" and the subjectivists of similar stripe. To praise this sort of devious subjectivism as pure Calvinism demonstrates that De Koster never understood his "Uncle John."[11]

In the Reformed tradition the teaching has always been that the Holy Spirit witnesses in and through the Word of God. If the Scripture teaches its own inerrancy then the Spirit cannot witness that there are errors in the Bible. It is obvious that the author of the Belgic Confession spoke about Scripture and its trustworthiness based upon what Scripture itself said. And any so-called inner witness of the Spirit to the contrary would have been known to be something other than the true witness of the Spirit.

The second point about Dr. De Koster's editorials has to do with the allegation made in *The Battle for the Bible* that the Christian Reformed Church in its American and Dutch manifestations has been infiltrated by an aberrant view of the Bible. Dr. De Koster admitted this to be true. His own admission indicates that *The Battle for the Bible* at least at this point was not "unseemly gossip." It was true. Editor De Koster said this:

Of course, because the Scriptures are the Word of God, we are joyously ready to confess ourselves "believing without doubt all things contained in them." Could any Christian, who seriously says "the Word of God," say anything less than that he believes all it says?
Yes, we are all aware that some do. Some choose which parts of the Bible are, in their judgment, to be accounted the Words of God; some even seem to choose which Words of God still oblige their acceptance. Such persons will have to answer for themselves. . . . It is, of course, the legitimate business of the Church to inquire if those ordained to speak for God to, and within, the Church discipline their speaking in terms of the Confessions. This was, in some sense, the issue at Synod last June in the instances mentioned before.[12]

Since Dr. De Koster has admitted there are those who do not believe in accord with the Belgic Confession, it is hardly worth the time and effort to discuss the incidental problems he adduced except as they arise in connection with some of Dr. De Koster's critics who saw in his efforts an endeavor to whitewash the growing inerrancy defection in the Christian Reformed Church.

The Outlook

The Outlook is a conservative voice among the Christian Reformed people. It stands squarely on the confessional commitment of the denomination and is concerned about the departure from a belief in an inerrant Bible on the part of some clergy and some lay people in the denomination. After Lester De Koster opened his campaign against *The Battle for the Bible*, *The Outlook*, which had recommended the book, did not falter in its approbation and went further by running articles that challenged the editorials of Dr. De Koster. Edwin H. Palmer, the executive secretary of the *New International Version*, entered the fray. He took sharp exception to some of the views expressed by Dr. De Koster. First, he endorsed *The Battle for the Bible* saying that while he thought there were minor errors "the general thrust is perfect—right on target." He was very unhappy with Dr. De Koster's statements that "the first casualty in Dr. Harold Lindsell's *Battle for the Bible* is the Bible there on your table—that King James or RSV or whatever your translation is!" Dr. Palmer made clear that inerrancy relates to the autographs and that every translation has mistakes in it whether it be the King James, the RSV, or the New International Version. Such mistakes are of no serious consequence (for they never affect Christian doctrine). And yet even they were never in the autographs.

Dr. Palmer faulted Dr. De Koster for not realizing there is no confusion between the witness of the Holy Spirit and the grounds for believing the Bible is true. It is not a choice between rationalism and the witness of the Spirit. We are to present reasons for believing the Bible to be the Word of God and look to the Holy Spirit to take these reasons and use them to convince men that the Bible is the Word of God. Dr. Palmer concluded that "Once we begin to fiddle-faddle with the inspiration and inerrancy of all the Bible, we will begin to question Adam and Eve, Paradise and the fall (Kuitert), Jericho (Koole), or the resurrection of the saints at the crucifixion of Jesus (Baarda), or Paul's instruction about women (Prof. Jewett of Fuller) . . . and so on. . . . Yes, inerrancy—partial or total—is the crucial question."[13]

The Reformed Journal

The Reformed Journal is the periodical which speaks for those who want the Christian Reformed Church to move away from its original foundation. It is owned and operated by Eerdmans Publishing Company whose label at one time was a badge of orthodoxy.

James Daane

James Daane is one of the editors of *The Reformed Journal.* As we shall see later he has labored hard in connection with the younger evangelicals especially concerned for social action, to urge that biblical trustworthiness be limited to matters of faith and practice. He also has written against *The Battle for the Bible* with the claim that the basic argument for inerrancy is derived from the presupposition that God cannot lie, therefore the Bible is inerrant. He concludes that "an error is not a lie."[14] Therefore the existence of errors in Scripture does not mean that God has told us that which is not true.

This can be handled several ways. In the first place, Dr. Daane cannot say that error is not a lie. For example, if a statement in the Bible were to say that the death of Jesus Christ on Calvary was only an example, when many Scriptures say He died as a vicarious sacrifice, this erroneous statement would be more than an error. It would be an untrue statement. An untrue statement is perhaps a lie of ignorance although it is not less untrue because the one who told the untruth was unaware of His error. But God can hardly be unaware of any error. And for God to allow error in Scripture when He knows all the truth would be a matter of self-contradiction on His part.

Dr. Daane fails to perceive that any claim that God cannot lie does not come as a presupposition apart from Scripture. Evangelicals believe that God cannot lie precisely because the Bible says He cannot lie. And this is the witness of the Holy Spirit as well. More than that, however, the true reason why evangelicals believe the Bible to be inerrant is that the prophets and the apostles teach this doctrine of Scripture. It is not presupposed. It comes directly from the Word of God itself. In addition, biblical inerrancy is the teaching of the Lord Jesus. This is not a presupposition either. It is to be found in the corpus of Scripture, and we believe it because the Bible says it is so. The Spirit witnesses to us that the Bible is true in this and in all other points. We know who God is and what His attributes consist in precisely because He has chosen to disclose this to us, and He has done so through Scripture. Dr. Daane has concluded that "there is no basic difference between Buswell's, Carnell's and Lewis's apologetic approach to the Bible and Lindsell's. All demand that the Bible meet an extra-biblical standard."[15] He is incorrect so far as Lindsell's view is concerned. The Bible is true because the Bible says it is true. And we confess this because the Bible confesses it. Dr. Daane stated that "the Reformational view of the Bible is not an argument for the Bible, but a confession about the Bible, a confession of faith. And faith is not a matter of waiting to bet until the odds are posted."[16] The only question Dr. Daane must now answer is this: Since the Reformational view of the Bible is committed to its inerrancy, why doesn't Dr. Daane join the Reformers in this confession of faith?

In the Christian Reformed Church a now famous document, Report 44 on "The Nature and Extent of Biblical Authority," was published and a reply made to it by Cornelius Van Til of Westminster Theological Seminary. He made some interesting comments about James Daane. He wrote:

> For some years there have been leading theologians in the Christian Reformed Church who wanted to have it change its course in line with the activist principles of Soren Kierkegaard and Karl Barth. I may mention Dr. James Daane, a minister of the Christian Reformed Church, now teaching at Fuller Theological Seminary, by way of illustration. Having written his doctoral dissertation at the new Princeton Theological Seminary on Kierkegaard, Daane has spent a good deal of energy in the interest of getting the Christian Reformed Church to adopt a modern activist theology that would involve a change of direction from Bavinck toward Barth. Daane has adopted the modern philosophical notion of human "freedom" i.e. as independence from the "counsel of God" as his starting-point in theology. According to Daane, as for Kuitert, historic Reformed theology is deterministic and rationalistic. In its place we must have an open universe and an "ethical" i.e. non-conceptual theology. Apparently without any awareness of the fact that the modern freedom idea leads to self-stultification, Daane keeps urging the Christian Reformed Church, and with it the Reformed community as a whole, to forsake the historic Reformed Confessions with their view of a finished revelation of God in history through Christ and the Scriptures and to follow a theology based on the philosophy of such men as Immanuel Kant.
>
> The Christian Reformed Church has taken no direct notice of (cf., my *The Theology of James Daane*, 1959) the neo-orthodox theology propagated in its midst by one of its ministers in good standing but it is now taking indirect notice of it through its synodical action with the respect to the new Hermeneutic, so influential in the Reformed Churches in the Netherlands.[17]

So we turn now from Dr. Daane to one of the other editors of *The Reformed Journal* and his role in furthering the opinions Dr. Van Til talked about in his analysis of Report 44.

Harry Boer

The Reformed Journal has used its pages to spread the opinion of Harry Boer that the Bible has errors in it. He is a minister in the Christian Reformed Church and denies its confession on Scripture, and the church has done nothing about it.

His articles, following publication in *The Reformed Journal,* were put together in a paperback book which was published by Eerdmans. Dr. Boer is committed to the use of the historical-critical method. Thus he says: "It is relevant at this point in our discussion to take up the question of the infallibility of the Bible in its relationship to biblical criticism."[18] From there he discusses the use of the word *infallible* and proceeds to change its historic meaning (in line with the new hermeneutic). "An infallible message is, of course," he says, "a reliable and trustworthy message. But a reliable and trustworthy message is not necessarily an infallible one." He concludes that "there is a reason for the receding into the background of the word infallible as applied to Scripture and the rising into prominence of trustworthy and reliable. The reason is none other than the legitimate claims of higher criticism."[19] At this point it is significant to note that the Lausanne Congress of World Evangelization spoke of the Scripture as trustworthy. The word infallible was not used. But what is becoming clearer every day is that the word trustworthy in the vocabulary of men like Dr. Boer does not mean the same thing as the word infallible. In other words, something that is trustworthy and reliable is not necessarily infallible to use Dr. Boer's own phrase. This may be the reason why a number of people whom we know do not believe in an infallible Bible did sign the Lausanne Covenant. But what it meant to some it apparently did not mean to others.

Dr. Boer's argument against an infallible Bible starts with the use of the historical-critical method. And he realizes that this methodology has penetrated his own denomination. Therefore he could say: "In my own denomination the 1971 and 1972 reports on 'The Nature and Extent of Biblical Authority,' prepared for the Synod of the Christian Reformed Church, provide a striking illustration. The impact of higher criticism on the thinking of the authors is clearly evident. Scholarly integrity has therefore made it necessary to face rather frontally the fact that *many data in Scripture are not in harmony with each other*"[20] (my italics). Dr. Boer says, in effect, that the conclusions of higher criticism shall sit in judgment on the Bible, not the Bible on higher criticism. When the "assured results" of higher criticism appear to be in conflict with the

Bible then the conclusions of the critics take precedence over Scripture.

Harry Boer is not naïve. He knows the historical background with regard to the church and Scripture. He says: "As a result evangelical scholarship finds itself in a dilemma. The churches it serves *have traditionally* (my italics) adhered to the view that the Bible as God's Word cannot contain inconsistencies or disparities of any kind. When disparities appear they must in some way be harmonized out of existence. It is in this sense that the words infallibility and inerrancy are frequently applied to Scripture, not only popularly but also theologically."[21] Against this backdrop Dr. Boer says "The word 'inerrant' is also a misleading adjective. It connotes the unqualified absence of inconsistency or disparity of any kind whatever with respect to any data found in the Bible. Unlike reliability or trustworthiness it is an absolute word. But its absoluteness is applied to an aspect of Scripture that is not in fact inerrant. The Bible is infallible; it is not inerrant in the accepted sense of that word." Dr. Boer has himself arrived at an absolute position. He refuses to accept the possibility that in cases where he does not possess sufficient information to solve this or that problem he could well afford to suspend judgment and wait for the verdict of time and even eternity to reconcile apparent discrepancies. No, indeed. There *are* errors and that is that. The door is closed and the final pronouncement has been made. Because of this Dr. Boer must, of necessity, propose a change in the acknowledgedly historic view of the church with regard to inerrancy. He dismisses with hardly a word the notion that maybe some of the problems stem from the translations or copies and that the autographs might hold the key to solution. He asks the question: "When the data cannot reasonably be brought together, must we then appeal to the no longer existing original documents with their assumed correspondence in all respects?"[22] First, he cannot know that the autographs do not exist. He flatly says they don't. Second, he speaks of the "assumed correspondence" of the data in the autographs. He is not even ready to allow for the *possibility* that the autographs could be perfect in their correspondence. Evangelicals are often laughed at because they refer to autographs they have never seen. Now Dr. Boer is drawing opposite conclusions from autographs he has not seen either. Would not simple prudence suggest that God and Scripture be given the benefit of the doubt?

Dr. Boer asks and answers one question at the same time, for the answer is implicit in the question. He says, "Should we not rather understand the infallibility of the Scripture in such a way that it does *not* include the assumption [sic] that all data in Scripture are necessarily harmonizable?"[23] Here Dr. Boer has failed to grasp the fact that inerrancy is not an assumption. It is not something evangelicals have come by presuppositionally although there is room for other legitimate procedures. Inerrancy is valid because it is taught by the prophets, the apostles, and the Lord Jesus Christ Himself.

Dr. Boer says that to accept the new view of the Bible will help the Christian witness, for he wrote: "When we must reconcile disparities by constant and often artificial harmonizations, and by sundry assumptions, our witness to the infallibility of Scripture is bound to create a credibility gap."[24] He came to the conclusion that "the adoption of (Dr. Boer's) view of infallibility as its exclusive meaning will put many things into proper focus and perspective. It will relieve the Christian mind of a great deal of tension that is not only painful and unnecessary but also without merit or inherent justification."[25] Dr. Boer states, "it is not possible to demonstrate logically by proof, either internal or external to Scripture the infallibility of the Bible."[26] This is an absolute statement which, when weighed against his objections to absolutes within the human perspective and his own assumption that the humanness of the Bible must of necessity include error, sounds strange indeed. This is especially true, since he is saying that he can, by external facts, demonstrate that the Bible has error in it. He can do what those who hold to inerrancy cannot do, according to him, and this strikes the reader as an astounding claim.

The Christian Reformed Church, like so many of the other churches, faces a frontal attack on its theological integrity. This bodes ill for the future of this denomination.

Further Erosion

In *The Battle for the Bible* mention was made of H. M. Kuitert whose biblical convictions leave much to be desired. Since the writing of that book further information has come to light from overseas. P. Jongeling was interviewed for television in the Netherlands by Godfried Bomans, as was Professor Kuitert. They were not interviewed together, but Mr. Jongeling was asked in his interview what his reactions were to some of the remarks made by Dr. Kuitert. The interviews were published under the title *Gesprekken met Bekende Nederlanders (Conversations with Well-Known Dutch Persons).*

Mr. Bomans asked Professor Kuitert what he thought about life after death. The specific question was, "Do you have an opinion about life after death or has this also shifted in your thinking over the years?" Dr. Kuitert answered: "If I am honest, I have to admit that this has shifted and is still shifting. Naturally, I am familiar with all of the old conceptions, and I am enough of a theologian to know what this is all about and how it originated. At the same time I have to say that in my experienced world these concepts are gone. . . . I think one way or another you return to where you came from. With God, and how that happens is a great secret; once returned to God you will probably also be aware of how the children are doing and how the world will end. . . . It used to be that we believed that the graves would open. But you really cannot imagine that anymore, at least I cannot. But am I therefore a heretic? Of course not, and everyone I talk to about this tells me 'I cannot believe this either.' "[27]

Later Mr. Bomans interviewed P. Jongeling and made the following statement: "I refer, for example, to my talk with Professor Kuitert, a man, who we cannot say has not faith. He even is a professor of theology. He says, in this many words, and I remember it still: 'The resurrection of the dead, the raising out of the graves, no, that can stand there, but I no longer accept that.' What do you think about that?" Mr. Jongeling replied to Mr. Bomans this way: "It is one or the other. You must believe God's Word or you must deny it. You cannot go half way. It is one of the two. I had followed that talk then also. Kuitert said something like this: 'I don't believe man disappears to nothing, he will return to God, whereby I hope that there still will be something. That the graves open, I cannot accept.' This is in absolute conflict with God's Word." And

Mr. Jongeling went on to quote from 1 Corinthians 15 with the remark that "it's just as if someone like Kuitert were being spoken to."[28] So, Professor Kuitert's pilgrimage moves constantly away from Scripture. He no longer believes in the bodily resurrection of the dead.

Herman Dooyeweerd is a name to conjure up interesting images in one's imagination. His name is connected with the Toronto Institute. John M. Batteau, who is completing his doctoral work at Kampen, wrote this: "I do have an interesting quote from Herman Dooyeweerd. In 1977 a book was published by Tjeenk Willink of Zwolle (Holland) with the interviews with Dooyeweerd conducted in 1976. To a question put to him by the interviewer about the difference between the Word of God and the Bible, he answered:

> That's of course automatic (Dat spreekt toch zo vanzelf). You certainly cannot say that everything in the Bible is inspired (U kunt toch niet zeggen dat alles in de bijbel geinspireerd is). If the apostle Paul writes to his fellow-worker, Timothy that he has forgotten his travel-coat somewhere and asks if he will bring it when he comes, would one have to regard that text inspired because it's in the Bible . . .? Wouldn't that be an absurdity (Dat zou immers dwaasheid zijn)? (pp. 57-58).

In the same interview Dooyeweerd also showed his preference for a Sabellian modalistic God rather than the orthodox view of the Trinity:

> Now there's nowhere in the Bible where it says that there are three persons; that's been derived (Nou er staat in de bijbel nergens dat er drie personen zijn, dat is erbij gemaakt) . . . it is rather a number-analogy (. . . getalsanalogie). (p. 57)

"Sadly, Dooyeweerd's influence is strong among evangelical leaders in Holland. And, via the later Berkouwer, Barth's even stronger. But then, at the Free University (and everywhere else) Barth is regarded as a dyed-in-the-wool conservative."[29]

It is clear that the Christian Reformed Church on both sides of the Atlantic has been deeply infected with the same liberal virus which has been mentioned in other connections. Whether the lay people and those evangelicals who perceive the situation in its true dimension can do anything about it remains to be seen.

Young Life

The Young Life Institute in Colorado has been the institutional training center for staff members of Young Life. It was presided over by Paul King Jewett, whose influence has been widespread and who brought to the campus teachers with views similar to his own. William S. Starr, the former president of Young Life, wrote a booklet titled *Focus: Security*. Part of the purpose was to interact with *The Battle for the Bible* and the fact that the official board of Young Life was itself not of one mind about biblical inerrancy was a significant factor. The visibility given to Dr. Jewett and the Institute, no doubt, was part of the background situation. Bill Starr observed: "The spirit that emerges out of thinking such as that found in the *Battle for the Bible,* is creating fruits that simply are not persuasive. I do not believe that any view of Scripture can be a proper one if it becomes a divisive element in the church. There is something wrong with a doctrine that *divides* the Body. To me, Lindsell loses his perspective on Christ in his cause to protect the Bible. In his eagerness to be the guardian of the Scripture he forgets that the Lord has already provided a guardian in the Holy Spirit."[30] What should be said in response to this statement?

From the context in which Mr. Starr wrote it becomes clear that he is not in agreement with the doctrine of inerrancy; yet many supporters of Young Life hold to this view. Naturally he felt the need to create a bridge of understanding with those who support Young Life. But how Mr. Starr did this hurts rather than helps his situation. He manages to contradict himself and fog the glass so it cannot be seen through. For example, he wrote: "Nowhere in the Bible do we find the term 'Authority of Scripture.' That is a human invention."[31] He might have added that nowhere in Scripture do we find the term "Trinity" and from that one could conclude that the doctrine of the Trinity is a human invention. Any survey of the theological literature on inspiration and authority will supply all the information needed to validate the claim that the authority of Scripture is taught in Scripture.

Mr. Starr does say, "What we do have in Scripture is the Authority of Christ' only, which is always expressed in terms of power, power to do something, power to accomplish something in His name."[32] When the authority of Christ is preeminent, then it follows that one accepts what Christ taught. And He clearly taught the inerrancy of the Word of God. If we do not believe Him on this score why believe Him on other matters?

Bill Starr is concerned about doctrine that divides the church. So is everyone else. But doctrine always has and always will divide. Is he saying that we should have no doctrine because it divides? After all, doctrine divides the Christian from the Christian Scientists, Jehovah's Witnesses, Mormons, and the like. Doctrine divides Baptists from Methodists. Of course, it would be preferable to have complete agreement on all doctrinal matters. The real quesion is not whether doctrine divides; the real question is whether the doctrines we hold are true or false. If inerrancy is correct, then the problem lies with those who refuse to believe it—not with those who articulate it and defend it.

Almost every church today is being split wide open on what most evangelicals would agree are not fundamental questions, even though they are very important ones. I refer to the ordination of women, for example. Who is dividing the church on this issue—the ones who promote it or those who oppose it? Take the question of homosexuality. This is a highly divisive issue among Christians and in their churches. Who is dividing the churches—those who favor the legitimacy of homosexual conduct or those who say it is wrong? Take the question which comes close to Young Life. Their own Paul Jewett says that subordination of women in the marital bond is wrong. The churches, however, have held to subordination through the ages. Dr. Jewett's viewpoint is a relative newcomer. Who is dividing the churches over this issue? The answer, paradoxically, is this: whoever is teaching that which is wrong is the one who is dividing the church. If, in order to avoid division, one party must agree to that which his conscience forbids, a state of affairs has been brought into being which no longer allows for the right of conscience to rule. The only thing wrong with any doctrine which divides the church is a doctrine which is wrong to begin with. But if it is right, then those who oppose the right are the dividers, not those who are the defenders of the truth.

The Young Life situation has come into sharper focus since the publication of *The Battle for the Bible*. The latest issue of the Fuller Seminary catalog says that "The Institute of Youth Ministries was established in 1977 to combine the theological resources of the School of Theology with the field training expertise of Young Life Campaign, a leading national evangelical Christian outreach to high school youth. . . . Although the institute is designed primarily for persons preparing to serve on the staff of Young Life, other persons preparing for ministry with youth may pursue this concentration."[33] This has fixed the relationship of Young Life to Fuller Seminary in concrete. Instead of Dr. Jewett and a few others at the summer training grounds in Colorado they now have the full resources of Fuller Seminary, whose commitment against an inerrant Scripture is very clear indeed. This means that Young Life has attached itself to an institution which espouses anti-inerrancy, presided over by a president who has stated that the inerrancy viewpoint is actually unbiblical. If the latter is true then inerrantists, of course, are divisive. But since Fuller Seminary, by its president's statement, does not even say that inerrancy is a live option, the door is shut and the issue foreclosed. The handwriting is on the wall for Young Life.

The Evangelical Covenant Church of America

In *The Battle for the Bible* attention was drawn to the North Park Seminary, owned and operated by the Evangelical Covenant Church. From the church's own documents it was shown that biblical inerrancy has had short shrift in that denomination despite the fact that a substantial number of the people in the pews have always believed the Bible to be true in all its parts. The church's own investigation showed their seminary did not have faculty representation for inerrancy in the biblical area, and it was recommended that someone holding this viewpoint should be added to the faculty. This was done. But it left the seminary lopsided and the inerrancy viewpoint still has only token representation.

When *Theology, News and Notes* (Special Issue, 1976) was published by Fuller Theological Seminary, letters were included from various respondents. One of them was written by

Lloyd H. Ahlem, the president of North Park College and Theological Seminary. In it he said: "I have just read portions of Harold Lindsell's book which attempts to indict both of our schools. I also read your statement in response to the book (i.e. Dr. Hubbard's Convocation Address) and wanted to express appreciation for both the content of your statement and the manner in which it was stated...."[34] The letter is plain enough about the position of Dr. Ahlem. Dr. Hubbard said biblical inerrancy is "unbiblical," and he made it obvious that inerrancy is not an option. Dr. Hubbard neither holds to the view nor supports it. And he cannot if it is, as he says, "unbiblical." Thus Dr. Ahlem chose to align himself with the views of Dr. Hubbard. Since all *The Battle for the Bible* alleged was that North Park has been deeply infiltrated by the noninerrancy viewpoint, Dr. Ahlem's response is an admission that the "indictment" is correct.

Donald Dayton

No one on the North Park Seminary faculty has written more on the subject of inerrancy than has Donald W. Dayton, who holds a professorship there and is Director of the Mellander Library. He comes out of the Wesleyan holiness tradition, and is a graduate of Houghton College. Donald Dayton himself is completing the work for his doctorate at the University of Chicago and has close contacts with Martin Marty of *The Christian Century*, which has published some of his articles. Mr. Dayton does not hold to inerrancy, and his writings indicate that he considers himself a protagonist for the errancy viewpoint. At the same time he is certainly better informed than many who oppose inerrancy, and he has not fallen into the trap of disavowing some of the background facts which others do not know about or wish to overlook.

Mr. Dayton's article " 'The Battle for the Bible': Renewing the Inerrancy Debate" appeared in the November 10, 1976, issue of the *Century*. He stated that the inerrancy view of *The Battle* "derives, at least in its precise formulation, from the late 19th century writings of A. A. Hodge and B. B. Warfield, representatives of the so-called 'Princeton Theology' rooted in the earlier work of Charles Hodge and ultimately in the post-Reformation scholastic traditions, especially that of the Genevan François Turretin."[35] Since a number of the critics of the inerrancy position (e.g. David Hubbard) wrongly claim that it is the unique contribution of Messrs. Hodge and Warfield, it is refreshing to hear Donald Dayton make it clear that the "Princeton Theology" derives at least from Francois Turretin whose work in systematic theology was studied by Princetonians for generations before Drs. Hodge and Warfield came on the scene. What Mr. Dayton cannot agree to, however, is that Turretin's theology sprang from the theology of John Calvin. Nor does he seem willing to say that the Lutheran doctrine of inerrancy sprang from Martin Luther. Rather, it came from the Lutheran dogmaticians who followed the Reformer, as he thinks was the case in the Reformed tradition. Much work has been done on both John Calvin and Martin Luther with respect to their views on Scripture. Books for and against the view that they taught inerrancy have been published. Even if one were to opt for the claim that the Reformers themselves did not affirm inerrancy (but above all, there is nothing to show they admitted there are errors in Scripture—and this is important) yet the fact that the Lutheran and Reformed dogmaticians did shows that the view is no newcomer. It has centuries of history behind it even as the witness of the sixteenth-century Christian Reformed Church Confession and others do the same.

Mr. Dayton also states that "there is a sense in which he (Lindsell) has 'got the goods' on Fuller Theological Seminary and certain members of the ETS. These institutions were founded self-consciously to perpetuate a view of Scripture very close to Lindsell's. Their problem is whether the modern questions (some of them also ancient!) allow such a position to be maintained."[36] He also says that George Ladd "has testified that his work in biblical theology has led him to an explicit rejection of the older categories of the 'orthodox' tradition and their emphasis on 'propositional revelation.' "[37] In other words, Dr. Ladd has moved into the neoorthodox position which is a departure from traditional orthodoxy. In addition (and the president of North Park should heed him in this), he says that "Lindsell's analysis reveals an ironic weakness in underestimating the extent to which biblical criticism has penetrated the evangelical world. One finds evangelical scholars (at schools Lindsell describes as safe!) practicing, for example, 'redaction criticism' to separate genuine sayings of Jesus from the creation of the Evangelists—a task inconceivable under the older assumptions."[38] The "ironic weakness" was nothing more than an endeavor not to paint any darker picture than possible at the time. But Donald Dayton is quite correct in saying that the situation is worse than was stated in *The Battle for the Bible*.

Mr. Dayton perceives that the Fuller Seminary School of World Mission is in theological trouble. He wrote:

> Evangelicals are beginning to understand that the real questions about appropriating the Scripture are not so much matters of *doctrine* as they are of *hermeneutics*. . . . Such hermeneutical discussions receive added impulse from what may seem a strange source, the highly influential and popular "Church Growth Movement" (also centered at Fuller—in the School of World Missions). What appears on the surface to reaffirm many of the undesirable features of the 19th century movement actually carries in its bosom the means of the destruction of the metaphysics that lies behind Lindsell's doctrine of the Scriptures.[4] The high commitment of Church Growth teaching to the social sciences, especially anthropology, has led to incorporation of a large portion of relativism and pragmatism of the modern world view. In discussions of the 'indigenization' of the church in non-Western culture one hears that the New Testament itself is a particular indigenization and that the gospel message needs to be extracted from first century 'cultural clothing' to be reclothed in that of another age. Leaders within the Church Growth Movement have even spoken of 'Christian Marxists'. Despite the mouthings of traditional formulas, when these positions are given full theological explication, they will be found to express a fundamentally different view of the Bible—fully consistent with the radical part of evangelical fundamentalists but irreconcilable with Lindsell's understanding."[39]

None of this means that Donald Dayton favors inerrancy. But at least he does know where the errancy position leads and he sees where the defection is taking place. His own view shines through in his statement that *The Battle* "is actually a repristination of a particular timebound formulation of biblical authority that is being seen by increasing numbers of evangelicals to have become a positive hindrance to the understanding of the fuller and deeper significance of the Scriptures."[40]

This is what liberals said a generation ago as they sought to destroy the foundations on which historic orthodoxy rested. And this is what some of the neoevangelicals are saying to those who think the New Testament is normative even in matters of feminism, social action, homosexuality, and the marital bond. What Donald Dayton represents is what North Park Seminary represents, and this is something which goes far beyond the simple question of whether the Bible is free from error in matters of fact, history, and the cosmos. Anyone can see from Mr. Dayton's own analysis that other and far more significant theological issues are at stake. The matters to which he has made reference go right to the heart of faith and practice.

However, Donald Dayton has raised a question which is important in relation to the image of the Evangelical Covenant Church. He said in effect that *The Battle* failed to see that this denomination did not spring out of the "rationalism and intellectualism of the scholastic and confessional traditions."[41] Rather it was a movement steeped in pietism and not committed to inerrancy in its roots. It is quite true that the present statement of belief of the Covenant denomination does not commit it to inerrancy. But the statement does say the denomination adheres "to the affirmations of the Protestant Reformation regarding the Holy Scriptures, the Old and New Testament, as the Word of God and the only perfect rule for faith and practice." Certainly this statement says that Scripture and the Word of God are synonymous. And this is the crucial root of the matter. The historical-critical method starts with the assumption that it is wrong to identify Scripture with the Word of God. Rather the Word of God must be found in Scripture. But North Park Seminary uses and propagates the historical-critical method and thus falls into a major inconsistency. If the denomination wishes to be honest with itself and its constituency, the statement should be changed, for what it says it believes and what is practiced in its classrooms are not in accord with each other. Now, if all Scripture is the Word of God and there is error in it, it raises a host of questions having to do with revelation and inspiration. Clearly the denomination is presently based on a statement which comes far closer to inerrancy than it does to the views entertained by Donald

Dayton and other members of the seminary faculty. Paradoxically the catalog of North Park (1975-1977) said that

> The Evangelical Covenant Church in America has its roots in historical Christianity as it emerged in the Protestant Reformation, in the Biblical instruction of the Lutheran State Church of Sweden, and in the great spiritual awakenings of the nineteenth century.

Any cursory survey of the theology of the Lutheran State Church of Sweden before the advent of the higher critical method indicates the church's commitment to an inerrant Scripture. Apparently the Covenant church has decided to forsake that part of Lutheranism's teaching even though a substantial number of the people in the pew believe the Bible to be free from error. But a look at the historic background may be of help in understanding the roots out of which the Covenant denomination came.

Karl A. Olsson

Karl A. Olsson, former president of North Park, published an article titled "Controversy on Inspiration in the Covenant of Sweden" which comprised his own opinions and a translation of a speech by Lorentz Theodore Backman. Professor Backman was recommended for a teaching post in Bible at the seminary of the Covenant in Sweden by P. P. Waldenstrom. Dr. Olsson said: "He [Waldenstrom] did not live long enough to see the effect of Backman's appointment. If he had, he may have felt more kindly toward the much-maligned North Park or at least a little less critical of his own school. With the coming of Backman to Lidingö a new chapter was written into the theological history of the church. . . . But Backman's teaching at Lidingö introduced a new note—that of higher criticism. . . . Backman assumed his position at Lidingö in the fall of 1917. Already in October of that year he was being queried about his use of a text of Professor Erik Stave's book on the Old Testament. The mutterings continued, and in January, 1923, the executive board of the Covenant of Sweden discussed his teaching methods. . . . The annual meeting of 1923 accepted Backman's resignation."[42] Dr. Olsson's account is plain enough. Before Professor Backman came, the school had no higher criticism. He introduced it. He wrote a new chapter in the theological history of the church—a chapter from which the church there and in America has never fully recovered.

L. T. Backman, the professor in question, delivered an address titled "Our Position on the Bible." He said: "Among wide circles (sic—note how prevalent he says it was) of believers it has become popular to hold a biblicist theory (verbal inerrancy) in accordance with which the Bible is throughout an infallible book, free of all contradictions and mistakes. It is essentially this theory about the Bible, or something close to it which comes in conflict with the new [sic] science and thereby causes doubts and difficulties. . . ."[43] "But is it possible in our time to read the Scriptures as Jesus read the Old Testament?"[44] His answer was a resounding No. He said: "Another example is the historic conceptions which we find in the Bible. In several respects these conceptions are impossible to reconcile with the results of modern historical science. The so-called books of Moses, or the Pentateuch, are not a unified work written by Moses but the product of the development of many centuries. Many [sic] of the writings of the prophets are not derived from the particular prophet, which according to the Bible, is purported [sic] to be their author. . . . The history of Israel in several respects has had a different development than that which we encounter in the Biblical presentation. Also in this area we find a series of contradictions between the testimony of the Bible and the modern way of looking at things."[45]

Dr. Backman continued: "Many serious Christians . . . have been accustomed to see in the Bible a book inspired in every detail by the Holy Spirit, which for that reason is, throughout, God's infallible Word. In this divine book, no contradictions can exist and no error in fact. . . . It is this conception of the Bible which meets us in orthodox theology. . . . However basic the differences may be in the various theological camps of our day, these camps are united in their rejection of the orthodox theory of the Bible. [They cannot] retain any longer the old theory of the Scriptures as a book in every detail inspired by the Holy Spirit and hence throughout the infallible word of God."[46] The professor was clear enough. Not every detail in the Bible was inspired by the Spirit. Only some parts of the Bible were. There was an old and now outworn "theory" which was nothing more or less than that of inerrancy which he wanted his listeners to give up. Obviously the rejection and the resignation of the professor indicates that the Covenant of Sweden preferred the old view of inerrancy to the new view of errancy. With respect to the person of Jesus Dr. Backman said that "Jesus shared the point of view of his time." Moreover he asserted that for Jesus "it is not sinful to have a limited or invalid conception in questions of a purely scientific character and Jesus does not become less our Savior because in personally, ethically, and religiously indifferent questions he shared the conceptions of his time. . . . If Jesus shared the conceptions of his time relative to the Pentateuch, the author of Isaiah, the history of human antiquity, and the historic development of Israel, and if his attitude toward the Old Testament is to be exemplary for us, it would seem that we cannot accept the scientific viewpoint on these questions. . . . That Jesus is our example cannot mean that we must copy him slavishly. . . . If we make his position decisive in those questions which lie outside of the realm of our personal life, we make him an authority in an area where he never pretended to be authoritative."[47] So spake Professor Backman.

The Covenant of Sweden was the Covenant from which its counterpart in America was formed. The parent group ridded itself of Professor Backman and by that act rejected his viewpoint. It was Dr. Backman himself who, over and over again, alluded to the fact that verbal inerrancy was the common view. He was taking exception to that view and wanted people to come over to his viewpoint. And what he did in Sweden North Park scholars proceeded to do in America. They removed the American Covenant group from its old foundations even as the Covenant of Sweden was to lapse in the years after Dr. Backman. Covenant pietism was based on belief in a trustworthy Bible—in all of its parts, not to mention a Christology which believed whatever Jesus asserted.

One further word on Karl Olsson may help us to understand his own theological uncertainties. He left the North Park presidency, joining Faith at Work, which was founded by Bruce Larson. The latter certainly has had a helpful ministry to people who were troubled by the usual run of human difficulties, but the soundness of Larson's theological viewpoint and that of Faith at Work (with which he is no longer connected) leaves one at least perplexed when some of his writings are scanned. For example, in Bruce Larson's book *Ask Me to Dance* the following statement appears:

> What is the biblical view of the male/female role? Certainly God created two sexes, male and female, and called them good and meant them for one another. In the Old Testament and even in the New, the woman's role is clearly defined as inferior to that of the man. But I think we need to understand that the revelation came at a time when slavery was acceptable, Samaritans were judged inferior, and *live animals were killed to placate God. All of this occurred simply because man did not know any better* (my italics).
>
> How amazing that Paul, at the same time he speaks of women being silent in the church and submissive to men, also says, by the inspiration of the Holy Spirit, that in Christ there is neither male nor female, only a new creation. I'm not sure Paul even knew what he was saying. . . .[48]

Judging from statements like this Larson's theology leaves something to be desired from the biblical perspective.

In conclusion we should note the same interesting paradox which rises from the letter of the president of North Park, Dr. Ahlem, who expressed his unqualified agreement with the views of Dr. Hubbard of Fuller. Dr. Hubbard said that biblical inerrancy is an "unbiblical viewpoint." Dr. Ahlem by his agreement is saying that the great host of Covenanters who believe in inerrancy are in fact heretical at this point because inerrancy is unbiblical. This is a matter that the Covenant inerrantists should explore for the implications are so obvious they hardly need to be stated.

The Assemblies of God

The Assemblies of God denomination (A/G) was not mentioned in *The Battle for the Bible*. Events since the publication of the volume show that the Assemblies has also been infiltrated by a view of Scripture which negates inerrancy. Central to this discussion lies the claim of errantists that the Assemblies, historically, did not commence with a commitment to biblical inerrancy. Rather, they say that the denomination limited inerrancy to matters of faith and practice. Therefore the current effort by the leadership of the Assemblies to "force" (this is the attitude of the errantists) inerrancy down the throats of the people is ethically wrong and violates the tradition of the Assemblies from its inception. In its early days the Assemblies of God communion was not noted for its number of educated, sophisticated, and bright theological minds. Time has changed that. Today increasing numbers of A/G young people have graduated from college, taken master of divinity degrees from accredited theological seminaries, and have obtained doctorates from prestigious universities at home and abroad. Some of them have labored in the institutions of the church. Others have taken teaching posts at Union Theological Seminary of New York, Fuller Theological Seminary, and Gordon-Conwell Theological Seminary to mention a few.

Some of the younger scholars have begun *Agora (a magazine of Pentecostal opinion)* which is published in Costa Mesa, California, where an Assembly Bible college is located. It began publication in 1977. Its Summer 1978 issue was listed as Volume two, Number one. This magazine seeks to influence the Assemblies not to commit the denomination to inerrancy. At least one of the writers has stated that the current crisis rises from *The Battle for the Bible*, which is hardly in accord with the facts. Perhaps the most that can be said is that the book added to the already existing discussion and acted as a prod to bring about what had already been in process for some time. The case can be discussed by referring to the two-part series penned by Gerald T. Sheppard of Union Theological Seminary in New York of whom more will be said later in another connection. He holds the M. Div. degree from Fuller and the Ph. D. degree from Yale. He teaches Old Testament.

Professor Sheppard says that

Harold Lindsell, in *The Battle for the Bible* contends that a confession of "inerrancy" of Scripture in all matters, even if peripherally [sic] addressed, is required for one to claim that he or she is an evangelical. On the other hand, Fuller Theological Seminary and most (this is untrue—my observation) other organizations within the evangelical Free Church tradition affirm the "infallibility" of Scripture "in matters of faith and practice" without addressing the accuracy of information one might extract from Scripture on other subjects, e.g. astronomy, philology, botany, geology and

so forth. Although no other doctrine is held in serious dispute
between contending groups who differ on the "inerrancy" question, Lindsell wishes to make the doctrinal formulation of Scripture a divisive issue which would determine whether or not a
person is "evangelical." . . .
      . . . In 1970 the national executive presbytery of the A/G issued
a "position paper" which sides with Lindsell's particular brand of
"inerrancy." The lack of sensitivity to our pentecostal tradition in
that lengthy document is apparent in a variety of ways.[49]

Dr. Sheppard has confused or misused the facts in the case.
In the first place he does properly note that the A/G booklet to
which he refers was issued six years before *The Battle for the
Bible*. The A/G commitment in that booklet to inerrancy preceded anything I wrote six years later. If Dr. Sheppard had said
that Lindsell sided with the A/G's particular brand of inerrancy
he would have been more correct. Moreover, the A/G committed itself to biblical inerrancy as a denomination when it
joined the National Association of Evangelicals and that was
more than thirty years ago. Thus, the true fact is that the A/G
was committed to biblical inerrancy and was moving on that
track long before *The Battle for the Bible* ever appeared. This
observation, however, leaves unanswered the pivotal question
Dr. Sheppard really has asked. It is whether the A/G was
committed to biblical inerrancy from its beginnings or
whether this represents a real change of position; and if there
has been a change whether it is ethical to make it. These are
good questions and require some sort of rejoinder before
going on to other aspects of Dr. Sheppard's case.
      Dr. Sheppard supports the doctrinal commitment of Fuller
Seminary. If it was ethically proper for Fuller to change from
inerrancy to errancy then how can it be ethically wrong to
switch from errancy to inerrancy? However, this statement
must be understood properly. I am not saying that the A/G
believed in an errant Scripture in its beginnings. No one I
know has produced evidence to show that this is so. The most
that Dr. Sheppard and others can claim is that the A/G did not
address itself to the question. I doubt very much, however,
that more than a handful of the A/G people ever believed the
Bible had errors in it. The objectors to inerrancy seem to be
saying that the A/G in its early days limited the infallibility or
inerrancy to matters of "faith and conduct." Now if a commit-

ment to inerrancy in matters of faith and conduct means Scripture has errors in it in matters of astronomy, botany, and geology, it is obvious that one cannot say the Bible is inerrant in all its parts. So we come to the second point which must be made in connection with Dr. Sheppard's case.

Dr. Sheppard said that in the 1914 meeting of the emerging A/G it was stated that "the purpose of the new fellowship and its doctrine of Scripture was to 'recognize Scriptural methods and order for worship, unity . . . and to disapprove all unscriptural methods, doctrine and conduct, and approve all Scriptural truth and conduct. . . .' " Dr. Sheppard went on to quote E. N. Bell who wrote an editorial in *The Christian Evangel* in 1915 in which he warned against becoming "narrow and sectarian by creating unscriptural lines of fellowship or disfellowship."[50] Then Dr. Sheppard said:

> I cannot resist noting parenthetically that this early tension seems quite removed from the present identification with Lindsell's separatistic doctrine of Scripture which would constitute public proof to many that we have indeed become "narrow and sectarian by creating unscriptural lines of fellowship or disfellowship."[51]

Over and over again Dr. Sheppard speaks about the A/G and its "Official Doctrine of Scripture." This is all to the good, for Dr. Sheppard thus acknowledges that one's attitude toward the Bible is a matter of doctrine, that is, it has to do with faith. It therefore belongs in the same category as the Trinity, the deity of Christ, the vicarious atonement, and the like. His conclusion with respect to the doctrine of Scripture is that a commitment to inerrancy is unscriptural. If this judgment is correct then, of course, inerrancy is out of bounds. The inerrantists I know all think that this view *is taught* in Scripture. If it isn't taught, it should never be imposed on anyone. To teach what cannot be supported from Scripture is divisive indeed, but if it is taught in Scripture, it can hardly be divisive. So the real question for Dr. Sheppard and his cohorts is this: Is inerrancy taught in Scripture? Since he has stated that from the earliest days the emerging A/G believed that its people should "approve all Scriptural truth and conduct" it should of necessity approve inerrancy if it is taught in the Word of God. Surely it is either taught or it is not taught in the Bible. If Dr. Sheppard wants to make a case against a commitment to inerrancy, then he ought to do so on the basis of its either being denied in Scripture, or that Scripture is silent and speaks neither for or against it. This he will have difficulty doing. But Dr. Sheppard has a third difficulty which cannot be sidestepped.

In the beginning of his article Dr. Sheppard alleges that "no other doctrine is held in serious dispute between contending groups who differ on the 'inerrancy' question." That is, the only question at stake is that which deals with "astronomy, philology, botany, geology, and so forth." It is here that Dr. Sheppard could not be more mistaken. As a graduate of Fuller Seminary he should know better. It has on its faculty men who say that the early chapters of Genesis are not historical, that Jesus was wrong about the mustard seed, that Paul was wrong in his teaching about female subordination in the marital bond, that he did not author Ephesians, 1 and 2 Timothy, and Titus, and that Peter did not write 2 Peter. The same sort of situation exists in many other institutions which will be discussed in this volume. So the question hardly is limited to matters of geology and the like. Questions having to do with Deutero-Isaiah, a late date for Daniel, the nonhistoricity of Adam and Eve, and the claim that some of Jesus' words and deeds were never spoken by Him or performed by Him are part of the contemporary picture. The problem is *not* limited to the smaller matters that Dr. Sheppard talks about.

If anyone wants evidence to demonstrate that the A/G indeed has internal difficulties about inerrancy, one of the editorials in the Summer 1978 issue of *Agora* will supply it. Murray W. Dempster, one of the editors, wrote about "Errant Ethics and Inerrant Church Politics: A Scenario of Irony." The purpose of the editorial was to stop the effort to commit the A/G more formally to the doctrine of biblical inerrancy. Had the writer been a believer in inerrancy he would have had no difficulty with this move. One of his statements expresses his intense antagonism.

> The tentacles of inerrancy must be spread throughout the Springfield educational triumvirate—Central Bible College, Evangel College, and the Assemblies of God Graduate School. The "Official Position Paper" must be distributed to faculty members. Letters must be sent to appropriate members of the faculty

declaring inerrancy to be the A/G stand on Scripture. The fact that the inerrancy position has never been officially adopted by the General Council and made part of the "Statement of Fundamental Truths" suggests no restraints on such subtle forms of coercion. *How ironic that the ethics of such coercive exercise of ecclesiastical power are apparently quite compatible with a commitment to an inerrant Bible.*

As the next step, inerrancy must be spotlighted as the fearless guardian of doctrinal purity within the halls of higher learning. Suspect educators must be found—preferably those who utilize historical criticism—to demonstrate the validity of the Lindsell thesis that educators are dangerous germs spreading theological liberalism. The liberal arts college is the most likely place to locate such an academic scapegoat. Sure enough, a sacrificial lamb is found in the Evangel College thicket, openly probing the critical problems of Old Testament scholarship. A quick unilateral decision seems called for—"Rev. Miller, your contract will not be renewed." . . . And amidst these in-house shenanigans, not one murmur from the Evangel faculty or administration.[52]

These words speak for themselves. His use of the word "shenanigans" is unfortunate because the word implies trickery and underhandedness. This is a value judgment on the hearts of those the writer refers to. Lindsell has never said that educators are dangerous. He has said that educators who disbelieve the Bible and teach what the Bible denies are dangerous. There are thousands of first-rate educators who are wholly committed to what the Scripture proclaims. Moreover, the unrenewed contract of "Rev. Miller" statement contains no evidence of any kind to show that this person was indeed innocent. But the writer's conclusion is that the leadership of the A/G are scoundrels who searched to find a scapegoat who was innocent and then proceeded to railroad him out of a teaching post. Documentation of such charges should be produced before they are accepted. And even ecclesiastical officials are presumed to be innocent until they are found to be guilty. In any event the editorial is sufficient evidence to show the struggle now taking place in the A/G against a commitment made by the denomination years ago and which is now being challenged by the new breed of A/G scholars.

Inerrantists do not budge from their position, because they know that once surrender occurs at this point, it opens the door wide to denial of matters organically related to what Dr.

Sheppard thinks of as matters of faith and conduct. The position he is advocating is none other than that which underlies the historical-critical method. As soon as he opens some part of Scripture to error he must look for the canon in the canon. Scripture and the Word of God are no longer synonymous. Of this more will be said later. But before then a word must be spoken about the Church of the Nazarene.

The Church of the Nazarene

The Church of the Nazarene was formerly known as the Pentecostal Church of the Nazarene. In this sense it was dynamically associated with the Assemblies of God. In 1919 the word Pentecostal was dropped from the name and it became known as The Church of the Nazarene. It suffered from the same problems experienced by the Assemblies of God. Its people were not as highly educated as those in the mainline denominations. It was some years before its ministers were exposed to theological education beyond the Bible school or college level. It has been asserted that this denomination was not committed to biblical inerrancy in its formative years. Thus Paul Merritt Bassett could write an article titled: "The Fundamentalist Leavening of the Holiness Movement, 1914-1940 The Church of the Nazarene: A Case Study." In it he claims that

> The smell of battle hangs over those portions of H. Orton Wiley's *Christian Theology* (published in 1940) which have to do with the character and role of Scripture. . . . Wiley did enter the fray, declaring the unsuitability of either the liberal or the Fundamentalist positions with respect to the authority and inspiration of the Bible. . . . But he came in on cat's paws, and a generation or two of holiness preachers thought he was basically a Fundamentalist. The contrast between his position and the "received" position of the great majority was not perceived, though the clues are ample and Wiley does not dissemble.[53]

From this statement one can note immediately that "the great majority" *were* Fundamentalists and believed in an inerrant Scripture. Wiley may not have dissembled, but it surely sounds as though he did an undercover job nonetheless to get the "great majority" straightened out on their fundamentalist views. In its essence, Paul Basset claims that fundamentalism leavened the Holiness Movement and did so with respect to its commitment to inerrancy. What he does not say, and cannot say, is that the Nazarenes in the beginning had any great number of people who believed that the Bible contained error. Moreover, given the low estate of the educational and theological background of the church, it is difficult to suppose that too many people were really aware of the problem, and almost without exception the less-educated people held to belief in the complete truthfulness of Scripture. Indeed it is Mr. Bassett himself who says that a "generation or two of holiness preachers thought he (Wiley) was basically a Fundamentalist." And what could there be any more basic to the fundamentalist tradition than a belief in the inerrancy of the Word of God? In fact, fundamentalism came into being as a result of the rise of liberalism which had for its cardinal standpoint the denial of the trustworthiness of Scripture. And opposition to liberalism of necessity included a repudiation of that liberal view of the Bible.

In the conclusion of his article Paul Bassett did say:

> Fundamentalism could not leaven the whole lump. But it has continued to affect the Church of the Nazarene, especially as it has become more and more clear that she has inherited two basically incompatible points of view; not on some peripheral item, but with regard to the central issue of spiritual-theological authority.[54]

Dr. Bassett, who teaches at the Nazarene Theological Seminary, is clearly opposed to inerrancy. However, he does recognize that the viewpoints of the errantists *vis a vis* the inerrantists are basically incompatible. In addition, he properly notes that to many of the Nazarenes it was not formerly clear that there were two divergent viewpoints. And he states that fundamentalism has continued to affect the church. His own admission that the views of fundamentalism were the views of the great majority in the beginning tells the story. The Church of the Nazarene has been deeply infiltrated by an errancy view of the Bible which has been gathering strength. It is believed and taught in most if not all of its educational institutions. Professor Bassett recognizes that the issue is not peripheral; it is central.

The Church of the Nazarene has a statement about the Bible

in its *Constitution and Special Rules,* Article IV which reads:

> The Holy Scriptures. We believe in the plenary inspiration of the
> Holy Scriptures, by which we understand the sixty-six books of
> the Old and New Testaments, given by divine inspiration, iner-
> rantly revealing the will of God concerning us in all things neces-
> sary to our salvation, so that whatever is not contained therein is
> not to be injoined as an article of faith.[55]

The statement says the Bible is plenarily (that is, all, fully or
completely) inspired. If inspiration does not mean that what it
says can be trusted then inspiration has lost any credible content. If some of it is true and some of it is false even though all
of it is "inspired," we come full circle to the same conclusion.
We must somehow find the Word of God within Scripture,
because not all of Scripture can be the Word of God. Unless, of
course, we wish to say that the Word of God can err. If it can,
then we must still find the Word of God which does not err
and the Word of God which does err. This makes man the
judge as to which parts of Scripture can be trusted and which
cannot. The Bible ceases then to be authoritative. Indeed, the
great weakness of the Nazarene statement on Scripture lies in
its failure to say that it is authoritative. All the other things
said about Scripture can be true without Scripture being authoritative.

The same difficulty attends the statement of faith of The
Christian Holiness Association of which the Church of the
Nazarene is a part. It speaks about "the inspiration and infallibility of sacred Scripture" and has a large segment about
entire sanctification. But nowhere is there a commitment to
the authority of Scripture, inspired or not inspired. Interestingly enough a number of groups in the Holiness tradition
who believe in biblical inerrancy do speak about the Word of
God as authoritative. Houghton College's catalog statement
reads as follows: "We believe the Scriptures of the Old and
New Testaments are fully inspired of God, inerrant in the original writings, and that they are the supreme and final *authority*
for matter of faith and practice." Marion College's catalog says:
"We believe the books of the Old and New Testaments to
constitute the Holy Scriptures which are the inspired and infallible Word of God and are of supreme *authority* for faith and
practice." On the other hand the catalog of the Olivet

Nazarene College, in Kankakee, Illinois, follows its Nazarene pattern in its statement that "the Old Testament and the New Testament Scriptures, given by plenary inspiration, contain all the truth necessary to faith and Christian living." This statement is easily susceptible to neoorthodox views, because it signally fails to say that the Bible is the Word of God. It simply *contains* all the truth necessary to faith and Christian living. It says nothing about biblical authority. The Wesleyan Theological Society at least does say its adherents believe in the "unique inspiration of the Bible as the divine Word of God, the only infallible (i.e., 'absolutely trustworthy and unfailing in effectiveness or operation'—RHD), sufficient, and *authoritative* rule of faith and practice."

The Asbury Theological Seminary is part and parcel of the Holiness Movement and its faculty is involved in the Wesleyan Theological Society. An undated brochure used by Asbury Seminary contained the following statement:

The Faith We Proclaim

The subtle inroad of modernism has been made at the pivotal point which involves the theory concerning the INSPIRATION and INFALLIBILITY of the Holy Scriptures. It is at this point that the levee is first broken which releases the floodtide of questioning—uncertainty and even open denial of the INFALLIBIL-ITY of the HOLY SCRIPTURES AS THE WORD OF THE LIVING GOD. . . . In view of the fact that the nature of the theory held concerning the inspiration of the Scriptures may be the entering wedge for disturbing doubts, uncertainties and even denials of the records contained in the Scriptures, we affirm as a declaration of faith:

"We believe that the BIBLE IS THE WORD OF GOD, authentic in all matters relating to man's life, faith and salvation; and that as originally given, ITS MANUSCRIPTS WERE FREE FROM ACTUAL ERROR OF FACT IN ALL REGARDS, and that the available evidence concerning the original autographs is not contrary to this position."

. . . Our CHIEF MISSION is TO SPREAD SCRIPTURAL HOLINESS over the earth.

—A Brochure, undated, of Asbury Theological Seminary[56]

One can say without fear of contradiction that the denominations and institutions related to the National Holiness Association one way or another, and the Wesleyan Theological Society constitute a mixed bag with regard to biblical inerrancy. Some adhere to it strongly; others do not. Statements of faith of some of the institutions include a commitment to inerrancy; others are vague. None, so far as I can detect, actually says the Bible has errors in it. This can be deduced, however, if statements are made in which inerrancy is strictly limited to salvatory matters. But it cannot be reasonably deduced if statements restrict inerrancy or infallibility to matters of faith and practice or conduct. The reason is this. Matters of faith have to do with doctrine. One of the doctrines of the Bible is the doctrine of Scripture. If the Bible is infallible in matters of faith (or doctrine), then it must be infallible in its doctrine of Scripture as it would be in regard to the virgin birth, the deity of Christ, and the like. Thus, if there are errors in Scripture, then the doctrine of Scripture found in the Bible cannot teach that there are no errors. No statement about the Bible among the Wesleyan Holiness group says the Bible teaches there are errors in it. Given the cloudiness of today's situation, it would be well for any and all of those churches and institutions in this movement to say forthrightly whether the doctrine of Scripture teaches there are or there are not errors in the Bible. At least this would clear the air and let the world know where they stand on this important issue.

In the case of the Church of the Nazarene, Paul Bassett, professor of History of Christianity at the Nazarene Theological Seminary, has said his church has inherited two incompatible views on a subject which is not peripheral but central and significant. A house divided against itself cannot stand. The Church of the Nazarene should make plain which of the two incompatible viewpoints represents the church and its people.

Conclusion

Time and space limitations make it impossible to discuss other denominations and organizations which are beset by problems similar to those of the groups mentioned in this chapter. Therefore it should not be assumed that because this or that particular denomination, parachurch organization, or institution has been left unmentioned, it is not faced with the same question about the trustworthiness of the Bible. My files are filled with other information that has not been included. Word-of-mouth conversations have produced data which reinforce the allegation that evangelicalism has been deeply infiltrated by an aberrant view of the Bible. But without documentation which can be checked by the reader, or because some of the information is privileged and cannot be released, these data cannot be used. I have sought to give "chapter and verse" for every assertion made in this volume. If anyone can still believe there is no problem facing the evangelical world with respect to biblical authority, revelation, inspiration, and inerrancy such a conclusion can be drawn only in the face of a refusal to accept the hard facts.

NOTES

[1]National Association of Evangelical's promotional pamphlet, n.d.
[2]Jack Rogers, ed., *Biblical Authority* (Waco: Word, 1977), p. 179.
[3]Fred P. Thompson, Jr., "At Issue: The Wrong War," in *United Evangelical Action*, Winter 1975, p. 8.
[4]Ibid., pp. 9-10.
[5]Ibid., p. 10.
[6]Ibid.
[7]Letter to the Editor, *United Evangelical Action*, Spring 1977, pp. 6, 38.
[8]*The Banner*, August 20, 1976, p. 7.
[9]Ibid., August 27, 1976, p. 6.
[10]Ibid.
[11]*News Bulletin*, October 1976, p. 3.
[12]*The Banner*, August 27, 1976, p. 7.
[13]*The Outlook*, January 1977, p. 5.
[14]James Daane, "The Odds on Inerrancy" in *The Reformed Journal*, December 1976, p. 5.
[15]Ibid., p. 6.
[16]Ibid.
[17]Cornelius Van Til, *The Nature and Extent of Biblical Authority*, unpublished manuscript, pp. 1-2.
[18]Harry R. Boer, "The Infallibility of the Bible and Higher Criticism" in *The Reformed Journal*, March 1976, p. 19.
[19]Ibid.
[20]Ibid.
[21]Ibid.
[22]Ibid., pp. 20-21.
[23]Ibid., p. 21.
[24]Ibid.
[25]Ibid.
[26]Ibid., p. 22.

[27]Bomans, *Gesprekken met Bekende Nederlanders*, pp. 44, 45.
[28]Ibid., pp. 88-91.
[29]Letter dated April 13, 1978.
[30]William S. Starr, *Focus: Security* (Colorado Springs: Young Life, n.d.), p. 10.
[31]Ibid., p. 11.
[32]Ibid.
[33]*Catalog*, 1978-80, Fuller Theological Seminary, p. 47.
[34]*Theology, News and Notes*, Special Issue, 1976, p. 30.
[35]Donald Dayton, " 'The Battle for the Bible': Renewing the Inerrancy Debate," in *The Christian Century*, November 10, 1976, p. 977.
[36]Ibid.
[37]Ibid., p. 978.
[38]Ibid.
[39]Ibid., p. 979.
[40]Ibid.,p. 977.
[41]Ibid.
[42]Karl A. Olsson, "A Controversy on Inspiration in the Covenant of Sweden," in *The Covenant Quarterly*, February 1966, Vol. XXIV, No. 1, pp. 3-4.
[43]L. T. Backman, "Our Position on the Bible," in *The Covenant Quarterly*, February 1966, Vol. XXIV, No. 1, pp. 6-7.
[44]Ibid., p. 8.
[45]Ibid., p. 9.
[46]Ibid., pp. 9-10.
[47]Ibid., pp. 13-14.
[48]Bruce Larson, *Ask Me to Dance* (Waco: Word, 1972), p. 93.
[49]Gerald T. Sheppard, "Scripture in the Pentecostal Tradition," in *Agora*, Volume one, Number four, 1978, p. 4.
[50]Ibid., p. 17.
[51]Ibid.
[52]Murray W. Dempster, "Errant Ethics and Inerrant Church Politics: A Scenario of Irony," in *Agora*, Summer 1978, pp. 3-4.
[53]Paul Merritt Bassett, "The Fundamentalist Leavening of the Holiness Movement, 1914-1940 The Church of the Nazarene: A Case Study," in *The Journal of the Wesleyan Theological Society*, Volume 13, Spring 1978, p. 65.
[54]Ibid., p. 85.
[55]*Manual of Church of the Nazarene* (Kansas City: Nazarene Publishing House, 1928).
[56]Mimeographed reproduction of brochure, carrying no date.

4

The Southern Baptist Convention: Moving Toward a Crisis

In chapter 5 of my book *The Battle for the Bible* I discussed the Southern Baptist Convention. In that chapter I stated that the Southern Baptist Convention now has in it a number of people who do not believe in biblical inerrancy. I made this allegation against the backdrop of the New Hampshire Confession of Faith, which has been generally accepted by the churches of the Convention. This confession was adopted by the messengers to the 1925 Convention and reaffirmed one way or another several times. The first article of this Confession speaks about the Bible and reads as follows:

> The Holy Bible was written by men divinely inspired and is the record of God's revelation of Himself to man. It is a perfect treasure of divine instruction. It has God for its author, salvation for its end, and truth, without any mixture of error, for its matter. It reveals the principles by which God judges us; and therefore is, and will remain to the end of the world, the true center of Christian union, and the supreme standard by which all human conduct, creeds, and religious opinions should be tried. The criterion by which the Bible is to be interpreted is Jesus Christ.[1]

It is important to note immediately that the confession does not rule out creeds. It simply states that creeds as well as religious opinions are to be judged by the Bible, not the Bible by man-made creeds. It also notes that the Bible needs to be interpreted or understood. In doing this, Jesus Christ is the criterion. And He is the One who said the "scripture cannot be broken" (John 10:35). He also told us: "Think not that I am come to abolish the law and the prophets; I have come not to abolish them but to fulfill them. For truly, I say to you, till heaven and earth pass away, not an iota, not a dot, will pass from the law until all is accomplished" (Matt. 5:17, 18).

Jesus in His life and teaching at no point expressed any reservations about the trustworthiness of the Bible. To be sure He was speaking of the Old Testament Scriptures, but He also preauthenticated the New Testament when He said to His disciples: "When the Spirit of truth comes, he will guide you into all the truth; for he will not speak on his own authority; but whatsoever he hears, he will speak, and he will declare to you the things that are to come" (John 16:13).

The Stance of the Southern Baptist Convention

The Southern Baptist Convention makes no claim to speak for local churches or for the people who are members of local congregations. Baptists accept the principle of soul liberty which is nothing less than the right of all people to believe as they choose. They have soul competency as well as soul liberty. But this does not mean that Baptists can believe what is not baptistic and still be Baptists, or that Baptists do not have a general consensus as to what constitutes true Baptist doctrine. Indeed, if Baptists do not generally agree about what they believe, confessions affirming Baptist beliefs are needless and perforce wrong. But in a multitude of ways Baptists make it plain that they are in general agreement about basis doctrines of the Christian faith. Of this more will be said later in this chapter. In the meantime, however, a few illustrations of the point I wish to make will suffice.

Baptist Ideals

The Southern Baptist Convention has printed and widely distributed a booklet titled *Baptist Ideals.*[2] The Sunday School Board printed this and it is still in use. Two segments of this statement are important here. The first has to do with the Bible. The booklet, on page 2, says the Bible is the Word of God, the Bible is authoritative, the Bible is the self-revelation of God, the Bible is inspired, and the Bible is trustworthy. The statement was prepared for the one hundred and fiftieth anniversary of the first Baptist national organization in America. It was written in 1964 by "Ralph A. Herring, chairman, and eighteen Southern Baptist Convention leaders and scholars."

At the end of the statement of Baptist ideals, point 9 speaks of self-criticism. It says:

> Both the local church and the denomination, if they are to remain healthy and fruitful, must accept the responsibility of constructive self-criticism. It would be damaging to our churches and to our denomination to deny the right to differ or to consider that our methods and policies are final and perfect. The work of our churches and of our denomination needs frequent re-evaluation to prevent the sterility of traditionalism. This is particularly true in the area of methods, but it also applies to historic principles and practices as they relate to contemporary life. This means that our churches and denominational institutions and agencies should defend and protect the right of our people to question and to criticize constructively.
>
> Healthy self-criticism will center on basic issues and will thus save us from the distintegrating effects of accusations and recrimination. For one to criticize does not necessarily mean that he is disloyal; his criticism may stem from a deep commitment to the welfare of the denomination. Such criticism will aim at growth toward full maturity both for the individual and the denomination.
>
> *Every Christian group, if it is to remain healthy and fruitful, must accept the responsibility of constructive self-criticism.*[3]

Any member of a local Southern Baptist church, then, has the right and responsibility to engage in criticism of any part of the Southern Baptist Convention where such criticism is needful. And I claim that right as a member of a cooperating congregation.

Herschel H. Hobbs

Dr. Herschel H. Hobbs is a former president of the Southern Baptist Convention. He is the pastor emeritus of the First Baptist Church of Oklahoma City, Oklahoma. He has been a speaker on the "Baptist Hour." He is regarded as one of the most kindly and broad-minded supporters of the Convention. It is not unusual for liberals to use his name in support of their freedom to disagree with his own evangelical viewpoint.

Dr. Hobbs wrote *A Layman's Handbook of Christian Doctrine*, published by Broadman Press, the Southern Baptist publishing house. In that book he made the following statement:

> "Inspiration" means to breathe in. It refers to God's act through the Holy Spirit whereby he enabled chosen men to receive and

record his revelation (2 Pet. 1:21). Second Timothy 3:16 reads, "All scripture is given by inspiration of God" or "God-breathed." Some see the Holy Spirit as giving the writers the exact words to use. Others see the Spirit as inspiring men, but leaving them free to choose their words. Since in parallel accounts on occasion the Gospel writers use different words (see *Kingdom of God* and *Needle*), the latter position seems to the writer to be the correct view. But both groups see the Spirit guarding the writers from error. The main thing is not the method but the product. And that is that the Bible is the Word of God, truth without any mixture of error for its substance. This, of course, refers to the original manuscripts. The Holy Spirit no more protects copyists than typesetters from error.[4]

This statement of Dr. Hobbs is consistent with the one on Scripture in the New Hampshire Confession of Faith. It is one with which the overwhelming majority of Southern Baptists would be in full agreement. It adds appreciably to the support for the claim that Southern Baptists generally do have a theological position that is orthodox and is derived from the Bible which is the source of their religious knowledge.

Theological Seminaries

To say Southern Baptists are a confessional people who have spelled out their particular beliefs in doctrinal statements is further demonstrated by the theological seminaries in the Convention. For example, the Southwestern Baptist Theological Seminary uses the New Hampshire Confession of Faith and affirms clearly that new faculty members are required to give assent to the statement of faith when they begin teaching at that institution. Adherence, however cautiously asserted, plainly demonstrates that doctrinal orthodoxy is a requirement for a faculty berth. However loudly some people say that Baptists adhere only to the Bible, this is incorrect with respect to the theological seminaries. All that any seminary would need to do, if that were truly the case, would be to have prospective faculty members simply assert that they believe the Bible without speaking about such matters as the Trinity, the virgin birth, the vicarious atonement, the bodily resurrection, the second coming of Jesus, baptism, and immersion.

The Southern Baptist Seminary at Louisville also has a doctrinal statement or confession. It is not the same as the New

Hampshire Confession of Faith, but it is somewhat similar. Wholly apart from any minor differences between the two statements of faith this much remains true. The Southern Baptist Seminary also requires all members of the faculty to assent to their "creed," if I may cautiously call it that. Their catalogs proclaim that signatures are affixed publicly by faculty members. What it does not appear to do, and that may be important, is this: it only assures the institution that at the time the faculty member signs the confession he believes those things stated therein—unless, of course, he is dishonest. But it does not appear to make any provision about what happens or should happen if a faculty member changes his viewpoints after he has signed the statement. This opens the door wide to possible abuse.

In the famous case of Professor Toy, this Old Testament professor did change his views.[5] But he was honest about the matter and informed the institution of the change. He subsequently left the institution, and later taught at Harvard University. Moreover, several decades ago some faculty members left the Southern Baptist Seminary (and the accreditation of the school was temporarily affected) because they were not in agreement with the doctrinal commitment of the school.

The Baptist Hymnal

The introduction to the popular and widely used Broadman *Baptist Hymnal* contains information that most Baptists never bother to read. The introduction includes a statement to the effect that in the preparation of the hymnal a subcommittee evaluated the "theological and doctrinal" contents of the hymns to be sure that they were in accord with Baptist beliefs. It says "Hymn texts were critically examined for theological accuracy and doctrinal soundness."[6] In other words, the committee was saying Southern Baptists believe certain truths which are derived from their study of Scripture. They wished to include in the hymnal *only* those songs that truly reflect what Baptists believe. This must mean that those not reflecting Baptist viewpoints were excluded from the hymnal. Thus any so-called Baptist who dissents from the theology of the hymnal is caught in a position of singing what he does not believe. His Baptist freedom has been abused, and he himself is being conditioned to believe what he does not. Clearly this state of affairs means that the Southern Baptist Convention, and rightly so, has gone beyond a simple affirmation of believing the Bible to a position where its hymnal is "creedal" whether Baptists realize it or not.

Critiques of *The Battle for the Bible*

The reader will perceive that two points stand out immediately. The first is that the Southern Baptist Convention does have a generally accepted theological viewpoint expressed in books, pamphlets, convention confessions, confessions adopted by theological seminaries, and the whole thrust of the *Baptist Hymnal*.

The second point is that *this* theological commitment of Southern Baptists has been breached. There are numbers of people who call themselves Southern Baptists who do not believe what Southern Baptists generally believe. I pointed this out in my previous book and supplied evidences to support the allegation. The results were interesting.

I have received numerous letters from Southern Baptists who, almost to a man, agree with my claim that the Southern Baptist Convention is being influenced from within to depart from its historic commitment to an inerrant Bible. But some who read my book were decidedly antagonistic. There is no need to enhance my book by publishing the complimentary opinions. I am interested, however, in making known some of the opinions of the critics who were unhappy with what I had done. I think the ones I shall mention are fair examples of those who have rejected my allegations in one fashion or another.

The Southwestern Journal of Theology

Professor William L. Hendricks of the Southwestern Seminary reviewed my book. Why he was selected to do so is an interesting question. So far as I know he is one of the least likely candidates for the title of "theological conservative" on the faculty. In any event the book was given to one whose sympathies do not lie in the same direction as mine.

I asserted that the errancy virus is to be found in all the great denominations, and among the smaller ones as well. Dr. Hendricks asked the rhetorical question: "Who then shall stand?" He asked the question with the view to concluding: "Apparently Lindsell speaks from a very small base while claiming to uphold the sole classical and orthodox view of Scripture." Professor Hendricks did not include himself among the small band of those who hold to inerrancy despite the fact, as we shall see, the Southwestern Seminary was created to teach the view I entertain, and he signed a doctrinal statement consenting to what he does not now apparently believe.

Dr. Hendricks could have noted that believers in inerrancy are not a small remnant even among Southern Baptists. I stated in my book that "at this moment in history the great bulk of the Southern Baptists are theologically orthodox and do believe that the Word of God is inerrant." Since there are more than thirteen million Southern Baptists, not including their children who have not been baptized, they constitute a very considerable constituency, which some of us hope will forever hold to biblical inerrancy.

I said in my book that "there is no Christian who has ever had a normal mind since Adam fell in the Garden of Eden." Dr. Hendricks responded that "It is to be hoped that the book does not fall into the hand of infidels of the ilk and type of Mark Twain and H. L. Mencken." What would they do with my assertion? I can only conclude that Dr. Hendricks rejects the biblical teaching that all men have been affected by the fall of Adam and have minds which have been depraved, distorted, and made worse by sin. The reading of any systematic theology will tell him that between the time a person is justified by faith in Christ and glorified at death, there is an interval in which sanctification is at work. Christians do draw closer to their prototype which is Jesus Christ, but they do not yet fully have the mind of Christ. Because of sin, we do not have normal minds by any means. The founding fathers of Southwestern Seminary could teach him about that.

Dr. Hendricks gave me credit for quoting my sources accurately. But he followed on to say that the title of the book should have been: "*Harold Lindsell's Battle for an A Priori View of the Infallibility and Inerrancy of the Bible as Defined by Himself and Possibly by a Few Neo-Evangelicals.*" In a moment I will show that the view of the Bible I am talking about is not just my view. It is the view of the New Hampshire Confession as well as that of the founder of the seminary where Dr. Hendricks has been teaching. And if, as he says, "The Bible says *nothing* (my italics) about infallibility and inerrancy" and if "Classical Christianity and orthodoxy have not meant what Lindsell apparently means by infallibility" then indeed I and most of my Southern Baptist brethren have been wrong. But if we are right, then he is the one who has discarded traditional Baptist views about the Bible. The reader can judge for himself from the evidences about to be cited.

Hendricks raises a question about my definition of truth and error, claiming the matter is more subtle and complex than I stated—which may indeed be true. He asserted that "Truth is Jesus Christ. . . . Error is to disbelieve in Christ, to disallow the biblical witness to him. . . . The primary source for these affirmations is the Gospel of John." But if the Gospel of John is not true, then Dr. Hendricks has a real problem about who Jesus is and why He came. Only if John's Gospel is true can we know that Jesus is truth. But Dr. Hendricks balks at an infallible Bible.

In his conclusion Professor Hendricks said, "It is painful that he (Lindsell) supposes the rest of the world is shifting rather than perceiving that it is he himself who is setting up a *new* (my italics) qualification for what it is to be genuinely evangelical" (and I will note later that men like Foy Valentine insist that Southern Baptists are not evangelicals to begin with). So wrote Dr. Hendricks about *The Battle for the Bible*.[7]

The Southern Baptist Seminary Review and Expositor

The treatment of *The Battle for the Bible* by Dr. Hendricks of Southwestern was rather mild compared to that which appeared in the Winter 1977 issue of the *Review and Expositor*, which is published by the faculty of the Southern Baptist Seminary at Louisville. The review was written by Bill Blackburn of Shelbyville, Kentucky, a graduate of Southern. The first portion of the review summarized the contents of my book. He came to the nub of the problem at the end. His comments are worth noting:

> What can be said in evaluation of this book? In short, it is atrocious. First, Lindsell has so defined his terms that only a very small

minority within Christendom could be classified as true blue believers, or "evangelicals." Second, as his predecessor at *Christianity Today,* Carl F. H. Henry, has said, "Lindsell is relying on theological atom bombing." This book was written with no irenic spirit. Of course, with his domino theory of theology—one concession to biblical inerrancy and the whole Bible is gone—his reasoning is that the end justifies the means. Third, the book is filled with half-truths, guilt by association, non sequiturs, quotations taken out of context, conclusions drawn from statements by others that one has no right to assume would be concluded by the author of the statement, sweeping generalizations, and misuse of scripture.

Good books on the nature and authority of the Bible are needed. Lindsell's book is not one. The reader would do well to turn instead to more balanced and constructive books such as Smart's *The Strange Silence of the Bible in the Church* or Beegle's *Scripture, Tradition and Infallibility.*[8]

Mr. Blackburn has dissociated himself completely from biblical inerrancy. That is plain. His commendation of the book *Scripture, Tradition and Infallibility* by Dewey Beegle (as well as the volume by Smart) who is openly and honestly opposed to biblical inerrancy, and who thinks there are theological as well as historical and scientific errors in the Bible, should be sufficient to decide how far Mr. Blackburn has strayed from the New Hampshire Confession of Faith and Southern Baptist views. Further observations about this approach will come later when I consider specifically the case of the Southern Baptist Seminary as a paradigm of the infection which has crept into the Southern Baptist Convention.

Duke McCall of Southern Seminary at Louisville

Dr. Duke McCall is the president of the Southern Baptist Theological Seminary of Louisville, Kentucky, which is the oldest seminary of the Southern Baptist Convention. Shortly after the publication of *The Battle for the Bible* Dr. McCall published his thoughts on the subject of biblical inerrancy in the school publication *The Tie.*[9] In the June 1976 issue President McCall said that the author of *The Battle for the Bible* (I am a member of a Southern Baptist Church) "will neither destroy the heresy he opposes nor divide the Southern Baptist Convention with this silly game with words." In his conclusion he said that "some men would rather fight than become the children of God." Strong words indeed!

Duke McCall thinks more snakes have been stirred up than can be killed. They arise because I "fight under the flag of inerrancy, infallibility, and verbal inspiration" of the Bible. He said I mean "to slay those who will not use some of the battle slogans of the new Fighting Fundamentalism." He argued that for me to say the Bible is without error in the autographs and to admit that a few copyists' errors may have slipped into the copying process is to destroy the argument for inerrancy. He stated that "even a master of imaginative rhetoric must know that you cannot say there are mistakes, but there are no mistakes, there are errors but there are no errors, fallible men have been infallible scholars." This is an illuminating statement, for it fairly represents Dr. McCall's own position.

Dr. McCall has said two things about the case for biblical inerrancy. He said it is wrong in principle to assert that the original books of the Bible were wholly trustworthy if the copies of those books have some copyists' errors in them. That is not a new question and has been answered many times. Work on the text of the Bible has narrowed down copyists' problems so that it can be said that to all intents and purposes we have a *very* trustworthy Scripture. Moreover, the places where there are textual problems in no way compromise the Scripture at any important point. However, Dr. McCall failed to note that the view of error-free autographs is the teaching of Jesus, and was brought about by the work of the Holy Spirit in the hearts of the writers. No believer in inerrancy can disagree with Dr. McCall's statement that "Studying the Bible will open hearts to the miraculous workings of the Holy Spirit." And the Westminster Confession of Faith (taken over in the Philadelphia Confession of Faith by Baptists) says it is this working power of the Holy Spirit which convinces men the Bible is true in all its parts.

What Dr. McCall objects to, and this is signally important, is the claim that "fallible men have been infallible scholars." Quite so! Inerrantists do say that the Holy Spirit used fallible men so that when they wrote Scripture they became infallible. And what they wrote was true in all its parts. This is what makes inspiration inspiration. If all inspiration does is assure us we have a Bible which is partly true and partly false, we are in trouble, for this can also be said of all other books. In what, then, would inspiration consist? The important point to note is that Dr. McCall is saying that *even in the autographs* we do not have an infallible Word, for fallible men under the inspiration of the Holy Spirit do not become infallible. And if the original Scriptures are not infallible, then the copies can be no better than the originals. But Dr. McCall is left with a still greater problem. If fallible men did not become infallible when they wrote Scripture, (unless McCall will qualify his statement by asserting that fallible men did become infallible when writing theologically), we cannot even say that their theological statements are to be trusted. Once Dr. McCall says there are only some infallible statements in the Bible, we must then seek to find the infallible Word of God in fallible Scripture, and of this I shall have more to say in another chapter on the use of the historical-critical method.

The *Louisville Courier-Journal* ran an article about Southern Seminary as a result of *The Battle for the Bible*.[10] This article said my book "prompted the president of the Southern Baptist Seminary, Dr. Duke McCall, to shed his kid gloves and come out counter punching." The author quoted *The Tie* article in which Dr. McCall said that "It is a case of the right-wing position becoming the wrong-wing. . . . Lindsell's accusations regarding the seminary are pure poppycock" (defined in the dictionary as "empty talk"; "bosh" —in which case the word has a specific meaning and we are right back to the question of verbal inspiration that Dr. McCall opposes so far as Scripture is concerned).

The newspaper reported that Dr. McCall would not invite me to speak on campus, although he has invited numerous liberals to speak there. He stated that he opposed any public debate "since the outcome would be determined by which one of us would play demagogue best [sic]. I wouldn't avoid a discussion with him but the question is, are we discussing this issue to determine the truth or are we discussing it to entertain an audience?" Moreover Dr. McCall said: "And, frankly, I don't feel we would want to give Lindsell a platform after he raised those questions about us that could have been answered with one phone call. But I think it served his book's purpose better to have questions than answers. He's selling division. He means to divide evangelicals. To have him here would be a waste of breath because he wouldn't change me and I wouldn't change him."

In the December 20, 1976, issue of *The Christian News* a Lutheran, Raymond F. Surburg, made an analysis of Dr. McCall's statements.[11] This article is especially significant because it was written by one who stands outside the Baptist camp and who comes to the issue with no denominational prejudice or with any intention "to divide" the Southern Baptist Convention. Part of this analysis appears in Appendix I of this volume for those who would like to read this observer's appraisal of the contemporary scene. Now back to Dr. McCall.

A year after the appearance of Dr. McCall's famous "snakes" article in *The Tie*, he made reference to a letter he received from an unnamed brother who asked him three questions: (1) Do you believe that God inspired every Word of the original manuscripts? (2) Do you believe there were any errors in the original manuscripts? (3) Do you believe that Adam and Eve were the first two human beings and that they gave birth to Cain, Abel, Seth, and other sons and daughters?[12] Dr. McCall's reaction was illuminating. He said:

> I sometimes get mail of such vicious intention that I am tempted to borrow this famous old response: "Some illiterate moron has written the enclosed vicious and unwarranted letter and has signed your name. I hope you can find out who did it and stop this slanderous letter-writing."
>
> But what Christian purpose would be served thereby? Only my hostility would be ventilated. Then, silence is golden. I meant to ignore the . . . letter . . . but seminary students kept asking me what I had written. . . .

President McCall responded to the letter by asking three questions in return: (1) Do you believe that God lost control of the Scriptures after the disappearance of the original manuscripts? (2) Do you believe the original manuscripts are the only inerrant and, therefore the only reliable, trustworthy Scriptures? (3) Where did Cain get his wife? Dr. McCall was obviously vexed by the letter he had received. I assume it had come from a Southern Baptist. The Louisville seminary is a

Southern Baptist institution. Any Baptist has a right to ask questions about any seminary. And the president owes the writer the courtesy of telling him what the institution stands for. The closest Dr. McCall came to a response was to generalize on the nature of biblical revelation, but he never answered any of the three questions posed in the inquirer's letter. How then should the reader interpret the response of Dr. McCall?

A fascinating sidelight opens the door to further understanding of Southern Baptist's influence through the glasses of Foy Valentine who is described in a newspaper article as "a liberal activist who has long headed the denomination's Christian Life Commission."[13] Dr. McCall at least had identified himself and his institution as evangelical. But Foy Valentine said "Southern Baptists are not evangelicals." This is strange language for one who would quickly declare that no one can speak for Southern Baptists as a whole. But Dr. Valentine went on to affirm that the word *evangelical* is "a Yankee word. They (northern evangelicals) want to claim us because we are big and successful and growing every year. But we have our own traditions, our own hymns, and more students in our seminaries than they have in all theirs put together. We don't share their politics or their fussy fundamentalism, and we don't want to get involved in their theological witch-hunts." The writer then said, "One of the 'witch-hunts' Valentine is referring to is a developing battle over the 'inerrancy' of the Bible, *Newsweek* said. This, it explained, 'is an evangelical refinement of the old fundamentalist doctrine which holds that the Bible is literally true in everything it says—about science and history as well as the central Gospel message.' "

Answering the Critics

I have tried to present as fairly as possible the reactions to *The Battle for the Bible* among some Southern Baptists who disagree with what I wrote. Some mention should also be made of the fact that few, if any, Southern Baptist bookstores stocked my book.

Basically the question has surfaced whether I provided sufficient documentation for my thesis that Southern Baptists have been infiltrated by an aberrant view of the Bible. If I am wrong then I owe an apology to men like Duke McCall and others. And there are multitudes of people who also owe similar apologies, because they hold the same views I do.

Southern Baptists have six theological seminaries whose trustees are elected by the convention. Probably the two most outstanding institutions are the Southern Baptist Seminary in Louisville and the Southwestern Baptist Theological Seminary in Fort Worth, Texas. At least they are the largest. Southern Seminary, being the oldest institution has played a distinctive and significant role in Southern Baptist life. Multitudes of its graduates serve local congregations and teach in Baptist colleges and universities. Its graduates are found on the faculties of all the theological seminaries. In one sense it can be said that a school like Southeastern Baptist Theological Seminary (Wake Forest, North Carolina) is the lengthened shadow of Louisville. Most of its founding faculty members were graduates of Louisville.

Surely one would suppose that the Southern Baptist Convention has enough seminaries in which to train all the men it needs for its churches. This is said even though thousands of churches are pastored by non-seminary graduates. But the truth is that numbers of Southern Baptists are unhappy about the direction in which their seminaries are moving. This is not something I invented. All I did was to disclose the obvious; that there is substantial dissatisfaction with existing theological seminaries on the part of loyal Baptists. And they have done something about it.

Dr. W. A. Criswell is pastor of the First Baptist Church of Dallas, Texas, the largest congregation in the convention. He is a former president of the Convention. His stand for an inerrant Scripture has brought him the opposition of many of the more liberal scholars in the convention. He has been dissatisfied with the college and seminary situation, and because of this the First Baptist Church houses a new institution designed to train men and women for the ministry. There would have been no need for him to open the doors of a competing institution if the existing ones were satisfactorily doing the job they were created to do.

Dr. B. Gray Allison and others began the Mid-America Baptist Theological Seminary in Memphis, Tennessee. He was formerly a member of the faculty of the New Orleans Baptist Theological Seminary. Surely the testimony of his own experience in Southern Baptist institutions regarding the theological shift should be seriously considered. This new institution trains Southern Baptist people, and the school is supported by Southern Baptist money, although it is independent of and does not secure any monies from, the cooperative program of the denomination. The school simply says it exists to offer Southern Baptists an option in seminary education. The option, simply stated, is this: The institution is staffed by people who are wholly committed to an inerrant Scripture. All the professors believe and teach in accordance with this conviction. The school enthusiastically endorses the Baptist Faith and Message confession of 1925. It has no intention of being divisive, but the failure of the denominational seminaries to stand without apology for historic Baptist orthodoxy was regarded as ample reason for the creation of a new institution. The growth of this school shows that multitudes of Southern Baptists agree there is a problem in the convention.

The establishment of the Luther Rice Seminary by Dr. Robert Witty almost two decades ago was occasioned by a desire to train Baptists in residence and by extension in a way not then done by the denominational schools. But it also was created to reflect traditional Baptist orthodoxy which was not being adequately expressed in existing institutions. This Jacksonville, Florida, school meets a growing need and its graduates are among those who lead the denomination in baptisms and church growth. This school has an ecumenical ministry that embraces virtually every mainline denomination and reaches out across the globe. The absence of forward-looking conservative leadership from the existing denominational channels is highlighted by this unique venture in theological education.

I propose, now, to do two things. First, I will demonstrate from the writings of the early leaders of the Southwestern Baptist Theological Seminary in Texas and of the Southern Baptist Theological Seminary in Kentucky what they believed about the Bible. When I have done that I propose to give visibility to the views of some of the Southern Baptist Theological Seminary faculty members and graduates as a paradigm to demonstrate conclusively there is a theological problem having to do with the Bible that no honest understanding of the situation can deny.

I choose to emphasize the Louisville Seminary for several reasons. First, Dr. McCall has publically stated that my allegation of the infiltration of an aberrant view of the Bible with respect to Louisville is poppycock. He has stated that a simple telephone call to Louisville, presumably to him, would have settled an issue that thousands of other Southern Baptists know about, and would not be satisfied with by a phone call in the light of the manifold evidences of departure from orthodoxy. Second, I have limited myself to Louisville because a crosscut analysis of all the institutions, collegiate and theological, would be impossible in this small book. Moreover, time limitations and the length of this book have kept me from more exhaustive inquiry, since I am writing abo t more groups than Southern Baptists. All I need to do to establish my point that Southern Baptists have been infected is to show how Louisville is the archetype of this infection. Later on, I will devote a part of this work to a discussion of the historical-critical method which lies at the heart of the problem among Southern Baptists and elsewhere. To these ends I now direct my attention, first to the seminary in Fort Worth.

Southwestern Baptist Theological Seminary

The 1976/77 *Bulletin* of the Southwestern Baptist Theological Seminary carried a section devoted to the background and origins of the institution. This is what was said:

> Nearly seven decades ago B. H. Carroll had a dream. In it he visualized a graduate institution providing trained leadership for the churches of America's spiritual frontiers.
>
> Sixty-nine years ago his dream became a reality. Southwestern Baptist Theological Seminary was an outgrowth of the theological department of Baylor University, Waco, Texas, established in 1901. In 1905, the department became Baylor Theological Seminary with five professors.
>
> The Baptist General Convention of Texas, authorized the separation of the seminary from Baylor University in 1907, gave it a new name, The Southwestern Baptist Theological Seminary, and a separate board of trustees.
>
> The seminary was actually chartered on March 14, 1908, and

functioned on the Waco campus until the summer of 1910. Several Texas cities made strong bids for the site of the new institution, but Fort Worth citizens provided a campus site and enough money to build the first building which was named Fort Worth Hall in honor of its new location.

In 1925, control of the seminary passed from the Texas convention to the Southern Baptist Convention. . . .

The seminary has had five presidents in its sixty-nine year history. B. H. Carroll, the first president, served from the embryonic stages of the school until his death in November, 1914. L. R. Scarborough, elected president in February, 1915, retired in 1942. . . .[14]

Since B. H. Carroll was the founder of what has become the largest theological seminary in the world, two questions must be asked and answered. The first is: What was the view of Dr. Carroll with respect to the Scriptures? Second: If his view of the Word of God included a commitment to verbal, plenary inerrancy, was this view shared by the denomination as well as by the Baptist General Convention of Texas? In this regard we must also ask whether what Dr. Carroll believed and taught was in agreement with the New Hampshire Confession of Faith adopted by the Southern Baptist Convention in 1925. If it was not, what were the differences between his beliefs and those of the New Hampshire Confession of Faith?

Dr. Carroll wrote a book titled *Inspiration of the Bible*. It was published posthumously in 1930. In it he brought into sharp focus his own thoughts and convictions about the Word of God. This volume should be republished today and read by tens of thousands of Baptists so that they would better understand the theological roots from which they have sprung. The following excerpts are from Dr. Carroll's book, and it is plain to see that he believed in an inerrant and wholly trustworthy Scripture.

B. H. Carroll on the Bible

Inspiration

It has always been a matter of profound surprise to me that anybody should ever question the verbal inspiration of the Bible. The whole thing had to be written in words. Words are signs of ideas, and if the words are not inspired, then there is no way of getting at anything in connection with inspiration. If I am free to pick up the Bible and read something and say, "That is inspired," then read something else and say, "That is not inspired," and someone else does not agree with me as to which is and which is not inspired, it leaves the whole thing unsettled as to whether any of it is inspired.

What is the object of inspiration? It is to put accurately, in human words, ideas from God. If the words are not inspired, how am I to know how much to reject, and how to find out whether anything is from God? When you hear the silly talk that the Bible "contains" the word of God and is not the word of God, you hear a fool's talk. I don't care if he is a Doctor of Divinity, a President of a University covered with medals from universities of Europe and the United States, it is fool-talk. There can be no inspiration of the book without the inspiration of the words of the book.

Very briefly I have summed up proof of the inspiration of the Old Testament and of the inspiration of the New Testament, and now I will give you some scriptures on both Testaments together. Hebrews 1:1, 2:1, 2:[15]

"God, having of old time spoken unto the fathers in the prophets by divers portions and in divers manners, hath at the end of these days spoken unto us in his Son."

In old times there were inspired men; but the culmination or completion is in the Son. That covers both. Hebrews 5:12 also covers both:

"When by reason of the time ye ought to be teachers, ye have need again that someone teach you the rudiments of the first principles of the oracles of God."

Here the New Testament is called "oracles" as well as the Old Testament. Those were Christian people who had learned the first principles of the oracles of God and stopped. Another passage is I Peter 4:11: "If any man speaketh, speaking as it were oracles of God." Peter is here talking about the Old and New Testaments. If a man gets up to speak, let him remember that there is a standard, and that that standard is fixed. He must speak according to the oracles of God. These Scriptures cover both.

Now let us consider some observations:

The Holy Spirit and Scripture

First, the books of the Bible are not by the will of man. Not one of the books of either the Old or the New Testaments would ever have come into being except by the inspiration of God. I want to give you a searching proof on that, found in I Peter 1:10, 11:

"Concerning which salvation the prophets sought and searched diligently, who prophesied of the grace that should come unto you: searching what time or what manner of time the Spirit of Christ which was in them did point unto, when it testified beforehand the sufferings of Christ, and the glories which should follow them."

Here are men moved by the Spirit of God to record certain things about the future, and they themselves did not understand it. They studied their own prophecies just as we study them. They knew that God had inspired them to say these things, but they did not understand, e.g., God instructed a prophet to say that the Messiah should come forth out of Bethlehem of Judea. God inspired each and every item concerning the Messiah. To show that these things did not come from the will of man, the man himself could not explain them. It was a matter of study and investigation to find out what these signified. They found out that their prophecies were meant for the future, that is, for us.

The second observation is that the propelling power in the speaking or writing was an impulse from the Holy Spirit. They, the inspired men, became instruments by which the Holy Spirit spoke or wrote. Take, for instance, that declaration in II Samuel 23:2, where David said:

"The Spirit of Jehovah spake by me, and his word was upon my tongue."

In Acts 1:16 we find that the utterances of David were being studied. We have a declaration that the Holy Sprit spake by the mouth of David concerning Judas; and in the third chapter of Acts we have another declaration of the same kind. Always the speaker or writer was an instrument of the Holy Spirit.

The third observation is that this influence of the Holy Spirit guided the men in the selection of material, even where that material came from some other book, even an uninspired book, the Spirit guiding in selecting and omitting material.

From such declarations as John 20:30, 31, and 21:25, we learn that Christ did many things, that if all were written it would make a book as big as the world; that what has been written was written for a certain purpose. The Holy Spirit inspired Matthew, Mark, Luke and John to select from the deeds and words of Jesus that which God wanted written; not to take everything He said, but only that which was necessary to accomplish the purpose.

The fourth observation is that inspiration is absolutely necessary in order to awaken the power of remembrance. John 2:22 says that after His resurrection they remembered what He had said, that is, the Sprit called it to remembrance.

To illustrate, take the speeches of Christ, viz.: that address delivered at Capernaum on the Bread of Life, the Sermon on the

Mount and, particularly, the fourteenth, fifteenth and sixteenth chapters of John.

There were no shorthand reporters in those days and there is not a man on earth who could, after a lapse of fifty years, recall *verbatim et literatim* what Christ said, and yet John, without a shadow of hesitancy, goes on and gives page after page of what Christ said just after the institution of the Lord's Supper. Inspiration in that case was exercised in awakening the memory so that John could reproduce these great orations of Christ.

Of the orations of Paul, take that speech recorded in Acts 13, an exceedingly remarkable speech, or the one recorded in Acts 26, or the one on Mars' Hill, in chapter 17, one of the most finished productions that the world has ever seen. Inspiration enabled Luke to report exactly what Paul said. Luke never could have done that unassisted. Luke, as a man, might have given the substance, but that is not the substance, it is an elaborate report, the sense depending upon the words used.

The fifth observation is that inspiration was to make additions to the Scriptures until they were completed, in order that the standard may be a perfect treasure, incapable of being added to, unsusceptible of diminution; we want what is there, all that is there, and no more than is there; therefore, when we come to the last book of the Bible, this is said which, in a sense, applies to the whole Bible:[16]

"I testify that every man that heareth the words of the prophecy of this book, If any man shall add unto them, God shall add unto him the plagues which are written in this book: and if any man shall take away from the words of the book of this prophecy, God shall take away his part from the tree of life, and out of the holy city, which are written in this book." —Rev. 22:18, 19.

The goals of inspiration

It was the design of inspiration to give us a perfect system of revealed truth, whose words are inspired. As an example of verbal inspiration, take Paul's argument, based on the "seed" in the singular number. Everything in the interpretation depends upon the number of that noun. Apart from verbal inspiration, how on earth would Paul hinge an argument on whether a word is singular or plural?

The next observation is that inspiration was to give different views of the same person or thing by different writers, each perfect according to its viewpoint, but incomplete so far as the whole is concerned, all views being necessary in order to complete the view. There is a Gospel by Mark, written for the Romans, beginning with the public ministry of Christ. Then there are the Gospels of Matthew, Luke and John, and a Gospel by Paul. Each of them is perfect according to the plan which the Spirit put in the mind of the writer. They are perfect so far as the whole thing is concerned. We have to put them side by side in order to get a complete view of the life of our Lord. That is what we mean by harmonical study. Each is infallibly correct, but it takes the blended view of all to make the whole thing.[17]

The Genesis account of creation

Apart from inspiration, no man on earth can account for Genesis. Just see in what small space there is given the history of the world up to chapter 11—how much is left out. We see the same plan all through the book. It first takes up the wicked descendants, gives their genealogy a little way, then sidetracks them and takes up the true line. Then of their descendants it follows the wicked first a short way and eliminates them and goes back and takes up the true line and elaborates that. That principle goes all through the Bible.[18]

The infallibility of Scripture

Now we come to an important point. When these inspired declarations were written, they were absolutely infallible. Take these Scriptures: John 10:35, "The scripture cannot be broken;" Matthew 5:18, "Till heaven and earth shall pass away, one jot or tittle shall in no wise pass away from the law, till all things be accomplished"; Acts 1:15, "It was needful that the scripture should be fulfilled."

That is one of the most important points in connection with inspiration, viz.: that the inspired word is irrefragable, infallible; that all the powers of the world cannot break one "thus saith the Lord."[19]

Right understanding about inspiration

Let me say further that only the original text of the books of the Bible is inspired, not the copy or translation.

Second, the inspiration of the Bible does not mean that God said and did all that is said and done in the Bible; some of it the devil did and said. Much of it wicked men did and said.

The inspiration means that the record of what is said and done is correct. It does not mean that everything that God did and said is recorded. It does not mean that everything recorded is of equal importance, but every part of it is necessary to the purpose of the record, and no part is unimportant. One part is no more inspired than any other part.

It is perfectly foolish to talk about degrees of inspiration. What Jesus said in the flesh, as we find it in the four Gospels, is no more His word than what the inspired prophet or apostle said.

Answers to objections

Here are some objections:

First, "only the originals are inspired, and we have only copies." The answer to that is that God would not inspire a book and take no care of the book. His providence has preserved the Bible in a way that no other book has been preserved.

The second objection is, "We are dependent upon scholars to determine what is the real text of the Bible." The answer is that only an infinitesimal part of it is dependent upon scholars for the ascertainment of the true text, and if every bit of that were blotted out it would not destroy the Holy Scriptures.[20]

Plenary and verbal inspiration

The Bible is the Word of God.

All the Bible is the Word of God.

A great many people say, "I think the Word of God is in the Bible, but I don't believe that all of the Bible is the Word of God; it contains the Word of God, but it is not the Word of God."

My objection to this is that it would require inspiration to tell the spots in it that were inspired. It would call for an inspiration more difficult than the kind that I talk about, in order to turn the pages of the Bible and find out which part is the Word of God.

"Oh," says one man, "I can pick them out." But can you satisfy Mr. B.? He can pick them out, too, but he doesn't agree with you. So whatever you do when you preach, don't preach a spotted inspiration, or you will have to find an inspired man to find the spots.

In other words, with reference to the Scriptures, inspiration is plenary, which means full and complete, hence my question is, "Do you believe in the plenary inspiration of the Bible?" If the inspiration is complete, it must be plenary.

My next question is this: "Do you believe in plenary verbal inspiration?"

I do, for the simple reason that the words are mere signs of ideas, and I don't know how to get at the idea except through the words. If the words don't tell, how shall I know? Sometimes the word is a very small one, maybe only one letter or a mere element. The word with one letter—the smallest letter—shows the inspiration of the Old Testament. The man that put that there was inspired.

Take the words of Jesus. He says, "Not one jot or tittle of that law shall ever fail."

The "jot" is the smallest letter in the Hebrew alphabet and the "tittle" is a small turn or projection of a Hebrew letter. He says the heavens may fall, but not one jot or tittle of that law shall fail. Then He says that the Scriptures cannot be broken. What is it that cannot be broken? Whatever is written cannot be broken if it is *theopneustos*. But the word is not inspired if it is not *theopneustos*, which means God-breathed, or God-inspired.[21]

Science and the Bible

I will now take up what some people have regarded as an insuperable obstacle in the way of accepting the inspiration of the Scriptures. They say that if the Bible is inspired, and all of its records are accurate, and that there is not errancy in it, then it puts a man of science in the position that he must choose between science and the Bible, their teachings being diverse.

To this man I would say that he is mistaken, and I would challenge him or any other man to show one solitary contradiction between science and the Bible.

But he must confine himself to science.

Science is something known, something proven. He must not bring up his speculative theories, his mental vagaries, and call them science. I challenge him to bring up a single contradiction between the teaching of Scripture and real science.

I have seen that tested on the first chapter of Genesis. That gives an account of the creation of the universe, the formation of the earth, and the creation of man, and to this very day science—not science as represented by some men who try to set the teachings of science over against the Bible by butting their heads against the accounts in Genesis, Job, certain of the Psalms, and Paul's declarations at Athens—but true science is and has ever been in harmony with the Scriptures.

The Word of God stands today grasping the hand of all real science just like the coat-of-arms of the State of Kentucky—"United we stand, divided we fall."

Now I will give you some science: When I was a young fellow, just before the Civil War, a great political emergency arose—the question of slavery—and men not only discussed it from political standpoints, but they began to discuss it from Bible standpoints, and then scientific standpoints, and there was published in the city of New York a daily paper, and because of its peculiar views on the subject of slavery, it attained a circulation of many thousands.

Just before the war a series of articles was published in that paper to prove that the Negro and the Caucasian, by scientific demonstration, did not have a common origin—that it was impossible in the light of science that all men came from one man. If that is true, that puts the Bible in default, for if anything in the world is taught in the Bible, it is the unity of the race.

It certainly does teach that the human race descended from Adam, and that the plan of salvation is based upon that fact, and all human redemption is based upon the fact that all these lost descendents of the first Adam are redeemed and saved in the Second Adam.

About this time two doctors, in Mobile, Alabama, who saw the question from a Southern standpoint, published a very large book, and they contradicted the articles which were published in the New York daily. They saw a conflict between science and the Bible. Well, all that was necessary in that case was not to move the Bible into the scientific camp, but let the Bible stand, and see all the scientists trooping back to get under the Bible-tent; so, I have even lived to see the time come when facts not only prove to the world that scientists are ready to demonstrate the unity of the human race, but that they, like the Indian, stood so straight up that they leaned over, and they went so far as to state that all beings had a common origin—not only man, but monkeys and man; not only monkeys and man, but elephants and man; not only elephants and man, but jellyfish and man; not only jellyfish and man, but cabbage heads and man. Now, all that is necessary is not to move the Bible, but just let it stand.

I have lived to see the theory of Charles Darwin die again as Paul saw it die in its original habitation where it was proclaimed by its advocates in Athens, Corinth and Rome, and today the best advocates of science are just as ready to denounce Darwin as I am.[22]

Joshua and the sun that stood still

I have had scientists bring up that instance of Joshua commanding the sun to stand still. Some preachers skip that chapter, and I am sorry for them. They had better read it just as it is. They had better take it just as it reads.

Only a few weeks ago I saw in a book of great power, an absolute demonstration of what would have been projected as a result if the sun and the moon had stopped, and I have certainly seen it demonstrated that it would not have occurred.

But suppose they put God into the account; if they would just put God in there, that would be a guarantee. He would know how to manage it. I suppose we all believe in an all-powerful God; He could take care of the situation, unless we have a God who finds some things too much for Him. I suppose He could manage that little affair just as He could raise a dead man to life that had gone into corruption.[23]

Supposed contradictions

When I was a boy I thought I had found a thousand contradictions in the Bible. In the old Bible of my young manhood I marked them. Well, I had then nearly a thousand more contradictions than I have now. I do not see them now; they are not there. There are perhaps a half dozen in the Bible that I cannot explain satisfactorily to myself. I don't say that my explanation of all the others would satisfy everybody. There are some that I cannot explain satisfactorily to myself; but since I have seen nine hundred and ninety-four out of the thousand coalesce and harmonize like two streams mingling, I am disposed to think that if I had more sense I could harmonize those other six; and even if I forever fail to harmonize them, God knows better than I know, and that when I know perfectly just as I now know only in part, and only a very small part, I will be able to understand that. . . .[24]

No one can doubt where B. H. Carroll, the founder of Southwestern Baptist Theological Seminary, stood on the issue of the Scriptures. He held to verbal, plenary or full inerrancy. This was the platform on which the seminary was built. This was the heartthrob of a great man whose views were the views of Southern Baptists generally. He was succeeded by Dr. Lee R. Scarborough. In Dr. Scarborough's *Gospel Messages* he tells of a conversation he had with Dr. Carroll before his death. This is his own account of part of the conversation:

I was in his room and he . . . looked me in the face. There were times when he looked like he was forty feet high. And he looked into my face and said, "My boy, on this Hill orthodoxy, the old faith is making one of its last stands and I want to deliver you a charge, and I do it in the blood of Jesus Christ." He said, "You will be elected president of the seminary. I want you, if there ever comes heresy in your faculty, to take it to your faculty. If they won't hear you, take it to the trustees. If they won't hear you, take it to the conventions that appointed them. If they won't hear you, take it to the common Baptists. They will hear you. And," he said, "I charge you in the name of Jesus Christ to keep it lashed to the old Gospel of Jesus Christ." As long as I have influence in that institution, by the grace of God, I will stand by the old Book.[25]

The years have gone by. Presidents have come and gone. A new era has begun with the election of Russell H. Dilday, Jr., to the presidency of Southwestern. He came from the pastorate of the Second Ponce de Leon Baptist Church of Atlanta, Georgia. Richard Quebedeaux in his book *The Worldly Evangelicals* listed this church "at the left of the convention's theological spectrum." I wrote to Dr. Dilday indicating I was writing this book and asked him where he stood with respect to Scripture. His reply was reassuring. This is what he said:

> All of our faculty and administrative staff at Southwestern have given their firm commitment to the statement of belief which says in part: "The Holy Bible was written by men divinely inspired and is the record of God's revelation of Himself to man. It is a perfect treasure of divine instruction. It has God for its author, salvation for its end, and truth, without any mixture of error, for its matter. It reveals the principles by which God judges us; and therefore is, and will remain to the end of the world, the true center of Christian union, and the supreme standard by which all human conduct, creeds, and religious opinions should be tried. The criterion by which the Bible is to be interpreted is Jesus Christ."

This statement, of course, comes from the New Hampshire Confession of Faith. If Southwestern, under Dr. Dilday's leadership, holds to this in theory and in practice the Seminary will forge forward in the days ahead. And its literary production will challenge the obvious departures from this viewpoint on the part of Southern Baptist colleges and seminaries. Indeed, Southwestern could provide dynamic leadership for the recovery of the view of the Bible on which the convention was established.

There are members of the Southwestern faculty who do hold the view of B. H. Carroll. Dr. Hendricks, who wrote the review of *The Battle for the Bible,* made it clear that he is not numbered among them. The flag that Dr. Carroll raised has been lowered. What will the future of the largest theological seminary in the world be like?

The Southern Baptist Theological Seminary

Now I turn my attention to Louisville, the oldest Southern

Baptist seminary, and in so many ways the leader in theological education among them. What was the view of the early fathers with respect to the Bible and did they, like Dr. Carroll, raise the standard for inerrancy? Two of the founding fathers of Louisville were Basil Manly and James Petigru Boyce. Both of them held to biblical inerrancy. John Sampey, Old Testament professor and president of the seminary, followed in their train and held the line on a trustworthy Scripture. I will consider their written statements.

Basil Manly on Scripture

Dr. Manly wrote *The Bible Doctrine of Inspiration Explained and Vindicated.* It was published in 1891. The title itself indicates there was indeed a problem of biblical infallibility raised by the advent of German higher criticism which had crossed the Atlantic to America. Dr. Manly opposed the basic proposition that underlies the historical-critical method—namely that Scripture and the Word of God are not synonymous. He believed that all the Bible is the Word of God. He also said: "The Bible is God's Word to man, throughout; yet at the same time it is really and thoroughly man's composition." He held to the same view of Scripture expressed by F. L. Patton of Princeton who said in his book *Inspiration* that

> The books of the Bible . . . were composed by men who acted under the influence of the Holy Ghost to such an extent that they were preserved from every error of fact, of doctrine, of judgment; and these were so influenced in the choice of language that the very words they used were the words of God.[26]

Dr. Manly also believed that the view of the Bible he espoused was the view of the church through the ages. George T. Ladd was an able opponent of Manly's view. Manly quoted him, an opponent, to demonstrate that although he denied inerrancy yet he had to agree that it was the church's view generally. Of Dr. Ladd, Professor Manly wrote:

> Dr. Ladd . . . the most elaborate, and probably the ablest of all the recent assailants of the strict doctrine of the Inspiration of Sacred Scripture, admits that the view of inspiration which he regards as incorrect because "incompatible with the real authorship of the Biblical writers . . . has doubtless been, on the whole, most generally prevalent" in the Christian Church.[27]

Is the Bible the Word of God?

Dr. Manly vigorously resisted the view that the Bible only contains the Word of God. He said:

> Among those who would change the statement "The Bible *is* the Word of God" into "The Bible *contains* the Word of God" may be named LeClerc and Grotius, whose views may be readily traced back to Maimonides, the celebrated Jewish Rabbi of the Middle Ages.[28]

Then he added:

> Professor George T. Ladd, in his most recent learned and able work on the Doctrine of Sacred Scripture, vehemently maintains the distinction between the Bible and the Word of God. "Its most untenable extremes (those of the Post-Reformation dogma) are all traceable to the fundamental misconception which identifies the Bible and the Word of God" (Ladd, Vol. II, p. 178).[29]

Dr. Manly went on the say that

> The doctrine which we hold is that commonly styled PLENARY INSPIRATION or FULL INSPIRATION. It is that the Bible as a whole is the Word of God, so that every part of Scripture is both infallible truth and divine authority.[30]

Moreover, Dr. Manly said that while the writers of Scripture did not enjoy perfect knowledge on all subjects; they did enjoy "infallibility and divine authority in their official utterances." And they were not infallible in conduct. In other words, he protected their fallen humanity, agreed that they were sinful men like all of us, but that as instruments of the Holy Spirit they were uniquely endowed with respect to the writing of Scripture so that this product bears the marks of the divine and constitutes nothing but truth.

Judging the Bible

Basil Manly was concerned that men should not sit in judgment on the Word of God. Rather, the Word of God was to sit in judgment on men. He quoted with approval a statement made by Bannerman concerning this:

> He comes to the Bible, and sits over its contents in the attitude of a judge who is to decide for himself what in it is true and worthy

to be believed, and what in it is false and deserving to be rejected; not in the attitude of the disciple who, within the limits of the inspired record, feels himself at Jesus' feet, to receive every word that cometh out of his mouth. . . . The assurance that the Bible is the Word of God, and not simply containing it, in more or less of its human language, is one fitted to solemnize the soul with a holy fear, and a devout submission to its declarations as the very utterances of God. The assurance, on the contrary, that the truths of revelation are mingled, in a manner unknown and indeterminate, with the defects of the record, is one which reverses the attitude, and brings man as a master to sit in judgment on the Bible as summoned to his bar, and bound to render up to him a confession of its errors, and not a declaration of its one and authoritative truth.—Bannerman, p. 107. Compare pp. 241, 242.[31]

On the transmission of the Bible: copyists and mistakes

In response to the question whether the Bible we now have (and I mark well that it is one of the points made by Duke McCall the president of Southern) has been preserved in such a manner that no errors or mistakes by copyists have entered the picture, Dr. Manly has a word to say. But what is important is that the inerrancy of the Bible pertains to the autographs, not to the copies.

The inspiration which we affirm is that of the original text of Scripture, and therefore does not deny that there may have been errors in copying. We have no assurance, nor the slightest reason to suppose, that the supernatural guardianship which insured the correctness of the original record was continued and renewed every time anybody undertook to make a copy of it. The accuracy of our present copies is a separate question, dependent on the ordinary rules of historical evidence in such matters. This is what is examined in the science of Text Criticism.

There has been indeed a providential guardianship over the Word, by which it has been preserved remarkably incorrupt, and singularly attested as being substantially the same that proceeded from the original writers. The results of the Herculean labors of modern critics make it evident that, in about a dozen important passages, and in very many unimportant ones, there is reasonable ground for correcting the commonly received text. In a number of others, there is room for discussion as to the true reading. But when all these known errors are corrected, and all those doubtful readings are set aside, it is evident that there is no change as to any leading doctrine or fact of the Gospel.[32]

Dr. Manly addressed the question:

"Why so strenuous for exact inspiration of the words, when you admit there may have been errors of transcription? What do you gain?"

We answer, we gain all the difference there is between an inspired and an uninspired original; all the difference between a document truly divine and authoritative to begin with—though the copies or translations may have in minute particulars varied from it—and a document faulty and unreliable at the outset, and never really divine.[33]

If there are "textual uncertainties," as we frankly admit, there are also textual certainties; and these are simple enough for guidance through the snares of earth and to the glories of heaven.[1]

On this subject the emphatic testimony of Westcott and Hort, the most recent, and certainly among the most competent of text critics, is adequate, without further discussion. They say:—

"With regard to the great bulk of the words of the New Testament, as of most other ancient writings, there is no variation or other ground of doubt, and therefore no room for textual criticism; and here therefore an editor is merely a transcriber. The same may be said with substantial truth respecting those various readings which have never been received, and in all probability never will be received, into any printed text. The proportion of words virtually accepted on all hands as raised above doubt is very great, not less, on a rough computation, than seven eighths of the whole. The remaining eighth, therefore, formed in great part by changes of order and other comparative trivialities, constitutes the whole area of criticism. If the principles followed in the present edition are sound, this area may be very greatly reduced. Recognizing to the full the duty of abstinence from peremptory decision in cases where the evidence leaves the judgment in suspense between two or more readings, we find that, setting aside differences of orthography, the words in our opinion still subject to doubt only make up about one sixtieth of the whole New Testament. In this second estimate the proportion of comparatively trivial variations is beyond measure larger than in the former; so that the amount of what can in any sense be called substantial variation is but a small fraction of the whole residuary variation, and can hardly form more than a thousandth part of the entire text."—*The New Testament in Greek,* II. 2.

Dr. Ezra Abbot, of Harvard, who ranked among the first textual critics, and was not hampered by orthodox bias (being a Unitarian), asserted that "no Christian doctrine or duty rests on those portions of the text which are affected by differences in the manuscripts; still less is anything *essential* in Christianity touched by the various readings. They do, to be sure, affect the bearing of a few passages on the doctrine of the Trinity; but the truth or falsity of the doctrine by no means depends upon the reading of those passages." The same scholar spoke on the subject more fully, with special reference to the English Revision: —

"This host of various readings may startle one who is not acquainted with the subject, and he may imagine that the whole text of the New Testament is thus rendered uncertain. But a careful analysis will show that nineteen twentieths of these are of no more consequence than the palpable errata in the first proof of a modern printer; they have so little authority, or are so manifestly false, that they may be at once dismissed from consideration. Of those which remain, probably nine tenths are of no importance as regards the sense; the differences either cannot be represented in a translation, or affect the form of expression merely, not the essential meaning of the sentence. Though the corrections made by the revisers in the Greek text of the New Testament followed by our translators probably exceeded two thousand, hardly one tenth of them, perhaps not one twentieth, will be noted by the ordinary reader. Of the small residue, many are indeed of sufficient interest and importance to constitute one of the strongest reasons for making a new revision, which should no longer suffer the known errors of copyists to take the place of the words of the evangelists and apostles. But the chief value of the work accomplished by the self-denying scholars who have spent so much time and labor in the search for manuscripts, and in their collation or publication, does not consist, after all, in the corrections of the text which have resulted from the researches. These corrections may affect a few of the passages which have been relied on for the support of certain doctrines, but not to such an extent as essentially to alter the state of the argument. Still less is any question of Christian duty touched by the multitude of various readings. The greatest service which the scholars who have devoted themselves to critical studies and the collection of critical materials have rendered has been the establishment of the fact that, on the whole, the New Testament writings have come down to us in a text remarkably free from important corruptions, even in the late and inferior manuscripts on which the so-called 'received text' was founded; while the helps which we now possess for restoring it to its primitive purity far exceed those which we enjoy in the case of any eminent classical author whose works have come down to us. The multitude of 'various readings,' which to the thoughtless or ignorant seem so alarming, is simply the result of the extraordinary richness and variety of our critical resources."—Sunday School Times, May 28, 1881.[34]

Basil Manly was fully aware of the implications flowing from the conclusions of the higher critics. He saw how these conclusions struck at the root of biblical inspiration and made such a view impossible if these conclusions were correct. He maintained that the choice lay between the opinions of the critics and the teaching of the Bible about its own inspiration and trustworthiness. The following extracts speak about Genesis, Daniel, and 2 Peter. And the issue today has not changed one iota since Dr. Manly's day. The basic battle is the same.

The Mosiac authorship of the body of the Pentateuch (aside from the addition to Deuteronomy which records his death, and possibly a few brief notes, geographical or historical, which may have been inserted by some later hand) seems to us of profound importance. It is so thoroughly assumed and recognized elsewhere in Scripture, that to deny it leads naturally, we think, to a denial of the reality of Old Testament history, and to a subversal of the whole scheme and system of divine revelation. If the Pentateuch, as we are told by some, is "not a work, but a growth," of exceedingly composite authorship and mainly post-exilian origin; if it is a compound of Babylonish legends and pious frauds, whether gotten up for selfish interest, or class aggrandizement, or with broader and more patriotic purpose; if it not only gives indications, as we think it does, of diverse sources traditional or documentary, employed under divine direction by Moses himself, but also contains, as we think it does not, contradictions and marks of falsehood; if Moses himself is, as some contend, a mythical personage, and the Exodus never actually occurred as described;—we can scarcely vindicate the verity of the subsequent history, or the allusions of Jesus and the Apostles to these writings.

So, if the genuineness of Daniel is successfully assailed, and it must be dragged down from the position of a true history and prophecy to be a legend of the era of the Maccabees,—a *vaticinium post eventum,* a fiction designed to inspire the patriotic ardor of the Jewish rebels against Antiochus Epiphanes,—we cannot, it seems to us, logically stop short with that; but must either exscind it from the Canon, in spite of its recognition by Jews and Christians and by our Lord himself, or else maintain such moral enormities as an honest lie, a fraud of divine origin.

If Second Peter, for instance, be clearly ascertained to be not genuine, not by the Apostle Peter, we should not regard it as inspired, or as any part of God's Word. It professes to be from "Simon Peter"; if it is not, but from some other author, it bears a falsehood on its face. It is a fraud. And there is no room for "pious frauds," or any other sort of fraud, in the Word of God.[35]

It is of more than passing interest in connection with Basil Manly that James Leo Garrett wrote an article, "Representative Modern Baptist Understanding of Biblical Interpretation," which appeared in the *Review and Expositor* (Vol. LXXI, No. 2. Spring 1974). In this Southern Baptist Seminary journal he discussed four Baptist theologians of whom Basil Manly was the only Southern Baptist. The others were Augustus Hopkins Strong, William Newton Clarke, and Henry Wheeler Robinson. Of them he said:

> ... the four Baptist authors taken chronologically, manifested an increasing awareness of the cruciality of the relationship between biblical criticism and biblical inspiration. *Manly showed the least awareness* (my italics), Clarke was profoundly changed by the conflice [sic] between the two, and Robinson evidenced the most comprehensive solutions to problems connected with this relationship. Thirdly, Manly, Strong, Clarke, and Robinson all treated biblical inspiration in close connection with biblical reliability and biblical authority, while drawing different conclusions.
> Finally, biblical inspiration is a concept or teaching that has been considered important to Baptists during the last hundred years, although its importance may have waned in the last quarter of a century and this fact serves to pose the needed question as to the future of biblical inspiration for and among Baptists and other Christians (p. 195).

Certainly Manly did not manifest an unawareness of the relationship between biblical criticism and biblical inspiration. One of his strengths was his perception of the dangers of biblical criticism and its incompatibility with biblical inerrancy. He deliberately chose biblical inerrancy over biblical criticism. But this article is important, for it shows the change that has taken place, marked by a departure from biblical inerrancy to a lower viewpoint. Duke McCall of Southern Seminary should read his own *Review and Expositor* carefully, for this article in

itself reveals the chasm between the Louisville of today and of
Basil Manly's day.

James Petigru Boyce,
systematic theologian at Southern Seminary

James Petigru Boyce was one of Southern Baptist's most distinguished scholars and seminary educators. He published a
book titled *Abstract of Theology* which was revised by his successor in the chair of systematic theology at Southern Seminary. This indicates, of course, the consent of Professor Kerfoot, who was Dr. Boyce's replacement, to the views of his
mentor. James Boyce did not differ in his views from those of
Dr. Manly, and both of them were among the founding fathers
of Southern Seminary. Here is what Dr. Boyce had to say: "The
subject of inspiration, for special reasons, has been remanded
in this special seminary to the department of Biblical Introduction." But he could hardly avoid the subject of inspiration as a
theologian and added:

> No other book has ever been found more reliable whenever its
> statements could be tested. It carries upon its face everywhere the
> verisimilitude of truth. Its own testimony is with most persons who
> read it an all-sufficient evidence of its truthfulness.

> We may argue *a priori* as to the character of this revelation as
> follows: a. It must come from God . . . b. It must be suited to our
> present condition . . . c. It must be secured from all possibility of
> error so that its teachings may be relied on with equal, if not
> greater, confidence than those of reason.[36]

John R. Sampey, Old Testament scholar and
president of Southern Seminary

Dr. Sampey taught Old Testament Interpretation at Louisville for many years. He published his *Syllabus for Old Testament Study* in 1903, long enough ago to identify him with the
historic position of Southern Baptists on Scripture. Dr. Sampey spoke of the difference between the radical and the conservative approaches to the Word of God. He identified with
the conservative viewpoint. He said:

> As to the inspiration of the Bible. Conservatives hold that the
> writers were preserved from all errors by the inbreathed Spirit.
> Radicals reject such a theory with scorn. Some liberals believe in a

sort of inspiration which heightened the spiritual perceptions of the Scriptural writers, but did not preserve them from error.

Dr. Sampey went on to say that those in the conservative tradition believe that what Jesus said puts an end to further argument. Here it is:

> Whereas Radicals set aside His authority entirely, and Moderate Liberals point to the limitations of His knowledge as a man, Jesus has Himself said that the Scriptures cannot be broken (John 10:35). If Radical critics break the Scriptures, they will also break the authority of Jesus as our Divine *Teacher.*[37]

These observations from the early teachers of the Southern Baptist Seminary at Louisville show beyond question what the view of Scripture was at that period in the history of Southern Baptists. Theologically there were no basic differences between the views held by B. H. Carroll, the founder of Southwestern, and those of the faculty at Louisville. However, this did not mean there were no problems. Crawford Howell Toy, mentioned earlier, was a Hebrew scholar on the Louisville faculty. He had studied in Germany and had become enchanted with the historical-critical methodology. The time came when he realized he was in disagreement with the confession of faith of the seminary.

The Toy case

Dr. Toy told the seminary he accepted the theological message of the Bible. But he believed the writers were men of their times who wrote what we now know is not true in matters of science, such as astronomy, and in matters of geography. He knew and agreed that his new position was not in accord with the fundamental principles of the institution, so he brought the matter before the administration and the board of trustees. The outcome was his departure from the halls of Louisville. Afterward he joined the faculty of Harvard College, and his later views marked a far more radical departure from Scripture than they had at the time his case was decided by the Louisville trustees. The point to be noted is that the institution declared itself in favor of an inerrant Scripture and that inerrancy extended to historical, geographical, and scientific matters as well as to matters of faith and practice. And the seminary did something about his unorthodoxy.

A call to Southern Baptists

I have already indicated that the journals of the Southern Baptist Seminary and Southwestern Seminary took exception to my allegation that Southern Baptists have been infiltrated by an aberrant view of the Bible—that is, there are those who deny inerrancy as it was taught and believed in the early days of these institutions. But Duke McCall of the Southern Seminary has loudly declared that my allegations are "poppycock." I now propose to concentrate on the faculty and graduates of Southern Seminary to show there has been a deep infiltration and a marked departure from the faith of the Louisville fathers with respect to the Bible and its truthfulness.

I am not saying every member of the Louisville faculty no longer believes in biblical inerrancy. Nor am I saying no graduate of Louisville holds to it. I am saying that the graduates of an institution tend to reflect the views of their teachers. I am saying there are Louisville faculty members who not only endorse the historical-critical method but who have applied that methodology to the Bible and consequently do not believe the Bible is true in all its parts.

Southern Baptist laymen should know what the situation is. Then they can reflect on it and decide whether they wish to correct the inbalance or whether to assent to the positions taken by Louisville faculty and graduates. The Louisville seminary is *only one* example of the point I am making. It is not to be supposed that using Louisville as an example implies no other seminary has been infiltrated by a wrong view of the Bible. How widespread and far reaching the departure from an inerrant Scripture is, I cannot say with exactness. But I wonder if there is a Southern Baptist seminary which stands to a man for inerrancy, and I know that the colleges and universities traditionally associated with Southern Baptists are not free from the problem.

Every Southern Baptist seminary owes it to the constituency of the convention to let the people know exactly where it stands on the issue of inerrancy. The seminaries belong to the convention and their trustees are selected by the convention. They are supposed to represent and reflect the commitment of the people in the pews. The people have spoken again and again through their messengers to the annual meetings of the convention which it did again in Atlanta last year. They are the ones who must decide whether the convention will be inclusive; whether the institutions of the convention should allow diametrically opposing viewpoints about the Bible to exist, be believed by faculty members, and be taught by them in the classrooms. If the people in the pews accept an inclusive policy, then at least the air will be cleared and those who hold to an inerrant Book can either remain in a fellowship which is openly divided or demit that fellowship for one which is in agreement with their belief in a trustworthy Bible. If Southern Baptists take the former course and allow for opposing viewpoints to be regarded as legitimate, then the Faith and Message statement of 1925 which has been reaffirmed again and again should be voted out and some substitute statement adopted in its place. Then the world can know where Southern Baptists stand. However, if the convention favors the retention of its long-standing commitment, then those who do not embrace it so far as Scripture is concerned should honorably seek employment elsewhere in situations more in line with their theological viewpoints.

I will now produce evidences to support the claim that some Southern Baptists deny the traditional approach of our forefathers about Scripture. And the evidence shows that the Louisville seminary is in disagreement with the views of its own founding fathers.

The Documentation for the Claim That Biblical Inerrancy Has Been Abandoned

Is the Bible a Human Book?

The Broadman Press published the volume *Is the Bible a Human Book?* in 1970. It was put together by Wayne Ward of Southern Seminary and Joseph F. Green. A number of the contributors had direct or indirect relationships with the Southern Baptist Seminary. The book shows that some of the contributors rejected the traditional view of Southern Baptists about the infallibility or inerrancy of the Bible. The coeditors frankly stated that there are those (and they could only mean Southern Baptists) who do not believe in biblical inerrancy. They said:

How shall we deal with the claim of some that the Bible indeed does contain errors? Must faith insist on the total[sic] inerrancy of the Bible, or can it survive a Bible that shows both human and divine characteristics?[38]

We can perceive immediately the editors were implying that because the Bible was written by human hands it must have errors in it. This, they said, is a human characteristic. In taking this stand they effectively denied the overshadowing presence of the Holy Spirit who was the One who kept the writers from error.

James Flamming, pastor of the First Baptist Church of Abilene, Texas, wrote a chapter titled "Could God Trust Human Hands?" He said:

Mark begins his Gospel in a hurry and has scarcely begun until he joins a quote from Malachi with a quote from Isaiah (1:2-3). Matthew and Luke both correct this in their account of the same event. Later, in the paragraph dealing with the controversy concerning sabbath laws, Mark has Abiathar as high priest when it was his father Ahimelech (I Sam. 21:1-6; Mark 2:23-28).

Some, incidentally, have been quick to say that only the original manuscripts were perfect and errors could have crept into later manuscripts. Here it seems to have worked the other way around. The later manuscripts, for example, correct the error in Mark 1:2-3, simply saying the "prophets," as reflected in the King James Version. . . .

Now what possible difference could these two incidental misquotes make to the redemptive work of Christ? None at all! But there is a measure of comfort in these pieces of humanity the Holy Spirit allowed to be sprinkled throughout the writings. If God could use Mark with sixth grade grammar, and an occasional misquote from the Old Testament, maybe he can use me too.[39]

Dr. Flamming added this sentence:

If God is as obsessed with perfection as we are, God could hardly trust man to write the Bible, for nothing man touches ever comes close to perfection (Rom. 3:23).[40]

This is a remarkable conclusion, for he is saying the Bible does not come close to perfection. Why then should we trust it, particularly those parts we cannot check?

John R. Claypool, former pastor of the Cresent Hill Baptist Church in Louisville, said:

On the basis of this and many other conflicting accounts alone, many serious students of the Bible have rejected the dictation theory and all of its claims to literal infallibility and inerrancy. I join them in this rejection, but for reasons deeper than errors in Scripture.

This is why it borders on the heretical to speak of the Bible as the final authority in all matters religious. Again and again the Almighty is pleased to take the Bible and transform its testimony into luminous encounter, but such an event is always of his initiative and through his power. The book then becomes his word to us in an intensely personal way.

This is why the mistakes and errors and conflicting opinions of the biblical record do not invalidate it for me but rather testify to its authenticity. If God had chosen to drop down out of the sky with instant truth as a way of saving us, then we could expect an inerrant and infallible book. But he has not chosen to do so![41]

It was at the Crescent Hill Baptist Church of Louisville that Dean William Hull of Louisville seminary delivered his now famous sermon against biblical inerrancy. But Dr. Claypool, the former pastor of the church, is known not only for his observations just cited, but also for his dissertation written in fulfillment of the requirements for a doctorate at Southern Baptist Seminary. This unpublished dissertation is titled *The Problem of Hell in Contemporary Theology* (May 1959, 284 pp.). In the conclusion of the dissertation Dr. Claypool made observations that most Southern Baptists would regard to be unbiblical. He said, "we are convinced that the Biblical writers wholeheartedly assumed that all men would survive the shock of physical death and would continue to exist in some form in the after-life" (see pp. 262-269). But what will the fate of men be in that afterlife?

Dr. Claypool went on to ask whether those without Christ suffer everlasting punishment or annihilation. He inquired: "Will it be conscious everlasting punishment or will it be ultimate extinction?" He added: "In trying to answer this question we readily admit that we are entering into the realm of speculation." In other words, the Bible does not tell us what the condition of the unsaved dead will be like. Dr. Claypool said he was not going *against* the teachings of Scripture; "we are simply going *beyond* them," whatever that means. There are, said Dr. Claypool, in his dissertation, three grave objections to everlasting punishment:

> First, it hardly seems fair to mete everlasting punishment for sins
> committed in time. Even when the infinite majesty of the God
> against whom the sin is committed is duly considered, the conse-
> quences seem out of proportion to the offense. Second, this posi-
> tion leads to an eternal dualism in the spiritual universe. Evil is not
> totally destroyed, but only confined and appropriately punished.
> ⸱Instead of God's finally winning a total victory over evil, the end of
> things results in an eternal stalemate. Third, the everlasting
> punishment of wicked individuals serves no constructive purpose
> for God or for man. If the point of no return has been reached
> . . . what purpose is there in perpetuating this kind of existence?
> . . . we are reluctant to accept the *theory* (my italics) of everlasting
> punishment.

Dr. Claypool went on to discuss annihilation and said that
"when the alternates (he means alternatives) are narrowed
down to Conditionalism and Eternalism, we would have to
favor Conditionalism. Again the question of purpose is the
decisive issue. We believe that free men can make wrong
choices, and in so doing render themselves forever unfit and
incapable for God's intention. When this point is reached, it
seems more consistent with God's nature of purposeful love
that such individuals cease to exist than for them to continue
forever in a state of helpless torment. . . . We admit that this
second conclusion (i.e. annihilationism) is speculative and
that it is anything but a self-evident truth. However, we feel
that the solution it offers meets the inherent problems better
than the idea of eternal punishment."

Now back to the book *Is the Bible a Human Book?*

Wayne Ward, a Louisville professor and coeditor of the volume, wrote a chapter "Stories that Teach." In it he spoke about
the creation narrative in Genesis. He declared:

> Just as misguided is the attempt of every literalistic minds to make
> every detail of these stories literal fact. . . . Some people are deter-
> mined to make the "serpent" in Genesis 3 a literal snake. . . .
> People who insist on making him a literal snake are denying the
> Bible itself.[42]

John M. Lewis, pastor of the First Baptist Church of Raleigh,
N. C., also wrote about the creation narrative in his chapter
"The Bible and Human Science." This is his interpretation:

Many Bible students realize that there are two accounts of creation in Genesis. . . . The older account in Genesis 2 is more primitive and childlike in its concepts and picturizations of God. Here man is created before any other living creatures.

This latter story from the Hebrew writer again marks a tremendous advance in the scientific understanding of ancient man. If one tries to take these (creation) accounts as literal scientific truth he does violence to the real intent of the Bible itself.

It is a drastic mistake to make the limited science of the biblical writer part of the revelation of himself which God is giving. If one does this, later scientific discoveries will undermine trust in the Bible as a book of truth.

The church assumed, falsely, that Darwin's theory undermined the biblical story of the creation of man. Unfortunately, this still presents a problem for those who cannot distinguish between the *process* and the *purpose* of creation (pp. 96-98).

Brooks Hays, one-time president of the Southern Baptist Convention, is a politician by background and a layman. Yet he represents the kind of viewpoint common to the Southern Seminary outlook. Mr. Hays wrote a chapter "What the Bible Means to Me." In that chapter he said:

I must say at the outset that I do not accept all of the Bible as literally true. (I do not believe, for example, that God ever ordered the slaughter of one's enemies.)

Modern Christians having experienced freedom in individual interpretations of the Scripture need not fear that biblical authority will be diluted by this freedom. Such fear is the chief cause of the irrational and unhistoric position of a few literalists who claim "verbal inerrancy" of the writings. On its face this is antibiblical— for it tends to make an idol of printed pages. Bibliolatry is as dangerous as any other form of idolatry.

Our faith is fragile if we let these fears shake our cherished Baptist belief that no organizational or official position may impose a rigid view upon individual believers.[43]

The volume *Is the Bible a Human Book?* tells us its own story. It shows how deeply the aberrant view of the Bible has penetrated the Southern Baptist fellowship. It allowed Brooks Hays' unfortunate claim to stand that inerrancy is an "irrational and unhistoric position of a few literalists who claim 'verbal inerrancy' of the writings. On its face this is antibiblical." The component parts of Mr. Hays' statements are nonsense. They are palpably false. But Mr. Hays did something which is even worse. He raised the specter that someone might impose "a rigid view upon individual believers" and shake a cherished Baptist belief that no organizational or official position may do this. Is he saying that for Southern Baptists to insist that members and churches must be trinitarian rather than unitarian is wrong in principle? Is there *nothing* which Baptists can insist on in order for you and me to retain the title of Baptist? Obviously his position is unacceptable, for if it were correct then no one could impose on any Baptist church such "rigid" views as believers' baptism, baptism by immersion, and congregational government.

Frank Stagg

Professor Frank Stagg of Louisville seminary previously taught at New Orleans Baptist Theological Seminary. Here he was known for his quasi-orthodox view of the Trinity and for his strong opposition to the substitutionary atonement of Jesus Christ. In the case of the former, his view, as we shall see, is at best modalistic, and in regard to the latter he thinks the moral influence theory of the Atonement is the correct one. But he is known also for his use of and promotion of the historical-critical method which lies at the heart of the struggle against biblical infallibility. A study of his writings yields a fruitful harvest of views which run counter to traditional Baptist standards.

Dr. Stagg reviewed the book *The Meaning of the New Testament* by Barclay M. Newman, a Broadman Press publication. In this review he said:

> Although the author does not belabor the reader with critical problems, he does not draw back from them, even where positions taken are not traditional, as in the recognition of the composite nature of Second Corinthians (222 ff.) and a possible second century dating for Second Peter (p. 289). Critical in methodology, the book is constructive in intent and effect. Broadman Press is to be commended for enlisting this able writer in providing this informative and incisive book.[43]

Dr. Stagg contributed to a book dealing with speaking in tongues. He wrote a chapter titled "Glossolalia in the New Testament." When speaking about the Acts of the Apostles Dr.

Stagg delved into source analysis, presenting the positions of those who reconstruct the text of Acts assuming that parts of the book are original and other parts are not. Some say, to use Stagg's own phrase and his own apparent agreement, that "Luke's account of the Pentecostal experience [is] a secondary version which hides what really occurred."[44]

Professor Stagg discussed "Sources and Acts 2," followed later by the "Conclusions from Source Analysis." This involves the use of the historical-critical methodology that diminishes Scripture. He finally stated: "The search for sources is a valid one, but nothing like a consensus has been achieved. In my judgment, *until* (my italics) something more conclusive is demonstrated, the Lucan account in Acts as we have it must be our working base." Professor Stagg accepts source criticism, and is willing to say this part of Acts is not Lucan if and when source criticism can make a valid case. He only waits for something more conclusive which is opposite from the views of those who stand or fall on Scripture as we have it, not on the basis of the higher critical method sitting in judgment on the Bible.[45]

In his *New Testament Theology* Dr. Stagg shows his antitrinitarian stance. He wrote:

> Thus the Spirit is the continuing presence of Jesus Christ (John 20:22). Paul could write of the risen Christ and the Holy Spirit in such a way as to make the terms almost interchangeable (Rom. 8:9f.).[46]

Then Dr. Stagg said:

> The New Testament knows God as Father, Son, and Holy Spirit, yet it knows God as one alone. One may suggest that in his transcendence he is known as Father, in his immanence as Holy Spirit, and in his ultimate presence and self-disclosure as Son. Yet to offer metaphysical questions and to offer rationales about the Trinity is to attempt to go beyond the New Testament. Its writers only know that the "incredible" had happened: the God of the ages had visited earth in the person of Jesus of Nazareth, and after the death of Jesus he continued his presence as the Holy Spirit. It is the uniqueness of the New Testament that the Father and the Spirit are understood in terms of Jesus Christ.[47]

The use of the phrase "God as Father, Son, and Holy Spirit" is quite different from saying "God the Father, God the Son, and

God the Holy Spirit." Nowhere did Professor Stagg say there are three distinct persons in the Trinity with one essence. Rather the one God manifests himself as Father, as Son, and as Holy Spirit. This is modalism.

Dr. Stagg was affirming source criticism when he said:

> The characteristic self-designation of Jesus in the New Testament is the intriguing though elusive title "The Son of man." This title is present in each major stratum of the Gospels: Mark, Q (non-Marcan material common to Matthew and Luke), M (material peculiar to Matthew), L (material peculiar to Luke), and John.[48]

Moreover, he supported the composite authorship of Isaiah. "It was," he says, "from Daniel 7 and *Deutero-Isaiah* (my italics) that he (Jesus) drew these figures."[49]

Along with a modal Trinity Professor Stagg could not bring himself to accept the vicarious atonement of Jesus Christ. At the same time he made assertions which further demonstrate his defective view of the Trinity. Here are his words:

> The cry of Jesus on the cross, "My God, my God, why hast thou forsaken me?" is by some taken as an actual abandonment of the Son by the Father, or a giving over of the Son to his fate. Such an interpretation suggests the impossible idea of two Gods at Golgotha. It would represent the Son friendly to man and the Father hostile. Such division between the Father and Son is forbidden in the New Testament and especially protested in the Fourth Gospel. However insoluble the cry may be to us, it must not be interpreted as to contradict the New Testament insistence upon the oneness of Father and Son. . . . It seems best to understand the cry as that of one who was truly human and who felt forsaken.[50]

Dr. Stagg enlarged on his objections to the expiatory, propitiatory death of Jesus in a variety of ways of which the following are examples:

> Jesus *paid* to liberate us from our sin. Of course he paid no one, neither the Father nor the Devil. He simply paid. . . . Neither (propitiation and expiation) is satisfactory. Because propitiation is so linked to pagan ideas of the appeasement of God, it is not suitable for translating New Testament ideas. Expiation is not satisfactory, but it is not so definitely linked to pagan usage. It is not sound *exegesis* to obscure by the *pagan* (my italics) idea of propitiation or appeasement the biblical emphasis upon the initiative of God in man's salvation. . . . God does not await appease-

ment. . . . The problem of estrangement is in man, not in God. . . . Calvin taught that God was our enemy until he was reconciled to us by Christ, writing that Christ satisfied and propitiated the Father "by this intercession his wrath has been appeased." But this is Calvin, not Holy Writ. This is Calvin, and he spoke no infallible word.

> The Father does not need to punish the Son in order to win the right to forgive. . . . Sin in the New Testament is not viewed as an entity which can be offset by a good act; it is a broken relationship which must be restored, a *sickness* (my italics) which must be cured.[51]

> It goes far beyond the writer of Hebrews to add the idea that this death (of Jesus) was an appeasement or satisfaction offered to the Father. . . . If in Jesus is the supreme manifestation of God, then at the cross we are to see God—the Father and the Son—in suffering, redeeming love. We are not to see an angry Father being appeased or satisfied by the sacrifice of a loving Son. Rather at the cross we see the Father in the Son.[52]

> Substitution is a serviceable term for the death of Jesus if properly employed To transfer to it all that belongs to the word in common usage is to obscure the New Testament doctrine. In modern sports, a player may be taken from the game and be replaced by a "substitute." But Jesus never becomes our substitute in that sense.[53]

What shall I say about the views of Dr. Stagg? If his views are orthodox then millions of Southern Baptists are unorthodox. If the death of Christ was not vicarious and did not render satisfaction to offended deity, then the *Baptist Hymnal,* as well as the writings of men like A. T. Robertson, Basil Manly, B. H. Carroll, and literally thousands of Southern Baptist pastors, must be removed from Southern Baptist literature. Scores of Sunday school lessons have told millions of students what is not true. And if the orthodox view of the Trinity is now unorthodox, then let the Southern Baptist Convention change its Faith and Message commitment toward unitarianism. This one thing I know: Modalism or unitarianism cannot be a viable alternative to trinitarianism without doing violence to one or the other of these views. And since trinitarianism has always been one of the Baptist distinctives, to change to modalism or straight unitarianism is to forsake the faith of our fathers.

William E. Hull

In *The Battle for the Bible* I mentioned Dr. William Hull, a graduate of the Southern Baptist Seminary, a professor, then Dean of the graduate school, and now pastor of the First Baptist Church of Shreveport, Louisiana. Dr. Hull is still being mentioned as a likely successor to Duke McCall upon his retirement. It was Dr. Hull who preached the famous sermon I mentioned at the Crescent Hill Baptist Church in Louisville. In this sermon, which was reprinted in the December 1970 issue of *The Baptist Program*, he clearly stated that he did not believe in an inerrant Bible.

Dr. Hull, in his inaugural address at the Louisville seminary, spoke on the subject "The Relevance of the New Testament." In the address he said: "It is not exaggerated to claim that for the first time in almost twenty centuries we have been able to recreate the New Testament situation with reasonable clarity and objectivity."[54] He went on to say that "Liberals and conservatives alike have had to learn the stubborn truth that there simply is no disembodied, timeless revelation which transcends the historical particularity in which it was originally expressed. A great gulf is fixed between the first century and the twentieth which makes it impossible to uproot biblical truth from the context with which it forms a living whole."[55] He added that "although the chief Apostle (Paul) was determined to preach the only true gospel, his kerygma was inescapably conditioned by the circumstances in which he labored."[56] To cap it all Professor Hull went on to say that "the Christian message in any age is seen not as a set of self-contained, timeless propositions, but as the address of God set over against the world in dialogue, a confrontation in which truth is disclosed in encounter."[57] This is a characteristic emphasis of neoorthodoxy—the existential divine-human encounter as the only valid way to religious knowledge.

All of this may be summed up by saying that for twenty centuries the saints of God read the Bible, understood its contents, and accepted the notion that truth is timeless, objective, transcendent, and equally valid and useful for all ages. The source critics, the form critics, and the redaction critics now tell us something different. So different in fact, that Dr. Hull can say "our message today is not represented as being the same as the New Testament message, any more than our modern world is identical with the first century world."[58] And "we are not to say to Louisville the same thing that Paul said to Corinth. . . ."[59] Many pastors and millions of people will be surprised to learn that what Paul preached cannot be preached today. And yet it *is* being done all the time, and thousands of people are coming to know Jesus without the benefit of the higher critics and without any awareness of Dr. Hull's pontifical dictum that "the forceful idiom of one generation becomes the tired cliché of the next."[60]

In October of 1969 Dr. Hull delivered his inaugural address as Dean of the School of Theology of Southern Seminary. In that address he acknowledged his indebtedness to Bultmann, C. H. Dodd, Emil Brunner, Sören Kierkegaard and Dietrich Bonhoeffer.[61] Their influence led him to agree with Kyle Haselden (deceased former editor of the *Christian Century*) in his phrase, "God is now coming to be seen as Lord of the 'flux' as well as of 'fidelity'."[62] Moreover, he stated that he has gone far beyond those "who in the name of 'classical learning' or the 'sole sufficiency of the Bible' or the 'historic Baptist position' would have us only study the past."[63] This will come as a surprise to Baptists who think God delivered a once-for-all message that never changes, that needs no updating, that can be understood and believed by this generation and a thousand more to come if the Lord tarries. And it is the preaching of the "historic Baptist position" that has made the Southern Baptist Convention the largest non-Catholic denomination in the U.S.A. and filled its seminary halls with more students than virtually all of the other denominations combined.

On February 23, 1968, William Hull delivered an address to the members of the Association of Baptist Professors of Religion of which he was president. In that address he noted that "with the passing of the torch to younger hands, one notes a growing impatience to go beyond the tired cautions of an earlier era. . . . We cannot worry forever with the millennium, or verbal inspiration, or the Scofield Bible. For an increasing number of restless spirits, it is time to move on."[64]

Professor Hull moved to denigrate the King James Version and to highlight "Today's English Version," also known as

"Good News for Modern Man." It was here that Professor Hull dropped his bomb. He asked this question: "What are the implications of widespread SBC acceptance of the TEV (Today's English Version)? To begin with, we have here the employment of a much more daring translation theory than that adopted by the RSV. . . . Of course, Southern Baptists do not yet realize all of this. . . . Shout it not from the housetops, but the TEV is clearly incompatible with traditional notions of verbal inspiration, and the theologies built thereon. It could be that Southern Baptists will embrace the TEV with their hearts before they grasp the implications with their heads."[65]

In regard to the "Good News for Modern Man" something else should be said, so that Southern Baptists may have a clearer picture of what has really happened. This translation, produced by the American Bible Society, worked on by a Louisville graduate, Robert Bratcher, is now being sold with introductions to each book of the Bible. This is something the American Bible Society has never done before. And what it has done is to many informed Christians disturbing. These introductions are fully in line with the higher critical methodology which undercuts the trustworthiness of the Bible. The introductions are skillfully put together to brainwash the reader without his being aware of what is happening. For example, none of the material contained in the introductions to the Pentateuch gives the reader the faintest notion that any portion of the five books of Moses was written by Moses. The introduction to the Book of Isaiah plainly states there were three Isaiahs, and the two who wrote Isaiah 40-66 did so *after* the events prophesied actually took place. The Book of Daniel is late dated at 168 B.C., after the events occurred which are prophesied in the book. None of the Gospels are said to have been written by Matthew, Mark, Luke, or John. When it comes to Pauline Epistles the readers will look in vain for any hint that Paul wrote Ephesians, 1 and 2 Timothy, and Titus, or that Peter wrote 1 and 2 Peter. At least the introductions do say that Paul wrote Romans, 1 and 2 Corinthians, and Galatians. The writers of the introductions are subtle when they speak about the authorship of the Pauline or Petrine letters that liberals say he never wrote for they always speak about "the author" without ever naming Paul or Peter.

Dr. Hull bestowed his highest praise for the modern critics at the end of his speech. He spoke of the "freest spirits in the various communions." "If anything, those great pioneers who have opened new frontiers to theological *progress* (my italics) have done so, not by abandoning their denominational commitments, but by subjecting them to a searching critique in order to *recover* (my italics—the word should no doubt really be *discover* or *invent*) the deepest truths worthy of sharing with others. Has this not been the profoundest contribution of Bultmann as Lutheran, Barth as Reformed, Robinson and Pike as Anglican, and Rahner and Küng as Catholic?"[66]

Now for a final word about William Hull. In the Summer 1967 issue of the *Review and Expositor* appears an article titled "The New Quest for the Historical Jesus." In it Dr. Hull agreed that all of the former quests have failed. It did not occur to him that further quests will also fail. He said, "the new questers continue to use the scientific disciplines of form, source, redaction, linguistic, and textual criticism." "Bornkamm can expunge from the Gospels any questionable accretions, such as most if not all of the messianic titles attributed to Jesus." ". . . the new questers would readily agree that the form of the Christian kerygma differed considerably from the message of Jesus."[67] In other words, the New Testament presents differing and inconsistent viewpoints. The message of Jesus and that of the church in the New Testament are not wholly compatible.

The New Quest "utilizes most, if not all, of the critical procedures developed by the Old Quest. The primary difference stems from the way in which the question is put to the texts and the separate research results are fused into a composite picture."[68] He later added: "The New Quest contributes to this task by seeking to discover what Jesus *must* (my italics) have said and done to create the self-understanding reflected in the Gospels. . . ."[69] "Unless I can see God in the life of Jesus, in the truths he taught, the decisions he made, the deeds he did, it will not finally suffice to believe in him simply because Peter and Paul concluded that he was the Son of God."[70] But since redaction criticism which Dr. Hull employs assures us that the gospel writers were writing theology and in so doing they put into Jesus' mouth words He never spoke and attributed to Him deeds He never performed, how are we to know what He really said and did, if indeed the written Word of God is not accurate?

Dr. Hull is a fair sample of Louisville seminary—he was nurtured there, he taught there, he was dean there, he has been defended by President Duke McCall. Louisville today is *not* the Louisville of the founding fathers.

Dale Moody

In the Summer 1967 issue of the *Review and Expositor* an article titled "Tabletalk on Theology Tomorrow" appeared under the byline of Dale Moody. He is a long-tenured professor at the Louisville seminary. Some of the remarks in this article will illustrate the allegation that Louisville harbors those who are not in agreement with what Baptists generally believe.

Dr. Moody talked about man in relation to evolution. He said:

> Conflict between science and religion is far from over. State laws against the teaching of evolution still exist, and some religious leaders would like to pass others. On the one hand, children are learning about man 1.75 million years ago, or even 2.5 million years, while they read religious literature and hear sermons about the first man being made about six thousand years ago. This condition is not able to continue. Biblical interpretation must reckon with science or prove it wrong, and the latter is not likely.[71]

Professor Moody went on to negate the notion that Adam and Eve were the first human pair. There were many others according to him. He wrote:

> Adjustment of biblical faith to modern science is not as catastrophic as many imagine. The most catastrophic thing for fundamentalism, still very much alive, is to adjust to the historical study of Scripture. The story of Cain in Genesis, an ancient Kenite account preserved by the Yahwist writer of Israel's first history, has statements impossible to harmonize with the assumption that only three human beings were left after the death of Abel. The origin of Cain's wife is an old debate, but the mark of Cain assumes the presence of other tribes that would attack Cain as he went as a vagabond through the earth. It is little help to hear the fundamentalists explain how this would be done by his brothers and sisters born later or his nieces and nephews. The famous four

(Adam and Eve, Cain and Abel) are only representative human beings at the dawn of civilization, not the only human beings. There is plenty of room here for L. S. B. Leackey's [sic] discoveries in *Adam's Ancestors.*

It is true that the later Adam story in Genesis 2, 3 (JE) makes no mention of other people, but it is possible to interpret Adam and Eve as representatives and symbolic human beings rather than the only human beings. Adam in Genesis 5:2, an even later story, is Collective Man ("he called their name Adam"), and it is this collective or corporate concept that is followed by Paul in the New Testament.

A symbolic interpretation of Adam and Eve yields profound insight. Adam is made from earth, but this does not rule out the long process described by scientific anthropology. The Hebrews believed God created every man, not just the first man, and they knew very well that this did not rule out the biological process in a mother's womb (cf. Job 10:9-11). Why should conservative Christianity attempt to rule out the long biological process described with no little evidence from scientific anthropology?[72]

When speaking of the doctrine of perseverance Dr. Moody put strange fire on the altar and knocked down ancient landmarks erected by the church fathers and accepted and preached by those in the Reformed tradition to this hour. He said that most Baptists have generally believed in "eternal security" or the "perseverance of the Saints." If I were to put it another way, it might be stated "once saved, always saved." It is a doctrine held to tenaciously by the greatest Baptist preacher of them all, Charles Haddon Spurgeon, who had a masterful sermon on the subject. He freely acknowledged that men might backslide. But he argued from Scripture that backsliders would be restored before death; for none who believe in Jesus can perish. Dr. Moody took a mighty swipe at this doctrine and in the process used an old saw that even a young Sunday school pupil could answer. This is his statement:

> Perhaps the most difficult subjects related to salvation began with the distortions of Augustine, and these were not sufficiently modified in Protestantism. Perseverance is a term not even mentioned in the New Testament, yet the complex of ideas surrounding it have been called "great Bible doctrine." What New Testament theologian thinks he finds any one of Augustine's five ideas (total depravity, unconditional election, limited atonement, irre-

sistible grace, the gift of perseverance) by the exegetical approach? Even evangelical Calvinism has long ago discarded the first four, yet the fifth hangs on. New Testament exegetes as conservative as A. T. Robertson and F. F. Bruce have not hesitated to say the concept of apostasy (falling away) is central in Hebrews. Now conservative Calvinism that teaches that all children born in a Christian household are regenerate finds an impossible conflict with the doctrine of perseverance when it sees great numbers of such children growing up to be atheists. The whole system requires reinterpretation today, but violent emotionalism makes it hard to get a hearing.[73]

When speaking of predestination, a doctrine held by many Presbyterians and Baptists, Dr. Moody came up with some interesting observations about the defects of Augustine and some biblical exegesis that many could challenge. He said:

> Predestination, the second term associated with Augustine's doctrine of salvation, is a New Testament word, but the historical blunder by which it was grounded in creation rather than Christ has missed the New Testament meaning. Predestination is "in Christ." Christ himself is the object of predestination, and we are predestined "in him" (Eph. 1:3-5). The distinction between "in creation" and "in Christ" is the difference between a doctrine deadly for evangelism and one dynamic unto the gospel of salvation. This dynamic doctrine will never be recovered as long as Presbyterians and Baptists put the Westminster Confession of 1947 [sic] and the Second London Confession of 1677 above the New Testament. Real reform is needed to deliver us from the dead hand of Augustine via Calvinism.[74]

Dr. Moody could not have been aware of what would happen in the ensuing period between the writing of his essay and present-day circumstances. A number of Presbyterian churches have turned again to the Reformation teachings of Augustine through Calvin and the doctrine of predestination has not hindered evangelism. Numbers of people have come to a saving knowledge of Jesus Christ under such preaching. Spurgeon held to the doctrine of predestination and large numbers of people were saved under his preaching. The Great Awakening was sparked by the preaching of George Whitefield who was a predestinarian and by Jonathan Edwards who was one also. Others were saved under the preaching of John Wesley who was an Arminian. If people could get converted under the preaching of predestinarians in ages gone by there is no reason to suppose that it will not or cannot happen again. Both Arminians and Calvinists can be, have been, and are, evangelistic.

Dr. Moody's conclusion positions Louisville Seminary in a mold far removed from that of most Baptists. He thinks it

is sufficient to say that the theological ferment of the present may be fruitful for the future if there is freedom to discuss the great issues of the faith and to relate them to the pressing personal and social problems that beset the church in an age of revolution. No evasive and oppressive conservatism will be adequate for the theological task of the future.[75]

Dale Moody reviewed John Macquarrie's book, *Principles of Christian Theology*, in the Fall 1968 issue of the *Review and Expositor*. In that review he said:

In Part Two (Symbolic Theology) the restatement of the "Triune God" (Ch. IX) in terms of being is very suggestive. God is the primordial being, the Son is expressive being, and the Spirit is unitive being. This reminds one of the God of process philosophy who is described as primordial deity and consequent deity in relation to the principle of concretion. No symbol, ancient or modern, can capture the full content of the divine mystery, but efforts of this type do help people to see the importance of the Holy Trinity when they have repudiated the popular distortion that sounds much like Peter, James and John on an astrodome.

More than any systematic theology now in print this one has common ground for conversation among all Christians and with those outside the camp.[76]

Louisville Professors and Isaiah

Back in 1947, J. Wash Watts wrote *A Survey of Old Testament Teaching*. In that volume he made clear the significance of the unity of the Book of Isaiah. The word of warning he expressed has been ignored by Louisville's teachers. He said:

It appears impossible to prove conclusively that there was only one Isaiah or more than one. Internal evidence is the only kind we have, and that seems insufficient to close the argument.

We cannot afford, however, to dismiss this question of authorship as unimportant. Careful examination of the effects of one's decision as to authorship upon one's appraisal of the teachings of the book should surely awaken students to the vital importance of the subject. Theoretically, it is easy to say that it does not matter. Practically, the effect is tremendous. Commentators' interpretations of the teaching concerning Israel's destiny, concerning Messiah's work and person, and concerning the plan of salvation seem to vary with their decisions on this point.[77]

Dr. Watts might have considered as decisive the attribution of John in the fourth Gospel to the Isaianic authorship of the second half of that book. But at least he was saying there is no hard evidence to deny the Isaianic authorship of the book. Why not then give the benefit of the doubt to the traditional view that Isaiah did indeed author the whole prophecy? But the Louisville professors accept two Isaiahs.

Page H. Kelley of the Louisville faculty reviewed Ralph Elliott's book on the Old Testament. He remarked that Elliott "moves with ease through recent research into the nature of Yahweh's covenant with Israel, the Servant figure in Deutero-Isaiah and Job. . . ." Here is his recognition of the two Isaiahs.

About Marvin E. Tate's *King and Messiah in Isaiah of Jerusalem* in the *Review and Expositor* this was said:

> This article is concerned with selected portions of Isaiah 1-39, often entitled "First Isaiah." However, chapters 1-39 are composite and almost certainly are not to be traced back in their entirety to the eighth-century Isaiah. Within 1-39 the consensus of scholars is to find authentic words in chapters 1-12 and 28-32 (though there are insufficient grounds to deny various sections of chapters 13-23 to the prophet).[78]

Donald Williams in the same issue of the Louisville magazine said:

> Few biblical scholars today would deny the correctness of the identification of Isaiah 40-55 as the work of an anonymous prophet during the period of the Babylonian Exile. In addition, other chapters of the book of Isaiah may be attributed to this prophet, e.g. chapters 34-35 and 60-62. . . . More precisely, the date for the beginning of the work of the Exilic Isaiah may be set during the early years of the conquests of Cyrus, i.e., the fall of Sardis in 547 B.C. The end of the prophet's ministry certainly parallels the fall of Babylon. . . .

Then there is the footnote which says: "The term 'Exilic Isaiah' is used as a synonym for such other designations as 'Deutero-Isaiah' and 'Second-Isaiah'."[79]

Page Kelley in his book *Judgment and Redemption in Isaiah* said "the evidence cited above has convinced most scholars that the book of Isaiah came from two prophets—Isaiah of the eighth century and an anonymous prophet of the exile. Each one who studies Isaiah must weigh the evidence and be convinced in his own mind. It is possible for scholars to disagree in their views regarding the unity of the book but still agree that it is the inspired Word Of God."[80]

He also appeared to agree with the argument that:

> Since the prophets always spoke directly to their own times, of what interest would it have been to the contemporaries of Isaiah to hear of Babylon and the campaigns of Cyrus? Israel's enemy in the eighth century B.C. was Assyria, not Babylon. A good rule of thumb for dating a prophecy is that it must be earlier than that which it predicts, but later than that which it presupposes. Chapters 40-66 presuppose that Israel is in exile, but predict that the exile will soon be over and that Israel will be restored to her land. These chapters should, therefore, be dated later than 587 B.C., but earlier than 538 B.C.[81]

From all of this material on the Book of Isaiah it is clear that Louisville indeed favors two Isaiahs rather than one. This brings with it the kind of problem foreseen by Dr. Watts. But more than that, it hits hard at the credibility of the Gospel of John. John 12:38 says that Isaiah 53 is the word of Isaiah the prophet and not some second "Isaiah" who wrote several centuries after Isaiah himself was dead. The construction of the Greek makes it clear that John was referring specifically to Isaiah. In other words, so far as John was concerned he was saying that Isaiah 53 is the very word of the prophet Isaiah himself and no other. Once the Isaianic authorship of chapters 40-66 is denied it also requires a denial of the accuracy or truthfulness of the testimony of John to Isaianic authorship of the whole Book of Isaiah.

The Book of Deuteronomy

Louisville professors also conclude that the fifth book of the Pentateuch, which has been regarded by the church through the ages as the product of Moses, is of much later date, and while it contains Mosaic material it is the product of redactors centuries later. Professor Donald Williams of Louisville in

Deuteronomy in Modern Study bought the higher critical views
and said parts of Deuteronomy were written centuries after
Moses (von Rad, a liberal commentator, speaks this way).
"This section [of Deuteronomy] was not written until after the
worship of the Canaanite Baals and the Assyrian astral
cults became acute, i.e., early seventh century B.C. Other
sections of this core have yielded to similar investigations."
Concerning Deuteronomy he also spoke of the "so-called
'Song of Moses' and the so-called 'Blessing of Moses'." Dr.
Williams continued in the same vein:

> Since the rise of nineteenth century critical scholarship, the
> Mosaic authorship of Deuteronomy has been denied. . . . Another
> long-standing affirmation is that Deuteronomy is a unique body of
> material which is distinct from the other Pentateuchal books: the
> vocabulary, style of writing, and theology separate Deuteronomy
> from the books that precede it.
> Classically, Deuteronomy has been associated with the reform
> of King Josiah in 622-621 B.C., since the aims of that reform
> enumerated in 2 Kings 22-23 find parallels in the core of
> Deuteronomy (5-26). . . .[82]

Dr. Williams nowhere suggested that Moses was the author of
Deuteronomy and he gave credence to the liberal views of von
Rad who is almost the patron saint of Old Testament teachers
in many theological seminaries.

Roy L. Honeycutt said of Deuteronomy:

> It is assumed herein that Deuteronomy arose in incipient form
> during the time of Moses, and continued within the worship cen-
> ter(s) as a living, growing body of oral tradition, interspersed with
> written legal materials, until the work of the final redactor in
> perhaps the sixth or seventh centuries B. C. How much material
> may be legitimately ascribed to Moses remains questionable.[83]

Professor Marvin E. Tate stated that "the theology of the
land rests upon a third still more basic foundation in Deuteronomic historiography. Von Rad has demonstrated that
there is a theological schema in the Deuteronomistic presentation of history in Joshua-Kings."[84]

Clyde Francisco of Louisville said about *The Song of Moses:*
"The Song is of uncertain age. In its present form it is later
than the time of Moses, but there is no way of telling his
original relation to it. Its basic message could well be his."[85]

Professor G. R. Beasley-Murray

Professor Beasley-Murray wrote a commentary on the general epistles of James, 1 Peter, Jude, and 2 Peter. This was part of the series edited by William Barclay and F. F. Bruce. In his treatment of 2 Peter Dr. Beasley-Murray states that the epistle was not written by Peter. The line of his argument is this. He says that 2 Peter 2 and Jude 4-16 are parallel. The question is whether the author of Peter knew of Jude and was referring to that book or whether Jude knew of 2 Peter and was referring to it. Dr. Beasley-Murray states that Jude was written no earlier than A.D. 80 and that 2 Peter came *after* that, for it has a dependence on Jude. But the apostle Peter was dead before A.D. 80. Therefore he could not have written 2 Peter even though the book itself claims to have been written by him. Dr. Beasley-Murray properly asks this question: "How can we believe that a book of the Bible claiming to be from an apostle is a *forgery?*"[86]

Dr. Beasley-Murray's answer is that the book was not written by Peter, but it is not a forgery. "It must be insisted," he says, "that a religious book of the Hebrew-Christian tradition written in the name of another is not a forgery. To describe it thus does a cruel injustice to many godly men who so wrote. . . ." Then Dr. Beasley-Murray concludes in agreement with opinions of other scholars that "the date of 2 Peter is commonly set in the second quarter of the 2nd century."[87] What shall we say to all this?

On its face it appears that the unknown author of 2 Peter felt that using Peter's name would give the epistle an acceptance it would not otherwise receive if his own name was attached to it. But this argument falls to the ground, because the Book of Hebrews bears no author's name and yet it was received by the church. On the other hand, if it is true that the epistle would have been received had the true author's name not been appended to it, the need for pseudonymity is gone. Therefore the former reason must be true. This means the unknown author deliberately and with malice aforethought used Peter's name to lead the reader to suppose the epistle came from that apostle; that is, so that it would be accepted as genuine. Such an argument may pass in the literary world, but surely not in the world of the spirit. And since the Holy Spirit is the true author of Scripture, for Him to bend so low and to use such deception would be completely needless and utterly demeaning to the divine majesty. If the Holy Spirit could make the Book of Hebrews to be recognized by the church even with no author's name attached He could have made 2 Peter similarly authoritative to the church without any author's name attached, or even with the real author's name (not Peter's) given. The modern critics who deny Petrine authorship commit still another folly. They argue that the intrinsic value of the letter is in no sense impaired by the fact that it was written by someone other than Peter. If this is true it follows that the use of the true author's name would not result in any impairment of the intrinsic message. So what is there to be gained by using Peter's name? If the higher critic is correct that the message is unimpaired, appending Peter's name is unnecessary, inappropriate, and really useless—unless, of course, the use of the name was absolutely essential—which the critics do not allege.

An ordinary reader would suppose that Peter was the author of the epistle. Since this is true, what is to be gained by saying Peter did not write the letter? Nothing is gained and much is lost. By denying Petrine authorship, the door is opened to regard any and all other parts of Scripture as suspect and spurious. It engenders doubt and distrust in the mind of the reader who can never be sure that what he reads in other places is true or false. Moreover, a denial of Petrine authorship means that we are told something which is not factual. If this is not factual, other apparently factual parts of Scripture may turn out to be unfactual after all. Biblical inerrancy falls to the ground, and the doctrine of inspiration suffers a mortal blow.

Robert S. Alley of the University of Richmond

Professor Robert Alley is one of the Southern Baptist Seminary's radical products. He is a teacher at the University of Richmond, which consistently honors Baptist professors and administrators with honorary doctorates. It has been receiving support from the state convention of Virginia in the amount of around $200,000 a year. I wrote about Dr. Alley in *The Battle for the Bible*. Recently he has added to his notoriety by proclaiming that Jesus is not God, the second person of the Trinity.

The Richmond *News Leader* reported Dr. Alley as saying: "I see Jesus as really a Jew. I don't imagine for a minute that He would have had the audacity to claim the deity for himself. I think (the Bible) passages where He talks about the Son of God are later additions—what the church said about Him."[88] The address was made by Dr. Alley in Richmond's First Unitarian Church to a group of self-proclaimed atheists. Even though Virginia is known for a liberality greater than that to be found among Southern Baptists generally, this was too much for some of them.

Dr. Alley was shifted from the Religion department to another department of the University. The president of the University, E. Bruce Heilman, apologized for Dr. Alley's statements and tried to pour oil on the troubled waters. Students and faculty members joined in the fray and the old cry of academic freedom, tenure, and Baptist liberty were heard again and again. The president left the public with the impression that even if he wanted to do something about the case of Dr. Alley, accreditation, tenure, and academic freedom made harsh action impossible. Dr. Alley remains in good standing among Southern Baptists. His ordination has not been withdrawn and he is still salaried by the University of Richmond. He, of course, has gone far beyond most of the people whose views I have quoted so far. But his position follows logically once one starts with the presuppositions he uses. As a follower of Bultmann, and user of the historical-critical methodology, he has made the quantum leap that others have not yet made.

The starting point for Dr. Alley's current opinions lies in his use of the historical-critical method. And this is the method generally employed at the Southern Baptist Seminary at Louisville. This methodology was used liberally in the *Broadman Bible Commentary* too. As one reads the doctoral dissertations written by Louisville graduates it becomes clear that they have been taught this methodology, and it underlies their scholarly efforts. One illustration will suffice to indicate the attitude of which I am speaking. In 1942 George Allen West, Jr., wrote his Th.D. thesis on *John and Form Criticism*. In it he said: "I cannot go so far as to accept the skepticism of Bultmann, nor the dogmatism of Barnes, nor the conservatism of Drummond. . . . I believe that Form Criticism is here to stay and that it must not take away from, but add to, the work and value of Historical Criticism."[89]

The Louisville Student Body

One of the most illuminating studies of the student body of the Southern Baptist Seminary at Louisville was made by Noel Wesley Hollyfield, Jr. He received the Master of Theology degree from Louisville in 1976. His thesis, in partial fulfillment of the requirements for the degree, was titled: "A Sociological Analysis of the Degrees of 'Christian Orthodoxy' Among Selected Students in the Southern Baptist Theological Seminary." The thesis was read and approved by a committee consisting of G. Willis Bennett, chairman, E. Glenn Hinson, and Henlee Barnette. The acceptance of the thesis indicates that the committee was satisfied that the contents were accurate and the conclusions validated. This thesis should be widely distributed among the lay people of the Convention. One would hope that the trustees of the Seminary would read it with special care. The thesis is the best available evidence to further confirm the allegation that Louisville has been deeply infiltrated by nonevangelical beliefs.

The study has some special features about it which are noteworthy. The author made a comparison between the students of the Louisville school and those at Southwestern. He also interacted with the well-known Glock and Stark study. All we need here is to report some of the basic findings of the research. Mr. Hollyfield surveyed Diploma students, Master of Divinity students, Graduate students, and Doctor of Ministry students. He used his own study and that of Robert C. Thompson ("A Research Note on the Diversity Among American Protestants: A Southern Baptist Example," *Review of Religious Research*, 15, No. 2 [Winter, 1974], 87-92). In Table 13 Noel Hollyfield gave the statistics for Southwestern and Louisville students in response to certain theological questions. The table cited the "percentages of Southern Baptists giving most 'orthodox' response on selected questions in the studies of Thompson, Hollyfield. . . ."

A sample breakdown of student response for those who

were studying for the Master of Divinity program tells the more complete story. One of the questions was this: "Does the devil actually exist?" There were four possible answers the respondent could choose from. He could say the statement was

	Diploma		M.Div.		Graduate		D.Min.
	Thom.	Holl.	Thom.	Holl.	Thom.	Holl.	Holl.
Belief in God	100.0	100.0	94.0	71.0	71.4	63.0	75.0
Divinity of Jesus	100.0	100.0	100.0	79.0	90.4	63.0	80.0
Belief in Biblical Miracles	100.0	96.0	94.0	54.0	76.2	37.0	80.0
Belief in Life Beyond Death	100.0	100.0	94.0	82.0	81.0	53.0	95.0
Belief in Virgin Birth	100.0	96.0	94.0	55.0	71.4	32.0	85.0
Belief in the Existence of the Devil	100.0	96.0	97.0	58.0	81.0	37.0	75.0
Belief that Jesus Walked on Water	100.0	96.0	90.6	54.0	85.7	22.0	80.0
Overall Average %	100.0	97.7	94.8	64.7	79.6	43.9	81.4
Sample Size	21	23	33	128	21	19	20

"completely true," "probably true," "probably not true" and "definitely not true." The answers given were: 6% said the statement was not true; 16% said it was probably not true; 20% said it was probably true; 58% said it was completely true.

Another statement said "Jesus was born of a virgin." And 55% said this was completely true; 22% said it was probably true; 17% said it was probably not true; 6% said it was definitely not true. Another statement said "Jesus walked on water." And 17% said it was probably not true and 6% it was definitely not true.

In response to the question about "holding the Bible to be God's truth," 39% said it was absolutely necessary; 21% said it was probably necessary; 25% said it was possibly not necessary; and 23% said it was not necessary.

The author of this student survey concluded that "Thompson found that the average student at the Southwestern Baptist Theological Seminary tended to be very much more 'orthodox' that the average theology student was found to be in the present study (i.e. at Louisville)." Moreover, Mr. Hollyfield concluded that "a trend toward doctrinal liberalism was discovered in the Th. M-Ph.D students. . . ."

The weight of this evidence is such that no one can fault it. The survey was made by a Louisville student and the thesis was accepted and approved for the degree by a seminary committee. Thus it can be said the students as well as the faculty of Louisville have been infiltrated by theological unorthodoxy. It appears that Louisville draws numbers of students who are liberal to begin with. But the admission procedures do not keep them from enrollment. Mr. Hollyfield's survey also shows that there is further erosion which occurs between the time the students enroll and just before they graduate.

When 23% of the M. Div. students believe that "holding the Bible to be God's truth" is not necessary there is a real problem. And when approximately 25% say Jesus either was not born of a virgin (6%) or that the virgin birth is probably not true (17%) there is a theological problem. Since all of the churches which contribute to the Convention budget also are giving money to the theological seminaries they are, in some measure, supporting unbelief in these institutions and are doing nothing to correct the situation or to protect the churches from being shepherded by those whose unorthodoxy is apparent and who will turn Baptists away from their heritage.

Tying the Pieces Together

The Southern Baptist Convention met in Atlanta, Georgia, in June of 1978. A number of apparently unrelated circumstances rose which, when placed together, form an interesting pattern. They tell their own story and mark the progress of the infection which has overtaken the convention and its institutions.

Prior to the 1978 convention Professor E. Glenn Hinson, a professor at Louisville, wrote an article for the *Christian Century*. In his article he said the Southern Baptists take in "conservative to liberal theology . . . John Birch to Norman Thomas politics, laissez-faire to Marxist economics, pragmatism to idealism."[90] Before the convention opened, the soon-to-be reelected president Jimmy Allen was reported in the press as saying: "I think Southern Baptists are staying with the Bible. The people who are in our evangelism and missions forefront are people who believe in the authority and accuracy of the Bible."[91] The importance of these apparently unrelated remarks is significant.

Dr. McCall of the Southern Baptist Seminary said my allegations about the infiltration of theological liberalism in Baptist seminaries were "poppycock." In the *Christian Century* article one of his own professors seemed to feel otherwise. He said there *are* liberals in the Southern Baptist Convention. Along comes Jimmy Allen who says that the people in evangelism and missions are Bible believers. And there is some reason to think his statement is fairly correct. In that case, where then are the liberals to be found? If they are in the pulpits, we must remember they are the product of Southern Baptist colleges and seminaries. If they are in the seminaries, and they are, then there is no poppycock about the existence of the problem. But another incident is quite conclusive.

Dr. McCall's own *Review and Expositor* in the Spring 1978 issue, dealt with "The Problem of Authority in Church and Society." One of his professors, Walter B. Shurden, wrote on the subject, "The Problem of Authority in the Southern Baptist Convention." He drew attention to the Elliott controversy of 1962-63. Then he spoke of *The Broadman Bible Commentary* controversy of 1970. Both had to do with liberalism, one in a published book, *The Message of Genesis,* and the other the Genesis commentary in the Broadman series which had been written by G. Henton Davies. Professor Shurden did not hesitate to face the problem squarely, to admit its existence, and to specify what lay at the heart of the two controversies.

In the Elliott case and in the *Broadman Bible Commentary* case the Southern Baptist Convention, meaning the pastors and lay people attending the conventions, voted against Dr. Elliott and against the Genesis commentary of Dr. Davies. Since both of these issues dealt with the Book of Genesis, and since both of the authors undercut the traditional conservative viewpoint of Southern Baptists, it should be unmistakable that the vote of the convention was against liberalism. But Dr. Shurden comes up with the unhappy fact that the Southern Baptists spoke out of both sides of their mouths at the same time. They said two different things that cannot be harmonized; two things that are antithetical. Dr. Shurden stated this quite perceptively:

> The issue regarding the Bible for the Southern Baptists is clear. Will Southern Baptists be able to follow the historical-critical approach to the study of the Bible or is the "plenary verbal-literalist" route the only one open? We usually end up "non-settling" the issue by saying both things at the same time. Like a character in Aesop's Fables we blow both hot and cold air from our mouths at the same time. Witness, for example, what happened in the Elliott Controversy. We banned a book, fired a professor, then affirmed the methodology the professor used to write the banned book. Witness number two: in the Broadman fight we banned a book, ridded ourselves of the man who wrote it, then rewrote it with a professor (Louisville's professor Clyde Francisco) who, while not agreeing entirely with the first man, nevertheless affirmed his methodology and scholarship. . . .
>
> The real reason we live with it—at least up to this point—is because denominational unity is more important to most Southern Baptists than theological arguments about the Bible[92]

There can be no doubt that Professor Shurden is correct in saying that the locus of the controversy lies in the use of the historical-critical methodology *vis a vis* the "plenary verbal-literalist" approach to the Bible. Unfortunately, he has mis-labelled the latter, which should rather be denominated the historical view of the church through the ages, which says that the Bible is free from all error in the whole and in the part. What is amazing is that Professors Shurden and Hinson along with most of the faculty members at the Southern Baptist Seminary in Louisville know what the problem is and where the battle is being fought, while their president, Duke McCall, and Jimmy Allen, the president of the Southern Baptist Convention, do not.

It is my own judgment that the messengers to the Southern Baptist Conventions know they believe the Bible. And again in the 1978 convention the messengers reiterated their stand that God is the author of the Scripture and that the Scripture is free from all error. But what the messengers have not seen clearly is that the Bible is being attacked and denigrated in their own seminaries and pulpits precisely because some of their scholars use a historical-critical methodology which starts with the assumption that Scripture and the Word of God are not synonymous. I believe that if the messengers to any future convention understand the true nature of the struggle they will cast their vote for the Bible and against the use of the historical-critical method which undermines the trustworthiness and authority of Scripture.

Moreover, the churches and the institutions which place their confidence in the "sure results of the higher critical method" turn out to be the ones whose missionary and evangelistic passion becomes seriously diluted. The most liberal seminaries and colleges of the Southern Baptist Convention are not the ones whose students flock to the mission fields, nor do they build churches by evangelistic methods. And all of this leads me to ask the question:

What of the Future?

I have sought to show that Southern Baptists stand at a crossroads with respect to their traditional understanding of the Bible. There are people who number themselves among Southern Baptists who do not hold to that view of the Bible I have shown to have been held by the founding fathers of Southwestern and Southern Baptist Theological Seminaries. I have provided decisive evidence to show that in those same seminaries conclusions have been drawn by their teaching staff concerning authorships, dates, and truthfulness of the text of the Bible as we have it that puts the authority of the Bible upon a different foundation from what it used to occupy. This trend has produced serious division among Southern Baptists and it will increase the friction in the days ahead if nothing is done to correct the decline of trust in an inerrant Bible.

I have provided documentation about people whose views show they do not and cannot accept biblical inerrancy. I have no quarrel with these people as persons. I am not saying they are conscious hypocrites, but I do think they are inconsistent. This inconsistency must be called to the attention of all concerned so that they can reverse their movement away from historic Baptist orthodoxy if they choose to do so. If this is not done, it will gravely impair the witness of Southern Baptists, and ultimately produce disastrous consequences. I realize some Southern Baptists think the modern situation makes it impossible to hold to the faith of our fathers as we have known it for centuries. They do not think themselves disloyal to remain within the convention as they seek to change the theological foundations. Indeed, some of them sincerely believe they are doing the majority a favor by enlightening them in ways they have not understood heretofore. This attitude is expressed in a statement made by a Louisville graduate, Temp Sparkman. He wrote:

> Are there some beliefs in your church's statement of faith that you do not agree with? Are there some words in the hymns of your church that you do not agree with? If so, welcome to a large club. You have much company, and have always had.
>
> This kind of intellectual problem has led many to change denominations and has caused ministers to change to secular employment. So conscientious have these persons been about belief, they have thought it dishonest to stay in a church where things were being said that they could not agree with.
>
> One way to deal with this kind of crisis is to remember that doctrine is never fixed once and for all. It is always changing, though perhaps not within the time-span of your intellectual crisis or even within your lifetime. But over the long haul, doctrine does and will continue to change. This means that a person might be

able to stay in a church during a time when many of the expressed beliefs are contrary to what he believes. He can do that honestly because he knows that those beliefs can be changed. And more, he can have a part in encouraging the change.

Your feelings may run too deep for this kind of waiting. But if you can accept the fact that you have a role to play in bringing about changes though you may not live to seem them realized, you can at least have the satisfaction of raising some relevant questions.

Then there is another point to be made. In your brief life you cannot be responsible for the whole theology of the church. If you can accept this kind of reasoning it will make it possible for you to repeat statements of faith with some clear conscience. It is not in dishonesty that you do this kind of thing. It is an admission that at the doctrinal level we cannot have every statement or belief agree in every detail with what we believe.[93]

Mr. Sparkman leaves unanswered the basic question Southern Baptists sooner or later must answer: What is it Baptists believe that remains forever unchangeable? What is it we believe that can never be negotiable? Does it include the doctrine that the Bible is the Word of God written in its entirety and is inerrant in all its parts?

Dr. Foy Valentine tells the press that Southern Baptists are not evangelicals. Dr. Dilday, the president of Southwestern Seminary, says they are. Dr. William Pinson, president of Golden Gate Baptist Theological Seminary asks: "Can Baptists Survive the Evangelicals?" Among the rising evangelical schools he names Mid-America Seminary, Luther Rice Seminary, and the Criswell Bible Institute. He seems to be joining Dr. Valentine in leaving open the question whether Southern Baptists are evangelicals. He talks sorrowfully about witch hunts, scapegoats, alienated Baptists, and the like. At the heart of the issue he discusses are the theological differences that divide Southern Baptists, the centerpiece of which is whether the Bible is true in all its parts.

The future of Southern Baptists depends, in a large measure, on how they resolve that problem.

NOTES

[1]Newton Brown, ed., *The Baptist Church Manual* (Philadelphia: American

Baptist Publication Society, 1945), p. 5.

[2]*Baptist Ideals* (Nashville: Baptist Sunday School Board, 1964.)

[3]Ibid., p. 18, 19.

[4]Herschel Hobbs, *A Layman's Handbook of Christian Doctrine* (Nashville: Broadman) p. 126.

[5]Harold Lindsell, *The Battle for the Bible* (Grand Rapids: Zondervan, 1976), p. 95ff.

[6]*Baptist Hymnal* (Nashville: Broadman, 1970), viii.

[7]*Southwestern Journal of Theology.*

[8]*Review and Expositor* (Louisville: Southern Baptist Theological Seminary, Winter 1977), pp. 106-107.

[9]*The Tie* (Louisville: The Southern Baptist Theological Seminary, June 1976), p. 10.

[10]*The Banner* (Grand Rapids: The Christian Reformed Church, August 27, 1976), p. 16.

[11]*The Christian News,* December 20, 1976, p. 9.

[12]Ibid. (June 1977), p. 7.

[13]The Minneapolis *Star* (Minneapolis, October 30, 1976), 4A.

[14]*Bulletin* (Forth Worth: Southwestern Baptist Theological Seminary, 1976-77), p. 6.

[15]B. H. Carroll, Inspiration of the Bible (New York: Revell, 1930), p. 20.

[16]Ibid., pp. 21-23.

[17]Ibid., p. 24.

[18]Ibid., pp. 24-25.

[19]Ibid., p. 25.

[20]Ibid., pp. 26-27.

[21]Ibid., pp. 54-55.

[22]Ibid., pp. 116-18.

[23]Ibid., p. 119.

[24]Ibid., p. 121.

[25]Lee R. Scarborough, *Gospel Messages* (Nashville: Sunday School Board, 1922), pp. 227-28.

[26]Basil Manly, *The Bible Doctrine of Inspiration Explained and Vindicated* (New York: Armstrong, 1891), p. 26.

[27]Ibid., p. 27.

[28]Ibid., p. 48f.

[29]Ibid., p. 49.

[30]Ibid., p. 59.

[31]Ibid., p. 16.

[32]Ibid., p. 82.

[33]Ibid., p. 222.

[34]Ibid., pp. 222-25.

[35]Ibid., p. 225f.

[36]James Petigru Boyce, *Abstract of Theology,* revised by Kerfoot (Philadelphia: American Baptist Publication Society, 1899), pp. 35, 36, 37.

[37]John R. Sampey, *Syllabus for Old Testament Study* (Nashville: Broadman, 1903), pp. 58, 59.

[38]Wayne E. Ward and Joseph F. Green, *Is the Bible a Human Book?*

(Nashville: Broadman, 1970), p. 5.

[39]Ibid.

[40]Ibid.

[41]Ibid., pp. 27, 28, 29.

[42]Ibid., p. 78.

[43]Ibid., pp. 131, 134.

[43]*Review and Expositor*, Vol. LXIV, No. 3, Summer 1967.

[44]Frank Stagg, E. Glenn Hinson, Wayne E. Oates, *Glossolalia: Tongue Speaking in Biblical, Historical, and Psychological Perspective* (Nashville: Abingdon, 1967), p. 26.

[45]Ibid., p. 29, 30.

[46]Frank Stagg, *New Testament Theology* (Nashville: Broadman, 1962), p. 39.

[47]Ibid.

[48]Ibid., p. 44.

[49]Ibid., p. 59.

[50]Ibid., p. 131.

[51]Ibid., pp. 140, 141.

[52]Ibid., p. 144.

[53]Ibid., p. 145.

[54]William E. Hull, "The Relevance of the New Testament," *Review and Expositor* (Vol. LXII, No. 2, Spring 1965), p. 188.

[55]Ibid., p. 190.

[56]Ibid., p. 191.

[57]Ibid., p. 192.

[58]Ibid., p. 194.

[59]Ibid., p. 195.

[60]Ibid., p. 199.

[61]William E. Hull, *The Integrity of the Theological Curriculum* (Louisville: The Southern Baptist Theological Seminary, 1969), pp. 2, 3.

[62]Ibid., p. 4.

[63]Ibid., p. 5.

[64]William E. Hull, *Southern Baptist Biblical Scholarship: Harbingers of Hope* (typescript of address presented to Southern Baptist Theological Seminary by President Duke McCall, 1968), p. 2.

[65]Ibid., pp. 3, 4.

[66]Ibid., p. 7.

[67]William E. Hull, "The New Quest of the Historical Jesus," *Review and Expositor* (Vol. LXIV, No. 3, Summer 1967), p. 335.

[68]Ibid., p. 333.

[69]Ibid., p. 334.

[70]Ibid., p. 339.

[71]Dale Moody, "Tabletalk on Theology Tomorrow," *Review and Expositor* (Vol. LXIV, No. 3, Summer 1967).

[72]Ibid., p. 345.

[73]Ibid., p. 354.

[74]Ibid., pp. 354, 355.

[75]Ibid., p. 356.

[76]*Review and Expositor* (Vol. LXV, No. 4, Fall 1968), p. 501.

[77]J. Wash Watts, *A Survey of Old Testament Teaching*, Vol. II (Nashville: Broadman, 1947), p. 150.

[78]*Review and Expositor* (Vol. LXV, No. 4, Fall 1968), p. 409.

[79]Ibid., p. 423.

[80]Page H. Kelley, *Judgment and Redemption in Isaiah* (Nashville: Broadman, 1968), p. 15.

[81]Ibid., p. 13.

[82]*Review and Expositor* (Vol. LXI, No. 4, Fall 1964), p. 266.

[83]Ibid., p. 288.

[84]Ibid., p. 317.

[85]Ibid., p. 328.

[86]G. R. Beasley-Murray, *The General Epistles: James, 1 Peter, Jude, 2 Peter* (London: Lutterworth Press, 1965), pp. 82-83.

[87]Ibid., pp. 83-84.

[88]*Baptist Press*, December 14, 1977.

[89]George Allen West, Jr., *John and Form Criticism* (Th. D. thesis: Southern Baptist Theological Seminary, 1942), p. 176.

[90]*The Atlanta Journal and Constitution*, June 11, 1978, p. 12B.

[91]Ibid., p. 13B.

[92]*Review and Expositor* (Vol. LXXV, No. 2, Spring 1978), p. 225.

[93]Temp Sparkman, *Being a Disciple* (Nashville: Broadman, 1972), pp. 30-32.

5

Fuller Theological Seminary:
A Seminary at Bay

The situation at the Fuller Theological Seminary has worsened since the publication of *The Battle for the Bible*. Prior to and since the publication of the book, Fuller Seminary has waged a vigorous campaign to offset its impact. This was not unexpected. In fact, it has served a useful purpose. First, it shows that the institution has taken the situation seriously. Second, the school has worked hard to blunt the edge of criticism. And third, it has tried to forge a strong coalition to support it theologically and promotionally. Above all, it wishes to retain the label *evangelical*. None of this is surprising. But how it was done, what its case consists in, and what further signs there are of quickening erosion and capitulation need exploration. Before I approach this task I must first restate what the central thesis of *The Battle for the Bible* was in the case of Fuller Seminary.

Basically I made three observations about the seminary. The first two were factual, and their rightness or wrongness can be appraised from the evidences given. The third was prophetic. The first allegation had to do with the changing of the doctrinal statement of the school. I charged that Fuller Seminary has been infiltrated by an aberrant view of Scripture. It had started as an institution committed to biblical inerrancy. That is undeniable. Drs. Wilbur Smith, Carl F. H. Henry, Harold John Ockenga, and myself can bear and have borne testimony to that fact. It is corroborated by the confession of faith that was formulated and became the foundation stone of the school. In that confession, Article 2 said that the Bible is "free from error in the whole and in the part." The statement made clear that this was true of the autographs for it said "as originally given." This allowed for the possibility of copyists' errors, few though they might be.

The new statement of Fuller reads:

> Scripture is an essential part and trustworthy record of this divine disclosure. All the books of the Old and New Testament, given by divine inspiration, are the written word of God, the only infallible rule of faith and practice. They are to be interpreted according to their context and in reverent obedience to the Lord who speaks through them in living power.[1]

In the new statement, Fuller Seminary no longer says that the Bible "is the infallible Word of God, the only infallible rule of faith and practice." It simply says the Bible is the word (lower-cased) of God, and then adds that infallibility is limited to matters of faith and practice. Thus whatever does not constitute a matter of faith and practice can contain error. I alleged that Fuller Seminary has given up its cherished belief in an inerrant or infallible Scripture. And I adduced evidences to prove that allegation.

Second, I charged that Fuller Seminary has taken the second step. It has gone beyond a denial of infallibility in matters of history, science, and the cosmos to a place where members of the faculty now deny the truth of Scripture in matters of faith and practice. Specifically I alleged that Paul King Jewett in his book *Man as Male and Female* said that the apostle Paul's teaching in Ephesians about the marital bond is in disagreement with his teaching in Galatians 3:28. He clearly stated that what Paul said in the Book of Ephesians is wrong.[2] We shall see in a moment how Fuller has responded to this challenge.

The third major point I made about Fuller Seminary was in the form of a prophecy. I asserted that once an institution surrenders biblical inerrancy it will sooner or later scrap other basic doctrines of the Christian faith. I asserted in the 1976 book that it has already happened at Fuller. And I pointed to the case of Paul King Jewett. I also said that down the road, Fuller Seminary will make further concessions and allow for other more marked departures from historic orthodoxy. It is against a backdrop of two factual allegations and one prophetic prediction that the reactions of Fuller Seminary must be seen. And to those reactions I now proceed.

Dr. Hubbard's Convocation Address

Before *The Battle for the Bible* was in the bookstores, Dr. Hubbard, the Fuller president, had access to the page proofs. He called a Seminary Convocation for April 8, 1976. At the convocation he delivered his address titled: "Reflections on Fuller's Theological Position and Role in the Church." In that speech Dr. Hubbard said "the good ship Fuller is headed once more into the winds of controversy." He said that my book was built on the thesis that "The Bible itself and the history of the Christian church support an interpretation of inerrancy that includes not only the intent of the biblical authors and their theological teachings but also every detail of geography, history, and science; second, the conviction that only those churches, institutions, and individuals who adhere to that definition of inerrancy can remain true to the evangelical faith."[3]

Dr. Hubbard went on to say that "evangelical unity has been threatened by what I must consider narrow definitions of the term evangelical." He added by way of a punch line that I was offering an alternative to Fuller's approach that looks "like a scholarship turned defensive, a churchmanship turned divisive, a historiography turned selective, a personal pique turned vindictive."[4] These were rather strong words, but the strong words at no point dealt with the evidences presented to show Fuller Seminary had indeed departed from its original intent and purpose. However, President Hubbard was plain enough at one point. He said: "My deepest concern about Dr. Lindsell's book is not that it criticizes Fuller, but that its inadequate and unbiblical view of Scripture will divide our evangelical fellowship worldwide."[5] I note with care his statement that biblical inerrancy is an unbiblical view of Scripture. Concerning this, several points should be made.

Under date of December 13, 1962, Dr. Hubbard wrote to Roger Voskuyl, then president of Westmont College, on whose faculty David Hubbard was a member. He had been called into question by the Board of Trustees because of an Old Testament introduction syllabus he was using which had been written by himself and Robert Laurin (now deceased). That syllabus adopted a number of higher critical viewpoints that were in conflict with the Westmont statement of faith. Dr. Hubbard told Dr. Voskuyl what it was he believed, and said he could use his statement anyway he pleased. He told Dr. Voskuyl he could share it with the Board of Trustees and any one else. In that statement Dr. Hubbard said:

> Earlier this semester I willingly signed the Westmont Statement of Faith and again, as I have annually since 1957, affirmed my belief in the *plenary, verbal inspiration* of the Scriptures. I believe that the Bible is exactly what God wanted it to be to the very word, that it is infallible in its teaching, completely accurate in its historical statements, and fully authoritative in matters of faith and practice. . . .
>
> In summary, let me say that I have read carefully the statement of our colleagues at Wheaton concerning the matter of faith and fellowship and that I agree wholeheartedly with the spirit, intent, tone and content of that statement.[6]

Wheaton College, then and now, is committed to an inerrant Scripture in the autographs and has also added an addendum specifying the immediate creation of Adam and Eve so as to rule out theistic evolution. I would not for one moment say that Dr. Hubbard signed the Westmont statement of faith with tongue in cheek. But several excerpts taken from the syllabus he coauthored with Robert Laurin will be found highly significant in this connection. The quotations are taken from a section of the syllabus written by Dr. Laurin. But the statements did not deter Dr. Hubbard from using the syllabus in class. Dr. Laurin wrote about the role of God in inspiration. This is what he said:

> The words of Paul to Timothy about inspiration say that the purpose of God's "breath" in the composition and collecting of Scripture is religious. The function of Scripture is not to give scientific information about the creation of the world or the structure of man; it is not to give us a history of ancient nations or of the people of Israel; it is not to provide us with a historical geography of various peoples. The witness of the New Testament is that the purpose of the Old Testament (and thus of the New as well) is to make better men and women out of us in terms of our relationship to God. It is to equip us "for every good work," to lead us to life with God. In a word, the Bible's purpose is purely and simply religious, or put another way, it intends to depict *Heilsgeschichte* ("salvation history").

Thus "inspiration" is that work of the Holy Spirit (how he operated we do not know) on the writers and collectors of the Bible, so that what is recorded and preserved is profitable for the purposes for which God intended, namely, to lead men to life with Him. So the Bible is infallible in terms of its purpose—the message about God and about man's need. Inspiration preserves revelation.[7]

It can be seen immediately that these views do not follow the pattern of those Old Testament scholars who are orthodox. But there are further questionable implications to be garnered from this particular essay. For example:

But it is clear that the Old Testament as a whole differs from modern standards of accuracy in historical and scientific statements.

This can be seen best, perhaps, in parallel accounts. As is well known the first two chapters of Genesis contain two accounts of creation, 1:1-2:4a and 2:4b-25. They do not agree on all details, such as the order of creation or the condition of the material God used in forming the world. If historical reporting were intended, the events should parallel. But since the purpose of Scripture is theological, historical or chronological considerations are secondary. "Chapter 1 emphasizes that God did it, primarily showing *power* behind creation and the monotheistic nature of that power. The emphasis of chapter 2 is that though God is *Lord* over it, his creation was to be a *fellowship* between him and man." (Dr. Laurin was quoting R. H. Elliott here— that Elliott whose book was repudiated by the Southern Baptist Convention, and the Elliott who was dismissed from Mid-Western Baptist Seminary—my observation.) Indeed when the Bible speaks of the nature of the universe it often does so with the descriptive scientific terminology of its day—a flat earth, a solid sky, windows in the sky through which the rain came (Gen. 1:7; 7:1; Ps. 74:14; 104:26).

The parallel accounts in Samuel-Kings and Chronicles are famous for their differences. For example, I Kings 15:11, 14 says, "and Asa did that which was right in the eyes of the Lord . . . but the high places were not taken away." But II Chronicles 14:2, 5 reports, "and Asa did that which was good and right in the eyes of the Lord his God . . . and he took away out of all the cities of Judah the high places." (Cf. also I Kgs. 22:43 and II Chron. 17:6; II Sam. 24:24 and I Chron. 21:25.)

The New Testament also illustrates this fact. Matthew 27:5 and Acts 1:18 give us two different accounts of the death of Judas. Matthew refers Zechariah's prophecy regarding the use of thirty pieces of silver to Jeremiah (Matt. 27:9; Zech. 11:12, 13). Jesus is reported to have identified the high priest at the time when David took the consecrated bread as Abiathar (Mk. 2:26), but the Old Testament tells us his name was Ahimelech (I Sam. 21:1). And the most obvious example of this disregard for precise accuracy in historical detail is the general method of the Synoptics in reporting the life of Jesus. When the Gospels put different words in the mouth of Jesus on the same occasion he obviously could not have used all forms at the same time. For example, Matthew 13:31 reports Jesus as speaking of "the kingdom of heaven," while Mark 4:30 says that he used the expression "the kingdom of God." Jesus did not use both.

Though there are many ways of resolving some of the alleged contradictions, the best solution to this problem is to understand the role of inspiration. God's purpose is not to give us *scientifically* accurate history or cosmology or other matters. Also, inspiration was never intended to guarantee the accuracy of the source material used by the biblical writers. They used the ordinary sources of information—documents and oral tradition. The Holy Spirit, as the empirical evidence compels us to admit, was not concerned with correcting these sources when they were in error on historical or scientific statements. Inspiration has as its goal the preservation of that which will lead us to life in Christ. It is in terms of its spiritual claims that we must demand infallibility of Scripture.[8]

How does this relate to Dr. Hubbard? After all, he did not write this section of the syllabus of which he was coauthor. He only used it in class. Of course he could have stopped the use of those parts of the syllabus which were unsatisfactory. Or he could have used some other Old Testament Introduction. It was the use of this syllabus that the Board of Trustees forbade in the Westmont classroom because it was defective. It said the Bible has errors in it. It advocated in that and other sections what were nothing more or less than straight liberal views.

In the mimeographed release I just mentioned Dr. Hubbard explained that he and Dr. Laurin did have differences of opinion, and they were going to discontinue the coauthorship which had come about by reason of Dr. Hubbard's invitation to Dr. Laurin to join him in the writing of the book. Dr. Hubbard was loath to stop the use of the syllabus in the classroom and made several suggestions, one of which was to replace the chapter on Daniel. This is what Dr. Hubbard wrote to Dr. Voskuyl:

In no way should anything that I have said be interpreted as impugning the scholarly integrity, the theological competence, or the orthodoxy of Dr. Laurin. Few Old Testament scholars that I know combine his dedication to Christian service with a profound insight into the word of God. We have a difference of opinion as to how wide the boundaries of orthodoxy should be set, *but there is not a trace of liberalism or neo-orthodoxy involved* (my italics). Let me be frank and say that anyone who thinks there is is not fully conversant either with Dr. Laurin's position or with the theological meaning of these two terms. (Dec. 13, 1962)

No one can misunderstand what Dr. Hubbard was saying. According to him Dr. Laurin was perfectly orthodox. There was no trace [sic] of either liberalism or neoorthodoxy in what he had said. Whatever differences he had with Dr. Laurin did not pertain to orthodoxy—only how far the circumference of the circle of orthodoxy should be. But Dr. Laurin's circumference, which was larger than that professed by Dr. Hubbard, was still orthodox. Dr. Laurin was not unorthodox when he said the Old Testament declares that the earth is flat. He was not unorthodox when he stated God did not intend to give us "scientifically accurate history or cosmology or other matters." If God gave us inaccurate history and inaccurate cosmology as Dr. Laurin alleged, it was still orthodox according to David Hubbard himself, because at no point was he "impugning . . . the orthodoxy of Dr. Laurin." If the late date for Daniel, the nonhistoricity of Adam and Eve, and the like are perfectly orthodox, then the intrinsic meaning of the word *orthodoxy* has been seriously diluted. In view of what Dr. Hubbard said in 1962, why should it come as a surprise to anyone that in 1976 in connection with the publication of *The Battle for the Bible* Dr. Hubbard should say that the view of the Bible I espouse is unbiblical? What is quite clear, however, is that Dr. Hubbard could not have come to Fuller Seminary as president in 1963 without either misunderstanding the Fuller Seminary statement of faith or interpreting it in a way that gave him a clear conscience. But if the statement which was in effect at that time was such that the view of Dr. Laurin could come under its umbrella, what was the need for changing it later? So now we come back to what Dr. Hubbard did after he gave his convocation address in the spring of 1976.

Theology, News and Notes

Dr. Hubbard was not content to let the matter rest there. He followed up his convocation address with a special 1976 issue of *Theology, News and Notes*. This was a thirty-two page booklet devoted to "The Authority of Scripture at Fuller." The title was not exactly in accord with the contents. Clark Pinnock was called to their support in the publication of his article "The Inerrancy Debate among the Evangelicals." This article was simply a review of *The Battle for the Bible* in which he registered his objection to the book. It was here that Dr. Pinnock referred to the Lausanne statement "in all that it affirms" with his watered-down interpretation of its meaning. But he did not hesitate to state that there are errors in the Bible. He said that "in confusing the facts of the Abraham story in Acts 7 we fault neither Stephen for citing the facts as he recalled them nor Luke for recording what he believed Stephen said; where Job cites the errant opinions of liars; where the chronicler recounts figures quite different from those used in parallel passages, his intention being only to set forth the record as he found it in the public archives. . . ."[9] So we see Dr. Pinnock in retreat from the strong stand he took in his earlier book *Biblical Revelation* published by Moody Press in 1971.

Dr. Paul S. Rees of World Vision and former president of the National Association of Evangelicals was called in also. His article from a World Vision publication, "Are We Trying to Outdo the Reformers?" included the assertion that "no statement of the exact mode of inspiration is entitled to the status of a criterion for evangelical faith."[10] I do not know who was asking that question, or what bearing it had upon the allegation that Fuller Seminary had departed from its commitment to inerrancy. Whether one decides that the Scriptures were dictated or given by the overshadowing influence of the Holy Spirit who superintended the writers of the Bible is of academic interest. What is important is what inspiration *did*, not *how* it worked. Either the resultant product, however it was done, was free from error or it was marred by errors. Dr. Rees and Dr. Pinnock were drafted to participate in Fuller Seminary's third effort to counteract the impact of *The Battle for the Bible*.

Theology, News and Notes ran a review of my book written by Donald Dayton of the North Park Seminary. This review was reprinted from *The Other Side*, a magazine which does not hold to inerrancy. The review was what one would expect.[11] Mr. Dayton himself does not believe in biblical inerrancy and has indicated to me that he thought my historical summary in this present book should face the Wesleyan question about which nothing was said in the first book. He argued that the Nazarene denomination, for example, has never been committed to biblical inerrancy, and they seem to be doing very well. Since I have already commented on Mr. Dayton I need say nothing further about this subject now. William LaSor, a former colleague of mine, devoted much space to his own recollections of the history of Fuller Seminary under the title: "Life under Tension—Fuller Seminary and 'The Battle for the Bible'." Unfortunately Dr. LaSor centered his article on personalities and his remembrance of incidents which called forth specific denials from Charles Woodbridge, Carl F. H. Henry, and Edward Johnson. (See, *Theology, News and Notes*, March 1977, pp. 22ff.) The intent of the article was designed to defuse the problem, an effort which did not come off very well. He himself made a rather odd observation about the original confession of faith of the seminary:

> The Statement of Faith was adopted, and we all were asked to sign it. Bela Vasady refused and was most "disappointed" with me because I was willing to sign it. I had already made my decision to cast my lot with Fuller Seminary, and I felt there was nothing to be gained by refusing to sign the Statement.[12]

The reason Dr. Vasady refused to sign the statement was simple. He objected to inerrancy. As a Presbyterian he of course already believed the Bible to be the infallible rule of faith and practice. Thus what Dr. LaSor said by way of explanation for his own signing of the statement makes no sense. In his later assertion he opened himself to criticism:

> There were others on the faculty who were as aware of the problems as I was, including Ed Carnell and Everett Harrison. We all understood "in the whole and in the part" to be interpreted as placing the whole of Scripture above the parts.[13]

Dr. LaSor appears to be saying that his view and that of Dr.

Vasady were no different. Yet he signed the statement of faith without mental reservation as though he believed it. Dr. Carnell is dead and cannot speak, but I do not for one moment think he would accept this statement about himself by Dr. LaSor. I have reason to think that Dr. Harrison does not do so either. But since Dr. Vasady was separated from the Fuller faculty precisely because he did not believe the Bible to be infallible in matters of history, science, and the cosmos, it is patently foolish to suppose that "error in the whole and in the part" could be interpreted so as to make legitimate what occasioned Dr. Vasady's departure.

President Hubbard contributed his own article "What We Believe and Teach" to the ongoing discussion. This was reprinted in pamphlet form and widely distributed. It is worth reading if for no other reason than that it supports fully my allegation that the seminary has given up biblical inerrancy. Dr. Hubbard beat the bushes without success. Some of his statements had nothing whatever to do with the issue at stake, an issue he never got around to answering. He said, for example: "We are convinced that this investigation of the context and purpose is essential to a correct understanding of any portion of God's word." No one would object to such a statement. Nor would anyone deny that "the emphasis be placed where the Bible itself places it—on its message of salvation and its instruction for living. . . ." But when Dr. Hubbard added "not on its details of geography or science, though we acknowledge the wonderful reliability of the Bible as a historical source book,"[14] he got to the point at which Fuller Seminary was being called into question. No one, at that time, was saying that Fuller Seminary no longer believed the virgin birth, the vicarious atonement, the deity of Christ, or even the bodily resurrection of Jesus. What was said was that Fuller Seminary had opened the door by denying the reliability of the Bible in matters of fact, history, and science. Of course Fuller Seminary, then and now, believes that some historical facts, scientific statements, and cosmological statements in the Bible are true, but not *all* such statements.

Perhaps without intention Dr. Hubbard gave away the game when he chose to discuss the use of the word "inerrancy."

We recognize the importance that the word "inerrancy" has attained in the thinking of many of our scholarly colleagues and the institutions they serve. We appreciate the way in which most of them use the term to affirm that the Scripture is indeed God's trustworthy word in all it affirms (note here the deliberate introduction of the phrase "all it affirms" in line with the Lausanne statement which has been so much abused [my observation]). When inerrancy refers to what the Holy Spirit is saying to the churches through biblical writers, we support its use. Where the focus switches to an *undue* (my italics) emphasis on matters like the chronological details, the precise sequence of events, the numerical allusions, we would consider the term misleading and inappropriate.[15]

Here Dr. Hubbard gave away his case. Inerrancy is satisfactory so long as it does not include chronology, allusions to numerical figures, or matters of science and the cosmos. He simply cannot accept a Bible which is inerrant in *all* its parts.

The Case of Paul King Jewett

Of all the articles in the special issue of *Theology, News and Notes,* none is more important than those pertaining to Dr. Jewett. Everyone interested in the Fuller situation should get a copy and read it carefully. In it, the reader will find the full confirmation of my second allegation: that Fuller Seminary has breached its new statement of faith in the case of Paul King Jewett who denies the infallibility of Scripture in regard to a matter of faith and practice. The seminary itself has now borne testimony to this fact. Dr. Jewett has said that in Ephesians 5 the apostle Paul tells us that which is not true. He has argued that Ephesians 5 conflicts with Galatians 3:28. He thinks Paul in Ephesians has given us a rabbinic ruling which is really false teaching when measured by Galatians. He does it on the basis of the use of "the analogy of faith" principle in the interpretation of Scripture. An *ad hoc* committee was appointed by the board to investigate Dr. Jewett's book *Man as Male and Female.* Their report was published in *Theology, News and Notes.* In their findings and recommendations the committee had this to say:

The Committee acknowledges that some application of the "analogy of faith" hermeneutic may be consistent with Article 3 (i.e. of the Fuller Seminary current doctrinal statement), but does not feel that this principle permitted the texts of Scripture (specifically Gen. 1:27, Gal. 3:28, I Cor, 11, 1 Tim. 2, and Eph. 5) to be handled in the manner in which Dr. Jewett followed.[16]

A little later the committee said:

> Dr. Jewett's approach to the authority of the Apostle Paul has left him and the Seminary vulnerable to misunderstanding and responsible criticism. To the extent that Dr. Jewett may be interpreted to say that St. Paul's teaching in I Corinthians 11, I Timothy 2, and Ephesians 5 was in error, or that St. Paul was a faulty theologian at these points in interpreting the Old Testament, the Committee sharply disagreed with him.[17]

The Committee pronounced adverse judgment on Dr. Jewett. When its careful phrasing is looked at the Committee said Dr. Jewett had breached the doctrinal statement of Fuller Seminary. Now the question was, What would the Committee recommend be done about it? Here was their answer:

> The Committee, while maintaining its disagreements with and regret of some portions of *Man as Male and Female*, which appear to question the authority of the Apostle Paul (and it is well to note that later we will see that at least one of Dr. Jewett's colleagues does not believe that Paul wrote the book of Ephesians in the first place [my comment]), recommends that the Seminary take no other action in the light of Dr. Jewett's proven integrity, his longstanding contribution to the upholding and teaching of the biblical faith at Fuller, and his reassurance of loyalty to the Fuller doctrinal standards.[18]

Here is a tangled mass of conflicting data which forms no coherent pattern. Dr. Jewett, they agreed, was guilty. The Seminary doctrinal statement had been breached. But they said Dr. Jewett is a man of integrity, a good teacher, and a long-time employee of the school. So they sacrificed the statement of faith on this basis to permit the continuance on the faculty of a man who openly contradicted the confession to which he appended his signature. But since he did not really think he had done anything wrong, even though the committee did, they agreed to forget the whole matter!

One of the Fuller trustees added his word: "The committee and the Seminary are intent on affirming the complete inspiration of Scripture in the words used by Scripture itself, and on continuing their quest to learn more fully what it means."[19] In other words, the completely inspired Bible has no untruth in it in a matter of faith and practice, but they will do nothing about the professor who says that it *does* contain such untruth, even though the seminary is committed to a trustworthy Scripture limited to matters of faith and practice (even if not in matters of historical or scientific fact). But we shall see shortly that Dr. Jewett is not alone, and if he were to be separated from the institution, there are others of whom he, the students, the trustees, and the administration have knowledge who would also have to be separated from the school. It would constitute a wholesale departure and breakup of the faculty if it were to be carried out.

Biblical Authority

The third barrage of Fuller Seminary against *The Battle for the Bible* was released with the publication of the book *Biblical Authority*, edited by Jack Rogers of the Fuller faculty. Published by Word Books of Waco, Texas, the back jacket of this paperback book says:

> The "Battle for the Bible" today threatens evangelicalism with schism. Here, by a group of authors of unquestioned faith and integrity, is urgent reading. Concentrating on the saving purpose of the Bible they present a responsible alternate view in the conflict over the precise nature of biblical infallibility. They demonstrate their unswerving belief in the truth and trustworthiness of God's Word, and they follow the biblical materials implicitly as the guide to our understanding of the meaning of God's message and the human means through which it is given.[20]

A sense of humor at this point is helpful. The question "Who are the schismatics?" should certainly be asked and answered. I have not changed my position. I left Fuller Seminary because it had changed its position. If all who have scrapped inerrancy were to leave the churches and institutions which are on record with respect to a commitment to inerrancy, the threat of schism would be removed. But if they remain and tension and schism are threatened, the threat comes from those who have violated or abandoned their belief in inerrancy. I would be happy to learn of situations in which believers in inerrancy can rightly be called schismatics. The true schismatics are to be found in those places where groups, de-nominations, or organizations are controlled by a doctrinal commitment to inerrancy to which they cannot assent with integrity. Charles E. Fuller certainly believed when he brought Fuller Theological Seminary into existence that it would forever stand for an inerrant Bible, even as he had so stood when he was chairman of the Board of Trustees of the Bible Institute of Los Angeles and when he preached on the "Old Fashioned Revival Hour."

The Fuller book *Biblical Authority* has chapters in it written by seven people, two of whom are on the Fuller faculty—David Hubbard and Jack Rogers. The other five are Paul Rees, Clark Pinnock, Berkeley Mickelsen, Bernard Ramm, and Earl Palmer. Some of the contributors stated they believed in bibli-cal inerrancy; some contributed chapters that had little to do with the current controversy. But those who profess inerrancy must face the onus of the charge made by David Hubbard (already mentioned above) that inerrancy is unbiblical. In that event the Fuller book must have in it contributors who are unbiblical. Why the seminary would use such men to help their cause can be explained only on the basis of the incipient inclusiveness of the Fuller approach, or a willingness to go along with inerrantists who support Fuller because they are also latitudinarian at this point.

The contradiction is further complicated by present Fuller faculty members (such as Geoffrey Bromiley) who still believe in the same inerrancy the seminary was formerly committed to. Thus Dr. Hubbard has in effect indicted some of his own faculty members for holding an unbiblical view of Scripture. This being the case, he now has faculty members who should be separated from the institution for holding a view of the Bible that he says is heretical. For whatever is unbiblical is heretical.

An Evangelical Response to Biblical Authority

It would be impossible for me to speak to all of the issues raised by the Fuller Seminary volume, *Biblical Authority*. By the time this volume sees the light of day other evangelical scholars will already have done that. The reader can follow the discussion about inerrancy by scanning the volume titled *The*

Foundation of Biblical Authority (Zondervan), published in the fall of 1978. Among the authors who have replied sequentially to each chapter in the Fuller book are Francis Schaeffer, John Gerstner, J. I. Packer, Gleason L. Archer, R. C. Sproul, James Boice, and Kenneth Kantzer. This is a *Who's Who* in evangelical life. It indicates how strong the conviction is that the Bible is inerrant and how noted evangelicals are willing to respond to the current challenge.

Professor Norman Geisler of the Trinity Evangelical Divinity School reviewed the Fuller book for *Christianity Today*. His acute observations will certainly acquaint the reader with the summary of the book's contents and his appraisal of the work on the whole. I have placed this review in the Appendix so that interested readers can have a general summary of the book's theses. I have also included in the Appendix the review of the book by Robert Preus who is the president of the Concordia Lutheran Theological Seminary of Fort Wayne, Indiana. for my own purposes, I will speak to items raised by the chapters written by the two Fuller Seminary faculty members which appear in the volume—Jack Rogers and David Hubbard.

Jack Rogers

Jack Rogers has performed one notable service in the matter of biblical inerrancy. His chapter in the Fuller book reveals that he does not believe in inerrancy and he uses every possible device to show that church leaders through the ages didn't believe in an infallible Bible in matters of science. Thus he writes:

> Augustine, Calvin, Rutherford, and Bavinck, for example, all specifically deny that the Bible should be looked to as an authority in matters of science. To claim them in support of a modern inerrancy theory is to trivialize their central concern that the Bible is our sole authority on salvation and the living of a Christian life.[21]

This statement by Professor Rogers is deceptive and misleading. I do not know anyone who argues that the Bible is a textbook on science. All that inerrancy proclaims is that when the human authors of Scripture wrote about scientific matters they did not tell us what is untrue. Indeed, the Scriptures say little about science when compared to the vastness of the subject. Thus the only question is whether the Bible, when speaking about matters of science, even though that be a tiny fragment of its content, tells us what is not true. Dr. Rogers is saying that the Bible indeed is inaccurate in scientific matters. His whole argument is based on that presupposition. So all he does is validate the claim I made in *The Battle for the Bible:* namely, that in the beginning, Fuller Seminary believed the Bible to be free from all error in the whole and in the part. Now it believes there are some errors, and some of those errors pertain to scientific matters. Why then should Fuller Seminary allow the publication of a book which admits the truth of what I alleged, and at the same time try to give the impression that there has been no change? This seems to be a clear self-contradiction.

Dr. Rogers quotes with obvious commendation the point made by Professor Berkouwer:

> Berkouwer acknowledged the "serious motivation" of advocates of scientific and historical inerrancy, but concluded: "in the end it will damage reverence for Scripture more than it will further it." [22]

From there Dr. Rogers goes on to assert something which is true but in so doing he draws a false conclusion with respect to inerrancy. He quotes Berkouwer to the effect that the purpose of God in Scripture is "to witness of the salvation of God unto faith." Of course the main purpose of the Bible is salvatory. Which evangelical has ever denied that? And surely it is true that the Bible has for its great objective bringing men face to face with Jesus Christ so that they may inherit eternal life when they believe in Him. But because all of this is true, it does not follow that in matters not directly related to the main purpose of Scripture the Word of God tells us what is not true. If all the Bible is the Word of God as Messrs. Rogers and Hubbard would have us believe, then we have an errant Word of God and an inerrant Word of God, and each man must decide for himself what is true and what is not. In that framework, then, when it is said that all of Scripture is inspired by the Holy Spirit two things follow as matters of logical necessity. The first is that the Holy Spirit inspires error. The second is that the Word of God contains falsehood along with its truth. This in turn suggests that God is the author of error.

If so, the Bible cannot be a trustworthy revelation of divine truth.

Dr. Rogers states that "it is historically irresponsible to claim that for two thousand years Christians have believed that the authority of the Bible entails a modern concept of inerrancy in scientific and historical details."[23] And then Dr. Rogers makes mention of Augustine, Calvin, Rutherford, and Bavinck. We must take a look at these men.

Augustine

It is an error for Professor Rogers to assert that Augustine specifically denied that the Bible should be looked to as an authority in matters of science. Augustine regarded the Bible as being free from error in all of its parts. If Dr. Rogers will not accept the testimony of Augustine at this point there is no way he can be convinced of anything, for Augustine is very plain on the matter. His attitude and understanding of biblical inerrancy is significant:

"The Faith will totter if the authority of the Holy Scriptures loses its hold on men. We must surrender ourselves to the authority of Holy Scripture, for it can neither mislead nor be misled." "The question," says Barry, " 'Why Christ Himself did not write any book' is answered by Augustine in these remarkable words. 'His members gave out the knowledge which they had received through the dictation of the Head; whatever He willed us to read concerning His own words and acts, He bade them write, *as through they were His own very words.*' More unguardedly still, Augustine teaches that we see in the Gospels the very Hand of the Lord which He wore in His own Body. . . . There are no contradictions of each other's writings in the Books of the Four Evangelists. 'We must demonstrate that the Four Sacred writers are not at variance with each other. For our opponents . . . frequently maintain that discrepancies are found in the Evangelists'. . . . Freely do I admit to you, my friend, that I have learnt to ascribe to those Books which are of Canonical rank, and only to them, such reverence and honour, that I firmly believe that no single error due to the author is found in any one of them. And when I am confronted in these Books with anything that seems to be at variance with truth, I do not hesitate to put it down either to the use of an incorrect text, or to the failure of a commentator rightly to explain the words, or to my own mistaken understanding of the passage" (Barry, op. cit., pp. 140ff).

Augustine went further than a simple belief in an inerrant Bible. He argued strongly about the consequences of undermining that viewpoint. In one of his letters to Jerome, he said that once you admit a single error in the Bible you open the door to a floodtide of unbelief.

For it seems to me that most disastrous consequences must follow upon our believing that anything false is found in the sacred books: that is to say, that the men by whom the Scripture has been given to us, and committed to writing, did put down in these books anything false. It is one question whether it may be at any time the duty of a good man to deceive, but it is another question whether it can have been the duty of a writer of Holy Scripture to deceive: nay, it is not another question—it is no question at all. For if you once admit into such a high sanctuary of authority one false statement as made in the way of duty, there will not be left a single sentence of those books which, if appearing to any one difficult in practice or hard to believe, may not by the same fatal rule be explained away, as a statement in which, intentionally, and under a sense of duty, the author declared what was not true. . . .

For my part, I would devote all the strength which the Lord grants me, to show that every one of those texts which are wont to be quoted in defence of the expediency of falsehood ought to be otherwise understood, in order that everywhere the sure truth of these passages themselves may be consistently maintained. For as statements adduced in evidence must not be false, neither ought they to favour falsehood. This, however, I leave to your own judgment. For if you apply more thorough attention to the passage, perhaps you will see it much more readily than I have done. To this more careful study that piety will move you, by which you discern that the authority of the divine Scriptures becomes unsettled (so that every one may believe what he wishes, and reject what he does not wish) if this be once admitted, that the men by whom these things have been delivered unto us, could in their writings state some things which were not true, from considerations of duty; unless, perchance, you propose to furnish us with certain rules by which we may know when a falsehood might or might not become a duty. If this can be done, I beg you to set forth these rules with reasonings which may be neither equivocal nor precarious (A Select Library of the Nicene and Post-Nicene Fathers of the Christian Church, First Series, Vol. I, [New York: The Christian Literature Company, 1892], pp. 252-53).[24]

Surely I should give Professor Rogers the benefit of the

doubt and assume that his statement about Augustine was made in ignorance. But it is no longer possible for him to be in doubt. Augustine was saying that *all* of Scripture is without error. And it was he who advocated the idea that once an error is found, you open the door wide to many errors and lose your authority. This position, laughed at by Dr. Rogers in the case of B. B. Warfield, was not the invention of either B. B. Warfield or Charles Hodge. It goes back at least to Augustine. And that is almost a millennium and a half before Drs. Warfield and Hodge addressed the question.

John Calvin

In the case of John Calvin, Jack Rogers chose ambiguous statements from his writings so as to make it appear that he did not hold to inerrancy. Dr. Rogers indicates that he read *The Battle for the Bible*. In that book I quoted generously from the doctoral dissertation, *The Knowledge of God in Calvin's Theology* by Edward A. Dowey, Jr. Dr. Dowey supplied abundant evidence to show that Calvin believed in an inerrant Bible. He went on to suggest that dictation might have been the view of John Calvin so far as the divine method of inditing Scripture is concerned. Professor Rogers makes no reference to this Columbia University dissertation written by a Presbyterian. I cannot doubt that this failure to do so is evidence that he is unable to answer Dr. Dowey. So he merely overlooks him. Here are several quotes from Dr. Dowey to refresh the reader's mind on the subject:

> To Calvin the theologian an error in Scripture is unthinkable. If he [Calvin] betrays his position at all, it is apparently in assuming *a priori* that no errors can be allowed to reflect upon the inerrancy of the original documents. Here are Calvin's own words: "For if we consider how slippery is the human mind . . . how prone to all kinds of error . . . we perceive how necessary is such a repository of heavenly doctrine, that it will neither perish by forgetfulness, nor vanish in error, nor be corrupted by the audacity of men." . . . When he does admit an undeniable error of grammar or of fact, without exception he attributes it to copyists, never to the inspired writer. . . . There is no hint anywhere in Calvin's writings that the original text contained any flaws at all.[25]

This judgment is particularly significant coming from an

analyst who was himself uncommitted to biblical inerrancy. Dr. Dowey was a prime mover in drawing up the revised Confession of 1967 for the Presbyterian Church UPUSA. So we see in the case of John Calvin that Dr. Rogers makes a fallacious claim—that Calvin specifically denied that the Bible should be looked to as trustworthy in matters of science. Indeed John Calvin never referred to the Bible as a scientific textbook, but neither did he believe that the Bible contained scientific error. Thus whenever the Bible speaks about matters having to do with science, it does not tell us what is not true.

Samuel Rutherford

Dr. Rogers claims that Samuel Rutherford also denied that the Bible should be looked to as an authority in matters of science. And since he was one of the leading lights in the construction of the Westminster Confession of Faith, Rogers goes on to conclude that the Confession does not stand for inerrancy. This is a *non sequitur* if for no other reason than that once again Jack Rogers makes an unwarranted deduction: because Samuel Rutherford did not regard the Bible as an authority on scientific matters this meant he believed there were errors in the Bible. By no means does this follow. For an understanding of Samuel Rutherford we need to backtrack to the days of Charles Augustus Briggs who was one of the leading opponents of B. B. Warfield and Charles Hodge back in the 1890s. He wrote a book *Whither* in which he argued just as Jack Rogers argues that the framers of the Westminster Confession of Faith did not write inerrancy into the Confession. Dr. Briggs used all his skills to show that the leading lights of the Westminster Assembly did not believe in an inerrant Bible. He did not have to wait long for an answer.

B. B. Warfield wrote a response to Charles Briggs, titled "The Doctrine of Inspiration of the Westminster Divines." This, along with five other essays, was printed in a volume titled *The Westminster Assembly and Its Work*. Dr. Briggs, in his work, tried to show that a number of leading Westminster divines did not believe in inerrancy. Dr. Rogers uses Samuel Rutherford as his prime example because he was one of the leading lights of the Assembly. But his case, as well as the case put together by Dr. Briggs, falls to the ground under the capable onslaught of B. B. Warfield. It so happens that Dr. Warfield cut the ground beneath Dr. Briggs's feet. Had Dr. Rogers acquainted himself thoroughly with the work of B. B. Warfield he could never say that the views of Samuel Rutherford show he did not believe in inerrancy.

At one time Samuel Rutherford engaged in a disputation with John Goodwin who wrote things he disapproved of. Dr. Briggs so managed his selective quotations that he concluded Samuel Rutherford did not believe in inerrancy. But B. B. Warfield supplied sufficient evidences to show that this was not so. Samuel Rutherford surely did not hold that the Bible was a textbook on science, and he did not think the Word of God was an authority in matters of science any more than I do. But this did not mean that he thought there were errors in the Bible when it spoke about scientific matters. B. B. Warfield made that plain as we shall now see:

(Rutherford) urges that Goodwin's argument "makes as much against Christ, and the Apostles, as against us," for they too had but copies of the Old Testament, the scribes and translators of which were "then [no] more then now, immediately inspired Prophets," and were consequently liable to error, so that "if ye remove an unerring providence, who doubts but men might adde . . . or subtract, and so vitiate the fountaine sense? and omit points, change consonants, which in the Hebrew and Greek, both might quite alter the sense?" Yet both Christ and the apostles appeal to the Scriptures freely, with such phrases as "as David saith" and the like, staking their trustworthiness on the true transmission. Nor will he allow the argument that it is the inerrancy of the quoters, not of the text quoted, which is our safeguard in such cases. This, he says, presumes "that Christ and the Apostles might, and did finde errours, and misprintings even in written [i.e. manuscript] Scripture, which might reduce the Church in after ages to an invincible ignorance in matters of faith, and yet they gave no notice of the Church thereof" (p. 367).

To Rutherford, therefore, all the Scriptures, whether in matters fundamental or not, were written by God (p. 373); he quotes them with the formula, "The Holy Ghost saith" (pp. 353, 354 bis); he declares that the writers of the New Testament were "immediately inspired" (p. 368), a phrase of quite technical and unmistakable meaning; represents it as the part of an apostate to deny "all the Scriptures to be the word of God" (p. 349); and looks upon them as written under an influence which preserved

them from error and mistake (pp. 362, 366, etc.), and as constitut-
ing a more sure word than an immediate oracle from heaven (p.
193). In the immediately preceding words to those which Dr.
Briggs extracts, he declares that "The Scripture resolves our faith
on, *Thus saith the Lord,*" which is "the only authoritie that all the
Prophets alledge, and *Paul*"; and adds that, if it were so as Mr.
Goodwin averred, "all our certainty of faith" would be gone;
wherefore he praises God that "we have βεβαιότερον λόγον *a
more sure word or Prophesie,* surer then that which was heard
on the Mount for our direction, and the establishing of our
faithe."[11]

It is an interesting indication of the universality of high views of
inspiration, that John Goodwin, Rutherford's adversary in this
treatise, himself held them. So far as the points we are here interested in are concerned, indeed, the dispute was little more than
a logomachy, since Rutherford and his friends admitted that the
providential preservation of Scripture is not so perfect but that
some errors have found their way into the several copies, and that
the translations are only in a derived sense the word of God, and
only so far forth as they truly represent the originals; while Goodwin was ready to allow that God's providence is active in preserving the manuscript transmission substantially pure, and that the
truth of God is adequately conveyed in any good translation. In
Goodwin's reply to his assailants it is made abundantly apparent
that he, too, believed in the inerrancy of the autographs, his objection to calling copies and translations the word of God, in every
sense, turning just on this—that no one extant copy or translation
is errorlessly the word of God.[26]

Thus we may see from the research and learning of B. B.
Warfield that Samuel Rutherford did hold to an inerrant Scrip-
ture and that included matters having to do with science. Dr.
Rogers is incorrect again. That brings us to Herman Bavinck.

Herman Bavinck

In the case of Herman Bavinck, Dr. Rogers quotes him as follows:

The writers of Holy Scripture probably knew no more than their
contemporaries in all of these sciences, geology, zoology,
physiology, medicine, etc. And it was not necessary either. For
Holy Scripture uses the language of daily experience which is
always true and remains so. If the Scripture had in place of it used
the language of the school and had spoken with scientific exact-

ness, it would have stood in the way of its own authority.

Later on he quotes Bavinck as saying:

> The real object to which the Holy Spirit gives witness in the hearts of the believers is no other than the *divinitas* of the truth, poured out on us in Christ. Historical, chronological, and geographical data are never in themselves, the object of the witness of the Holy Spirit.[27]

So it is from quotations like this that Dr. Rogers concludes Bavinck did not hold to inerrancy in matters having to do with science. But these quotations prove nothing of the sort. The professor would have been better advised to inquire whether Herman Bavinck disclosed what his view of Scripture was. And he did this indeed.

I asked the Reverend Doctor Jerome De Jong of the Faith Reformed Church in South Holland, Illinois, about Herman Bavinck. He has expertise in this field and reads the Dutch language as only a Dutchman can. His reply was very informative. Dr. Bavinck did make a statement about his view of the Bible. And all other statements must be understood within the context of his belief in inerrancy. He wrote:

> But like the human in Christ, no matter how weak and lowly, yet free from sin, so also is the Scripture "conceived without error." Human in all parts yet also totally divine.[28]

Dr. Rogers' fourth illustration falls to the ground. Once again, while it may be true that Herman Bavinck believed the Bible should not be looked to as an authority in matters of science, he was not saying there are errors in Scripture about things pertaining to science. He held to an inerrant Scripture, and that included matters scientific as well as theological or historical.

I could understand Dr. Rogers if he were to say that the church through the ages believed in an inerrant Scripture but that he himself does not now do so. But to assert that inerrancy was not the view historically held by the church in scientific and historical details is to do violence to the facts. He has merely bypassed the testimony of even the Roman Catholic Church which, as I showed in *The Battle for the Bible,* holds tenaciously to an inerrant Scripture and that in matters historical and scientific as well.

Dr. Rogers has also bypassed the witness of the American Lutheran Church, the Lutheran Church-Missouri Synod, and the Wisconsin Evangelical Lutheran Synod. He has bypassed the New Hampshire Confession of Faith, and the witness of scholars like George Duncan Barry (*The Inspiration and Authority of Holy Scripture*) who himself did not believe in errancy, but who wrote that the witness of the church for the five centuries after Christ was in favor of an infallible or inerrant Scripture.

Fuller and the Reformed Tradition

Anyone who reads *Biblical Authority* will come away from it with the distinct impression that Fuller Seminary's approach to the inerrancy of the Bible is thought of almost without exception in terms of the Reformed tradition, the Westminster Confession of Faith, and the Princeton theology. This is tragic because it overlooks the contribution of other protestant groups and also that of the Catholic Church, not to mention Eastern and Russian Orthodoxy. If it has made the Princeton theology so central to its position, Fuller Seminary has become parochial. The reader should note too that in *The Debate about the Bible,* the author, Stephen T. Davis, is also a Presbyterian and he treats the whole subject within the context of the Princeton theology.

Jack Rogers makes the assertion that "the false equation of the theory of inerrancy with the position of the Westminster Confession was never repudiated."[29] This is a provocative conclusion first because Rogers calls it a "false equation." By this he means that the Westminster Confession did not embrace inerrancy but only trustworthiness having to do with matters of faith and practice. This is amazing for the following reasons. First, the so-called Princeton theology did not have its beginnings with Drs. Hodge and Warfield. It began with François Turretin whose *Institutio* was used as a standard text for systematic theology until Charles Hodge's *Systematic Theology* made its appearance. The claim of Charles Briggs that Turretin's book had become the theological textbook and that "the Westminster Divines were ignored" may have an element of truth in it, but it overlooks the reason why this was the case. The Westminster divines simply did not produce a systematic theology that was in any way comparable with that of Turretin. And it may be added that when Charles Hodge's *Systematic Theology* replaced the *Institutio* of Turretin it occupied such a singular place in the academic world that it is still being sold and read by many people today. Professor Briggs was actually claiming that the theology of François Turretin was not in agreement with that of the Westminster divines. And he never made a case for that theory. All that Dr. Rogers did was to rehash the discredited claims of Charles Briggs and that too upon a much more slender scholarly basis.

One comes away from the thesis of Jack Rogers (and that of David Hubbard) with the distinct impression that the Princeton theology was responsible for the rise of the biblical inerrancy school of thought in the United Sates. The only trouble with that evaluation is that it misreads the situation. The Princeton divines did have a powerful influence, but it was not an influence which determined the direction of other equally or more powerful denominations in the United States. Southern Baptists, for example, paid little attention to Messrs. Warfield and Hodge. The Lutherans hardly knew of their existence. In fact, the Lutheran Church-Missouri Synod, which was of German background, felt that Reformed Theology was a threat to its own foundation and heritage. And rightly so, for some of the German Lutherans were influenced by the Reformed tradition. But it was European, not American, Reformed theology that endangered German Lutherans.

Moreover the Episcopal Church and the Methodist bodies had little in common with the Princeton theology and its leaders. It is doubtful that Methodism was in any measure indebted to Princeton for its theological convictions. The Catholic and Orthodox communions were unaware of Princeton, but they had one thing in common with Princeton: they held to biblical inerrancy as they did before, during, and after the Reformation.

If one is to believe Dr. Rogers, then it must be said that François Turretin, Charles Hodge, B. B. Warfield, the General Assembly of the Presbyterian Church over a long period of time, and untold hundreds of thousands of Presbyterians, misunderstood John Calvin and the Westminster Confession of Faith. These people, however, were not the ones who misunderstood the situation. The challenge to biblical inerrancy came with the rise of the historical-critical method in the last two centuries. And the chief opponents of biblical inerrancy at all times have been those who did not wish to believe the Bible. Let it not be supposed that the real issue in the inerrancy struggle has to do with minutiae of Scripture—matters of the cosmos, chronology, and science. Whoever reads the Westminster divines, for example, will not find they questioned the historicity of Adam and Eve, or thought there were two Isaiahs, or said that Daniel was composed in 168 B.C., or that Paul did not write Ephesians or the Pastorals, and that there was no virgin birth and no bodily resurrection of Jesus from the dead. It was the sort of people who embraced these departures from the obvious interpretations of Scripture who were at the heart of the struggle over inerrancy. And Dr. Rogers and Fuller Theological Seminary are deeply involved in a departure from some things about which Scripture is plain, and that departure is becoming increasingly obvious—as we shall presently show.

David Hubbard

The first and the last chapters of *Biblical Authority* were written by Fuller Seminary paid employees. The first chapter, (for Paul Rees' contribution was a Foreword) was written by Jack Rogers, and I have already discussed that. The last chapter was written by President David Hubbard. It is expected that the president of an institution do all in his power to protect and shore up the standing of the school he represents. In Dr. Hubbard's chapter we find a potpourri of conflicting data, an *ad hominem* appeal for peace rather than purity, and an attempt to identify himself and his institution with evangelicalism. His chapter is titled: "The Current Tensions: Is There a Way Out?" He presumes there is a way out. This emerges clearly despite the rhetorical verbiage. The way out is to forget inerrancy as it applies to "every detail of every kind of statement of Scripture"[30] and to scrap the mentality that dares to suggest that the existence of a proved error places one on a slide that insures a further diminution of biblical authority. He speaks quite feelingly of people who, threatened by this intolerant mentality have "felt forced either to give up their system of belief or to give up their sense of intellectual integrity."[31] He says that "a collapse of belief in that definition of inerrancy (literal inerrancy) may lead to a collapse of trust in the gospel itself."[32] The real question is whether inerrancy or the view represented by Dr. Hubbard and Fuller Seminary leads to the dismal results he forecasts. I think it can be established that the view of Fuller Seminary will result in the very disasters he posited as the outcome for those who believe in enerrancy. But first of all, it will be profitable to take a look at some of the arguments adduced by Dr. Hubbard in his essay.

Dr. Hubbard is correct in his statement that it was in the seventeenth century "for the first time, theological arguments began to focus on the inerrancy of Scripture as well as its sufficiency and clarity."[33] In *The Battle for the Bible* I made the assertion that each age has had to face and deal with different theological problems. The early church faced the christological problem having to do with the person of the preincarnate and the incarnate Jesus. The outcome influenced the church to this moment. Jesus was acknowledged as the Second Person of the Trinity, the eternal Son who was from everlasting to everlasting. There was no time when He did not exist. It was also perceived that the incarnate Christ was one person with two natures, a perfectly human nature and a divine nature, and they were not mingled or fused.

The anthropological controversy dealt with the nature of man and involved Augustine and Pelagius. Was man sick or was he dead? Pelagianism held the former, Augustinianism the latter. Later, in the time of the Reformation, the doctrinal issue of the moment was justification by faith alone versus justification by faith plus good works. The threefold declaration of that age was *sola Scriptura, sola gratia, sola fide*. But in our age the great theological question under debate has to do with the Word of God written, its nature and its inerrancy. The beginnings of the inerrancy battle do go back to the eighteenth century, but it was in the nineteenth century that the full flower of the new disease became apparent and had to be coped with. A pattern that existed in all the previous controversies appeared again. This is an important factor in any consideration of inerrancy.

Theologically speaking, whenever a controversy arose, it did so usually because the people of God had not previously formulated clear-cut apologetic statements about it. Normally, no need existed to develop an apologetic about questions no one was asking. The rise of higher criticism had for its central thrust an innate antipathy toward unquestioned confidence in the Bible. As we shall see in another chapter, the heart of the controversy centered on the issue raised by Johann Semler, that it was theological heresy to say that Scripture and the Word of God are synonymous. Throughout its history the church had believed that Scripture and the Word of God meant the same thing. When one spoke of the Scripture he did so with the assumption that he was talking about the Word of God. The controversy, then, was to be fought over the question whether one had to search for the Word of God in Scripture or whether the Word of God was equivalent to the Scripture, together with all the implications of this theological affirmation.

Second, Dr. Hubbard says that when the Bible was called into question, those who sought to retain plenary inspiration did so by insisting "that if the inspiration of any part of the Bible were in doubt, the inspiration of the whole would be put in question." Then he says, "In the Calvinist wing of the church, Francis Turretin took a similar approach."[34] What is in some ways humorous is that Dr. Hubbard is saying implicitly that before this happened Christians believed in plenary inspiration and consequently in a fully trustworthy Bible. Certainly no Christian church that I know of in the 1800 years after Pentecost ever wrote a confession of faith or decreed in a church council of any kind that the Bible has errors in it. The Westminster Confession of Faith nowhere suggests that the Bible is errant. But let us make no mistake about the implications which flow from statements made by Drs. Rogers and Hubbard as well as by that earlier spokesman for errancy, Charles Augustus Briggs: they are saying that their belief that the Westminster Confession limited inerrancy to matters of faith and practice means the Confession is by implication admitting the presence of errors in the Bible. Surely if the church through the ages had said the Bible contains errors there would have been no need for the present controversy to arise since an errant Bible would have been nothing new. But the concept of an errant Bible against the backdrop of a trust in an inerrant Bible, which the church has promoted for centuries, was something new and did provoke the conflict.

Third, it is true, as Dr. Hubbard says that the defenders of inerrancy developed a fuller and more complete and detailed response in which they established the boundaries of the doctrine of Scripture. But they did not, at least for the reasons Dr. Hubbard seems to think, spend their time inferring "an inerrancy that extended to every detail of every kind of statement in Scripture."[35] What they did was this: they simply responded to the arguments advanced by the skeptics who sought in every way to prove that the Bible has errors in it. The chief reason why men like François Turretin, B. B. Warfield, Charles Hodge, and contemporary spokesmen deal with these so-called minor issues that do not directly pertain to salvatory matters is that the opponents keep dragging them up in order to show that the Bible cannot be trusted in all its parts. And we must remember that it is not the believers in inerrancy who proceed from there to the denial of other truths in Scripture that hit at vital elements of the Bible. Those who go on from the denial of matters having to do with history and science to larger and more significant deviations are those who began with the more simple denial of what appeared to be less important aspects and areas of the Word of God.

If Dr. Hubbard wants contemporary proof of this *modus operandi* all he needs to do is take a look at the article written by his fellow faculty member, William S. LaSor, in *Theology, News and Notes*. In this article Dr. LaSor points out what he thinks to be classic problems in the Bible which cause him to reject inerrancy. And the sequel is equally interesting. Just because he did this his former colleague, Dr. Gleason L. Archer, of the Trinity Evangelical Divinity School, chose to answer Dr. LaSor by writing his own article to show that Dr. LaSor is incorrect in supposing that the problems to which he makes reference are insoluble. Dr. Archer's article is entitled "Alleged Errors and Discrepancies in the Original Manuscripts of the Bible." Dr. Archer would not have had to write such an article, were it not for the fact that Dr. LaSor was calling the truthfulness of the Bible into question about these matters. And this has been and always will be the chronological sequence. Men like B. B. Warfield formulated their statements and wrote their apologies for the truthfulness of the Bible in areas where salvation was not directly involved because they knew from experience that the people who raised these questions were also those who proceeded from there to disbelief in important matters. If Dr. Hubbard cannot see this, he is disregarding the incontrovertible fact that this same process is at work in the Fuller Seminary faculty right now and is getting worse each year.

Dr. Hubbard proclaims, and in his proclamation provides reassurance for the uninitiated, that:

> While we have rightly treasured every book, every verse, every line, every word of the sixty-six sacred documents, we have not always been eager to hear what those words mean. Sometimes it is our [sic] very doctrine of literalistic inerrancy that has gotten in our way. If every verse is equally God's Word, then may we not look for a special, even hidden, meaning in every verse?[36]

Here one would suppose that Dr. Hubbard is saying that he believes what he has written. Of course, it is true that a person can believe in inerrancy and have a hardness of heart and fail to hear and heed what Scripture teaches. But it is not at all difficult to say that those who deny inerrancy by that very denial do exactly what he is talking against. No one of evangelical persuasion has ever said that "every verse is equally the Word of God" in the way Dr. Hubbard intimates. In fact, there are statements in the Bible which are nothing more than a fabric of lies. When Scripture records what Satan has said, we understand that Satan is a liar from the beginning and the truth is not in him. We also know, however, that the statements attributed to Satan were said by Satan and that we have a reliable record of what he said. On this basis we must regard even Satan's words as part of the record contained in the Word of God. All of the Bible is the Word of God, although not all parts of the Bible are of equal value. But this does not mean that the portions that are of lesser value are therefore riddled with error.

At this juncture I wish to say that Dr. Hubbard's statement about rightly treasuring every book, every verse, every line, and every word of the Bible leaves us wondering. Let me illustrate what I mean. In the New Testament the Books of Ephesians, 1 and 2 Timothy, and Titus claim to have been written by the apostle Paul. At least one member of Fuller's faculty says that Paul did not write these books. If that is treasuring every word of the Bible, the performance is poor. If I can delete from Scripture all those verses which assent or imply Pauline authorship, there is no logical reason why I may not delete many other things as well, including substantive salvatory doctrines. Some of Paul Jewett's own colleagues say he was utterly and completely wrong in saying that the apostle Paul was mistaken in a theological matter.

President Hubbard says also that the Bible is the Word of God, but he can only mean that that word is both true and false. He asks the question: "What proof do we need to know whether the Bible is the Word of God? Nothing but the Spirit of God speaking to us in Scripture."[37] No one is trying to or should diminish the witness of the Holy Spirit to our hearts that this Bible is the Word of God. Dr. Hubbard's statement, however, leaves open a problem that neither he nor I nor anyone else can run away from. No one can say that the Holy Spirit does or would witness to some people that the Bible has errors in it and then witness to others that it has no errors in it. I take it that Dr. Hubbard is affirming his own conviction that the Holy Spirit has witnessed to him that the Bible has errors in it. Lest anyone think this is a harsh indictment, let me add that nowhere since the publication of *The Battle for the Bible* has Dr. Hubbard or the Fuller Seminary ever said that it still believes that the Bible is free from all error. They say opposite. And so do others as well, as we shall see.

The nub of the current problem is not whether the Holy Spirit witnesses to our spirits that the Bible is true. The nub of the problem is whether the Spirit has witnessed to those of us who believe in inerrancy or to those who deny inerrancy. One group or the other cannot have the true witness of the spirit. One group is wrong and the other right. Even Dr. Hubbard is more than clear in this. He is the one who stated from the beginning of the current discussion on inerrancy that the view I and others maintain is unbiblical. If the view entertained by The Evangelical Theological Society, and the members of the International Council on Biblical Inerrancy, as well as by Augustine, Calvin, Luther, Spurgeon, the Lutheran Church-Missouri Synod, and thousands of Christians through the ages, is unbiblical, then we must conclude that somehow we have failed to heed the witness of the Holy Spirit who is Truth. And since all of these teachers and denominations have affirmed their belief in inerrancy from the clear teaching of Christ and His apostles, they too must require this correction from those who have found that this belief is "unbiblical"!

But Dr. Hubbard still must tell us what he means by the phrase "the Word of God." We cannot be at all sure of what he means by this term. He certainly does not mean that the Word of God is free from all error. He can only mean that while the Bible may be the Word of God, one still must decide what is true and what is not true in the Bible. This becomes the choice of each individual apart from a belief in biblical inerrancy, and there would always be disagreement as to what is true and what is not true in the Bible. Dr. Hubbard in his own statement about the work of the Holy Spirit has stated: "One of his [the Holy Spirit's] tasks in redemptive history was to inspire the Scriptures—all (my italics) of them."[38] But what does inspiration mean if it does not involve reliability? For Dr. Hubbard and those who follow his viewpoint, inspiration becomes devalued to such a dubious status that it means nothing more than that some parts of the Bible are true and other parts are false. And Dr. Hubbard must sit upon the judge's bench and decide which is valid and which is not. For this awesome responsibility he must produce the credentials of inerrant judgment on his own part.

But Dr. Hubbard endeavors to show that present-day inerrantists do not define error correctly. He writes:

> Yet time and again in the arguments presented by those who purport [sic.] to follow the Hodge-Warfield position words like *error*, or *inerrancy*, or *infallibility* are defined by secular, twentieth-century standards, sometimes with an appeal to Webster's Dictionary for support.[39]

I can only suppose that Dr. Hubbard refers to my use of Webster's dictionary in *The Battle for the Bible*. The implication is that current dictionary definitions are not reliable. He says earlier in his chapter that twentieth-century standards of accuracy have been imposed on books that God was pleased to inspire in ancient Oriental contexts, with their very different standards of accuracy. Claims have been made about the meaning of the text without recourse to the ancient documents of Egypt, Mesopotamia, and Ugarit which provide part of the background for understanding both the Bible's meaning and its uniqueness. This may have been excusable a hundred years ago at the beginnings of archeological and epigraphical research; it certainly is not in the last quarter of our century.[40]

Of course the meaning of words and words themselves change. We do not use "charity" for "love" today. We teach Greek and Hebrew in evangelical seminaries to enable students to exegete the Scriptures, for the purpose of finding out what the words really mean. Curiously the liberal theological seminaries forget Hebrew and Greek and fill the minds of their students with psychology, sociology, group dynamics, and the cultivation of interpersonal relations. Dr. Hubbard starts by assuming, but not proving, that the standards of accuracy of ancient cultures were not at all similar to standards in the twentieth century. Probably this is true about some things and untrue about others. When it comes to the facts of history I am loath to suppose that the standards differed so much. When the Old Testament says that a certain king reigned a certain number of years, the Israelite concept of a mathematical meaning was hardly different from what is followed today. The Israelites were perfectly aware of the seasons of the year, and they knew (modern archeological research has demonstrated) how to maintain quite accurate standards of dating.

The ancients had standards for weights and measures. Undoubtedly these standards were not as precise as some of ours are today. But our scales in general use are not much more accurate than theirs. And a foot on a yardstick today is probably neither more or less accurate than a cubit among the ancients (even though the exact length of the cubit may have varied from one locality to another). Certainly the Egyptians, in the building of the pyramids, were amazingly exact in their measurements. The stones the Jews used in building the temple were all hewed out far from the site of the temple itself. Yet when they were assembled on the foundations laid, they proved to be perfectly accurate and fitted exactly into place when the temple stones were assembled. Moreover two and two made four in the ancient world as it does today. The sun dial of Hezekiah, too, was undoubtedly as accurate as the sun dials we use today.

When Dr. Hubbard defines *error* he does so as follows:

> *Error* theologically must mean that which leads us astray from the will of God or the knowledge of his truth.[41]

However, this confuses the whole issue we are dealing with. If Dr. Hubbard's statement is read carefully, the reader will see that he is talking about matters theological. He is not talking about more mundane matters such as science, history, the cosmos, etc. He deliberately limits error to things concerning the will of God and the knowledge of His truth (whatever that latter phrase may mean). In the sense that Dr. Hubbard is talking about error I do not find myself in disagreement. I do believe that whatever leads us astray from the will of God or the knowledge of His truth is error. But what do I do if the facts of the Bible are not true? What if the Bible says a king reigned for twenty years and he really reigned only five years? What if the Scripture says a half million men were involved in military action and modern critics declare it could only have been a few thousand? Or what if the present-day scholars assure us that Adam and Eve were not historical persons, nor really the first human pair ever created, but are to be understood as merely fictional representatives of the human race? How do we reconcile this with Scripture which plainly tells us of their personal conversations with God and about the children they raised in their home? Or in the case of the Book of Daniel, the text of which professes to have been written by Daniel himself about 535 B.C., how am I to deal with the claim of the rationalist critics who say it was written around 168 B.C.? Or again, how about the truth factor involved when non-inerrantists affirm that Paul did not write some of the New Testament epistles whose text claims to have been written by him? How am I to respond when the reductionist critics say the Book of Jonah is mere fiction whereas Jesus certifies it to be historical (Matt. 12:40-42)? What about the antisupernaturalists who deny the virgin birth which is clearly recorded in Scripture?

Dr. Hubbard needs to refine his definition of error. To most of us error means simply this: error is that which is not factual

or true, whether it be theological error, scientific error, cosmological error, chronological error, or numerical error. Even
if the Lord Jesus were to say two and two make eight, that
would be an error. And if it is impossible for a human being to
remain in the belly of a fish for three days and three nights,
even miraculously, and emerge alive, then the Book of Jonah
tells us that which is not true. This is the issue with which we
are dealing. This is the question we must face and respond to.
I must question the tenability of Dr. Hubbard's claim to
loyal adherence to the principle that "every part of Scripture is
God-given and, therefore, profitable,"[42] in the face of Fuller
Seminary's demonstrable stand that some things in the Bible
are not true. I do not for one moment believe that demonstrable error is "profitable." All things in the Bible can be *profitable* to us only if they do not deceive. Truth is of the essence in
the Bible. If "Biblical errancy is not an option for most evanglicals," why then has Fuller Seminary opted for it? Further proof
that it has in fact opted for errancy will be furnished shortly.
   In dealing with Dr. Hubbard's viewpoint, one more item
requires attention before passing on to other matters. At the
end of his chapter he mentions the doctrinal statements of a
number of organizations and rightly points out that they do
not always make specific reference to inerrancy. He does this
to leave the reader with the impression that the Fuller Seminary statement on Scripture is similar to that of others who
have been thought to be committed to inerrancy. In response
to this I can only add the footnote that most of the organizations which he refers to almost surely had assumed inerrancy
as their basis when they constructed their doctrinal platforms.
They failed to make it explicit only because the issue had not
been called in question [*given the visibility*] the way it now has.
Therefore the need for the kind of precision Dr. Hubbard argues against was not at that time thought to be essential. By
way of example, he says that the statement of the National
Association of Evangelicals "we believe the Bible to be the
inspired, the only infallible, authoritative word of God" is
worth noting because it uses the word "infallible" rather than
the word "inerrant." The founders of the NAE will be surprised to learn now that infallible and inerrant are two distinct words that have different meanings. I drew attention to

the words of Daniel Fuller when I wrote *The Battle for the Bible*. He himself conceded (although President Hubbard wishes to repudiate what his own publication published) in the *Fuller Theological Seminary Bulletin* (Vol. XVIII, No. 1, March 1968), "We assert the Bible's authority by the use of such words as *infallible, inerrant, true,* and *trustworthy*. There is no basic difference between these words. To say that the Bible is true is to assert its infallibility." Which of the two men are we to believe?

Perhaps his most intriguing comment pertains to the Moody Bible Institute. It so happens that Moody has stood for biblical inerrancy for almost a century. Dr. Hubbard has this to say:

> Perhaps more surprising is the fact that the center of the doctrinal stance of one of the great Bible schools of our land is on verbal inspiration, with no mention of inerrancy: "The Bible, including both the Old and New Testaments, is a divine revelation, the original autographs of which were verbally inspired by the Holy Spirit."[43]

Dr. Hubbard, of course, implies that the Moody statement's failure to mention the word inerrancy means that Moody Bible Institute is not committed to inerrancy. Nothing could be further from the truth. The Moody Bible Institute has *always* stood for biblical inerrancy; it does today. Its trustees are fully familiar with Dr. Hubbard's statement. They also know something by hard experience. Doctrinal statements never guarantee continuing belief in biblical inerrancy even if it is included in a doctrinal statement. Witness the example of Fuller Theological Seminary itself. It included the precise words "free from all error in the whole and in the part" as part of its original statement. But this did not preserve the institution from abandoning inerrancy. Moody does not have the word "inerrant" in the original statement, but it has preserved the firm adherence to inerrancy nonetheless. Just recently, according to my best information, the trustees of MBI have added a parenthesis affirming inerrancy in explicit terms in the wording of their doctrinal statement so that no one can take Dr. Hubbard's deduction seriously. Moody still holds to biblical inerrancy, and does so more firmly than ever.

So much for the Fuller book, *Biblical Authority*. The time has come for me to demonstrate that Fuller Seminary is now in worse shape theologically then it was when I wrote *The Battle for the Bible*. This may be a slightly inaccurate statement in the sense that the disease may have been there before, but it was not yet as visible then as it is today. In any event, I shall provide further explanations of materials alluded to in my earlier book and expand on the matter with information so explicit, you will recognize the fact that Fuller has not only departed from biblical inerrancy on matters of historical fact, or of science and the cosmos; it has also compromised or abrogated its revised statement which asserts belief in the infallibility or inerrancy of the Bible with respect to matters of faith and practice.

Daniel P. Fuller

I have already mentioned the case of Professor Daniel Fuller in *The Battle for the Bible*. There I drew attention to the fact that he asserted that the Bible consists of revelational and non-revelational materials. He claimed that non-revelational materials can have errors in them. More than a year after the publication of my book Dr. Fuller wrote an article entitled "I Was Just Thinking" which appeared in *Today's Christian*, a publication of the radio broadcast, "The Joyful Sound," which originated with Charles E. Fuller as "The Old Fashioned Revival Hour." Daniel Fuller is the president of the Fuller Evangelistic Association and the Director of "The Joyful Sound." He is professor of hermeneutics at Fuller Theological Seminary. He and Dr. Hubbard are apparently in disagreement about certain facts of the doctrine of biblical authority.

Dr. Hubbard, for example, does not approve the word "inerrancy" (as we have already seen), and thinks that the definitions found in twentieth-century dictionaries are not to be trusted. Dr. Fuller, on the other hand, said in his article just mentioned that "people have been understandably alarmed by the statement" made by Lindsell that he, Dan Fuller, does "not believe the Bible to be free from all error in the whole and in the part." Then Dr. Fuller stated: "I have always affirmed the complete inerrancy of the Bible."[44] Now that sounds excellent (even though it appears to clash with Hubbard's rejection of the term), but is it correct and do the facts support it? Before I discuss this and other matters connected with Professor Fuller's position one enlightening item should be mentioned. The Fuller Evangelistic Association has a doctrinal statement. It is the statement which was adopted by Fuller Theological Seminary some time ago. It does not differ from their early statement and has never yet been changed, that I know of. This statement explicitly affirms that the Bible is free from all error in the whole and in the part. Both Dr. Hubbard and Dr. Fuller are part of that organization. This means they are signing two different doctrinal statements, one of which affirms inerrancy and one which does not. We also know that Dr. Hubbard frankly disavows inerrancy and even declares this view to be "unbiblical." Yet as the speaker on "The Joyful Sound" he identifies himself with the doctrinal statement he has signed but apparently does not believe.

In the article mentioned above, Daniel Fuller agreed with an assertion I made, but which Dr. Hubbard has opposed. Dr. Fuller said: "If even one of its (i.e. the Bible's) statements could be in error, the truth of any of its statements becomes questionable." This too was the position of B. B. Warfield, but it is a position which Jack Rogers, David Hubbard, Stephen Davis, Clark Pinnock, and Bernard Ramm cannot fully subscribe to.

In Dr. Fuller's article he returns to the issues raised by his dictum on a discussion of the mustard seed statement of Jesus (Matt. 13:32)—a matter which I had discussed in my first book. And once again Dr. Fuller distinguishes between those things that are revelational and those that are not. Here is his statement:

> For example, Jesus called attention to the mustard seed, which "is the smallest of all seeds, but when it is grown it is the greatest of shrubs and becomes a tree . . ." (Matthew 13:32). None of Jesus' hearers need a revelation from God to know this. In making this statement Jesus was repeating the popular conception that the mustard seed was the smallest seed. None of us today need a revelation from God to know if mustard seeds are the smallest; botanical research is quite adequate to the task. But Jesus spoke of the smallness of the mustard seed, not to teach us botany, but to provide us with an illustration of the fact, known only by revelation, that the kingdom of God would have a very widespread influence, even though it started from very small beginnings. So the illustration of the mustard seed greatly helps the communica-

tion of revelational truth. But the illustration itself is a matter of common knowledge and not revelational.[45]

The substance of Dr. Fuller's argument is this: Jesus said something that we now know is not true. Modern botanical experts tell us that the mustard seed is not actually the smallest seed known to modern science. Then he adds:

Jesus was nevertheless guilty of no error in affirming that it was, because his intention was not to teach botany but to reveal things God wants us to know, so that we can be saved. I affirm that the Bible is totally without error. All of its writers perfectly fulfilled the Bible's purpose of setting forth the whole counsel of God, because each one was always protected from error in that he spoke or wrote under the verbal inspiration of the Holy Spirit.[46]

Note carefully Dr. Fuller's assertion that "Jesus was nevertheless guilty of no error in *affirming*" (my italics) that the mustard seed is the smallest of all seeds. Now the word "affirm" means "to state positively with confidence: declare as a fact." Daniel Fuller said Jesus did this. And He was wrong, yet it is not an error! He then said of me: "For him, the Bible would be in error if any of its statements—in the original documents, which no longer exist (and where Dr. Fuller got this knowledge I do not know)—did not fit the facts." That is true but obviously he does not accept it. Anything that is not intrinsic to the author's intention may then be full of mistakes and yet there would not be mistakes after all. This is Dr. Fuller's line of reasoning. And whoever wishes to accept that kind of logic is at liberty to do so, but in the process he turns things upside down. In any event, Dr. Fuller says he believes and always has believed in inerrancy, but at the same time he says there are errors in the Bible. I regret Dr. Fuller's notion that I affirmed that Jesus said the mustard seed is the smallest of all seeds. I did nothing of the kind. All that Jesus said was that this was the smallest of the seeds cultivated by his learners in their gardens or fields—which was the context in which He was speaking. No one can convict that statement of error.

Paul King Jewett

I mentioned Dr. Jewett earlier in connection with *Theology, News and Notes,* in which the report appeared about the investigation of Dr. Jewett and the verdict which was rendered. I am referring to him now in another connection. This relates to his classroom teaching and his view of biblical inerrancy.

If anyone wants further confirmation of Dr. Jewett's departure from an inerrant Bible he can find it in his mimeographed paper distributed as a Bulletin in Systematic Theology I. It is titled *The Doctrine of Scripture: The Divine Word in Human Words.* Dr. Jewett is plain enough in this essay. He says: "Of course the Holy Spirit, who inspired Stephen (Acts 6:10), *could* have kept him from such a slip of memory just as he *could* have recalled to Paul's memory the names of all whom he had baptized at Corinth (I Cor. 1:16). But *did* he? That is the question. Yet it is hardly a serious question. It would seem obvious that, as Calvin would say, the Holy Spirit is not *concerned* with such matters. Common sense—which has its place in theology— teaches us this much."[47] So said Dr. Jewett who at one time accepted inerrancy.

James Daane

Dr. James Daane is a Fuller professor who comes from the Christian Reformed Church, which has its headquarters in Grand Rapids, Michigan. This denomination is facing the same infiltration of an aberrant view of the Bible, not only in its American institutions, but also in Holland where Professors Berkouwer and Kuitert have exercised a tremendous influence to the discredit of biblical inerrancy. I shall be speaking of them in another chapter, but wish to mention Dr. Daane of Fuller as a vocal opponent of inerrancy. He is one of the editors of the *Reformed Journal* and is generally associated with the *avant garde* wing of his denomination.

In May of 1977 a group of so-called young evangelicals met in Chicago and drew up a document titled "The Chicago Call: An Appeal to Evangelicals." Forty-six professors, pastors, editors, and lay leaders attended the meeting. The *Religious News Service* reported that the Call was expected to "stir a good deal of discussion and controversy in the evangelical community." The report indicated that "two sections of the statement were particularly troublesome to the drafters—those dealing with the sacraments and the Scriptures." The RNS report went on to speak of the discussion on the Scriptures.

The section on the Scriptures also drew intense discussion. Dr.

James Daane, professor of theology and ministry at Fuller Theological Seminary, Pasadena, California, originally proposed that the section be worded in such a way as to repudiate the position of Dr. Harold Lindsell, editor of *Christianity Today*. Under this proposal, the statement would have affirmed the authority of the Scriptures "in any matter of salvation, doctrine and life," but not in other matters.

That aim was eventually given up when others in the discussion objected to a statement that would rule out a particular group. The section on the Bible, as approved, says: "We deplore our tendency to individualistic interpretation of Scripture. This undercuts the objective character of Biblical truth and denies the guidance of the Holy Spirit among His people through the ages."

Therefore, it continues, "we affirm that the Bible is to be interpreted in accordance with the best insights of historical and literary studies, under the guidance of the Holy Spirit, with respect for the historic understanding of the church. We affirm that the Scriptures, as the infallible Word of God, are the basis of authority in the church. We acknowledge that God uses the Scriptures to judge and to purify His Body. The church, illumined and guided by the Holy Spirit, must in every age interpret, proclaim and live out the Scriptures."[48]

Dr. Daane did not accomplish his objective. The exact opposite occurred, because the Chicago Call statement on the Bible is stronger than the Fuller Theological Seminary statement. The Call says that "we affirm the Scriptures as the infallible Word of God." Fuller says the Scriptures are the Word of God, but leaves out the qualifying and important word "infallible." They use infallible only in connection with faith and practice. All of this indicates that Dr. Daane not only does not believe in inerrancy but he also waged a campaign to have the Fuller viewpoint expressed in the declaration. Since he does not believe the Bible to be the infallible Word of God one wonders why he even permitted his name to be attached to the Call, since it included an important doctrinal statement he does not accept. This raises the age-old question of integrity and of this more will be said later. Dr. Daane's efforts simply reinforce the allegation I made in *The Battle for the Bible* that Fuller Seminary no longer holds to biblical inerrancy.

Ray Sherman Anderson

Ray Anderson is a graduate of Fuller Theological Seminary.

For some years he was a minister in the Evangelical Free Church of America serving a parish in Southern California. He left the pastorate to study under T. F. Torrance at Edinburgh in Scotland. When he had earned the Ph.D. degree he returned to America and became a member of the Westmont College faculty. He was a vigorous, vocal, and popular teacher. When the time came for him to be considered for tenure, it was not granted. Proceedings of this sort are generally masked in secrecy for good reasons, not the least of which is to protect both the individual involved and the institution itself. But it can be fairly inferred that theology was high on the list of the proceedings and there was dissatisfaction with what was contained in his doctoral dissertation on the part of the department in which he served.

Dr. Anderson's dissertation was published in book form by Eerdmans under the title *Historical Transcendence and the Reality of God*. The subject was one of import to T. F. Torrance who, by the way, has lectured at Fuller Seminary. Dr. Torrance goes beyond Karl Barth on the matter of transcendence. Dr. Barth, according to James D. Spiceland, who is on the philosophy faculty of Western Kentucky University, says "we are not capable of conceiving God, going on to say that God is not only invisible to the physical eye of man, he is also invisible to the spiritual eye." He added that "The Scottish theologian T. F. Torrance goes even farther than Barth in this." According to Professor Spiceland, T. F. Torrance says that "thinking or speaking of God is just impossible." This was the man under whom Dr. Anderson wrote his dissertation, and the subject had to do with this very topic.

Dr. Anderson's book was reviewed in the pages of *Christianity Today*. That review will be found in the Appendix. The review was written by Bruce Demarest, associate professor of systematic theology at the Conservative Baptist Seminary in Denver, Colorado. He said of this book:

> Having thus dismissed the traditional Christian conception of transcendence based on ontological knowledge of God, the author advances the alternative idea of "historical transcendence"—a concept rooted in the seminal thought of Bonhoeffer. . . .[49]

Professor Demarest raised the most serious question about Dr.

Anderson's fidelity to the thought world of Scripture. He said: "One suspects that operating within the post-Kantian tradition of skepticism in relation to the objective knowledge of the absolute God, the author himself has appropriated a philosophical scheme essentially alien to the thought world of the Scripture."

The reviewer concluded that Dr. Anderson's orientation is generally Barthian, and he "considers God to be 'wholly Other' and therefore both unthinkable and unknowable by the creature as thinking subject." But Professor Demarest was not the only reviewer to think Dr. Anderson's position to be non-traditional.

David E. Pfeifer reviewed Professor Anderson's book in the *Journal of the American Academy of Religion*. He said this about the work:

> The general thesis is that a return to historical transcendence (God's otherness) is required to restore our apprehension of the reality of God lost through the acceptance of immanent transcendence (God's non-separateness). Historical transcendence is understood through the study of the "inner logic" of the Incarnation. And that leads to lived transcendence. In lived transcendence "the reality of God impinges upon the world through the historical existence of the man who lives in the Spirit of God" (p. 229).
>
> Although kenosis (the idea Christ restricted his use of the divine attributes) is used as "a 'way into' the inner logic of the Incarnation" (p. 150), Anderson does not accept the usual kenotic position. His position seems to grow out of a quotation from R. G. Smith's *Collected Papers:* "The answer which is contained in the interior logic of the incarnation is that God is disclosed in and through the ordinary situations of our life and nowhere else. We encounter transcendence not as a theory of understanding the universe but as the very nature of our encounter with things and persons in this world" (p. 107).
>
> Anderson presents a challenge to both the Incarnationist and usual kenotic Christologies. His talk of confrontation and commitment make him resemble a Kierkegardian existentialist, although he does not so label himself.[50]

These quotations give us a rough idea of the opinions of the two reviewers of Dr. Anderson's book. They also inform us what the reason was for the refusal of Westmont to grant him tenure. And now he is a professor at Fuller Seminary.

Charles Kraft

Dr. Kraft is a professor in the School of World Mission at Fuller Seminary. Two illustrations will suffice to show the continuing Fuller drift away from the authority of Scripture. Dr. Kraft has been deeply involved in anthropological and sociological studies in relation to missions. Dr. J. Robertson McQuilkin, a missionary for many years in Japan and now president of Columbia Bible College, wrote an essay titled "The Behavioural Sciences under the Authority of Scripture." His burden included demonstrating that in some cases people who profess to be evangelical place the behavioral sciences over Scripture rather than under Scripture, with the result they undermine the Word of God. He made specific reference to Professor Kraft, who spoke to a group of mission leaders gathered in Marseilles, France. It was a consultation about reaching Muslims. Then Dr. McQuilkin quoted Dr. Kraft:

> What is necessary to faith, apparently, is some feeling of need or inadequacy that stimulates a person to turn in faith to God. (Likewise) meaninglessness in American culture too is a manifestation of the sin problem, the alienation problem. How do we get people who experience meaninglessness to feel guilty so they can repent and be saved? Well, what I'm saying is , we don't have to. God can save directly. . . .
>
> Similarly, he [the Muslim] doesn't have to be convinced of the death of Christ. He simply has to pledge allegiance and faith to God who worked out the details to make it possible for his faith response to take the place of a righteousness requirement. He may not, in fact, be able to believe in the death of Christ, especially if he knowingly places his faith in God through Christ, for within his frame of reference, if Christ died, God was defeated by men, and this, of course, is unthinkable. . . . Thus, if he is required to accept a historical and doctrinal truth as a precondition to salvation, he may reject that salvation for a reason which should be very intelligible, even to us outsiders. . . . He doesn't have to know the details, for knowledge does not save. He simply has to pledge in faith as much of himself as he can to as much of God as he understands, even the Muslim "Allah". . . . The concept of the Trinity can also in most cases be avoided. . . . It is interesting and discouraging to look back at the development of the Trinity, and to find out that this is a development that comes out of the appli-

cation of Greek ways of thinking to the Scripture. . . . The deity of Christ is a more difficult concept to handle. Since this doctrine is intimately related, in the informed Muslim's mind, to the doctrine of the Trinity on the one hand and the relative position of Christ and Mohammed on the other, we again cannot answer, "Yes" if he asks us if we believe in the doctrine. But we assuredly cannot answer "No" either. . . . The principle here is that a fraction of the truth well communicated is preferable to the antagonism engendered when a whole truth is totally rejected. . . . But we can, I believe, without denying Christ as we know him, start with his Arabic concept of the Judeo-Christian God as the proper object of saving faith.[51]

From Dr. Kraft's presentation Dr. McQuilkin concluded that

Kraft goes on to quote several scholars, who are considered evangelical, to the effect that people can be saved without a knowledge of Christ. Although Kraft's emphasis is on the initial approach to the Muslim and as such might be justified, he clearly indicates that a Muslim can be saved without a conviction of sin and without accepting the death of Christ as historically true. It would almost seem that for a Muslim to be saved all he would need was a consciousness of inadequacy and a sincere calling upon Allah to save him.

Although this is not the position commonly held by evangelical cultural anthropologists, it does illustrate graphically what happens when Scripture is not dynamically, functionally, pervasively in control.[52]

Dr. Kraft was involved in the Pan African Christian Leadership Assembly which met in Kenya in December of 1976. He conducted a workshop on the indigenous church and dropped a bombshell about polygamy. The writer of the report said:

Dr. Charles Kraft . . . regretted that missionaries "westernized African ways." He questioned the missionary/church position on polygamy, and in doing so released a bomb in the audience. He mentioned the Idi culture in Nigeria in which polygamy is given high respect and is a sign of leadership. He suggested that the church should start where the people are. Kraft asked, "Why did God take 2,000 years to eliminate polygamy?" He wondered why we should expect to eliminate it right away when we evangelize a foreign culture. Kraft did not specify whether he was talking of converted polygamists or whether a Christian convert could be allowed to become a polygamist in order to become a leader in the church. This lack of explanation confused and upset the participants and there were several responses from them suggesting that it is unbiblical for a polygamist to be a leader.

A black African layman pointed out wisely to Kraft that there is "a danger of having Westerners interpreting what is happening in Africa." To this, Kraft answered that only the Holy Spirit can interpret Scripture, not man. He does not want to speak for Africans, but wishes to activate research and find answers.

One delegate reminded Kraft that polygamy is not a respectable way of life, for if it were so, how come the polygamist had a "preferred wife leaving the other wives in a secondary position?"

At that point, Kraft realized his mistake and called a "moratorium" on the subject of polygamy for the rest of the workshop.[53]

In his conclusion the author of this piece observed:

> Personally, I was disappointed by the failure of the use of the Bible in some of the presentations in both the plenary sessions and workships, particularly by Prof. Mbiti, Dr. Charles Kraft and Dr. Bokeleale. They made statements which are not consistent with the inspired, infallible Bible which is the Word of God. It seems to me that PACLA, by bringing in this kind of speakers, brought syncretism through the front door, while some of the African Christians have been doing it secretly through the back door at night.
>
> Said Rev. Daidanso Ma Djongwe of Chad: "We more or less agree with what we have heard." But this is just what many found disturbing at PACLA. If the Word of God is truly authoritative, we cannot be "more or less" agreed. Africans must come to an agreement based on "what the Bible says". To fail to use heavily the Bible in our presentations is both unwise and dangerous.[54]

Ralph P. Martin

Ralph P. Martin is Professor of New Testament at Fuller Theological Seminary. He is the author of *New Testament Foundations: A Guide for Christian Students*. Some of his students informed me of his deviations from the orthodox understanding of the New Testament. One of them sent me a section of a syllabus he used in one of his classes. I wrote to the Fuller Seminary bookstore to buy a copy of the syllabus. In due time I received a letter from President Hubbard in which he refused to sell it to me. I tried again more than a year later with no success. But that difficulty has been alleviated for two reasons.

The first is that I ran across Dr. Martin's commentary on Ephesians in The Broadman Bible Commentary series. And second, Vol. II of his *New Testament Foundations* was released recently by Eerdmans. We can start with Dr. Martin's commentary on Ephesians. Virtually all liberal scholars say that Ephesians was not written by the apostle Paul. Dr. Martin has joined this chorus. Here are his words:

> The present writer has argued that it was a well-known disciple and companion of Paul who published this letter under the apostle's aegis either during his final imprisonment or after his death. He did so by gathering a compendium of Paul's teaching on the theme of Christ-in-his-church; and he added to this body of teaching a number of liturgical elements (prayers, hymns, and confessions of faith) drawn from the worshipping life of the apostolic communities with which he was himself familiar. . . . Paul's disciple has faithfully conveyed the substance of his master's teaching. But he has angled it in such a way that its thrust is set in the direction of some erroneous doctrine and practice which he seeks to dispel. . . . Or a third possibility, which we have adopted, the teaching of the epistle is Pauline but the composition and style of this letter were entrusted by the apostle to a colleague and amanuensis. . . . Our option is for Luke (and note here that Dr. Martin acknowledges his indebtedness for this to Peter Rhea Jones, "now of the Southern Baptist Theological Seminary, Louisville, Kentucky"—so this gives further evidence of Louisville's departure from orthodoxy). . . .[55]

Interestingly, Dr. Martin thinks Ephesians was written by Luke. And he thinks it possible that it was written after Paul was dead. This supposition makes for some strange difficulties. If this were so then the epistle misleads the readers into thinking that Paul is still alive and a prisoner as per Ephesians 4:1. Moreover there is at least one clear statement at the close of the letter which is out of keeping with the thought that it was written after Paul's death. It says: "Now that you also may know how I am and what I am doing, Tychicus the beloved brother and faithful minister in the Lord will tell you everything" (Eph. 6:21). As if this were not enough, for Luke (or whoever may be thought to have written the letter) to ascribe it to Paul when it was not, amounted to deception and fraud. After all, Luke had written the third Gospel and the Acts of the

Apostles. If Paul were dead there would be no reason in the world why Luke would not have said so, and told the Ephesians he was writing what Paul had instructed him to tell them—if that was indeed the case. But for him or anyone else to artfully lead the readers to think it was a genuine letter from Paul when it actually was not, would bring the canonicity of the book into serious question. To speak of biblical inspiration and then to suppose that the Holy Spirit was a party to such deception is utterly beyond imagination. But this is not the end of the story. Dr. Martin does not think Paul wrote the pastorals, i.e. 1 and 2 Timothy and Titus.

Professor Martin engages in guess work and patch-quilt organization to explain away the Pauline authorship of the Pastorals. He wrote in his new book *(New Testament Foundations, Vol. II:*

> Suppose that Tertius kept a set of Paul's "notes" on which Romans was based; the notes would have neither particles, prepositions, or even pronouns, and be written in abbreviated form.
>
> Let us imagine that this same procedure was followed in the case of the Pastorals. The original "notes" were destined for Timothy and Titus to aid them in their work as leaders at Ephesus and Crete, and items that are recognized as personal memoranda, travel notes, and intimate reflections formed the substance of these apostolic communications. Later the "notes" were edited by being written up and set in a form that made them more readable. To these statements of Paul's teaching were added materials such as hymns and creedal forms, based on what was common property in the Pauline churches. The completed wholes, compiled by such a man as Luke who was Paul's companion in Rome (2 Tim. 4:11), were later available to be sent off to churches in Asia and Crete at a time when there was need to reinforce the Pauline emissaries who were wrestling with false teaching and also needing special reminders of what the apostle had taught.[56]
>
> We would thus value these documents for the light they cast on the closing years of Paul's ministry and by the extension of a situation that arose in the Pauline churches and appreciate them as indicating how a devoted Paulinist (Luke or someone else) used his master's teaching and example to confront situations that were embryonic in Paul's lifetime which Paul had foreseen and which emerged in the Aegean region in the time immediately following his death as already envisaged in Acts 20:29-32 in

Paul's address to the Ephesian church leaders.[57]

The fanciful inventions of Dr. Martin to explain away the true Pauline authorship of the Pastorals are more difficult to accept than the simple claims of the letters that they are from the hand of the apostle. If Dr. Martin is correct, and the Pastorals were not written by Paul but by Luke or someone else, we are faced with the same problem of the integrity of the editor or composer who claims to be Paul speaking and who lets every reader so suppose. Even today it would be impossible for anyone to read the Pastorals without coming away from them with the impression that they were written by Paul. This is so patent that when anyone comes to believe they were not written by the apostle, he opens a wide door to disbelief as well as to doubt concerning the integrity of the Word of God. No honest man, then or now, would do what Dr. Martin thinks was done. Professor Martin is a firm advocate of the historical-critical method with its anti-biblical presuppositions; he has capitulated to liberal thinking.

The story does not stop with the Pauline corpus. Dr. Martin also has doubts about 1 and 2 Peter. His conclusions about 1 Peter are mixed, but at least he thinks it possible that it may have come from the apostle himself. But he does not accept the salutation at the beginning of the letter, for if he did he would conclude without question that it was penned by Peter. He wrote:

> We may now venture a conclusion concerning the Epistle's authorship and provenance. . . . And, as we noted, there is specific evidence of the use of a scribe and (possibly) an editor in 5:12. Also, the unspecified description of the persecutions is in keeping with a setting in the 60's. . . . The place of publication was almost certainly Rome. . . . We may conclude that, given the apostolic authorship whether direct or indirect, the Roman origin of this Epistle stands without serious challenge.[58]

The conclusions of Dr. Martin about 2 Peter are clear and negative. He said:

> While the document gives the appearance of being "written in the form of a testament of Peter" there is no strict requirement to take it as written personally by Peter the apostle or published prior to A.D. 64/65, when (tradition has it) Peter perished as a Roman martyr. . . .[59]

Barker, Lane, and Michaels write: "Posthumous publication in Peter's name does not necessarily imply any intent to deceive. If the tradition behind Second Peter is genuinely Petrine, then the only kind of compiler of the material who might be guilty of deception would be the one who presumptuously signed *his own* name to the apostle's teaching." (The same conclusion stands in regard to the origin of Ephesians and from the Pastorals.)

The conclusion is that in 2 Peter we are faced with a later expression of the apostolic gospel, extended and modified to counter the problems raised by the inroad of a gnosticizing antinomianism. The writer builds his case on the deposit of apostolic teaching he has inherited and applies it to his own day. Yet it is apostolic truth and, to that extent, Peter's name and aegis can be claimed for it.[60]

Dr. Martin does not believe that Peter wrote this second epistle even though the letter itself declares that Peter was the author. Any uninstructed reader of the letter would assume that it was written by Peter. It leaves unanswered the question why the anonymous writer stated that the corpus was Peter's while he, the author, was the real composer of the letter. To allege that this sort of thing was commonplace to that period of history will not hold water. The only way a man like Dr. Martin can deny the Petrine authorship is to bring to bear on the epistle outside information which causes him to cast judgment against the letter, rather than letting the plain attribution in the salutation remain as being true and honest. When Dr. Martin works from within the text of Peter's second letter and claims that it is stylistically non-Petrine, he cannot then escape the conclusion that the unknown author was trying to get his readers to believe that the composition was Petrine and he so attributes it. This amounts to rank deception and automatically calls into question the canonicity of the book.

Dr. Robert Mounce, Dean of Arts and Humanities at Western Kentucky University, reviewed Ralph Martin's book, which I have just discussed, in *The Reformed Journal* (October 1978, p. 29). He said:

The only surprise that meets us is Martin's view of the authorship of Ephesians. He holds that while the teaching is definitely Pauline, the compilation and publication of the work was done by Luke (pp. 224, 227-33). . . . the Pastorals are apparently assigned to a "devoted Paulinist." . . .

No clear conclusion is given for the authorship of 1 Peter, James, and the Johannine materials. 2 Peter and Jude, however, are clearly assigned to a period in the history of the church subsequent to the death of the apostles.

Dr. Mounce's conclusions bulwark what I have said and make clear that Dr. Martin rejects what the books in question affirm with respect to their authorship.

Dr. Martin was on sabbatical leave during the latter part of 1976. His travels took him to London, where he addressed a meeting for ministers and Christian workers on October 26. The gathering was arranged by the Evangelical Alliance and the place of meeting was the London Bible College, where Dr. Martin used to teach. Incidentally, it should be mentioned here that Dr. Martin is recognized by the leadership of the London Bible College as having departed from their traditional outlook on the Bible. In any event, it is also interesting to note that the London Bible College, generally recognized as one of Britain's most conservative institutions, has on its faculty now an Old Testament teacher who can hardly be called conservative.

Leslie Allen, a London Bible College teacher, wrote a commentary on Joel, Obadiah, Jonah, and Micah. His discussion of these minor prophets is cast within the S. R. Driver context which includes acceptance of the higher critical approach to Scripture. One major illustration from this commentary will suffice to show the penetration of liberal scholarship into the London Bible College. Professor Allen said that Jonah is a book of fiction, not a book of fact. He wrote:

> It is best to confine the definition of the literary form of the book to that of a parable with certain allegorical features. Rabbinic parables sought not only to interpret OT texts but to explore God's dealings with man, and in this second regard the little book of Jonah stands out as an illustrious ancestor.[61]

Of course this approach must take into account the fact that Jesus used the Book of Jonah to speak about His own three days and three nights in the grave. Dr. Allen acknowledged that Von Orelli held that "It is not indeed proved with conclusive necessity that, if the resurrection of Jesus was a physical fact, Jonah's abode in the fish's belly must also be just as historical." Dr. Allen bought this viewpoint and went on to give his own testimony that conclusively undermines the historicity of the book. He said:

> In this regard it is important to note a feature which will be shown in the later section on the sign of Jonah, that it is not strict exegesis that is reflected in Jesus' use of the narrative of Jonah and the fish, but the popular Jewish understanding, which the Lord took up and employed as a vehicle for truth concerning himself. If this is so, it is quite possible to maintain that his reference merely reflects the contemporary view without necessarily endorsing it for the student of the OT. Moreover, allowance must be made for a figurative element in the teaching of Jesus, an element Western literalists (!) have notoriously found difficulty in grasping. If a modern preacher would not be at fault if he challenged his congregation with a reference to Lady MacBeth or Oliver Twist, could not Jesus have alluded in much the same manner to a well-known story to reinforce his own distinctive message?[62]

Dr. Gleason Archer, an Old Testament professor at Trinity Evangelical Divinity School, observed to me:

> You may judge for yourself whether Allen does not in effect charge Christ with a kind of duplicity in endorsing "the contemporary view" of the authenticity of *Jonah* as factually accurate and historical, whereas in point of fact it is but a pious piece of fiction—a "parable with certain allegorical features." Christ's alluding to Jonah's fictional experience as a type of His own nonfictional burial and resurrection is said to be parallel to one's mentioning some analogy in *MacBeth* and *Oliver Twist*. This is precisely the position of Robert Pfeiffer, Otto Eissfeldt and all the rest. From the evangelical perspective I can hardly see how this work can be described as "an excellent commentary"![63]

In fairness to the London Bible College I know they are disturbed by what Professor Allen has done. There seem to be difficulties that hamper their doing anything about it at the moment. What those difficulties are in particular I do not know. But if they include the old ones of tenure and academic freedom, then no evangelical institution can be safeguarded against intrusion of alien views. I was in Taiwan during the summer of 1977, and there I happened to meet a graduate of the London Bible College. In the ensuing conversation it was apparent that he and the students at the college knew all about Allen and his nonevangelical teaching. They were well aware of his higher critical orientation and his depreciation of the Old Testament in favor of liberal views.

The Evangelical Alliance issued a press release after Dr. Martin finished his speech at the London Bible College. They quoted Dr. Martin as claiming that "the attempt to make the inerrancy of the Bible the touchstone of evangelical orthodoxy is a retrograde and divisive movement in American church life." According to Dr. Martin "American fundamentalism had been dogmatic, dispensational, and often divisive in the 1920's and '30's," the release stated. "In the last ten or twelve years there had emerged a new wing of 'neo-evangelicals' who were more open to modern science and to other groups within the church." *The Battle for the Bible* "aimed to take the evangelical mainstream back to where the neo-evangelicals had left it, and argued that a belief in biblical inerrancy was an essential mark of the true evangelical; if this were lost, other vital truths were soon lost also. Dr. Martin criticized Dr. Lindsell for setting up inerrancy as a standard the biblical data did not themselves require. . . . The 'domino theory' that if biblical inerrancy were lost, other vital truths would then be lost, was just not true. Dr. Lindsell was trying to put the clock back to the 1920's and '30's, whereas today's theological battles were being fought on other fronts."[64]

All that needs to be said here is that Dr. Martin was waging a campaign against what had been the original viewpoint of Fuller Seminary about the Bible. I must ceaselessly remind those interested in the current debate that all I said about Fuller Seminary was that the institution used to believe in inerrancy, but it does no more. Dr. Ockenga, the co-founder of Fuller, says this is so. Drs. Carl F. H. Henry, Charles Woodbridge, and Gleason Archer all say the same thing. Dr. Martin is fighting against inerrancy, something that President Hubbard has done also, but in a more sophisticated and confusing way. Thus Dr. Hubbard could say: "My colleagues join with me in expressing serious questions about those who have doubts about *any portion* of the Bible" and he speaks of "the trustworthiness of the entire canon" of Scripture. In his institutional advertising Dr. Hubbard has said his school seeks to train men and women "who are controlled in their living and thinking by the infallible authority of the Sacred Scriptures." How do these things square with the statements of Dr. Martin?

Is it not obvious that Dr. Martin and others are *not* controlled in their thinking by "the infallible authority of the sacred Scriptures"? Is it not true that Fuller does not believe in "the trustworthiness of the entire canon" of Scripture? If they did, then they would believe that Ephesians and the Pastorals were written by Paul. And all of them would believe that the words of Paul in Ephesians constitute true teaching about the functional subordination of wives in the marital bond. They would also believe that Jesus did not tell us that which isn't true even in minor matters like the mustard seed. And they would believe that polygamy is wrong and cannot be justified.

Fuller Seminary Graduates

The graduates of an institution usually give full proof of the teaching they received from the school in which they studied. According to Dr. LaSor's observations the leaven was present when David Hubbard, Daniel Fuller, and Ray Anderson were students. They went from Fuller to graduate study overseas and were promptly converted to the neoorthodoxy and liberalism of their professors. They returned to Fuller Seminary having moved farther to the left than any of their teachers at Fuller. And now their students in turn begin to reflect their views. If my third thesis is correct, that once an institution breaches its commitment to biblical inerrancy it leads, sooner or later, to a full-scale flight from orthodoxy (as we have noted in the case of so many other theological seminaries), then Fuller Seminary is due for marked changes in the days ahead.

Gerald T. Sheppard

Gerald Sheppard is a graduate of Fuller Theological Seminary with a doctorate from Yale. He now is an Assistant Professor of Old Testament at Union Theological Seminary in New York City. He wrote an article titled "Biblical Hermeneutics: The Academic Language of Evangelical Identity." It was published in the Winter 1977 issue of the *Union Seminary Quarterly Review*. This essay should be read widely, not only because it places the Fuller situation in better perspective, but also because it shows how deep has been the infiltration of liberalism into the evangelical fold. Dr. Sheppard ranged widely in his essay but I will quote from it specifically as it relates to Fuller Seminary. And its importance increases because Dr. Sheppard is an alumnus of the school. Professor Sheppard traces the rise of the present controversy over Scripture declaring that it is really a hermeneutical problem. He mentions the Fuller Seminary response and the orchestration of a campaign to retain the evangelical image. Then Dr. Sheppard says:

> One of the most consistent responses to Lindsell in the addresses by President Hubbard has been to distinguish Fuller's position from the two non-evangelical alternatives of "neo-orthodoxy" and "liberalism." By anachronistically setting Fuller in opposition to movements no longer robustly definitive of theology currently in vogue at the so-called "liberal" seminaries, Hubbard hopes to reassert the older, sharper identity of being "evanglical." . . .
> Despite these strident affirmations of biblical infallibility, responses from Fuller demonstrate a serious inconsistency in distinguishing evangelicalism from neo-orthodoxy. The contradiction in identity becomes quite pronounced when Hubbard weakens his distinction by the observation that after the impact of Karl Barth, Emil Brunner, Oscar Cullmann, and Walter Eichrodt, ". . . *the battle between fundamentalists and liberals which characterized the American church in the first half of our century is more a matter of ancient history*" (italics his). The paradox that Barth, Brunner, Cullmann, and Eichrodt provide more attractive models at Fuller for an "evangelical" approach to Scripture than do the fundamentalists and that they are at the same time major representatives of "neo-orthodoxy" has yet to find resolution.[65]

Dr. Sheppard goes on to suggest that Fuller's problem may be deeper than the institution itself realizes. He says:

> By defining evangelicals over against the purported "neo-orthodoxy" of other seminaries, Hubbard has sought, likewise, to protect Fuller's uniquely marketable "evangelical" status without forfeiting her new ecumenical spirit. Nevertheless, the obscurity in a distinction between the terms "inerrancy" and "infallibility," coupled with the uncertainty over whether scholars like Karl Barth are "evangelical" or "neo-orthodox," suggests that many of the clear theological differences between Fuller and the so-called non-evangelical seminaries have already seriously broken down.[66]

Professor Sheppard has caught the true picture. Fuller Seminary not only has capitulated with regard to biblical inerrancy. It has also moved straight toward the camp of neoorthodoxy which it claims to repudiate. Dr. Sheppard went on to talk about the feminist situation *vis a vis* the published works of Paul Jewett and Virginia Mollenkott. The latter's book was reviewed in *The Other Side* by John Alexander. Mrs. Mollenkott and Paul Jewett followed the culturally conditioned pattern to repudiate Paul's teaching about female subordination in the marital bond even though Dr. Jewett's pattern differed somewhat from that of Mrs. Mollenkott. Dr. Alexander, the editor of *The Other Side,* caught the implications of what Mrs. Mollenkott was saying. Dr. Sheppard recorded his words:

> I am gradually moving toward your (Mrs. Mollenkott's) position, and after this discussion it may be less gradual. But if I wind up where you are, I am seriously considering resigning from *The Other Side.* Throughout our history, as I said at the beginning, our stance has been to call America and the church back to the Bible . . . that is one very important thing which accepting your position makes hard to do.[67]

Dr. Alexander understood the situation perfectly. The position of Mrs. Mollenkott and Dr. Jewett invalidates any call back to the Bible because their position denies overtly what the Bible teaches, and relativizes Scriptures according to their personal tastes or preferences. Immediately after having quoted this observation by Dr. Alexander in relation to Mrs. Mollenkott, Dr. Sheppard made the application to Fuller. Here is what he said:

> Consequently, the crisis in the older evangelical view of Scripture is even more pronounced than Lindsell indicates in his selective review of a few seminaries. The hermeneutical language used in evangelical apologetics is being strained to its limits. Despite all of Hubbard's arguments to the contrary, Fuller, as well as most of the seminaries which Lindsell regards as truly "evangelical," are no longer in united opposition to neo-orthodoxy. In my opinion, just at the time when other so-called non-evangelical seminaries are moving into a post-neo-orthodox period, seminaries like Fuller are dramatically relaunching the old Biblical Theology Movement. With the influx of historical criticism in the seminaries, would not the labels used by evangelicals suggest by their own

definitions that a type of conservative "neo-orthodoxy" is already commonplace among them? Ironically, rather than viewing evangelical seminaries as an alternative to the neo-orthodox ones, historians must ask if evangelical seminaries are not quickly becoming the neo-orthodox centers of North American theology.[68]

In *The Battle for the Bible* I did not say that Fuller Seminary had gone over to neoorthodoxy. It was in my mind, but I hoped my book might cause Fuller to reconsider its posture and openly move away from the tendency toward neoorthodoxy even though it was doing in its praxis what Dr. Hubbard was repudiating in his public relations. I think Dr. Sheppard has analyzed the situation with remarkable accuracy, and I agree with him that my own work may well have underestimated the penetration of neoorthodoxy as well as a denial of inerrancy in the evangelical camp. One thing remains to be said about Dr. Sheppard's provocative essay. It has to do with a footnote. Speaking of neoorthodoxy he properly recognized that

Although neoorthodox scholars rejected the dogmatics of liberalism, their re-discovery of Reformation theology is distinguished from the earlier Protestant Orthodoxy precisely by their acceptance of the historical critical methodologies won through the period of "old liberalism."

Professor Sheppard went on to add:

. . . the most significant New Testament scholar in the evangelical complex is George Eldon Ladd. He sets his own work in continuity with the Biblical Theology Movement and has recently produced the only English New Testament Theology to appear in seventy years. Martin Kahler provides, with Oscar Cullmann, the chief clues for Ladd's own relativizing of historical criticism and its implications for theology. Hence, his approach is not like that of the orthodox period but operates fully within the modern categories of neo-orthodoxy. His theology is "evangelical" for its confessional orientation to the right of Bultmann, but not for its offering a position outside of a neo-orthodox response to biblical criticism. Thus, Donald Dayton can realistically view Ladd's theoretical position as "largely neo-orthodox". . . .[69]

Dr. Sheppard has put his finger on the critical issue, what might be called the point at which the fulcrum is employed to move from orthodoxy to nonorthodoxy. The fulcrum is the historical-critical methodology. It represents the distinctive distinguishing mark that separates orthodoxy from nonorthodoxy. Fuller Seminary's basic problem lies in its acceptance and use of the historical-critical methodology which begins with its denial of an inerrant Bible before it moves on to deny other great affirmations of historic orthodoxy. Later on, the historical-critical methodology will come in for review.

Whither Fuller Seminary?

I have now updated the case I made in 1976 in which I asserted that Fuller Seminary has departed from its original commitment to biblical inerrancy. Whoever wishes to think Fuller Seminary has not changed can do so. It is fruitless to engage in discussions with those whose minds are made up. However, I still need to make some concluding observations about the future of Fuller Seminary.

The sharper the battle the more likely one's sanctification is apt to be tried. It is difficult enough to love those who love you. It is harder to love those with whom you are in disagreement. I remember a columnist who said that to uncover that which people want to keep under the rug is not likely to bring one plaudits from those whose rug has been lifted for the public to see what lies beneath it.

If Fuller Seminary were to return to the original foundation on which it was begun it would necessitate the dismissal of a large number of faculty members. It would require the reorganization of the school of theology, the school of mission, and the school of psychology. Dr. Quebedeaux's observations happen to be true.[70] All three divisions of the seminary are now involved in the departure from orthodoxy. There is no reason to think the Board of Trustees, or at least the majority, understand the true nature of the problem. One cannot expect the administration to undo what has taken it more than a decade and a half to bring about. Therefore the only hope is the Board. If the Board was unwilling to do anything about the Paul Jewett case, it is unreasonable to think it will do anything about the other instances to which reference has been made. If the Seminary can swallow what men like Drs. Martin, Kraft, Jewett, and others have written, it should not be too difficult to wink at further concessions. The board itself is not of one mind to begin with, and President Hubbard is skillful and persuasive in maintaining the evangelical badge while changing the historic meaning of the term and investing it with insights compatible with the historical-critical methodology.

Given the state of theological education in most of the major denominational seminaries, Fuller still looks outwardly to be conservative. And it is, when compared to the postneoorthodoxy new liberalism that goes far beyond the old liberalism in temperament and in its departure from orthodoxy. For the time being Fuller can return to the major denominations graduates who will be an improvement on what many seminaries are turning out. How long this state will continue no one can tell. A crunch may come when Fuller Seminary conceivably could find the doors shut to its graduates in the more liberal denominations and shut among the conservatives.

Institutions are long lived in any event. And the seminaries which were at one time conservative have moved from orthodoxy to liberalism to neoorthodoxy and now to the *doxy* of the current day. Most of them have survived. Fuller will survive too. But it will not attract genuine evangelicals the way it used to. On the other hand Fuller has one factor in its favor. Other evangelical seminaries are in motion to the left. What we may see emerge is a threefold catalog of theological institutions: (1) those who remain distinctively evangelical and cling to biblical inerrancy; (2) those like Fuller who try to ride two horses at the same time and keep at least part of the evangelical public convinced they are orthodox; (3) those who have forsaken even neoorthodoxy and have identified themselves vigorously with the new liberalism which gives the appearance of being very hostile to orthodoxy and may be anxious, as James Barr is,[71] to tame it or render it functionally inoperative.

NOTES

[1]Harold Lindsell, *The Battle for the Bible* (Grand Rapids: Zondervan, 1976), p. 116.
    [2]Ibid., 118.
    [3]David Allan Hubbard, *Reflections on Fuller's Theological Position and Role in the Church* (Pasadena: Fuller Seminary—printed typepage, April 8, 1976), pp. 1, 3.
    [4]Ibid., p. 7.

⁵Ibid., p. 11.

⁶Mimeographed Memo from Dr. Hubbard to Dr. Voskuyl, dated December 13, 1962.

⁷David Hubbard and Robert Laurin, *The Old Testament: A Survey* (mimeographed syllabus), from the chapter titled "The Authority of the Old Testament," pp. 16, 17.

⁸Ibid., pp. 17, 18.

⁹*Theology, News and Notes* (Pasadena: Fuller Seminary, 1976 Special Issue), p. 12.

¹⁰Ibid., p. 14.

¹¹Ibid., pp. 18, 19.

¹²Ibid., p. 8. The Fuller people claim that I am disenchanted with the school because I was not chosen to become president. This canard has been repeated many times. It is interesting, in view of the fact that I have been offered five presidencies in the course of my career and turned all of them down.

¹³Ibid.

¹⁴Ibid., pp. 3, 4.

¹⁵Ibid., p. 4.

¹⁶Ibid., p. 21.

¹⁷Ibid.

¹⁸Ibid.

¹⁹Ibid., p. 22.

²⁰Jack Rogers, ed., *Biblical Authority* (Waco: Word, 1977).

²¹Ibid., pp. 44, 45.

²²Ibid., p. 44.

²³Ibid.

²⁴Harold Lindsell, *God's Incomparable Word* (Minneapolis: World Wide Publications, 1977), pp. 54, 55.

²⁵Lindsell, *The Battle for the Bible*, p. 60.

²⁶Benjamin Breckinridge Warfield, *The Westminster Assembly and its Work* (New York: Oxford University Press, 1931), pp. 270, 271.

²⁷Rogers, p. 43.

²⁸Herman Bavinck, *Gereformeerde Dogmatiek* (Kampen: J. H. Kok, 1928, Vol. I, p. 406.

²⁹Rogers, p. 41.

³⁰Ibid., p. 156

³¹Ibid., p. 158.

³²Ibid., p. 159.

³³Ibid., p. 154.

³⁴Ibid.

³⁵Ibid., p. 156.

³⁶Ibid., p. 160.

³⁷Ibid., p. 166.

³⁸Ibid.

³⁹Ibid., p. 167.

⁴⁰Ibid., p. 160.

⁴¹Ibid., p. 168.

⁴²Ibid., p. 171.

[43]Ibid., p. 179.

[44]*Today's Christian*, Vol. 6, No. 9, September 1977, p. 4.

[45]Ibid.

[46]Ibid.

[47]Paul Jewett, *Bulletin, Systematic Theology: The Doctrine of Scripture*, p. 7.

[48]*Religious News Service*, Friday, May 6, 1977, p. 15.

[49]*Christianity Today*, November 19, 1976, p. 240.

[50]*Journal of the American Academy of Religion*, Volume XLV, Number Three, September 1977, p. 391.

[51]*The Journal of the Evangelical Theological Society*, March 1977, p. 40.

[52]Ibid.

[53]*Perception* (Nairobi: Association of Evanglicals of Africa and Madagascar, April 1977), pp. 6, 7.

[54]Ibid., p. 11.

[55]Ralph P. Martin, "Ephesians" in *The Broadman Bible Commentary* (Nashville: Broadman, Vol. VI), p. 125, 126, 128, 129.

[56]Ralph P. Martin, *New Testament Foundations: A Guide for Christian Students* (Grand Rapids: Eerdmans, 1978), p. 303.

[57]Ibid., p. 306.

[58]Ibid., pp. 334, 335.

[59]Ibid., p. 384.

[60]Ibid., p. 388

[61]Leslie Allen, *The Book of Joel, Obadiah, Jonah and Micah* (Grand Rapids: Eerdmans, 1976), p. 181.

[62]Ibid., p. 180.

[63]Letter to the Editor, *Christianity Today*, dated March 17, 1977.

[64]News Release, Evangelical Alliance, October 29, 1976, pp. 1, 2.

[65]Gerald T. Sheppard, "Biblical Hermeneutics: The Academic Language of Evangelical Identity" in *Union Seminary Quarterly Review*, Volume XXXII, Number 2, Winter 1977, p. 89.

[66]Ibid., p. 90.

[67]Ibid., p. 91.

[68]Ibid.

[69]Ibid., p. 94.

[70]Richard Quebedeaux, *The Worldly Evangelicals* (San Francisco: Harper and Row, 1978), p. 85.

[71]See here his *Fundamentalism* (London: SCM Press, 1977) which was reviewed in depth by Carl Henry in a three-piece series in *Christianity Today*, beginning June 2, 1978.

6

The Lutheran Church—
Missouri Synod:
A Battle Fought and Won

Of all the major North American denominations numbering more than a million members only two emerged from the Liberal-Fundamentalist controversy without serious theological erosion. They were the Southern Baptist Convention and the Lutheran Church-Missouri Synod. This does not mean they had no problems. They emerged from the storm committed to theological orthodoxy, whereas the other major denominations capitulated to theological liberalism and became inclusivist churches. In recent years these two denominations have been under assault. The Lutheran Church-Missouri Synod faced the more severe barrage. A crisis situation developed, and in the ensuing struggle orthodoxy won a pivotal battle although it would be premature to say that orthodoxy has won the war.

To the best of my knowledge the victory of orthodoxy in the Missouri Synod is the only case of its kind in twentieth-century American Christianity. The story has been told in two significant books, both written from within the denomination. The so-called "moderates" who lost the battle will, no doubt, deny the truth of what is contained in these two books. Although the stories may vary between the conservatives and the moderates (which term "moderates" is in my opinion a mislabel—they are generally liberals) the basic facts are there for all to see. Perhaps the Missouri story will help evangelicals in other places as they wage their own battles for theological orthodoxy. But one thing we can be sure of. Wherever struggles like this erupt they lead to bloody confrontations and fissures of one kind or another.

Lutheran Backgrounds

It is unfortunate but it is true, that wherever there has been an issue of any kind there have always been two or more opposing opinions on the subject. For example, in the Alger Hiss case, some books have been written condemning him and others absolving him from his guilt. The Kennedy assassination has given rise to a number of differing opinions as to whether it was a plot or the work of one individual; whether Cuba, the Soviet Union, or neither was involved in the murder. The Rosenburg case illustrates the same thing. Some think they were innocent and others that they were guilty. In the Christian realm a similar situation exists with respect to Martin Luther. Books have been written to prove that he believed the Bible to be free from error. Others have been written in an attempt to prove that such was not the case. Certainly one cannot arrive at a definitive conclusion on the basis of the number of people who hold to either view. What then?

My reading of Martin Luther has led me to conclude that he did hold to an inerrant Scripture. I get tired of the old cliché used by so many to cut the ground from beneath the claim to inerrancy for Martin Luther. I refer to the "James is a strawy epistle" argument. People who use this fail to recognize the difference between inerrancy and canonicity. Martin Luther surely asked the question whether James was canonical. But once its canonicity was accepted, inerrancy followed. There are some who say that the Lutheran dogmaticians who came after the Reformer were responsible for establishing the concept of inerrancy among Lutherans. Let's suppose for a moment that Luther did not teach inerrancy. If he did not, it is quite clear that he did not teach the Bible has errors in it. In that event the dogmaticians who taught inerrancy cannot be faulted as though they taught something Martin Luther denied. The worst that can be attributed to them is that they advanced Lutheran theology by considering a subject about which Martin Luther had made no formal commitment. And there is nothing intrinsically wrong with that.

For hundreds of years Lutherans have had the opportunity to read and study the writings of the Reformer and his followers. In the light of this, so far as American Lutheranism is concerned, one must face one intractable fact. Except for the Lutheran Church in America all of the significant Lutheran denominations have held to biblical inerrancy. The LCA is a relatively recent emergent which came into being in 1962. It was made up largely of the United Lutheran Church in America, the Augustana Evangelical Lutheran Church, the Finnish Evangelical Lutheran Church, and the American Evanglical Lutheran Church. Its doctrinal statement did not include a commitment to an inerrant Scripture. The reason for this failure is not difficult to identify. By the time these Lutheran bodies became one they had been deeply infiltrated with the historical-critical method of interpretation which repudiates the view that Scripture and the Word of God are synonymous. What of the other major Lutheran bodies?

The American Lutheran Church has its headquarters in Minneapolis. It comprises a union of the earlier American Lutheran Church, the Evangelical Lutheran Church, and the United Evangelical Lutheran Church. Three national churches made up of Germans, Norwegians, and Danes united to form the new denomination. Earlier, in 1925, the "Minneapolis Theses" were produced and included in them was a statement about the Bible. The "Theses" accepted the canonical Scriptures "as a whole and in all their parts as the divinely inspired, revealed, and inerrant Word of God."[1] When the union of three national churches was completed and a constitution drawn up in 1960, the same statement about the Bible was written into the constitution. Surely the new denomination representing three different national groups did not for one moment think it was doing anything which in any way contradicted the teaching of their founder, Martin Luther. They believed they were operating within the historic tradition of Lutheran orthodoxy.

A second Lutheran group which holds to inerrancy is the Wisconsin Evangelical Lutheran Synod. This group has published an official statement in pamphlet form titled *This We Believe*. Among the statements in this pamphlet the following are representative of Wisconsin's commitment:

We believe that in a miraculous way that goes beyond all human investigation God the Holy Ghost inspired these men to write His Word. These "holy men of God spoke as they were moved by the

Holy Ghost" (II Pet. 1:21). What they said, was spoken "not in the words which man's wisdom teacheth, but which the Holy Ghost teacheth" (I Cor. 2:13). Every thought they expressed, every word they used, was given them by the Holy Spirit by inspiration. St. Paul wrote to Timothy: "All scripture is given by inspiration of God" (II Tim. 3:16). We therefore believe in the verbal inspiration of the Scriptures, not a mechanical dictation, but a word-for-word inspiration. . . .

We believe that Scripture is a unified whole, true and without error in everything it says; for our Savior said "The Scripture cannot be broken" (John 10:35). . . .

We reject any thought that makes only part of Scripture God's Word, that allows for the possibility of factual error in Scripture, also in so-called nonreligious matters (for example, historical, geographical).

We reject all views that fail to acknowledge the Holy Scriptures as God's revelation and Word. We likewise reject all views that see in them merely a human record of God's revelation as he encounters man in history apart from the Scriptures, and so a record subject to human imperfections.

At the conclusion of *This We Believe*'s statement about Scripture these words appear: "This is what Scripture teaches about God and His Revelation. This we believe, teach, and confess."[2] And who can deny that this Lutheran body rightly believes it stands in the tradition of the great Reformer, Martin Luther?

The third group of Lutheran inerrantists is the Lutheran Church-Missouri Synod which has its headquarters in St. Louis, Missouri. The Missouri Synod Lutherans are generally of German background. From its inception, this church committed itself to an inerrant Scripture. Like most of the Lutheran churches, it held in highest esteem the Augsburg Confession as well as the Smalcald Articles, the two Catechisms of Luther, and the Formula of Concord. Lutherans were generally agreed that Luther himself held to an inerrant Scripture as has already been stated. But when doubt began to creep in, the Missouri Synod took steps to spell out more specifically under modern conditions the more exact nature of the denomination's commitment to a trustworthy Bible.

In 1932 the Missouri Synod adopted a *Brief Statement* of its doctrinal position. In 1947, at the centennial celebration of the denomination, the *Brief Statement* was incorporated in the official proceedings of the convention (Proceedings, 1932, p. 1548), although it was not made part of the Constitution. The first article of the *Brief Statement* said this about Scripture:

> 1. We teach that the Holy Scriptures differ from all other books in the world in that they are the Word of God. They are the Word of God because the holy men of God who write the Scriptures wrote only that which the Holy Ghost communicated to them by inspiration, 2 Tim. 3:16; 2 Pet. 1:21. We teach also that the verbal inspiration of the Scriptures is not a so-called "theological deduction," but that it is taught by direct statements of the Scriptures, 2 Tim. 3:16, John 10:35; Rom. 3:2; I Cor. 2:13. Since the Holy Scriptures are the Word of God, it goes without saying that they contain no errors or contradictions, but that they are in all their parts and words the infallible truth, also in those parts which treat of historical, geographical, and other secular matters, John 10:35.

The Missouri Synod has consistently believed and taught that its commitment to inerrancy is in accord with the teaching of Martin Luther. Again and again its publishing house has printed monographs supporting inerrancy and declaring that the view is that of Doctor Luther himself. Now I will consider what happened in the Missouri Synod, why it happened, how the struggle was fought, and what the outcome of the battle was.

The Source of the Conflict

The use of the historical-critical method lies at the center of the Missouri Synod's recent struggle. Professor Kurt E. Marquart has documented this fully. He wrote:

> The long lists of doctrinal differences sometimes compiled to show what finally brought the Synod's tensions to a seething climax at New Orleans in 1973 can be boiled down to two root issues: Scripture and the church. All else—Job, Jonah, JEPD, joining-fever, and JAOSP's (i.e. Dr. J. A. O. Preus) jurisdiction—are simply symptoms of the underlying divisions as to Scripture and the church.[3]

As to Scripture, Dr. Marquart said:

> It is clear that the Biblical Principle in the Missouri Synod crumbled under pressure from the historical-critical approach, which was naïvely mistaken simply for objective scholarship. . . . after

World War I the historical-critical principle began to conquer the leading Lutheran seminaries, first in the ULC and later in the ALC. Denial of the old doctrine of inspiration and inerrancy came to be tolerated in the Missouri Synod largely because Lutheran union received top priority.[4]

It is important to note what was intrinsic to the historical-critical method if we are to understand what happened in the Missouri Synod. Years before the boiling point was reached, one of Missouri's great leaders, Carl Walther, saw the way in which things were moving. He realized that the works of men like T. Harnack who embraced German higher criticism were bound to destroy the Missouri Synod's foundations. Dr. Marquart said that "A year before his death Walther paraphrased Luther's warning against Zwingli's clever device for manipulating Scripture, and applied this warning to the new 'conservative' view of the Bible":

> We must apply this to the so-called "divine-human character of Scripture" as that term is used by the modern-conservative theology: Beware, beware, I say, of this "divine-human Scripture"! It is a devil's mask; for at last it manufactures such a Bible after which I certainly would not care to be a Bible Christian, namely, that the Bible should henceforth be no more than any other good book, a book which I would have to read with constant sharp discrimination in order not to be led into error. For if I believe this, that the Bible contains errors, it is to me no longer a touchstone but itself stands in need of one. In a word, it is unspeakable what the devil seeks by this "divine-human Scripture."[5]

This same Carl Walther had written elsewhere:

> It is absolutely necessary that we maintain the doctrine of inspiration as taught by our orthodox dogmaticians. If the possibility that Scripture contained the least error were admitted, it would become the business of *man* to sift the truth from the error. That places man *over Scripture*, and Scripture is *no longer* the source and norm of doctrine. Human reason is made the *norma* of truth, and Scripture is degraded to the position of a *norma normata*. The least deviation from the old inspiration doctrine introduces a rationalistic germ into theology and infects the whole body of doctrine.[6]

Two observations are in order at this junction. The first is that the traditional Lutheran position on inerrancy was not the position of the Missouri Synod alone. It was also the position of the whole Synodical Conference. The leaven of the Sadducees was at work, however. Some Lutherans in Germany even then were saying in effect that "Holy Scripture remains God's Word for the Christian even when he has had to give up the doctrine of inspiration."[7] This same Dean Kier "argued that the Bible was a human book (a very familiar sound today among evangelicals), marked also by the defects and mistakes which attach to all human works. This, moreover, he claimed had been 'proved, not by the attacks of unbelief against God's Word, but by the historical-critical science about the Bible, which has been produced by Protestantism and is totally indispensable to it.' "[8]

The second observation relates to inerrancy and the oft-repeated fable that in America this view of the Bible was the product of the Princeton school of which B. B. Warfield and Charles Hodge were the leading progenitors. Lutheran orthodoxy was in no way indebted to Drs. Warfield and Hodge. It is doubtful that many, if any, Lutherans were familiar with the writings of the Princeton school if for no other reason than that they were certain that Reformed theology represented a dangerous deviation from traditional Lutheran theology. But they did share one thing in common: both the Lutherans and the Reformed peoples in America held to an inerrant Bible.

Doctrines or Documents

The departure of Missouri Lutherans from inerrancy to errancy on the part of some of their scholars was due to the use of the historical-critical method. But the use of this method involved a secondary issue that was perhaps no less important. This had to do with subscription to the Lutheran standards such as the Augsburg Confession and to the Book of Concord, which included a number of documents. Lutheran churches traditionally have been confessional churches as contrasted with Baptists, for example, who have not been. Baptists say that their only creed is the Bible. Lutheran and Presbyterian bodies, however, have always had confessions based upon the Bible. Those who were examined for ordination to these churches were required to subscribe to what their confessional standards iterated. With the advent of the historical-critical method, subscription to the creeds no longer meant what it used to because many who subscribed to them did not believe what the creeds taught. Some subscribers held to the documents, i.e., to the Confessions, but not to the doctrines taught in the confessions. In other words, some ministers hypocritically assented to confessions they did not believe. It was justified, of course, by the usual arguments such as the plea that those who wrote the creeds would agree with the new understanding if they were alive and had the advantage of the new learning. Or it was felt that the new breed of disbelievers were the *avant garde* leadership who had the truth unknown to their more troglodyte brothers. They were doing the people in the pew a favor by dissembling until they could educate them to accept the new understanding.

No one should dismiss the fact that the battle between the "moderates" and the conservatives in the Lutheran Church-Missouri Synod was fought over the question of subscription to the standards. The "moderates" constantly affirmed that ordinands only needed to say they accepted the standards after which they could preach and teach that which contravened the standards. Dr. Tietjen was a leader among those who elevated the standards to a place of preeminence. According to him, when talking about Lutheran unity all that was needed was "subscription to the Lutheran Confessions." But the Synodical Conference went beyond the Lutheran Confessions, insisting "on complete agreement in doctrine and practice."[9]

Professor H. E. Jacobs, on behalf of the Lutheran General Council, made this observation:

> The unity of the Church does not consist in the subscription to the same Confessions, but in the acceptance and teaching of the same doctrines. . . . It is well to notice that it is not the acceptance of the unaltered Augsburg Confession, but the acceptance of its *doctrines*, which determines the Lutheran character of a teacher or Church body. A man who has never seen it, is a Lutheran if he teaches the doctrines which it maintains. A man who makes his subscription to the Confession an object of especial boast, is no Lutheran, if "by equivocation or mental reservation," or even by excusable misunderstanding he depart from any of the doctrines therein clearly and professedly taught.[10]

No mistake should be made about the focal point of the

battle in the Missouri Synod. It centered in its professors in its colleges and seminaries who subscribed to the Augsburg Confession while teaching that which contradicted its doctrines. Men like Dr. Tietjen could swear on a stack of Bibles that they believed the Bible to be the infallible Word of God, but this did not keep them from teaching what the Bible does not allow. And this situation had its beginnings in the acceptance of the historical-critical method which ripped the Bible to shreds.

Missouri's problem, basically, was the same as the one all of the other churches faced earlier and surrenderd to. It is the same problem evangelicals face in our generation. They affirm their commitment to doctrinal platforms and then by equivocation, mental reservation, or misunderstanding deny in practice what they profess in principle. There are professors in Southern Baptist seminaries who sign doctrinal statements and then teach things the statements do not allow. This is currently the problem at Fuller Theological Seminary even after it changed its statement of faith, for the school now has on its faculty those who have breached the latest statement of faith in their classroom performances and in their writings. This is the problem facing the National Association of Evangelicals. This is the problem in the Christian Reformed Church. This is the problem in all the groups to which reference was made in *The Battle for the Bible*. And behind it lies this question: Can a church, or institution, survive and maintain its historic commitment when it winks at deviations and permits its people to teach that which contradicts its faith commitment? Martin Luther had an answer to this question and it needs to be written large over all the halls of learning and on the front door of every church in the nation. This is what he said:

> In philosophy a small error in the beginning leads to a very large error at the end. So in theology a small error overturns the whole doctrine. Therefore doctrine and life must be rigorously distinguished from each other. Doctrine is not ours but God's, Whose called servants we merely are. Therefore we may not yield or change even one tittle of it. . . . Accursed be that love which is preserved to the detriment of the doctrine of faith, before which all must yield, love, apostle, angel from heaven, etc. . . . If they believed that it is God's Word, they would not play with it like this, but hold it in the highest honour, and accord it faith without any

disputation or doubting. . . . For doctrine is our sole light, which enlightens and leads us and shows us the way to heaven. If it becomes wobbly in one part, it must necessarily become wobbly altogether. When that happens, love cannot help us. We can be saved without love and unity with the sacramentarians, but not without the pure doctrine and faith. . . . Doctrine is heaven, life is the earth. In life there are sin, error, impurity and misery. . . . But in doctrine, as there is no error in it, so also no need for forgiveness of sins. Therefore doctrine and life may by no means be equated. One tittle of doctrine counts for more than heaven and earth; therefore we do not tolerate that it be violated in the slightest. But when it comes to errors of life, we can overlook very much. But doctrine must not be sin, nor guilty, and does not belong in the Our Father, when we pray, "forgive us our trespasses." For it is not our doing, but God's very own Word, Who cannot sin nor do wrong. . . . Here it is not necessary, yes not good, to ask forgiveness of sins. . . . for it is God's and not my Word, which God neither should nor can forgive, but must confirm, praise, crown and say: You have taught aright, for I have spoken through you, and the Word is Mine. Whoever cannot boast that of his sermon, let him leave preaching alone, for he certainly lies and blasphemes God. . . . So life may well be sin and wrong, yes it is, alas, only too wrong; but doctrine must be absolutely straight and certain, without all sin. Therefore in the church nothing but alone the certain, pure, and sole Word of God may be preached. Where that is lacking, it is no longer the church, but the devil's school.[11]

The Concordia Seminary at St. Louis

Two of the most important institutions in the Missouri Synod struggle to retain historic orthodoxy were Valparaiso University and the Concordia Theological Seminary in St. Louis. The latter, of course, was the more important source of the infection since it was the institution in which the largest number of men were trained for ordination to the Christian ministry. But Concordia-St. Louis was taken over gradually and systematically by subversion from within as well as from without. It was in 1961 that Martin E. Marty, associate editor of the *Christian Century,* which to the best of my knowledge never employed an editor who was an evangelical, came out with a classic statement of the methodology to be employed for the takeover of the Synod. He publicly urged "the prophets" to work "from within" their denominations "for constructive subversion, encirclement, and infiltration, until anti-ecumenical forces bow to the evangelical weight of reunion." This same approach some years later prompted *Christianity Today* to refer to Marty's endorsement of "ecclesiastical Machiavellianism" and to comment: "Ministers who have taken denominational or-dination vows are increasingly faced with the question of personal honesty and integrity as they participate in a movement that ex-plicitly condemns denominations and aims at their merger into the ecumenical church. Applying the borrowed phrase "sociological Machiavellianism," Dr. Marty counsels a procedure that would actually promote "the ultimate death and transfiguration of these forms" while patiently "living in denominations and being faithful to their disciplines."[12]

This was the counsel of Martin E. Marty who was to be one of the founding fathers of the schismatic ELIM, which he and others promoted before and after they lost the battle for the control of the Missouri Synod. This was the Martin E. Marty who was a book award judge for Abingdon when *Sense and Nonsense* by Sten H. Stenson was selected for the Abingdon award. Marquart observed:

> The book "defended" the validity of Christianity and other reli-gions on the grounds of "the punlike character of miracle stories and religious legends." "Religious" language, in other words, is not to be taken literally, but is comparable to puns or "witti-cisms," which "are irrelevant to truth and falsity in the usual propositional sense." . . . Indeed, Bultmann is here cited to the effect that the evangelist St. John "while making free use of the tradition creates a figure of Jesus entirely from faith!" Stenson's total relativism is clear from these excerpts: "If a Jew comes to understand Torah, he will, in a sense, have risen above it, and can throw it away. . . . Likewise, when Christians come to understand Christ they will no longer need to cling to him as, literally, the only way to the Truth. This, among other things, is what the so-called death of God theologians have discovered. . . . both Judaism and Christianity are anti-idolatrous, self-destructive, and equally true in the manner of religious "wit."[13]

This blasphemous book received the high commendation of Martin E. Marty. He said: "It is a fresh presentation of the Christian faith, and of faith itself. I would be proud to hand it to bright people up and down my block and to colleagues in worlds of media or academy!" Dr. Marty posed as a "moderate" in the Missouri Synod. If this is what "moderates" stand for it would be difficult indeed to try to describe what a "liberal" would be like. Dr. Marty is a graduate of the St. Louis seminary.[14]

The St. Louis seminary did not become liberal overnight. It was planning and manipulation that produced the result. In a graduate class at the school the professor told his students about the historical background of the effort to change the Missouri Synod. This professor was one who later left Concordia when the exodus occurred. He joined "Seminex" (meaning *Seminary in exile*). In a July 1968 class he told the students

> . . . that the "progressive" movement got started in a smokefilled pastor's office in New York City in 1930 when 2 LCMS pastors . . . decided, after Synod had turned down the Chicago Theses and had authorized the drafting of the Brief Statement, that they would start a movement to "change Synod." Their goals were to prepare the LCMS for outreach into America by use of English (vs. German), and by moving Synod toward a more open doctrinal stance. To attain these goals they urged the election of conservative leaders (e.g., Behnken) who would listen to their suggestions of names for seminary presidents, professors . . . and other officials. [The professor] said he joined that growing *underground* (my italics) movement in 1940.[15]

The decay of Concordia occasioned by its surrender to liberalism must be understood within the context of the presidency of the institution and the presidency of the Missouri Synod. One of the functions of the president of the Synod was to keep his eye on the institutions of the church. John W. Behnken, just mentioned in connection with the progressive movement that went back to the "smoke-filled pastor's office in New York City," was elected president of the Synod in 1935. He occupied the office until 1962 when Oliver Harms took over. Dr. Harms was rejected by the Synod in favor of J. A. O. Preus in 1969. The deterioration of Concordia took place mainly during Dr. Behnken's presidency of the Synod. Dr. Alfred O. Fuerbringer was the president of the seminary from 1953 to 1969, and was directly responsible for what occurred there. He was replaced by John Tietjen in 1969 under strange circumstances about which we will hear more shortly. It was against this backdrop that the sad story of Concordia unfolded which led to the explosion early in the 1970s.

By 1950 it was obvious that Concordia of St. Louis had been infiltrated by neoorthodoxy and had committed itself to the use of the historical-critical methodology. The young intellectual, Jaroslav Pelikan, who later migrated to Yale University, published a book titled *From Luther to Kierkegaard*. In it he said the Lutheran Church "had been set on the wrong philosophical track already by Chemnitz and the Formula of Concord, that the German philosopher Immanuel Kant had destroyed the foundations of Lutheran Orthodoxy, and that Lutheranism now needed a new philosophy, namely that of Kierkegaard, to wit: 'Only that is true which is true for me.' . . . Indeed Pelikan himself came to pay glowing tribute to Schleiermacher, who figures as arch-heretic in Pieper's *Christian Dogmatics*, and even to the neo-pagan Paul Tillich, whose 'Protestant principle' abolishes the whole idea of God-given truth and doctrine. Pelikan served on the faculty of Concordia Seminary, St. Louis, from 1949 to 1953."[16]

Missouri's Concordia was deeply influenced by students who had gone to the leading graduate schools in America and abroad. Clifford Nelson had this to say:

> Many of these men, who found their way into teaching positions in major colleges and seminaries of the Lutheran churches, including Concordia Seminary (St. Louis), had been exposed to contemporary biblical research (Dodd, Hoskyns, Wright, Albright, Bultmann, G. Bornkamm, von Rad, *et al.*); to contemporary theologians such as Nygren, Aulen, Barth, Brunner, Tillich and the Niebuhrs; and to the Luther researches of Swedes, Germans, Englishmen and Americans (notably Wilhelm Pauck and Roland Bainton). *One result was that in the course of time students were exposed to a new brand of Lutheranism that was remarkably similar in all schools, whether in Chicago, Philadelphia, the Twin Cities, or St. Louis.*[17]

John Behnken

Dr. John Behnken was president of the Synod from 1935 until his retirement in 1962. From 1953 until 1969 Dr. Alfred Fuerbringer was president of Concordia Seminary at St. Louis. It was during the later years of Dr. Behnken's presidency that Concordia moved so far to the left, but as early as the middle thirties warning signs had been raised. In 1940 *The Confessional Lutheran* "battled on valiantly for nearly three decades under the energetic leadership of Pastor Paul Burgdorf. Dr. Behnken, as his memoirs indicate, saw little merit in those early warnings and responded accordingly. This tragic absence from the outset of any real meeting of the minds between the synodical administration and conservative critics was to cost the Synod dearly. Positions hardened, relations deteriorated, the theological situation worsened, yet remedial action was postponed."[18]

In 1961 and 1962 conservatives drew the administration's attention to the rapidly growing theological difficulties in the Synod. Two *Books of Documentation* were put together in which photocopies of the evidences concerning the progress of liberalism and ecumenism in the Synod were made available. Missouri Synod headquarters continued to tell the people in the pews that all was well and that doctrinal purity existed throughout the church. Dr. Behnken, now close to the end of his presidency, was "troubled about the situation, and he made no secret of it." In 1960 he said that the Conference principles had been violated and that

> Some of these men have not been disciplined as they should have been . . . Our meetings . . . and also this conclave have convinced me all the more that it is necessary to emphasize and put into practice firmer discipline. . . . We realize that the independent action on the part of a few—who by some are called intellectuals—has caused misgivings in the minds and hearts of our brethren within the Synodical Conference. We are sorry for these actions and we beg your pardon.[19]

Professor Marquart makes clear that Dr. Behnken did not become fully aware of how he had been misled until after he stepped down from the presidency of the Synod. Then he wrote to President Fuerbringer in 1966 directing his attention to twenty-eight questions about the historicity of persons and events in the Old Testament to which he wanted answers. He got no satisfactory response. In 1967 he made his correspondence public, sending copies to the District Presidents, seminary faculties, and boards of control. "The St. Louis faculty minutes for March 28, 1967 reveal no response except polite contempt: 'Dr. J. W. Behnken has directed some questions concerning phases of interpretation of Genesis to the faculty and to many others.' Period. Finish. And that was that! Fuerbringer, of course, had had the questions already since the previous summer, but they are not mentioned in the official record of his report to the faculty's opening retreat in September, 1966."[20]

Oliver Harms

Dr. Harms took over the presidency from Dr. Behnken in 1962. He was himself orthodox in his own theological convictions but he disregarded what his predecessor had learned in the school of hard knocks, and he did his best to reassure the constituency that all was well in Missouri. He said "Our studies make it clear that the Word of God with all of its doctrines is our sure and immovable constant. . . ." After 1962 many voices were raised in protest about what was happening in Missouri. At the end of 1965 Dr. Harms wrote to Dr. Fuerbringer recounting some of the evidences which had been adduced for the charges that Concordia at St. Louis was defective in its teaching. Dr. Harms suggested to Dr. Fuerbringer

> that perhaps a statement with which the faculty would agree but prepared and signed by the department heads would help. This statement should be a short statement, a simple one, one that addresses itself very directly to the points at issue . . . very straightforward, synod-stanced, and in complete agreement with Holy Scripture and the historic Lutheran Confessions, the Lord guiding us.[21]

The St. Louis faculty responded to Dr. Harms with a statement that was "nebulous in the context of the synodical controversy." A month later Dr. Harms went back to President Fuerbringer of the seminary by letter expressing the hope

> that the faculty would be willing to add clear rejections of errors which had been attributed to them, for example, that "the factuality and truthfulness of Scripture is denied," that "the Bible contains errors," and the denial of "the historical correctness of Genesis 1, 2, and 3" in deference to evolution. Harms even prepared a sample formulation, showing how his suggestions for clear rejections of errors might be incorporated into the text of the faculty statement of January 20.[22]

Dr. Harm's good intentions availed him nothing. Neither

the faculty nor the president of St. Louis were about to oblige him or the Synod itself. Dr. Fuerbringer wrote to Dr. Harms as follows:

> By and large, neither the sacred Scriptures nor the Lutheran symbolical books speak directly enough to some of the issues that your letter raises to enable our faculty to make the kind of statement that you desire without a great deal of careful reflection. Much of the discussion that is going on in our church-body and elsewhere in Christendom centers around the meaning of terms like "factuality," "historical correctness," "error," and "evolution." I believe that it will unquestionably be possible to formulate a consensus among the members of the faculty on any of these issues and we propose to address ourselves to them. At the same time, this will not, in my opinion, take place within any time limit that would be of help to you in your present situation.[23]

When Dr. Harms' effort came to nought he did not make an issue out of the matter. He closed ranks with the seminary and maintained that it did not teach false doctrine. Meanwhile warnings were being given to the Missouri Synod from a variety of sources. These came from within the United States, from sister churches of the Missouri Synod in Germany, and from Australia. Pressures were building up that were to lead to the sensational 1969 Denver conclave of the Missouri Synod. At that time Dr. Harms was voted out of office and Dr. J. A. O. Preus was elected in his place.

The Preus-Tietjen Era

The disturbers of the peace in the Missouri Synod were not unaware of the possibility that Dr. Preus would be elected president of the denomination. Thus before the Denver meeting at which Dr. Preus was elected, an unusual situation developed with regard to President Alfred Fuerbringer of Concordia at St. Louis. He was due for retirement. But his retirement was to take place after the Denver election. And if Dr. Preus was in the saddle as president of the Synod he would have a definite influence on the selection of the new president for the St. Louis school. In order to bring in John Tietjen, Dr. Fuerbringer, who had been largely responsible for the movement of Concordia to liberalism, decided to retire before the bylaws required him to do so. Thus it was possible to locate and elect his successor before the Denver meeting. Conservative candidates for the presidential office were available but they did not have a chance. The selection process was in the hands of four electors, two of whom were to go out of office at the July 1969 convention of the Synod. One of them was Dr. Harms, who was in a large measure responsible for the selection of John Tietjen to replace President Fuerbringer. John Tietjen was elected and "it marked the first time in the Synod that a Seminary president was chosen while his predecessor was still in office." Dr. Tietjen had taken his graduate study at Union Theological Seminary in New York City. At the time of his election he was Executive Secretary of the Department of Public Relations of the Lutheran Council in the USA. He was already known as a theological liberal and came into office at the same time the conservative Dr. Preus was elected to the presidency of the Synod. The theological differences between the two men were so obvious that a conflict was certain to erupt unless one or the other backed down. But since J. A. O. Preus was intent on preserving the orthodox position of the Synod, this meant trouble in the days ahead. And it was not long in coming.

"A Call to Openness and Trust"

One of the developments that was to help in precipitating the crisis was the publication of a document titled: "A Call to Openness and Trust." It was brought into being in January 1970 when a St. Louis group protested the fact that Richard Jungkuntz was not reappointed to the executive secretaryship of the Commission on Theology and Church Relations. At least three professors from the St. Louis Seminary were authors and signers of this document which stated:

> We specifically hold that differences concerning: (1) the manner of the creation of the universe by God, (2) the authorship and literary form of any books of the Bible, (3) the definition of the presence of Christ in the Lord's supper, (4) the moral obligation of Christians in individual or corporate action, (5) the question of factual error in the Bible, and (6) the role and authority of clergy in the church are not to be the basis for inclusion or exclusion of people among the true disciples of Jesus Christ or membership in the Missouri Synod.[24]

The document was not in accord with the historic position of the Missouri Synod. In the 1971 meeting of the Synod it was voted to repudiate the inaccuracies in the "Call to Openness and Trust," and those identified with it were called upon to assure the Synod publically "through the office of the President of the Synod that they are faithful to the confessional stance of the Synod. . . ." Nothing really came of this, although the vote itself showed the Synod was concerned about the trend away from orthodoxy in the denomination. Meanwhile some of the few conservative faculty members at St. Louis were raising their voices. All of this led to the appointment of a fact-finding committee to inquire into matters at the St. Louis Seminary.[25]

Dr. Robert Preus Speaks for the Minority

Obviously what was at stake was the use of the historical-critical method at the St. Louis school. One thing led to another so that when J. A. O. Preus issued a directive not to allow one of the St. Louis professors to teach courses in which he would have the opportunity to advocate his higher critical views of the Bible, Dr. Tietjen aimed a shot at the heart of the directive when he declined to carry it out. He told the student body of his decision in an official release on March 6, 1972. In that release he stated that it was impossible to operate a department of exegetical theology at a graduate school without the use of the historical-critical method. This called forth a reply from Dr. Robert Preus, a St. Louis faculty member, who said:

> When I joined this faculty the so-called historical-critical method was not employed but generally rejected by this faculty. A couple of exegetes might have advocated using certain aspects of it, but this was all. Now after fifteen years, during which the method has been quietly and gradually brought in, we are told that it is impossible to do exegesis at a seminary without using it.
>
> I must respond that as a called teacher at Concordia Seminary, committed to the Sacred Scriptures and the Lutheran Confessions, I cannot and will not use the historical-critical method as such for its false presuppositions and its false goals and conclusions. I have done this privately and publicly and in every possible forum, in joint faculty meetings and before the Council of Presidents, in my classes, in papers delivered throughout the Synod, in

periodicals and books and before our Board of Control. And I intend to do the same in the future in this school or anywhere else with the help of God.[26]

The Report of the Fact-finding Committee

The fact-finding committee appointed by Dr. Preus brought back the "Blue Book" which was a report of its findings on the St. Louis Seminary. The report said there were doctrinal problems at the school. This, of course, was not only apparent but was well known to anyone and everyone who had any knowledge of what was going on at the seminary. The committee did report "a distressing amount of diversity in the theological positions of various members of the faculty [some of which] represent significant departures from the position of the Synod." The report then documented what some of the professors at the seminary held or permitted:

1. A confusion on the doctrine of Scripture, especially its verbal inspiration and inerrancy, as well as disagreement on the relationship between the formal and material principles of Scripture.
2. A commitment to the use of the historical-critical method as a valid and preferred method for the interpretation of the Bible.
3. A possibility that many of the Old and New Testament stories are not really historical.
4. An acceptance that words attributed to Jesus in the Gospels were in fact never spoken by Him, but were later additions or interpretation made by the Christian community after the death of Jesus.
5. A reluctance to attribute Old Testament prophecies as pointing directly to Jesus Christ, that is, the minimalization of predictive prophecy in the Old Testament.
6. An insistence that Moses was not the author of the Pentateuch, Isaiah did not pen his entire book, and Paul may not have written all the books attributed to him in the New Testament.[27]

At the conclusion of the report the committee made the observation:

The Synod must face the grave issue of fundamental disagreement in the doctrine of the Holy Scriptures with its far-reaching implications for all of Christian faith and theology. It is a matter of utmost urgency, demanding the Synod's most serious study, its clearest judgment, and its decisive and swift action under the guidance of the Holy Spirit.[28]

Dr. Preus's Response and President Tietjen's Counteroffensive

There can be no doubt that J. A. O. Preus was made of stern stuff. He made this clear, and undoubtedly those who supported the candidacy of John Tietjen for the presidency of the St. Louis seminary knew they were headed for a confrontation with the president of the Synod. Dr. Preus said:

> The case now lies before the church. It is evident that the use of the historical-critical method has brought about changes both in our doctrinal stance, our certainty, and our attitudes toward doctrine. It is becoming clear that we have two theologies. With the influential position the Seminary holds in the church, its views will prevail unless the Synod directs otherwise and sees to it that its directives are implemented.[29]

Dr. Tietjen went on the offensive. In his turn he accused the president of the Synod and others of entertaining un-Lutheran doctrine. He spoke of the distortions and misrepresentations of the position of the faculty. This was patently false, although it was true enough that the position of the faculty majority and that of the fact-finding committee and Dr. Preus were totally opposed to each. But Dr. Preus was beyond any doubt on the side of what had been the traditional position of the Synod from the beginning. The Board of Control of the St. Louis seminary did nothing, despite the report of the fact-finding committee and of the response of the synodical president. This being the case, it was clear that the matter would have to be decided by the denomination at its meeting in New Orleans in 1973.

Meanwhile the Association of Theological Schools (earlier known as the American Association of Theological Schools) got into the act. A visiting team went to St. Louis ostensibly because the contract of Dr. Arlis Ehlen, who was off base theologically, was not renewed. Since Concordia was owned and operated by the denomination, it was a hasty move on the part of the ATS to enter into the fracas at that time, if it should have entered into it at any time. But anyone familiar with ecclesiastical procedures would know that this was one way of putting pressure on Dr. Preus and the Lutheran Church-

Missouri Synod. Concordia was placed on probation by the ATS.[30]

The Convention's Decision at New Orleans

The majority faculty at Concordia put out its own propaganda report in the booklet titled *Faithful to Our Calling, Faithful to Our Lord*. As a result confrontations of various kinds took place that further exacerbated the situation. Dr. Tietjen was in no sense ready to give in to the president of the Synod, and the president in turn had no other course of action than to bring the matter before the denomination itself. At New Orleans Dr. Preus was overwhelmingly reelected. And after that the convention adopted as an official doctrinal statement by a 652-455 vote the document the St. Louis faculty described as "having a spirit alien to Lutheran confessional theology." The resolution which the convention adopted read as follows:

> RESOLVED, That The Lutheran Church-Missouri Synod declare *A Statement of Scriptural and Confessional Principles*, in all its parts, to be Scriptural and in accord with the Lutheran Confessions, and therefore a formulation which derives its authority from the Word of God and which expresses the Synod's position on current doctrinal issues.[31]

This was a victory for the conservative wing of the Synod, but the opposition used the occasion to demonstrate against the majority vote. Hundreds of their delegates "streamed to the platform to have the secretary record their negative votes while they and others sang the first stanza of 'The Church's One Foundation is Jesus Christ her Lord.' This was the first of several well-planned and highly emotional demonstrations held in protest against convention resolutions."[32]

Further actions by the convention condemned the doctrinal position of the faculty of Concordia and the door was opened for the dismissal of John Tietjen from the presidency of the seminary. Dr. Tietjen himself stated "I have no doubt it will not be long before I am no longer President of the Seminary."[33]

The Majority Faculty Fight Back

The majority faculty published "A Declaration of Protest and Confession" after the Synod meeting at New Orleans. Within a short time "Evangelical Lutherans in Mission" (ELIM) was brought into being (and Martin Marty of the *Century* was right in the middle of the situation as one of the directors along with John Tietjen). Concordia faculty members were among the founding fathers of the dissident group and provided leadership for it. In view of the infiltration of an aberrant view of the Bible among evangelicals in Christendom it is of more than passing interest that the ELIM group used the word *evangelical* in its name. Its use suggests that the word has been debased and may no longer serve a useful purpose if it becomes an umbrella under which those who deny inerrancy and those who affirm it can support each other as though the question at stake is incidental and peripheral rather than central and determinative.

President Tietjen and the large majority of the faculty of Concordia made it apparent from the beginning that they were in a fight to the finish. What happened and how the dissidents conducted themselves was not accidental. It was planned and carried out with dispatch and efficiency. Public statements were released which could hardly be called reconciling. Public displays included the use of black armbands which had been prepared in advance, and the media were fed news which made the battle a nationwide issue.

In September of 1973 the Synod's Board of Directors learned that President Tietjen had participated in the formation of a new organization "Fund for Lutheran Theological Education, Inc." (FLUTE). The leadership of the denomination were not informed that this was happening and it was independent of the Synod, but it was promoted and controlled by people who were then very much inside the church. To an outsider, the formation of ELIM (which later was to become The Association of Evangelical Lutheran Churches) and FLUTE gave every appearance of the beginnings of a new schismatic church. While these things were transpiring, faculty and students were touring the country bringing the message of resistance and rebellion to the people in the pews.

The Suspension of John Tietjen and the "Exile"

On January 20, 1974 John Tietjen was suspended from his office as president. The suspension included the provision that "the contractual obligation of Concordia Seminary to Dr. John H. Tietjen shall continue until the aforesaid charges against him shall be resolved."[34] Dr. Tietjen immediately went public and the students entered the fray as though they were entitled to have a part in the proceedings. Dr. Tietjen called the proceedings against him a "sham," a "mockery," and a "charade." These were fighting words and could only mean that an impasse had been reached and the situation was irrecoverable. Events now moved swiftly and the last act of the drama was soon to take place.

The faculty moved rapidly, with President Tietjen's obvious knowledge and consent, to ring down the curtain and end the play. In February the faculty decided it would not finish out the academic year on the Concordia campus unless their demands were met. "They wanted to teach their own theological position and to run the Seminary their own way." Their letter to the Board of Control was nothing less than sheer revolt and rebellion. It read:

> We of the Faculty Majority and Executive Staff of Concordia Seminary are determined to complete the theological education of the students, and so we are agreed that instruction will resume on February 19, the day following your February meeting. You can bring peace and unity back to the campus and return students to their customary classrooms and duties on that date. You can do these things by affirming that the Scriptures of the Old and New Testaments are the written Word of God and the only rule and norm of teaching and practice and that the Lutheran Confessions are a correct exposition of the Word of God, by declaring that the Scriptures and Confessions alone are the doctrinal basis of The Lutheran Church-Missouri, and by recognizing that the Faculty Majority and Executive Staff teaches in accord with that doctrinal standard.
>
> You can show your agreement with the above in a series of simple actions which it is in your power to take: reinstate John H. Tietjen as president together with the department heads whom you removed; issue a contract to Paul Goetting so that his teaching may continue at our institution; reverse the retirement policy announced in November and the retirements affected by your January action. However, if positive steps are not taken to reverse the decisions of the past months, then on February 19 theological education, conducted by the Faculty Majority and Executive Staff, will begin again. We intend to remain loyal and responsible mem-

bers of the Lutheran Church-Missouri Synod. Our program of theological education will involve the same faculty and staff, the same student body, the same synodically-approved curriculum, and the same Lutheran Confessional commitment, but it will not be under your auspices and not at the customary location, until there is a satisfactory resolution of the issues facing us. Nevertheless instruction must and will resume, even while we wait such a resolution.[35]

The terms of the letter to the Board of Control were easy enough to understand. The Board was asked to give up the control of the institution into the hands of the Seminary faculty and John Tietjen. No room for negotiation was included. It was a hard ultimatum and it is difficult to suppose that those who drew it up thought there was any possibility of the Board abdicating its responsibility. Knowing this, the faculty had made preparations for a seminary-in-exile as they were to call it, and arrangements existed in principle for the use of off-campus facilities to continue a school which came to be known as Seminex. And sad to say, the ecclesiastical world rallied to the support of the revolters and lent support to them.

The larger part of the Concordia student body voted to go "into exile" with the faculty. A "funeral" service was held. Crosses were planted in the Seminary Quadrangle. A march out of the campus premises was held. And, of course, publicity was courted and the news circulated around the world. The students even boarded up Walther Arch on the seminary grounds using the word "exiled" as part of the charade. Perhaps the most humorous aspect of the mass departure was the return of the students and faculty members to eat lunch in the seminary cafeteria right after the exile march. In any event it was a *fait accompli*. Concordia Theological Seminary in St. Louis was gutted. Only five professors remained. A few students met in small groups on the campus. The Seminary in Exile was now a reality. And John Tietjen at the ELIM assembly in Chicago in August of 1974 could say:

The Lutheran Church-Missouri Synod we have known is dead. The institution that has given us life is no more. Its structures are hopelessly corrupt. Its leadership is morally bankrupt. Its rank and file members have chosen to ignore and overlook the evil.[36]

The Aftermath

The exodus of the dissidents from the Seminary campus was the climax of a battle which had been in progress for at least thirty years. It had been brought into sharp focus in 1969 when Dr. Preus was elected to the presidency of the Missouri Synod and Dr. Harms was ousted from office. At stake was the control of the denomination. At the center of the struggle was the theological orthodoxy of the denomination. Whatever the claims of the dissidents that it was a political and ecclesiastical battle rather than a theological one, it is a claim which is impossible to sustain. Of course the control of the denomination was involved. But the basic question was whether it was to be controlled by the orthodox or the liberals. And the use of the historical-critical method was the specific bone of contention between the opposing sides.

Churches were lost to the Synod as the new group consolidated and sought to create a new denomination. Speaking of the exodus of some of the churches one astute observer suggested that the problem was that not enough of them left the Synod. He was saying that some churches remained in the denomination which were not of the same mind and spirit as the great mass of clergy and laypeople. The rump movement was exactly that. It was small and of no real consequence. President Preus reported in April of 1978 that the church had lost 86,616 members and 111 congregations the previous year. He said that the statistics were "sad and unfortunate, certainly—but minimal compared to the dire predictions of the size of the split from the Synod some made a few years back." That year's loss plus earlier losses meant that 152 congregations had left the Synod, but in the last year 41 new congregations were started. When compared to the 6051 congregations that comprise the Synod the losses were fractional indeed. At the end of 1977 baptized membership in the Synod stood at 2,766,958 and confirmed membership was 2,052,180. The annual per capita giving of communicants in the Missouri Synod was $178.66 in 1977, the highest of the major Lutheran bodies.[37] The offshoot of the Missouri controversy, the Association of Evangelical Lutheran Churches, comprised only 116 churches of the total number that left. Its main integrating force was Seminex and that is now shrinking on the vine and promises to be a small and inconsequential factor in Lutheran life. The accrediting of Seminex by the Association of Theological Schools when it had neither property, library, assets, or endowments must stand as a first in the history of accrediting and will go down as a blight on that organization's otherwise distinguished career as an objective agency whose own standards were violated and misused when it came to Seminex.

An interesting side note about the Association of Evangelical Lutheran Churches came from its second convention in April of 1978 when it issued "a call for Lutheran Union." The document called upon "all Lutheran Church bodies in North America to join us in making a formal commitment to organic Church union in a design in which Lutheran life and mission may be consolidated at all levels." The document called for a consultation in 1979 "to establish an implementation process in which the people of the Church at the congregational and judicatory levels will have full participation."[38] The action had its bizarre aspects. A tiny fragment of churches that were schismatic to begin with was calling for the union of all Lutheran bodies when they were unable to keep the unity of the body of which they were part a few years earlier. It is consistent with the spirit manifested by the appeal to the media in the exodus earlier. It did gain the attention of the press and made the AELC a news item for a few days.

The Recovery of Concordia

In the few short years since the "exile" occurred the Concordia Seminary in St. Louis has enjoyed a new lease on life. A new faculty has been gathered, and the student body increases year by year. Dr. Ralph A. Bohlmann, the new president, and every member of the faculty hold to an inerrant Bible. Concordia Seminary is once again a thriving, vital, and effective institution. From the human perspective there was no way the battle for the institution and for the Synod could have been avoided. It was an exhausting and bruising battle for one reason: the infection was allowed to spread over a period of time as the dissident group was being strengthened year in and year out. If the matter had been dealt with when it was small in numbers and in influence it would have been a different matter.

The growth of the liberal movement in the Missouri Synod continued unabated for a few decades because the leadership of the Synod either did not see the signs on the horizon or because the presidents and the Board of Control of the Seminary did not have the courage to attack the problem and root out the disturbers of the peace. The dissidents knew the history of Christendom very well. They were well aware that all the major denominations except Missouri and the Southern Baptist Convention had gone through the same wringer and had been taken over by liberal leadership. They knew that among the theological seminaries of the major denominations, with the exception of the Southern Baptist Convention and the Missouri Synod, there was not to be found a single institution which could be said to be distinctively evangelical or orthodox. In view of the liberal track record of the past, John Tietjen and his faculty had the data of history to support their hopes that they would emerge victorious. Their mistake was that they failed to realize that there might be an exception to the historic pattern. And there was. It was the Lutheran Church-Missouri Synod.

What of the Future for Missouri?

The Missouri Synod has two theological seminaries, one at St. Louis and the other at Fort Wayne, Indiana. It is the only large denomination of which it can be said that all their seminaries and all their faculty members are committed to biblical inerrancy and do not accept or use the historical-critical method as a viable tool for theological education.

The reversal which has taken place in the Missouri Synod is the first such event in American Christianity in the twentieth century. No denomination of any consequence has gone from liberalism to conservatism. No denomination has responded to the threat of liberal takeover and dealt with it more strongly than Missouri. A battle for the soul of the Synod has been fought and won, but whether the war will be won is another matter. In the mid-twenties the General Assembly of the Presbyterian Church in the USA went on record affirming biblical inerrancy. But within ten years all that it did was annulled. Princeton Theological Seminary was reorganized. J. Gresham Machen and some of his conservative colleagues left to start the Westminster Theological Seminary. Today it would be difficult to find anyone on the Princeton faculty of whom it can be said he believes in biblical inerrancy as defined by the General Assemby in the 1920s. A battle was fought and won in the Presbyterian Church but the war was lost later. Today that church is an inclusivist body with an evangelical wing which can hardly be expected to turn any one of its theological seminaries into a citadel for orthodoxy.

The strong stand of the Missouri Synod for orthodoxy has attracted some to its side. The *Religious News Service* reported the case of a pastor and part of his congregation who left a Lutheran Church in America building in Indiana to become a mission of the Missouri Synod. The pastor, J. Kincaid Smith, spoke about the destructive and subtle heresy in the LCA which denigrates a literal approach to the Bible. He was opposed to the seventh- and eighth-grade teacher's guide for the LCA Sunday school which states that the purpose of the course is to help children understand it is no longer necessary to believe in the miraculous elements of the Bible. The LCA is undoubtedly the most liberal of the Lutheran groups and the only major body among the Lutherans which does not have inerrancy written into its confessional statement. The RNS report said:

> A 1973 graduate of the Hamma School of Theology at Wittenburg University, Pastor Smith found himself "empty" after two years in the ministry. His sermons and ministry were not providing for his parishioners "the fulfillment that is there for us in historic Christianity," he said. He realized, he said, that he never had received Christ in his heart, but had learned to ridicule such an idea as being simplistic and fundamentalist. As his faith deepened through Christ, he said, he saw that the Missouri Synod which he formerly ridiculed was on the right track. And his feeling that the Lord had placed him in the Lutheran Church in America to bring about peaceful change proved "untenable." . . . He and his new congregation feel that the Missouri Synod successfully reversed the tendency toward liberalism with its action replacing "moderately liberal" professors with conservative men at Concordia Seminary in St. Louis, Mo., in 1973. "To say that you are moderately liberal is like saying you are moderately pregnant," he said. "Even in that as time passes the condition becomes more obvious." "I believe that those differences between conservative Lutheran and liberal Lutheran positions is infinitely greater than

the differences which have historically divided us from other main-line denominations," Pastor Smith stated. "It is an impassable gulf."[39]

Missouri's Continuing Problem

Missouri's major problem right now is the reshaping of its colleges and universities. Some Lutheran collegiate institutions are orthodox; others are not. Some of the strongest supporters and defenders of the same viewpoint as that of the Concordia dissidents are found in Missouri Synod colleges and universities. And those voices are still in those institutions, teaching students who some day will be theological seminary students. However orthodox their seminary training may be, the influence and effect of wrong teaching at the collegiate level can manifest itself after the ordinands have entered the ministry and they can, in turn, become the founding fathers of another revolt. This means that eternal vigilance is required even if all the educational institutions at all levels are orthodox. There is also the danger of infection when students take graduate studies in neoorthodox and liberal graduate schools.

The case of Valparaiso University illustrates one of the remaining problems as yet unresolved. This is the nation's largest Lutheran institution of higher learning. Its president retired in August of 1978. Prior to his retirement his successor was named. It turned out to be Dr. Robert Schnabel who came to Valparaiso from Wartburg College, which is affiliated with the American Lutheran Church. Dr. Schnabel was president of Concordia College in Bronxville, New York, from 1971 to 1976. This is a Missouri Synod school. He left there after disagreements with "a conservative-dominated Board of Control."[40] How he will fit into the Missouri picture now that the Concordia battle has been won and liberalism uprooted in the seminaries remains to be seen. Until the colleges and universities of the Synod have been brought into a harmonious relationship with the teaching of the seminaries the problem of deviation from the orthodox stance of the denomination remains.

The Lutheran Church-Missouri still has a long way to go. But the first steps have been taken on the long road to renewal and to the reestablishment of the traditional orthodoxy of a great denomination. Much of the credit for the turnaround must go to the often maligned, misused, and abused J. A. O. Preus, the president of the Synod. It would be foolish to claim that this man has made no mistakes or that he is free from the warts and bumps most of us display to our discomfort. Whatever his shortcomings, he stands tall among the stalwarts whose names will be written in the books of history as defenders of the true faith who have risked all and suffered much for the cause of Christ and the Gospel. His depth of perception, his sense of his denomination's needs, and the resolute pursuit of his goals mark him off as an example to many who have similar battles to fight and goals to reach.

NOTES

[1]Kurt E. Marquart, *Anatomy of an Explosion* (Fort Wayne: Concordia, 1977), p. 102.
[2]*This We Believe* (Milwaukee: Northwestern Publishing House), pp. 4-6.
[3]Marquart, p. 4.
[4]Ibid., p. 5.
[5]Ibid., p. 41
[6]Ibid.
[7]Ibid.
[8]Ibid.
[9]Ibid., p. 29.
[10]Ibid., p. 30.
[11]Ibid., p. 76.
[12]Ibid., p. 80.
[13]Ibid., p. 123.
[14]Ibid.
[15]Ibid., p. 81.
[16]Ibid., pp. 108-109.
[17]Ibid., p. 109.
[18]Ibid., p. 88
[19]Ibid., p. 89.
[20]Ibid., pp. 89-90.
[21]Ibid., p. 92.
[22]Ibid.
[23]Ibid., pp. 92-93.
[24]The Board of Control, *Exodus from Concordia* (St. Louis: Concordia Seminary, 1977), p. 19.
[25]Ibid., p. 33.
[26]Ibid.
[27]Ibid., p. 35.
[28]Ibid.
[29]Ibid., pp. 35-36.

[30]Ibid., p. 43.
[31]Ibid., p. 53.
[32]Ibid.
[33]Ibid., p. 61.
[34]Ibid., p. 94.
[35]Ibid., p. 114.
[36]Ibid., p. 140.
[37]*Religious News Service*, April 17, 1978.
[38]Ibid.
[39]Ibid., January 27, 1977.
[40]Ibid., April 11, 1978.

7

The Historical-Critical Method: The Bible's Deadly Enemy

I have stated elsewhere that the historical-critical method is the Bible's greatest enemy. I am convinced that this is the case. But the documentation needs expansion for several reasons. One of them is that the church exists in history and is related to the movements of history, secular as well as religious. The church is not of the world, both with respect to its nature and its ultimate destiny, but it is in the world. It is to have an influence upon the world. At the same time, however, it is always possible for the world to have an influence upon the church. Since the world is constitutionally different from the church, the influence of the world upon the church is always and of necessity a debilitating influence which brings with it decline and decay for the church. The church in history has been repeatedly affected by the world, and this has brought with it times of backsliding or even apostasy from which there has been recovery by the intervention of the Spirit of God who has brought seasons of refreshing through revival and spiritual awakenings which have shaken the church and even the world.

Today the church is in a state of disarray. This, of course, does not mean that God is not at work saving people. There are all sorts of evangelistic outreach among the peoples of the world today. Multitudes are being saved in Latin America, in Africa, and even in America. The situation is rather dark in certain others places such as Europe. I do not know of a large nation in Europe where church attendance exceeds five per cent on any Sunday morning. The religious situation in Scandinavia, Britain, and Germany is especially dismaying. These are countries in which large numbers of the inhabitants were dynamically related to the churches in centuries gone by. Today the people in these nations are just as much in need of evangelization as are Muslims, Hindus, and Buddhists. On the surface, the situation in the United States appears much brighter, but the same inroads which brought about the current state of affairs in European churches is gradually overtaking the United States as well.

The disarray of the church today has not come upon it suddenly. It is the result of forces which have been at work for generations. The full flower of these working forces has come upon the church in this generation. For an understanding of what happened and how the present situation has come into being we must go back to the Renaissance. It was during this period of history that western culture changed its orientation basically, and in so doing turned away from the foundations on which it had rested for more than a thousand years. The Renaissance became the new leaven that was to permeate society and the church slowly and inexorably for several centuries. There are some things I cannot say, however. First, I cannot say that the influence of the Renaissance has reached its peak and has tapered or will taper off. Second, I cannot say there will be no divine intervention in which a radical change will turn the church and the world away from the Renaissance tradition to a theistic one which will reverse the present trend. I am sure, however, that the church is in grave trouble right now, and evangelicals have been and are being influenced by adverse forces in astonishing ways. I do not regard the evangelical situation with complacency, but of this I shall say more later when speaking about the future as I see it. Right now I must state what the Renaissance did which has so affected the church and how its influence is related to the historical-critical method.

The Renaissance

Paul Tournier wrote a provocative book titled *The Whole Person in a Broken World*. It is valuable partly because he has related psychology to religion and in doing this spoke from the perspective of one who has embraced the Christian faith. He said the Renaissance was the turning point for modern man, and showed how it brought about the current malaise of western culture. He did not hesitate to say that movements like fascism and communism spring from the Renaissance as well. Basically what the Renaissance did was this: it taught man an opposite view of the world from that which had prevailed in antiquity and the Middle Ages. In place of a world looked at through the eyeglasses of "a spiritual, religious, and poetic view" "it substituted a scientific, realistic, economic view."[1] "Abruptly humanity rejected that which it had hitherto allowed to guide it."[2]

We should not suppose that the conduct of men before the Renaissance was always in accord with the presuppositions on which life was based. There were immoral men, a variety of philosophies, a church that itself committed abominable deeds. But even while these things were happening, men everywhere agreed there were transcendent values which underlay all of life. For example, men may have committed fornication and adultery and surely there were homosexual activities. But their value system condemned these activities. The Renaissance, however, was to change all of this. Today, when people perform the same acts, they do so with this difference: they claim that what they do does not violate any canons of morality for they have discarded morality as known before the Renaissance.

Dr. Tournier concluded that

> The modern world has honestly decided to exclude everything emotional, moral, and religious. On November 10, 1619, in the course of a real mystical crisis, Descartes caught a glimpse of a new civilization in which men, in order to be able to tolerate themselves, would establish a science founded upon reason and common sense, a dependable science free from those moral value judgments which in his conviction had been the cause of all their previous controversies.[3]

Science was substituted in place of the moral and the religious. Science, of course, was morally neutral and supposedly completely objective. There were no inner realities such as spirit that had any bearing on man and his life on this planet. One could not start with the presupposition that there is any God to whom tribute must be paid or who ordered life and determined the destinies of men. Everything must be considered without the use of such nondemonstrable ideas. The

November-December 1977 issue of *Harvard Magazine* carried an article by one of Harvard's three most popular professors in terms of student enrollment, Eric J. Chaisson. His article was titled "The Scenario of Cosmic Evolution." The editor of the magazine included this statement about the article: "To make new discoveries about the origins of matter and life, modern science is synthesizing research from many disciplines." Except, of course, anything metaphysical or pertaining to a Creator. This is what Professor Chaisson said:

> Later, but only as recently as a few hundred years ago, man began to adopt a more critical stance toward himself and his universe, seeking to view the world *objectively* (my italics). With it, modern science was born, the first product of which was the Copernican crisis. The idea of the centrality of the earth was demolished forever (a non-scientific statement). Human beings came to feel they were marooned on a tiny particle of dust drifting aimlessly through a hostile universe. . . . Recent scientific developments . . . have demonstrated, that, as living creatures, we inhabit no very special place in the universe at all. . . .
>
> Who are we? Where did we come from? In essence, we are a combination of chemical elements, produced eons ago inside the fiery cores of massive stars. . . . The proper answers to these questions are evolutionary ones that enable us to relate ourselves to all forms of matter, indeed, to the whole material universe. . . . We are in a transition period that no Earth society has ever encountered. This is not a doomsday forecast, but a statement that social and political organizations appear unprepared to deal with the widespread changes necessary for our continued existence. How then can we survive? Actually it's easy. We simply become more intelligent! . . .
>
> The philosophy that we are the product of cosmic evolution is not a new one. It may be as old as that first *Homo sapiens* who contemplated existence. But as we enter into the last quarter of the twentieth century, for the first time we can begin to identify conceptually and test experimentally some of the subtle astrophysical and biochemical processes that enable us to recognize the cosmos as the ground and origin of our existence. . . . The cosmos is no longer cold and hostile—because it is *our* universe. It brought us forth and maintains our being. We are, in the very literal sense of the words, children of the universe.[4]

These statements are wholly inconsonant with the basic evolutionary hypothesis the author presupposes along with a series of opinionative but nonobjective observations, and are taken without a grain of salt by the academic community. For our purposes here what is important is that this *Weltanschauung* is the outgrowth of the underlying principles of the Renaissance. If the viewpoint espoused is true, then there are no objective values which can be deduced from it, and we are left high and dry. As a consequence the words of Paul Tournier became more significant:

> Thus modern man appears to be disgusted with the religion for which he nevertheless feels a homesickness. He has repressed it, banished it from his life, proclaimed the exclusion of everything beyond the reach of his senses. He has consummated a great rift between the spiritual and the temporal world. And ever since, he has lived in a tragic duality.[5]

Dr. Tournier goes on to note that there is "a fundamental demarcation between science and religion." They exist as separate domains and the boundary line between them should never be erased. "Today," said Dr. Tournier

> this scientific dogma is almost unanimously accepted. A man can believe what he wishes; this is only his affair. But as a scientific scholar, a builder of civilization he dare not give any consideration whatever to his faith. He must confine himself exclusively to the ground of objectivity. Faith is the domain of hypothesis which one can go on discussing forever. Only objectivity leads to sure and effective knowledge.[6]

The ideas that undergirded the Renaissance penetrated all of life. This penetration included the world of religious scholarship. One of the consequences may be seen in the rise of the school of comparative religion. In this area it quickly became popular to assume that religion is man's invention and that differing forms are equally valid, for no religion is unique and forever binding. Thus one seminary dean said several years ago:

> I'm not afraid of the plurality of truths. This doesn't mean that I don't make distinctions, but only that I hold it open that what is true for the Buddhist in his situation may be as valid for him as mine is for me.

Perhaps no other part of the western world accepted the ideas of the Renaissance more enthusiastically and with special reference to the Christian faith than the Germans. The notion of the scientific approach to the Bible became the watchword of the day. Consonant with Renaissance views the Bible was looked upon as a human book written by men who were creatures of their times. One needed to distinguish between what they said and what is true. Fortunately or unfortunately the German higher critics retained the idea of God and imagined that somehow He was able to communicate something about Himself to man through the agency of human writers who were no different from the rest of us. The Renaissance idea found lodgment in the mind of one German who became the real father of the historical-critical method. So we now turn our attention to Johann Semler.

Johann Salomo Semler

Johann Semler was born in 1725 at Saalfeld, Thuringia. He was the son of a Lutheran pietist pastor which fact influenced him adversely so that he came to detest Pietism. Strangely enough he was to occupy the chair of theology at Halle University which was of pietist background. Before that he taught at Coburg and Altdorf. In 1757 he succeeded Baumgarten as head of the theological faculty at Halle. He was the one who developed the principles of textual criticism of the Bible. He departed from the orthodoxy of his father when he challenged the idea of the verbal inspiration of the Scriptures, holding to a strictly historical interpretation of the Bible. Professor Eugene F. Klug had this to say about him and about the methodology he introduced into the blood stream of the church:

> The historical-critical approach to the Bible has its history, of course. Johann Salomo Semler (late 18th century) is usually designated as father of the technique which not only handled the Bible as an object for historical scrutiny and criticism, but also as a book little different from and no more holy than any other, and surely not to be equated with the Word of God. Very plainly he was saying that he rejected the divine inspiration of the text. This was but a symptom of his total theological stance, a tip of the iceberg so to speak. His was really a revolt against miracles and the supernatural in general, and against heaven in particular. God's supernatural activity in history simply was not in Semler's "book." Not unexpectedly, under his and others' hand, the Bible

text and content suffered deliberate vivisection. The surgery was quite often radical and overt, without benefit of anaesthesia for those directly affected by it in the churches.[7]

Gerhard Maier points out in his book *The End of the Historical-Critical Method* that the heart of what Professor Semler thought and propagated is contained in one sentence he wrote: "The root of the evil [in theology] is the interchangeable use of the terms 'Scripture' and 'Word of God'. "[8] By this Dr. Semler meant that the Bible or Scripture contains the Word of God, or that not all of Scripture *is* the Word of God. This meant that his goal from that point onward was to find the Word of God in Scripture.

I started this chapter by referring to the Renaissance, stating that today's situation can be understood only in the light of what happened as a result of that movement. Whether Professor Semler realized it or not he was a product of Renaissance thinking. He was a secularist in spirit. He approached the Bible as a scientist, with supposed objectivity and without bias. He did not therefore really acknowledge what had been the pre-Renaissance dictum that God had spoken and had not stuttered in His speech. He did allow that there is a Word of God but he set himself up as the determinator of what the Word of God is. And this is exactly what lies at the heart of the historical-critical method. Man is autonomous. He decides for himself what the Word of God is. Once this becomes true, then all men are faced with the problem of determining which man is correct in saying what parts of Scripture are the Word of God. It leaves forever open whether I choose to believe one critic over another since all of them disagree with each other.

It should be clear, for example, that if I accept the ruminations of Professor Bultmann I have immediately rejected the viewpoint of all the Reformers, the viewpoint of Augustine and the church fathers. I have effectively rejected the human authors of the Bible from Paul and Peter to Matthew, Mark, Luke, and John. Why then should I accept Dr. Bultmann and reject the others? This is a question which must be faced candidly.

J. I. Packer is surely one of evangelicalism's great British scholars. He authored a notable book titled *Fundamentalism and the Word of God*. Another book which is directly related to the present discussion was published in 1965 and is titled *God Speaks to Man–Revelation and the Bible*. Dr. Packer says that the churches have reached a point in which there is "a famine . . . of hearing the words of the Lord" (Amos 8:11f.). He said at no time since the Reformation has the church as a body been so unsure, tentative, and confused as to what they should believe and do. "Preaching is hazy; heads are muddled; hearts fret; doubts drain our strength. . . . We stand under the divine judgment. For us, too, the Word of God is in a real sense *lost*." Dr. Packer sees the source of the problem to be "biblical criticism." He is talking, of course, about the historical-critical method. He said:

> Liberal Theology, in its pride, has long insisted that we are wiser than our fathers about the Bible, and must not read it as they did, but must base our approach to it on the "assured results" of criticism, making due allowances for the human imperfections and errors of its authors. This insistence has a threefold effect. (1) It produces a new papalism—the infallibility of the scholars, from whom we learn what the "assured results" are. (2) It raises a doubt about every single Bible passage, as to whether it truly embodies revelation or not. (3) And it destroys the reverent, receptive, self-distrusting attitude of approach to the Bible, without which it cannot be known to be "God's Word written". . . . The result? The spiritual famine of which Amos spoke. God judges our pride by leaving us to the barrenness, hunger, and discomfort which flow from our self-induced inability to hear His Word.[9]

While Dr. Packer acknowledged some of the valuable results of much of modern careful Bible study he asked how it could at the same time be so destructive. Its mistake was that it separated the Bible from the Word of God. In short it was the error begun by Johann Semler and perpetuated in the historical-critical method to this hour. Inerrancy is impossible to accept once this deadly distinction is made. So speaks J. I. Packer, one of evangelicalism's most careful scholars.

The Historical-Critical Method Per Se

Grant Osborne of the Trinity Evangelical Divinity School observed: "The truth is that most scholars end up with conclusions remarkably similar to the presuppositions with which they begin their study."[10] The truth of this observation is patent. It applies to myself as it applies to everyone else. It behooves us to inquire about the presuppositions of those who employ the historical-critical methodology. This methodology is not neutral. It starts with a negative assumption. It says that nothing can be accepted as the Word of God in Scripture unless it can be proven to be so. In other words, unless it can be proved to be valid it must be considered invalid. Thus the higher critic comes to Scripture with doubt, not with faith. He comes with the wrong spirit. Whoever comes to the Bible with doubt will always find what he thinks to be good reasons to throw out at least some portions of the Book.

Anyone who thinks the historical-critical method is neutral is misinformed. Since its presuppositions are unacceptable to the evangelical mind this method cannot be used by the evangelical as it stands. The very use by the evangelical of the term, the historical-critical method, is a mistake when it comes to describing his own approach to Scripture. The only way he can use it is to invest it with a different meaning. But this can only confuse the uninformed. Moreover, it is not fair to those scholars who use it in the correct way with presuppositions which are different from those of the evangelical. It appears to me that modern evangelical scholars (and I may have been guilty of this myself) have played fast and loose with the term perhaps because they wanted acceptance by academia. They seem too often to desire to be members of the club which is nothing more than practicing an inclusiveness that undercuts the normativity of the evangelical theological position. This may be done, and often is, under the illusion that by this method the opponents of biblical inerrancy can be won over to the evangelical viewpoint. But practical experience suggests that rarely does this happen and the cost of such an approach is too expensive, for it gives credence and lends respectability to a method which is the deadly enemy of theological orthodoxy.

One question surfaces immediately, and how one answers the question will determine the direction his study and his conclusions will take. This is the question: Is the Bible above criticism or is it subject to the conclusions of men drawn from extrabiblical materials? Stated differently I might phrase it this way: Does the Bible sit in judgment on men or do men sit in judgment on the Bible? As soon as I negate anything the Scripture affirms I have by that decision made myself a judge of Scripture. If I reject a historical datum contained in the Bible, it can only mean that something outside the Bible is considered more definitive and more authoritative than the Bible. And whatever it is that is above the Bible must be superior to the Bible, so that its uniqueness is lost and its authority and truthfulness have been diminished.

At the heart of the historical-critical method lies the notion that the Bible is subject to something outside of it and this becomes superior to Scripture. I can illustrate it many ways. Every "critic" comes to the Bible asking a variety of questions. Among the questions both liberals and evangelicals ask is this one: Who wrote this book? Let's be specific: Who wrote the Book of Ephesians? The historical-critical advocate phrases the question differently. He asks: Did Paul write the Book of Ephesians? Asking the question this way demonstrates the negative spirit with which the questioner comes to the Book of Ephesians. Of one thing there can be no doubt. The Book of Ephesians itself claims to have been written by the apostle Paul. Therefore no responsible evangelical could ask the question as to whether Paul wrote the book. His faith approach to Scripture and his presupposition that it is truthful compel him to conclude that Paul wrote Ephesians. He can give the reasons why he believes Paul wrote the Book of Ephesians, but the question "Did Paul write the book?" is no question for him. He is shut up to Scripture. And it makes no difference whether the internal evidence of grammar, sentence structure, use of different words, and the like make it appear that Ephesians, for example, seems different from Galatians and on that basis one can deny Pauline authorship. An evangelical can and should struggle with the differences between one Pauline book and another. But the moment he uses these differences to conclude that Ephesians was not written by Paul he has surrendered his basic presupposition that the Bible is true in all its parts. If he brings external evidence to bear on the situation the result is the same. There are many scholars who do not believe that 2 Peter was written by the apostle Peter. They argue that its contents require a second-century date. Of course Peter was dead long before the second century dawned. And dead men don't write books. If 2 Peter was written in the second century A.D., it was not written by Peter. But if it claims to have been written by Peter when actually it was written in the second century, the claim to Petrine authorship is false. And no talk about some pseudonymous author using Peter's name because he was conveying petrine doctrine answers the question.

Why would some persons other than Paul or Peter use the names of these apostles when writing books attributed to them? If the unknown authors did so in order that their books be accepted by the churches that is rank deception. If the books could not stand in the names of the true authors then the product itself is questionable. Moreover, it is inconceivable that the Holy Spirit would be part of this deception, and it is an insult to the sovereignty of God to suggest that the use of the names of the true authors would invalidate the books. Wholly apart from authorship, the books in and of themselves would bear the divine imprimatur and that would be sufficient. A number of the books in the Bible carry no author's label. Yet they bear the divine seal of God upon them. The divine seal does not require that a pseudonymous name must be inserted to authenticate any book.

Another illustration of the illicit use of Scripture by advocates of the historical-critical method comes from the Book of Genesis. The simplest reading of Genesis and the rest of the Bible makes it plain that Adam and Eve are regarded as historic personages and the first parents of the human race. The genealogical tables include them, and their sons and grandsons are named as though they too were real persons. When critics declare that the biblical accounts here are myth or saga and not real history, they are allowing extrabiblical data and personal opinions or hermeneutical dodges to sit in judgment on the Bible. Any evangelical who does this has consciously or unconsciously applied principles inherent in the historical-critical methodology to Scripture. The alternative to special creation is the theory of evolution. A number of evangelical teachers in Christian institutions are theistic evolutionists. They teach this view in the classrooms of evangelical schools. There is no way the evolutionary hypothesis can be developed from the phenomena of Scripture without doing violence to the data. Paul Tournier quoted Professor P. Lemoine, curator of the Paris Museum, as saying: "Evolution is a kind of dogma in which its priests no longer believe, but which they preserve for the people. One must have the courage to say this. . . ."[11] Dr. Tournier later said that

> . . . . a dogmatic statement of the doctrine of evolution remains one of the challenges to the Christian faith. How can we believe the Bible, they think, when the very first pages are refuted by science? Our first father was not Adam, not a perfect man created in the image of God, but a poor, primitive, unintelligent product of blind animal evolution, a link between the apes and us. All the discoveries of paleontology, they think, contradict the world-view which is given to us in Genesis.[12]

Almost without exception those who employ the historical-critical methodology are evolutionists. This should come as no surprise because their basic presuppositions preclude accepting the Bible as trustworthy to begin with. What is surprising is that those called evangelicals sometimes employ the same methodology and arrive at the same conclusions and still think of themselves as genuine evangelicals.

In this connection the observations of C. S. Lewis are helpful. He pointed out the same truth stated above that the critics sit in judgment on Scripture rather than letting Scripture sit in judgment on them. C. S. Lewis himself was a literary critic and knew something about the discipline. But he had little confidence in the critics of Scripture and for good reasons. On the subversion of belief in the Word of God, Lewis said:

> The undermining of the old orthodoxy (Biblical authority) has been mainly the work of divines engaged in New Testament criticism. The authority of experts in that discipline is the authority in deference to whom we are asked to give up a huge mass of beliefs shared in common by the early Church, the Fathers, the Middle Ages, the Reformers, and even in the nineteenth century.[13]

He went on to evaluate the credibility of these twentieth-century critics and to explain why he had little faith in them:

> I want to explain what it is that makes me skeptical about this

authority. . . . First whatever these men may be as Biblical critics, I distrust them as critics. They seem to me to lack literary judgment, to be imperceptive about the very quality of the texts they are reading. . . . These men ask me to believe they can read between the lines of the old texts; the evidence is their obvious inability to read (in any sense worth discussing) the lines themselves. They claim to see Fern-seed and can't see an elephant ten yards away in broad daylight.[14]

Speaking about the prince of biblical demythologizers, Rudolph Bultmann, Dr. Lewis wrote:

Dr. Bultmann never wrote a gospel. Has the experience of his learned, specialized, and no doubt meritorious life really given him any power of seeing into the minds of those long dead men who were caught up in what, on any view, must be regarded as the central religious experience of the whole human race?[15]

Alluding to higher criticism's dismissal of miracles Professor Lewis said:

If one is speaking of authority, the united authority of all the Biblical critics in the world counts for nothing here. On this they speak simply as men; men who are obviously influenced by, and perhaps insufficiently critical of, the spirit of the age they grew up in.[16]

With respect to what the literary critics said of his own writing, C. S. Lewis added what might be the best postscript for any discussion of the historical-critical methodology:

My impression is that in the whole of my experience not one of these guesses has on any point been right; that the method (literary criticism) shows a record of 100 per cent failure.[17]

Unquestionably the users of the historical-critical methodology come out with answers which are in accord with their presuppositions, just as I come out with answers consistent with my presuppositions. The difference lies in the fact that at least I have an external, objective authority to which I can repair and against which I can measure not only my opinions but the opinions of all the critics and skeptics of all ages to discover whether what they have said is true. But the user of the historical-critical methodology ends up on a dead-end street. He has nothing but his own opinions on which to depend. And his opinions vary so widely from those held by

others who use the same methodology that nothing but confusion and uncertainty result from the use of this method that
nullifies Scripture while it subjects it to the whims of sinful
man.

Gerhard Maier

Gerhard Maier's book *The End of the Historical-Critical
Method* should be read by every one who professes to be a
Christian. In his book he has put his finger on the most crucial
issue troubling the church in our age—the question of authority. The destruction of external, objective authority based on
the Hebrew-Christian tradition was one of the results of
the Renaissance. That authority in turn was based upon the
self-revelation of God in the Old and New Testament Scriptures. The Renaissance with its emphasis on science
and reason without revelation could only regard the Bible
as a human book. This is what Johann Semler and those
who now follow the historical-critical method have done.
Inerrancy then is an impossible postulate, for anything
human must bear the marks of humanity, one of which is
error.

Professor Maier has contributed to the present dialogue by
making clear that which is central to the historical-critical
method. Starting with Johann Semler's statement that Scripture and the Word of God are not synonymous Dr. Maier
stated:

> It is evident that the attempt to dig out the Word of God in Scrip-
> ture, or what is genuine and binding in the Bible, inescapably
> leads to the obligation of finding "the canon in the canon." If one
> does not want to give himself up to subjective, arbitrary action,
> then objective standards, generally convincing, must be estab-
> lished.[18]

Dr. Maier went on to say that it is impossible for anyone to
discover the canon in the canon. He pointed out that there is
no agreement among the scholars as to the canon in the canon.
They disagree with each other and often cannot make up their
own minds on this question. They are always seeking without
ever finding, starting but never finishing, beginning a journey
but never arriving at the destination. Moreover, no one can
establish from the Bible any reason to endorse the conclusion

that there is a divine Scripture and a human Scripture. No one should misunderstand the title of Professor Maier's book. He is not saying that we have come to the end of the historical-critical method. He is saying what the end of the historical-critical method requires—the finding of the canon in the canon. And he states categorically that this cannot be done for a variety of reasons.

From the practical point of view Dr. Maier's work points up the problem facing the average reader of the Bible. He has never heard of the Graf-Wellhausen documentary hypothesis. JEPD means nothing to him. He doesn't often know scholars are saying that the first eleven chapters of Genesis are not historical. He has always thought the Book of Isaiah was written by the prophet Isaiah. He reads the Bible and thinks the Book of Daniel was written in advance of the events prophesied. He reads the Gospels and assumes that the words of Jesus were spoken by Him. He reads Ephesians, Titus, 1 and 2 Timothy and thinks they were written by Paul. Form and redaction criticism are meaningless terms to the same reader of the Bible. He doesn't even know he is supposed to find the canon in the canon. And if he did he wouldn't have the vaguest notion about how he would do this. How then is the Bible going to help people like this when the conclusions they draw from their reading of the Bible will be in conflict with most of the conclusions arrived at by the higher critics? The Bible has become the book of the critics, not the book of John Ploughman who is turning furrows in his field. Also, it is a book that has really been a closed book not known to men until the last two centuries when the historical-critical methodology opened the curtains and swept the cobwebs away. The Church Fathers and the Reformers will waken in the Resurrection (if there is one) to discover they had preached from a thousand pulpits that which was not true and they were no more than blind leaders of the blind.

At the end of his treatise Dr. Maier concluded that Scripture and the Word of God are synonymous and all of it is free from error. This is what he said:

> And beyond all doubt, Luther considered the *entire* Bible to be inspired. . . .What this signified for Luther is evident with exemplary clarity from his themes for debate under the title *De*

Fide (concerning faith) of 1535. No. 59 states: "For we are not all apostles, who by certain decree of God have been sent to us as infallible teachers." No. 60 reads: "Therefore not they, but we, who are without such a decree may err and fall in faith." According to this, the apostles in their statements in Scripture are infallible because God has sent them to us as teachers. Inspiration here aims at the infallibility and the certainty of the faith which depends on this Word. Inspiration lifts Scripture above all human utterances as well as above all access by human criticism and, notwithstanding the fact that it was written by men, gives it the attributes and the preeminence of divine discourse. "When God speaks through men, that is a far different thing than man speaking himself." From this Luther concludes: "So nothing but the divine words should be the first principles of Christians, but the words of all men are conclusions which are derived therefrom and must be led back to them and verified by them." From here we arrive in a straight line at the convictions and formulations of late orthodoxy after Luther, where we read in the *Examen* of Hollaz or the *Epitome* of Calixt: "Whatever Holy Scripture teaches is unfailingly true," supplemented and supported by the thesis: "In the most exact sense of the concept the Holy Scriptures are the Word of God."[19]

The Conscious and Unconscious Use of the Historical-Critical Method by Evangelicals

It now remains to consider how the principles of the historical-critical method are being applied in practice today and how this use effectively destroys scriptural infallibility and in effect forces the user to find "the canon in the canon."

Revelational and Non-Revelational Scripture

Some evangelicals are anxious to preserve the full trustworthiness of Scripture in matters of faith and practice. But they are convinced there are what I would call errors in Scripture for which provision must be made by constructing a doctrine of Scripture to accommodate this sort of thing. I made reference to this in another setting in *The Battle for the Bible*. There I used the illustration provided by the paper presented by Dr. Daniel Fuller to the Evangelical Theological Society at its annual meeting in Toronto, Canada, in December 1967. In his paper Dr. Fuller plainly said there are two kinds of Scripture—revelational and nonrevelational. He agreed that revelational

Scripture is wholly free from error. But nonrevelational Scripture has error in it. He did this within the context of the view of B. B. Warfield, a view which he properly and correctly expounded to the effect that all biblical statements "whether they pertain to knowledge that makes men wise unto salvation or to such subjects as botany, meteorology, or paleontology, are equally true."

Dr. Fuller, however, did not agree with B. B. Warfield, but felt that given the passage of time and greater knowledge B. B. Warfield, if he were alive today, would accept the slight change that he recommended. He said it this way:

> I am sure Warfield would agree that if the doctrinal verses explicitly taught only the inerrancy of revelational matters—matters that make men wise unto salvation—and that if the phenomena bore this out, loyalty to Biblical authority would demand that we define inerrancy accordingly.[20]

To define inerrancy in such a manner as suggested by Dr. Fuller would invalidate biblical inerrancy as it has been understood traditionally. To limit inerrancy as he suggests to revelational matters requires the ability to know which matters are revelational and which are not. And if nonrevelational matters are those which we can learn by ourselves then Dr. Fuller has given himself greater problems, because he has elsewhere referred to the differences in numbers in Chronicles over against Kings, and there is no way he can discover for himself, apart from Scripture, what the numbers were.

If parts of Scripture are nonrevelational they cannot be considered to be the Word of God in the same way revelational matters are. This means that Dr. Fuller and whoever follows this line of thought must, of necessity, find the canon in the canon. And they are right back into the historical-critical method which says that Scripture and the Word of God are not synonymous. This appears to be exactly what Dr. Fuller is saying.

Scripture and Science

There are self-proclaimed evangelicals who definitely think there are scientific errors in the Bible. I mentioned two in another connection: Dr. Robert Laurin in his Old Testament syllabus which he co-authored with David Hubbard included remarks that the Bible teaches a three-story universe as well as a flat earth. We know that the earth is not flat and no one believes in a three-story universe today. These are scientific matters in which the Bible and science seem to be at odds and science is thought to be correct. Perhaps this illustration is inadequate because I do not for one moment think the Bible says or intimates that the earth is flat. Nor do I think it says we live in a three-story universe. The reader should note that I have carefully refrained from saying the Bible "teaches" that the earth is flat. Someone might suppose if I stated it that way that I was weaseling out of the situation by asserting I believe that the Bible *says* the earth is flat but *does not teach* it. Of this more will be said shortly. If the Bible says something, the Bible also teaches it. Thus, if Jesus really said the mustard seed is the smallest of all seeds known to men then or now, He was stating something which is not true. If He said it, He affirmed it; and if He affirmed it, He taught it. But He neither said it nor taught it.

A few pages ago I referred to Adam and Eve and to evolution. I recently listened to a tape by Dale Moody of the Southern Baptist Seminary in Louisville. He was speaking about Adam and Eve, and dealt with the question where Cain got his wife. He did two things. He endorsed the evolutionary view (and this I already documented in the chapter on the Southern Baptist Convention). But he also made it clear that he does not think all men descended from the first man, Adam. This is consistent with what scientists commonly say, but it is at variance with what the Scripture says. So Dr. Moody prefers the "assured results" of scientific inquiry and allows science to sit in judgment on Scripture and nullify it.

In the cases I have just cited we can witness the use of the historical-critical method which leads, as night follows day, to the need for finding the canon in the canon. All of Scripture is not the Word of God unless God is the author of error, and I doubt that the people to whom I have made reference here would go that far.

Faith and Practice

The record shows that more and more evangelicals limit the trustworthiness of the Bible to matters of faith and practice.

One thing is apparent immediately. The argument that inerrancy or infallibility is limited to matters of faith and practice carries with it the guarantee that whatever is not related to faith and practice can have error in it. No person who believes in inerrancy would fail to say so. Nor would he limit infallibility or inerrancy to part of the Bible when in fact he believes all the Bible to be inerrant. Thus an inerrantist who would vote for an inerrancy limited to faith and practice would by that action operate on the basis of expediency rather than principle, and would make it impossible to discipline anyone who held to an errant Bible in nonsalvatory matters. Such a person would be placing his imprimatur on the rightness of disbelief in inerrancy, and even though he might be conscious of his equivocation he would by doing that be yielding to the historical-critical method requirement of finding the canon in the canon.

Once Scripture is breached and error acknowledged, holding to infallibility in matters of faith and practice loses credibility. One is automatically put into the position of having to determine what the matters of faith and practice really are. It becomes easy to eliminate from faith and practice anything that one dislikes for any reason. Is the miraculous, for example, a matter of faith? Is not the virgin birth expendable? Cannot it be supposed that what really is important is the Incarnation and that the means by which this was brought about is immaterial? And may it not be said, on the same basis, that the writers of their times believed like the people of their times, that Matthew and Luke were simply expressing an opinion they shared with the people of that day? Today we say there are no virgin births.

In our day we are witnessing the publication of scholarly works denying that Jesus is God. The doctrine of the Trinity is also under attack. Is it not simple to declare either that it is a mistake to suppose the Scripture teaches these things, or can it not be said that the Scripture says this but does not teach it? Whichever route one takes the result is the same. The search is on for discovering the canon in the canon and the presupposition which underlies the historical-critical method is in use again.

The situation is more clouded when we talk about matters of

Christian conduct, that is, ethical decisions. In some instances this involves hermeneutics, of which I shall speak in a moment. Biblical normativity over against sociological relativity also becomes a factor. What has happened among evangelicals is the same as that which has gripped the western world and is one of the results of the Renaissance. Cultural relativity prevails today, and this disease is intrinsic to the historical-critical method. By cultural relativity I mean that the mores of a people are a product of their own times and circumstances; what was normative for a culture in bygone days is not normative for us today. Moreover, even within a given culture the mores change as people change, and what was "wrong" yesterday may be "right" today. My particular concern here relates to the cultural standards of the Old Testament over against the New Testament and today's revolt against the standards of both the Old and the New Testaments.

Two illustrations will pinpoint the ethical problem and the normativity of the Bible in matters of practice or life. The first one is the role of women in marriage and the ancient dogma of female subordination to the husband. The other is homosexuality. Any objective approach to the phenomena of Scripture must result in the conclusion, first, that the Bible does teach the subordination of the wife to her husband. This is true in both the Old Testament and the New Testament. They also teach that homosexual conduct is intrinsically wrong and forever forbidden. But among evangelicals a case is being made in favor of women's liberation or egalitarianism so that female subordination in the marital bond is looked upon as an antiquated custom no longer binding on Christians. And homosexuality is being defended as an alternate lifestyle that is in accord with the will of God and has His divine sanction and blessing. The consequences of this approach should be perceived immediately.

Anyone who endorses homosexual conduct as legitimate, and egalitarianism in marriage for the Christian, has fallen into the syndrome of the historical-critical methodology. If what the Bible says about these two ethical and life-style matters is no longer binding then biblical normativity is lost. It is not the Word of God for us today, and we must then find the canon in the canon. But there is a worse consequence that should be shouted from the housetops. It is inconceivable that homosexual conduct, for example, should be right at one time and wrong at another unless situation ethics is true. It is not inconceivable, however, that some injunctions should be binding on God's people in the Old Testament but not on Christians in the New Testament. I have in mind dietary laws. The reason why this statement can be true is that the New Testament clearly says what Old Testament injunctions are no longer binding us, for example, in the Book of Hebrews. However, in the cases of homosexuality and female subordination the New Testament carries over the injunctions of the Old Testament, and there is no way these injunctions can be broken as far as the Bible is concerned unless there is a new revelation. But Christian orthodoxy has always affirmed that the canon of Scripture is closed and there is no further revelation from God in Scripture. Mormonism does provide for continuing revelation and this "church" has recently changed its long-standing prohibition against the negro in relation to the priesthood; but Mormonism does not stand within the boundaries of biblical orthodoxy.

If the Bible teaching about homosexuality is not binding, then that portion of the Bible which teaches this cannot be the Word of God. For the Word of God is true. This means that those who support egalitarianism in marriage and homosexual conduct have made the Word of God of none effect. Indeed, they cannot regard these sections of Scripture as the Word of God, and therefore they must find the canon in the canon. This they cannot do. Moreover, when it comes to matters of practice, no two people will think the same way on all of these matters. Whom then shall we trust? And why?

Heilsgeschichte Versus Historie

Another strait jacket imposed on Scripture is the one which asserts that the purpose of God is to save men at the expense of fact and biblical inerrancy. This view effectively divides the Scripture into two strands. Salvation history (which the Germans call *heilsgeschichte*) is what counts. History (*historie*), which deals with facts and figures, or the nuts and bolts, doesn't make any difference.

In this view, God infallibly accomplishes His purpose, which is to get men saved. He does it through an imperfect and fallible Word. No one, of course, should say God is not sovereign or that His purposes can be annulled. But to say salvation proceeds through God's own inspired vehicle the Bible and then to affirm the inspired vehicle cannot be trusted in all its parts is to deny any credible meaning to inspiration. But more than that.

If God is to accomplish His purpose infallibly, which is to save men, even that cannot come about unless there are some parts of the Bible which are both true in themselves and trustworthy. In other words, there must be statements in the Bible which are dependable. If there are not, then we are saved by a God we cannot be sure exists, who may or may not have had a Son, who may or may not have been born of the virgin Mary, who may or may not have died on the cross, who we think may possibly have risen from the dead, and on whom, possibly, we may or may not believe with no assurance that we have been saved. We only hope so.

Those who glibly talk about the infallible purpose of God must say there is either nothing at all in Scripture which is objectively true, or that there are parts of Scripture which are historical, true, and accurate. Whichever way they decide, they must end up either with no Scripture they can trust, or only some Scripture they can trust. If they limit what they can trust to some Scripture, they are right back with the advocates of the historical-critical methodology. They must find the Word of God they can trust in Scripture—i.e., the canon in the canon; and this is the old subjectivity, for no two higher critics have ever agreed on what the canon in the canon is.

Redaction Criticism

Redaction criticism is a late variant of form criticism, of which Rudolph Bultmann was perhaps the best-known exponent. His influence through his students has been extensive, and that influence has filtered through to evangelicals. In form criticism as it relates to the Gospels, the purpose is to get behind the purported words of Jesus to find out what He really said. This is based upon the conclusion that the gospel writers have recorded words Jesus never said and attributed to Him acts He never performed. The critics say the gospel writers were theologians, not historians, and in writing their Gospels, in order to accomplish their theological purpose, they attributed to Jesus words He actually never spoke and deeds He did not really perform. They did this in order to give credence to the theology they wished to develop.

If the Gospels are simply theology and not history, and if they tell us things about Jesus that never really happened, then they are not trustworthy history (even though they may be *heilsgeschichte* or salvation history but not *historie* or real history). This brings us right back to the historical-critical methodology in which it becomes necessary to get behind the Gospels in order to find out what Jesus really said and did. This does not necessarily mean He could not have said some of the words recorded in the Gospels or that He did not perform some of the acts attributed to Him. But which is which has to be discovered. When the conclusion is reached that the Gospels do not reflect true history the consequences are mindboggling. We simply do not know who the real Jesus was. This undermines Scripture and destroys the Christian faith as a historical vehicle. It opens the door wide to a thousand vagaries and brings us right back to trying to find the canon in the canon.

Hermeneutics

Hermeneutics by definition is the science of interpretation and explanation. It is a branch of theology which defines the laws applied by exegesis. Everyone who reads the Bible, consciously or unconsciously, uses hermeneutics, i.e., interprets the Bible. How one comes out in his understanding of the Bible depends on what laws he assigns to hermeneutics. Hermeneutics is not a discipline limited to the reading of the Bible. It applies to all literature. For example, one of the basic laws of hermeneutics is this: What is the author trying to say? A second law says the reader should interpret obscure passages in the light of those which are clear or perspicuous. A third principle is to ask what the genre of the writing is. Satire illustrates this particular form of writing, a form or genre so often misunderstood by the reader. I recall one issue of *Christianity Today* in which Gordon Haddon Clark wrote a piece of satire on higher criticism. Readers wrote back wanting to know why we published an essay by a liberal. Dr. Clark happens to be an outstanding conservative without a trace of liberalism in his veins. The reader was taken in because he failed to discern that the essay was pure satire and as such did not represent the viewpoint of Dr. Clark at all. I have learned that satire is a very dangerous genre in literature because it is so often misunderstood. The apostle Paul used satire on occasion.

Another hermeneutical principle which has undergirded evangelical interpretation of Scripture is that one accepts the Bible literally, that is, you take it at its face value. The literalist principle is regarded as an abomination by liberals. They love to say that fundamentalists are "wooden-headed literalists." They regard literalism as a bane, not a blessing. Of course one can make the Bible stand on its head if the principle of literalism is applied so that it interprets figures of speech literally. Jesus said, "I am the door." No one thinks that Jesus was a literal door, so this is obviously a figure of speech. But such examples as this do not invalidate the principle of literalism. One uses the principle wherever possible, recognizing that figures of speech are to be interpreted as figures of speech and are not to be regarded literally.

A word of caution needs to be inserted here for the benefit of evangelicals in the light of the new hermeneutic. However badly hermeneutics may be misused and misapplied, evangelicals should not and cannot throw it out. Everyone must use hermeneutics. What is important is that the right hermeneutics be used. In our day words have lost their meaning. Often words mean only what the speaker intends to put into them. Like Alice in Wonderland they say that words mean whatever they choose to make them mean. When this condition inheres communication is virtually impossible. Nowhere is this more perfectly illustrated than in communism. The communists use the same words evangelicals use. But they attach different meanings to the words. Anyone who does not know the meaning attached to the words used by the communists will draw wrong conclusions.

The word hermeneutics is itself a neutral word, simply a descriptive word. When it is invested with particulars, i.e., when the rules are laid down, it then becomes either good or bad depending upon the rules of interpretation you accept. The presuppositions that you bring to hermeneutics will shape the conclusions you draw when you study the Bible with the view to interpreting it. Those who use the historical-critical method start with a presupposition we have already stated— Scripture and the Word of God are not synonymous. This becomes one of the hermeneutical principles employed by the higher critic. The evangelical starts with the presupposition that Scripture and the Word of God are synonymous. This is part of his hermeneutical apparatus. The evangelical consequently takes all the Bible seriously. The historical-critical scholar first has to find the Word of God in Scripture before he can take it seriously. Since no two critical scholars have ever agreed as to what parts of Scripture are the Word of God, individual choice with all its sinful overtones becomes the order of the day. The hermeneutical situation is more involved than this, however. Even when evangelicals agree which basic principles govern their hermeneutics they still disagree with each other on many points. Some evangelicals baptize infants and others do not. Some hold that in the sacrament of the Lord's Supper (Baptists do not use the word *sacrament;* they prefer *ordinance*) Jesus Christ is symbolically present; others that He is spiritually present; and still others that He is really present. Some evangelicals are Arminians, others are Calvinists. Some are pacifists; others are not. Some are amillennialists; other are premillennialists. But evangelicals are agreed on the fundamentals of the Christian faith, and it is here that critical scholars differ from evangelicals.

There is an intimate and binding relationship between hermeneutics and such things as ethics, form criticism, redaction criticism, the Graf-Wellhausen hypothesis, as well as science. It behooves the evangelical to be acutely aware of these implications and to be certain that his hermeneutics does not cross the line which separates the historical-critical method from evangelical faith. When the evangelical crosses that line he either becomes an inconsistent evangelical whose heart is right but whose head is wrong; or he gives up his evangelical faith and joins the ranks of the higher critics. The evangelical must be interested in hermeneutics. He must be sure that he understands what the governing principles of his hermeneutics are. He must use those principles consistently. He must avoid falling into the errors of the historical-critical methodology.

When G. Bromley Oxnam, a bishop in the Methodist Church, said that God never ordered the slaughter of the Canaanites, a major part of his problem derived from a failure to employ a proper hermeneutical principle. When Dr. Davies in the now famous first volume of the *Broadman Bible Commentary* (Genesis) said that God never ordered Abraham to offer up Isaac as a burnt offering on Mount Moriah, he could do so only by sacrificing a basic hermeneutical principle—that is, to deny that which is plainly and obviously stated and taught in the Bible itself. If this can be done with that incident, then there are few incidents in the Bible which cannot be assaulted on precisely the same basis.

To say the Book of Jonah is fiction when Jesus Christ clearly regarded it as factual, the hermeneutical principle that what Jesus said is to be regarded as truth is abandoned. When the Pauline authorship of Ephesians, 1 and 2 Timothy, and Titus is abandoned, a basic hermeneutical principle has been sacrificed. Scripture can no longer be taken at its face value. To regard those parts of the Bible which are untrue as the Word of God makes no sense. The canon in the canon must be discovered, and however the non-Pauline authorship of these letters is explained away it still remains true that the Bible itself declares Paul was the author.

The Conclusion

In the final analysis the historical-critical method humanizes the Bible while it downgrades the divine authorship. It establishes hermeneutical principles foreign to the Christian faith. It radically changes the traditional understanding of the Bible so that until two hundred years ago no one really comprehended the Bible. It effectively nullifies the great confessions of the churches since the Reformation. Had this not been true there would have been no need for The Confession of 1967 in the United Presbyterian Church. This confession denies some of the important affirmations of the Westminster Confession. The confession of the United Church of Christ denies what is contained in the Savoy Declaration of 1658 which underlay historic Congregationalism. Worst of all, and this must be said again and again, it makes the Bible a closed book to the common man. He cannot read it and know what it means if the historical-critical conclusions are correct. No ordinary reader of the Bible could possibly come to these conclusion simply by reading it. The conclusion the common reader would draw would be antithetical to those of the higher critic. Also, the evangelical faith itself is mistaken if the historical-critical methodology is correct. To preach that Adam is a special and immediate creation of God and the first human being on the planet Earth is to bear false witness if this is untrue. To claim that God ordered Abraham to sacrifice Isaac on Mount Moriah is to bear false witness if it is not true. To claim that the Book of Jonah is fact when it is only fiction is to deceive the people to whom the evangelical preacher brings this message. To say that Jesus died on Calvary as a vicarious sacrifice when this is not true is to speak as a heretic and to mislead innocent people who believe this to be an essential component of their salvation. The issues at stake are momentous. They will not vanish away. The historical-critical method is indeed the great enemy of evangelical faith. It is a crucial issue and will not go away. How one accepts or rejects it makes a world of difference now and forever.

NOTES

[1]Paul Tournier, *The Whole Person in a Broken World* (New York: Harper and Row, 1977), p. 4.

[2]Ibid., p. 10.

[3]Ibid., p. 75.

[4]Eric J. Chaisson, "The Scenario of Cosmic Evolution" in *Harvard Magazine*, November-December 1977, pp. 21, 22, 32, 33.

[5]Tournier, p. 78.

[6]Ibid., p. 80.

[7]Gerhard Maier, *The End of the Historical-Critical Method* (St. Louis: Concordia, 1977), p. 8.

[8]Ibid., p. 15.

[9]J. I. Packer, *God Speaks to Man-Revelation and the Bible*, as quoted from *The Outlook*, June 1976, "Attack on the Bible," by Peter De Jong, pp. 25-26.

[10]Grant R. Osborne, "The Evangelical and *Traditiongeschichte*" in *Journal of the Evangelical Theological Society*, Volume 21, No. 2, June 1978, p. 121.

[11]Tournier, p. 107.
[12]Ibid., p. 110.
[13]C. S. Lewis, *Christian Reflections* (Grand Rapids: Eerdmans, 1967), p. 153.
[14]Ibid., p. 153, 154, 157, et passim.
[15]Ibid., p. 162.
[16]Ibid., p. 158.
[17]Ibid., pp. 159, 160.
[18]Gerhard Maier, p. 16.
[19]Ibid., p. 65.
[20]Harold Lindsell, *The Battle for the Bible* (Grand Rapids: Zondervan, 1976), p. 113.

8

What or Who is an Evangelical?: An Unresolved Dilemma

In *The Battle for the Bible* I asked the question whether one who denies biblical inerrancy should be considered an evangelical. This question is now an important issue in the continuing dialogue with regard to inerrancy. The reactions have been numerous and varied. It will help if I indicate what some of the reactions have been, so that there can be a fuller discussion of the matter.

Today an increasing number of evangelicals do not wish to make inerrancy a test for fellowship even though ordinary consistency requires an evangelical to believe in it. The term *evangelical* can and does mean different things to different people. Consequently its use in a variety of ways makes it more difficult to link it exclusively to inerrancy. Those who do not wish to make inerrancy a requirement for fellowship often argue that a strict application could produce undesirable divisions which could damage the Christian enterprise. This aspect of the subject is inflammatory and arouses passionate responses. At a time in history when evangelicals are front-page news they ask if it would not be better to forget inerrancy as a test for fellowship, assuming that it is just not *that* important. Any consideration of the inerrancy issue should take these factors into account.

Men like David Hubbard, Bernard Ramm, Clark Pinnock, and a host of others who want to be considered as evangelicals strongly deny that disbelief in inerrancy disqualifies anyone from the right to the label. Stephen T. Davis in his book *The Debate about the Bible* describes what he calls "divisive inerrantists" who believe in inerrancy and who say "that a person cannot be considered an evangelical Christian unless he believes in inerrancy." Of course, he is vehemently opposed to such people and has painted a dark picture of what can happen if "the divisive inerrantists win out and people like me (Dr. Davis) can no longer be considered evangelicals—what will this mean pragmatically?" From there Dr. Davis goes on to say:

> Will it mean that non-inerrantist professors can no longer be hired by certain undergraduate and theological faculties? Will it mean that non-inerrantist editors will be fired from editorial boards of religious publications?[1]

To this I have already replied but it should not be forgotten as I consider the adverse reactions of others I have just mentioned. The first order on the agenda, however, is to define what an evangelical is.

A Definition of an Evangelical

Sometimes the word *evangelical* has been employed to describe someone who is not a *Catholic,* that is, someone who is not connected with the Roman Catholic Church. Many German churches have traditionally employed the term *evangelical* in their church titles and still do even though there is little evangelical faith among many of them. North American denominations have often used the word *evangelical* in their official titles and still do. Several illustrations will suffice. The Evangelical Baptist Church of Canada, The Evangelical Church of North America, the Evangelical Congregational Church, The Evangelical Covenant Church of America, and The Evangelical Free Church of America. Some of the churches using the word *evangelical* are by no means evangelical in their theological convictions. So the word requires further definition.

It will be of interest to the reader to remember that James Barr in his book *Fundamentalism* identifies a number of different terms as the equivalent of the word *fundamentalist,* a word he constantly uses pejoratively and with disdain. In fact, he thinks that people of this type suffer from a severe pathological condition. He uses such terms as *evangelical, fundamentalist, conservative,* and *conservative evangelical* interchangeably. The burden of his book has for its central theme, biblical inerrancy, which he considers to be part of the fundamentalist tradition to which he is opposed. He clearly describes what he believes to be one of the central affirmations of this group of people whom he labels variously: they believe in the "total (a strange and needless word to use) infallibility and inerrancy of the Bible, not only in its doctrinal content, but also in historical details, dates, numbers of persons in battles, ascriptions of authorship, unity of books and such things."[2] Now this is a satisfactory and quite adequate definition of what people such as he describes in his book believe about the Bible.

Dr. Barr, in his own intensive drive to destroy the concept of inerrancy, has performed a notable service with respect to the current struggle among "evangelicals." Repeatedly he adduces evidences which reinforce a charge I leveled in *The Battle for the Bible*—that a number of evangelicals do not believe in inerrancy any more. His book serves two purposes. The first is his witness to the effect that evangelicals traditionally held to biblical inerrancy. The second is his detailed verification of the departure from biblical inerrancy on the part of those who have in the past professed to believe in it. He is saying that these people are inconsistent, and he wants them to acknowledge that they really agree with him that the Bible is an errant book. He makes an observation about Bernard Ramm which is a telling one. He notes that Dr. Ramm cannot swallow the idea of a great miracle in Joshua's long day when the sun stood still; i.e. the earth stopped rotating on its axis. But he hits Dr. Ramm hard for introducing supernatural explanations for other incidents which Dr. Barr considers no less impossible than Joshua's long day. Dr. Ramm, for example, finds it difficult to explain away the great fish account in the Book of Jonah and Jonah's three-day stay in the fish's belly. In this case Dr. Ramm says God performed a miracle. James Barr caustically assaults him when he says:

> From the wording of the King James text, "Now the Lord had prepared a great fish," Ramm extracts this imaginative account of a specially created creature, different from all other fishes or whales. No doubt it had a primitive form of air-conditioning for the well-being of the prophet. Perhaps it contained a writing desk with inkpot and pen, similar to those actually found at Qumran, so that the prophet could indite on the spot the prayer which he recited (Jonah 2). These are not exaggerations for comic effect: in sober truth there is absolutely nothing to control speculation once

the extreme (note the use of this pejorative word) supernaturalism of Ramm is accepted.

These last two instances are cases of very extreme supernaturalist interpretation. The general tendency, however, in conservative evangelical literature is in the opposite direction, and numerous cases have been cited. Far from it being the case that miracle and supernatural causation is a fully accepted principle of interpretation in conservative (note that Dr. Barr has used the term *conservative evangelical* and *conservative* scholarship as identical with fundamentalist) scholarship, that scholarship makes very considerable efforts to rationalize and to eliminate miracle, reducing it from its biblical dimensions (note here that he is saying that the Bible does bear witness to the miraculous even though he does not accept it) to something more like the picture of a deity who from time to time arranges favourable conjunctions of natural phenomena. . . . The rationalization and naturalization of miracle narratives in deist and liberal style is a quite normal and frequent feature of conservative interpretation.[3]

From Professor Barr's perspective it is clear that he regards biblical inerrancy as one of the major doctrinal beliefs of evangelicals, conservative evangelicals, fundamentalists, and conservatives. And he is correct. So it may be said that any definition of what evangelicals believe must include biblical inerrancy. But of this another word will be spoken shortly.

What other doctrinal beliefs belong to the term *evangelical*? Let's forget momentarily the material and the formal principles of the Reformation and simply list the major doctrines associated with evangelicalism in its historical form: the belief (1) that God is a Trinity, one in essence, subsisting in three persons, the Father, the Son, and the Holy Spirit; (2) that Jesus is the incarnate, virgin-born Son of God, sinless, holy, and the vicarious substitute for man's transgressions; (3) that Adam was the first man, he sinned in the garden of Eden and his transgression wrought disaster for the human race; (4) that Jesus rose in bodily form from the grave, ascended into heaven, and is coming again personally, visibly, and in power and great glory; (5) that salvation is by faith alone, without works of righteousness; (6) that there is a heaven and a hell. To these could be added other items of belief which would form a more complete statement of traditional evangelical convictions, but these are sufficient for our purposes.

It is not enough to assert that the foregoing articles of faith constitute a satisfactory definition of what evangelical belief consists in. The assertion must be followed by evidences to support that definition. If there were no people anywhere who believed these articles of faith it would be obviously ridiculous to say they comprise evangelical beliefs, but history comes to our support. Of course there are those who spurn the testimony of history. They turn their backs on what ought to be plain enough to any reasonable person. People of this sort will never be convinced no matter how high the stack of evidence is. This is illustrated in life a thousand times over. Some people do not believe that communism represents a threat to democracy or to the western world. Nothing one says seems to convince them. The same is true about evolution. No matter how much evidence one presents to convinced evolutionists many of them are wholly unsusceptible to the evidences. But for those who do regard history seriously, sufficient evidence exists for them to agree that evangelicalism is properly represented by the doctrinal affirmations I have mentioned.

The Westminster Confession of Faith includes all of the items mentioned in this section. The New Hampshire Confession of Faith does the same. The canons of the Synod of Dort do the same. The doctrinal commitments of any number of denominations include them: the Lutheran Church-Missouri Synod, the Evangelical Wisconsin Synod, the American Lutheran Church, the Christian and Missionary Alliance, the Christian Reformed Church, the Conservative Baptist Association of America, the Evangelical Free Church, the Southern Baptist Convention, and the various offshoots of the United Presbyterian Church and the Presbyterian Church in the south, to mention only a few. Many schools and parachurch organizations are also committed to these convictions: Westminster Theological Seminary, Wheaton College, Westmont College, Southwestern Baptist Theological Seminary, Moody Bible Institute, Campus Crusade for Christ, the InterVarsity Christian Fellowship, to name a few. The National Association of Evangelicals, the largest interdenominational evangelical church organization today in the United States, holds to these same convictions. So do all of the Bible institutes and Bible colleges. In short, from the historical perspective one can say that American evangelicals by and large hold to the theological convictions I have stated above.

When Does One Cease to Be an Evangelical?

If evangelicals consist of people who believe the tenets I have mentioned, when does one cease to be an evangelical? We can ask this question in two ways: (1) How many of the tenets of evangelicalism can one surrender without forfeiting the right to the use of the evangelical label? (2) Does the denial of any *one* of the basic evangelical tenets mean that a person has forfeited the right to the use of the term?

I take it that some of the people I have mentioned are saying that one does not cease to be an evangelical so long as he retains belief in all the basic doctrines of the faith except inerrancy, provided he believes the Bible to be the infallible or inerrant rule of faith and practice. Using this statement as a starting point, I think we can proceed with an examination of the viewpoint. Clearly, if one denies the virgin birth of Christ he denies what is plainly taught in the Bible and is a matter of faith. Ergo, such a person can hardly be called an evangelical however much he covets the use of the label. So also with the deity of Christ, the doctrine of the Trinity, the vicarious atonement, the bodily resurrection of Jesus from the dead, etc. The denial of any one of these means that such a person is not really an evangelical.

It seems to me that those who think the term *evangelical* can be applied to those who deny inerrancy in secondary matters but affirm inerrancy in matters of faith and practice run into several difficulties. I am assuming, of course, they would agree that whoever denies biblical inerrancy in matters of faith and practice cannot honestly be called *evangelical*. This means that men like Paul King Jewett of Fuller Seminary, whose own colleagues agreed that he was out of line and that he did deny a matter of faith and practice in his book *Man as Male and Female*, technically is not and cannot be termed an evangelical unless the term is stripped of any credible meaning.

Moreover, I assume that these same people would agree that men like Frank Stagg of Southern Baptist Seminary in Louisville, who deny the vicarious atonement, cannot be termed evangelical. But what will they do with someone like Ralph Martin of Fuller Seminary who claims to believe the Bible in matters of faith and practice and who may affirm his belief in all of the items, except inerrancy, that comprise evangelical belief? He does not believe that the books of Ephesians, 1 and 2 Timothy, and Titus were written by Paul. Nor does he believe Peter wrote 2 Peter. Is such a man an evangelical? Hardly. But if the principle which is involved in this instance is acceptable, and such a person as Dr. Martin can be called an evangelical then the application of it will surely produce the worst possible consequences. On the same basis one could deny the Isaianic authorship of Isaiah 40-66, the sixth-century date of Daniel, the Mosaic authorship of the entire Pentateuch as well as the historicity of Adam and Eve and other things, and still claim to be an evangelical. Indeed, one could deny the historicity of the Book of Jonah, claiming instead that it is fiction, not fact. In so doing the individual has not compromised any of the doctrines listed under the label of *evangelical* unless he has reference to the implication in the teaching of Jesus that Jonah was a real person who was incarcerated in the belly of a real fish for three days and nights. Perhaps on that basis, the testimony of Jesus having been breached, they might reasonably infer that whoever does this has a defective Christology and thus is not an evangelical. This is a delusion since the acceptance of this principle about the testimony of Jesus is a two-edged sword.

If the testimony of Jesus about Jonah is sufficient to deny the label of evangelical to those who think the book to be fiction, then it would also follow with respect to the doctrine of Scripture itself. Some who think a man can be an inconsistent *evangelical* so long as he holds to inerrancy in matters of faith and practice, also think that Jesus taught that all of the Bible is inerrant. Surely if the testimony of Jesus with respect to Jonah is not binding, why should not Jesus' testimony with regard to Scripture be disregarded too? So I must declare again that whoever denies inerrancy also denies the witness of Jesus Christ to the whole Bible. Those who deny the witness of Jesus Christ entertain an erroneous Christology. How can they then be considered evangelicals? And if one can extend to them the courtesy of the evangelical label even though they deny the witness of Jesus Christ, why should they not be given the same courtesy if or when they deny other things which Jesus taught with reference to His death, resurrection, and second coming? The doctrine of Scripture is no less a doctrine than is that of the virgin birth, the vicarious atonement, and the bodily resurrection.

John R. W. Stott spoke to the students at the 1973 triennial InterVarsity Missionary Convention. He delivered an address titled *The Authority of the Bible,* which is now in print. He based his argument for the full trustworthiness of Scripture mainly on the person of Jesus Christ and especially His lordship. In his booklet he said several times: "For him (Jesus) what Scripture said God said."[4] If all this means is that Scripture sometimes is true and sometimes is not then this statement doesn't make sense. Moreover, it is an offense to the nature of God who *is* truth. Dr. Stott realized that some people distinguish between God and the human writers of Scripture. He said:

> Even biblical scholars are sometimes most irresponsible in their treatment of the apostles. "That's Paul's view," they say, "or Peter's or John's. But this is mine. And my view is just as good as theirs, in fact better." But no. The teachings of the apostles is the teaching of Christ. To receive them is to receive Christ, to reject them is to reject Christ.[5]

If Dr. Stott is right in what he said, and I think he is, then men like Paul Jewett who say that what Paul taught in Ephesians about wifely subordination is wrong, must say that Jesus is wrong for the teaching of Paul is the teaching of Jesus. Dr. Stott went on to say:

> A Christian is somebody who not only confesses with his lips that Jesus is Lord, but brings every aspect of his life under the sovereign lordship of Jesus—his opinions, his beliefs, his standards, his values, his ambitions, everything!
>
> To us, then, submission to Scripture . . . is part and parcel of this submission to the lordship of Jesus. We cannot accommodate ourselves to the idea of a selective submission—for example, agreeing with Jesus in his doctrine of God but disagreeing with him in his doctrine of Scripture. . . . Selective submission is not true submission. . . .[6]

Dr. Stott argued that submission to the authority of Scripture "is fundamental to *Christian integrity*" (note that it is not secondary; it is *fundamental*). Then he said:

> Many would deny this and would even affirm the contrary. They regard the acceptance of biblical infallibility as actually untenable and therefore charge Christians who hold it with a lack of mental integrity, with intellectual obscurantism, schizophrenia or suicide, or with other horrid crimes![7]

Dr. Stott said categorically that "our view of Scripture depends on our loyalty to Christ." He asked this question:

> How then can we, the disciples of Jesus, possibly have a lower view of Scripture than our Teacher himself had? . . .
> There are only two possible escape routes from this obligation. The first is to say that Jesus did not know what he was talking about, that the incarnation imprisoned him in the limited mentality of a first-century Palestinian Jew, and that consequently he believed the Old Testament as they did, but that he, like them, was mistaken. The second is to say that Jesus did know what he was talking about, that he actually knew Scripture to be unreliable, but that he still affirmed its reliability because his contemporaries did and he did not want to upset them. According to the first explanation, Jesus' erroneous teaching was involuntary (he could not help it); according to the second it was deliberate. These theories portray Jesus as either deceived or a deceiver. They discredit the incarnate Son of God. They are incompatible both with his claims to speak what he knew (Jn. 3:11), to bear witness to the truth and to be the truth (Jn. 18:37; 14:6), and with his known hatred of all hypocrisy and deceit. They are totally unacceptable to anybody who has been led by the Holy Spirit to say "Jesus is Lord" (I Cor. 12:3). Over against these slanderous speculations we must continue to affirm that Jesus knew what he was teaching, that he meant it, and that what he taught and meant is true.[8]

From these remarks of Dr. Stott I ask myself again: Is he who denies inerrancy only an inconsistent evangelical or by this denial does he forfeit his right to the evangelical label? If the case made by Dr. Stott is correct then it seems to me such a person is not an evangelical. And for this reason. Inerrancy does not stand by itself. It is inextricably linked to the person of Christ. To deny inerrancy is to deny what Jesus believed, taught, and practiced. It is a denial of the lordship of Jesus Christ. And I do not think that he who denies the lordship of Jesus can be an evangelical.

Evangelical *Vis a Vis* Christian

No one has a copyright on the word *evangelical* nor is anyone's permission required to use the term. Numbers of those who, according to my understanding of the Word, use it to describe themselves will not forsake its use. The value inherent in it is too great. There's a great deal of mileage in the term. There is no way I or anyone else who accepts biblical inerrancy or infallibility can keep noninerrantists from the use of the label. Since they will not forego its use what should be done? Why not let the noninerrantists keep it for themselves while believers in inerrancy select another label? This was done when the *divinity* of Christ became so worthless that orthodox believers stopped using it and chose to speak of the *deity* of Christ instead.

Lest there be any misunderstanding, a word of explanation and caution must be inserted at this point. I do not equate the term *evangelical* with that of *Christian*. In other words I am not saying that one who limits inerrancy to matters of faith and practice cannot be a Christian. So far as one can judge, James Orr did not believe in inerrancy. But he otherwise affirmed the other basics of evangelical faith. Was he not a Christian? I would suppose he was, but I add quickly that a man can believe all the great doctrines of the Christian faith, including biblical inerrancy, and still be lost. The devils believe and tremble. Belief in the cardinal truths of the Christian faith does not bring salvation with it, but surely there can be no salvation without belief in at least some of the cardinal doctrines of the faith of a salvatory nature. There may be some who do not claim to be evangelicals who have saving faith in Christ and are thus justified. But that is not what I am discussing here. I am talking about the proper use of the term *evangelical* both with respect to its meaning and to its application in the Christian church. Carl Henry's conclusion that one of my statements implied that those who deny inerrancy are numbered among the tares is incorrect. If I worded my statement badly so that one could draw such a conclusion I correct it again.

One other observation is in order. The content of the term *evangelical* is more important than the word itself. Those who believe all of the doctrines I have included in the word *evangel-*

ical are evangelicals even if they know nothing about the word itself or if they refuse to apply the label to themselves. Contrariwise the one who uses the label but denies some or all of its contents is not an evangelical. Some Roman Catholics today are evangelicals even though the word itself is foreign to their vocabulary. Likewise a Jew who acknowledges Jesus as his Messiah and believes in Him is just as much a member of the body of Christ as any Christian, even though the Jew may not call himself a Christian. He has the substance even though he does not have the nomenclature. And some who call themselves Christians are not!

Christian Fellowship

One of my colleagues has stated that "the doctrine of inerrancy should not be made a test for Christian fellowship." This statement which is, no doubt, a reflection of a viewpoint found extensively among evangelicals, demands consideration. Unfortunately many of my brothers have not defined what they mean by the term *fellowship*. But we can sometimes tell what they do not mean when we take a hard look at their practice.

Most Christians engaged in secular pursuits have relationships with people who are not Christians. Most of us do business with unbelievers. We develop relationships. Even in social pursuits most Christians relate to friends, community neighbors, and others who are not Christians. Christian college students form friendships with non-Christians. In almost every area of life one can trace such relationships. But the fellowship in these relationships differs from the kind of fellowship Christians have with each other in their churches and in Christian groups. Perhaps we can speak of friendship when it pertains to unbelievers and fellowship when the people involved are Christians.

Certainly there is a sense in which Christians can, do, and should have friendly relationships with both Christians and unbelievers. But fellowship connotes more than that. It indicates a common bond which believers have with believers because of their common faith. Their common faith has content so that their fellowship is based upon this common content as well as the attractiveness of the individual to his fellow Christian. I can have fellowship with some Christians who hold views similar to mine, and I can find it difficult to have the same kind of fellowship with some who hold similar views but with whom the same kind of closeness never comes. Anyone who thinks that, given our present state of imperfection, all Christians can have the same kind of fellowship with all other Christians is sadly mistaken. Ideally there should be no differences with respect to fellowship. Practically there are. There are many fine Christian women who would not want to be married to me. There are good Christian women to whom I would not wish to be married as well. Thus the term fellowship has an elusive aspect about it which makes it difficult to pin down.

When I was on the faculties of Columbia Bible College, Northern Baptist Seminary, and Fuller Theological Seminary, those institutions would not hire teachers who did not believe in biblical inerrancy. But, if inerrancy, as some assert, should not be made a test of fellowship, can I really have fellowship with those I would not vote to hire as teachers, nor vote to ordain them to the Christian ministry, nor vote to call them to pastor a church in which I had my membership? Must I not say there are different kinds of fellowship, and if those who hold to limited inerrancy are excluded from certain institutions and local perishes do I not have a different kind of fellowship with them than I do with believers in inerrancy?

The Evangelical Theological Society has a doctrinal platform which consists of one proposition—subscription to biblical inerrancy. No one can become a member of that organization unless he willingly affirms his belief in inerrancy. Those who do not accept inerrancy are barred from its membership. What does this mean for fellowship? The National Association of Evangelicals has a commitment to biblical inerrancy. Individuals, denominations, and organizations which are in good standing in this association must profess a belief in biblical inerrancy. What does this do to fellowship when numbers of those who deny inerrancy cannot become participants in the organization?

Must we not face the truth that what has just been said about biblical inerrancy can also be said about many other aspects of the Christian faith? Baptist institutions will not employ those who believe in and practice infant baptism. Many organizations have committed themselves to premillennialism. Anyone who is an amillennialist or a postmillennialist is excluded. Indeed there are groups which require subscription to a secret-any-moment rapture for admission to their fellowship. Since there are all kinds of theological requirements laid down for admission to different groups, why should it appear strange that some should require a belief in an inerrant Scripture for admission? And whoever is excluded from any group for whatever theological reason is bound to feel that fellowship has been affected. Thus it seems to me that saying inerrancy should not be made a test for Christian *fellowship* means very little when those who say this do make it a test for admission to institutions, societies, for ordination, etc.

I have a sneaking suspicion that many evangelicals could have better fellowship, at least on the surface, with some people who do not subscribe to inerrancy than they can with some who do. I remain to be convinced that there is a necessary relationship between belief in biblical inerrancy and fellowship. Perhaps what is more important is how strongly people believe in the doctrine and how much they allow it to be a dominant motif in their relationship with other professing believers. All of this, however, leaves unanswered the important question. If a man does not believe in justification by faith alone, is he simply an inconsistent evangelical? And if a man does not believe in biblical inerrancy, is he simply an inconsistent evangelical? In the latter case I am willing to say that he can be a Christian, but I find it difficult to say he is an evangelical who is simply inconsistent.

The Broadening of the Term *Evangelical*

In my contacts with the World Council of Churches, I have found many who refuse to allow the term evangelical to remain the property of those who are theological fundamentalists in the best sense of that misused term. The ecumenists also want to use the term evangelical. Thus it came about that the ecumenists today call people like myself conservative evangelicals and others liberal evangelicals. In this way the adjectives *conservative* or *liberal* carry the freight rather than the word *evangelical.* It has helped to convince me that the term itself may have lost too much of its content to remain serviceable. Perhaps what we need is a new word and the suggestion was made by one well-known inerrantist that perhaps we ought to call ourselves *Orthodox Protestants.* This would distinguish us from those in the Catholic tradition and align us with those committed to historic orthodoxy. But more about that shortly.

Stephen T. Davis's Query

Professor Davis's question about the ultimate aim of what he calls the "divisive inerrantists" requires further elaboration. He thinks "the prospects are horrifying" if they gain control of groups whether they be denominations or institutions and proceed to eliminate those who do not hold to inerrancy. Moreover, he fears that the door to appointments would then be closed to people like himself who really don't care as much about the use of the term "evangelical" as they do about "the practical implications of divisive inerrancy."[9] Earlier I responded to this question raised by Dr. Davis, but there is still another side to it that must be considered. This has to do with the question of fellowship of which I have been speaking.

Dr. Davis has overlooked one very significant item in his argument. He should be apprised of the practice of non-evangelical theological seminaries which studiously refrain from appointing to their faculties anyone who believes in an inerrant Scripture. It could be illustrated this way. Every major denomination has evangelicals within it. The sizes of these groups vary. Certainly there are numbers of American Baptists who believe in an inerrant Bible. The United Presbyterians have strong churches and many people who hold to this viewpoint. The American Lutheran Church has a large body of evangelicals who believe in inerrancy. The Good News Movement in the United Methodist Church includes a body of people who believe in inerrancy. Asbury College and Asbury Theological Seminary have traditionally held to biblical inerrancy, but they are not denominationally controlled institutions. Anyone taking a look at the theological seminaries controlled by the major denominations which have in them those who hold to inerrancy will find inerrantists are not adequately represented on the faculties of most of these schools. And the same is true for most prestigious independent nonevangelical seminaries such as Harvard, Yale, Chicago, and Union of New York. One can look very hard and still will not find any articulate, vocal spokesmen for the inerrancy viewpoint. The Federated Theological Faculty of the University of Chicago had theological diversity as one of its major objectives. But when it came to practicing this diversity it ran into problems that forced it to abandon the objective especially as it related to evangelicals. We can search the rosters of this institution without discovering anyone who can be identified as a committed evangelical who holds to all the major doctrines of evangelicalism, including biblical inerrancy. Here is an interesting statement made by one who was intimately connected with the Chicago Federated Faculty:

It contained unregenerated, modified, and neo-orthodox liberals. Indeed, there was a deliberate effort made in new appointments to maintain a diversity of views. But if this process of self-education on the part of the faculty was to be continued, it soon became clear that certain types of mind would not fit into the Faculty circle. A man, for instance, might be a notable scholar and highly prized as a possible member of the faculty; and yet he would not be considered if he took the position that his ideas alone were valid, or if he declined to listen to the voice of alternate points of view. A doctrinaire stance like that would quickly destroy the basis on which the Faculty conducted its common intellectual life.[10]

This Federated Theological Faculty has indeed sheltered itself from at least one viewpoint—that of the true evangelical. This sort of person has been excluded from fellowship on a faculty so broad that the former president of the Chicago Theological Seminary which was part of the complex admitted there was room for the unregenerate but not for the evangelical. The greatest of all sins was to hold to dogma without apology and to propagate it as though other views were wrong.

Perhaps the greatest irony of all with respect to the University of Chicago lies in the fact that its charter (1890) states: "An institution . . . loyal to Christ and his Church, employing none but Christians in any department of instruction; a school not only evangelical but evangelistic, seeking to bring every student to Jesus Christ as Lord." The university is everything but this today.

I know of only one seminary connected with the United Presbyterian Church which has on its faculty one man who holds to biblical inerrancy. I do not know of a single such person on the faculties of the institutions connected with the United Methodist Church. I know of no such one on the faculties of the seminaries connected with the United Church of Christ. If there are any, their voices are not raised; they do not identify themselves with fellow inerrantists. If I have overlooked any, it can still be said they constitute a tiny proportion of the teachers in theological academia. Evangelicals, and especially those who hold to inerrancy, find no open doors to teaching posts in multitudes of institutions.

Dr. Davis bemoans the possibility that if "divisive inerrantists" ever get control they will do what the nonevangelical schools have been doing for so long. Evidently it all depends on whose ox has been gored. Unfortunately the movement always seems to be a one-way street away from inerrancy even in institutions which at one time or another were committed to it. The situation is bleak and there are no signs of a breakthrough in the opposite direction. There has been the one notable exception to which reference has already been made: the two theological seminaries connected with the Lutheran Church-Missouri Synod. Both of these institutions held to inerrancy by background. Concordia at St. Louis was infiltrated, but the coming of J. A. O. Preus to the presidency of the Synod changed the situation. Today the two Concordias are fully staffed by faculty members, all of whom believe in an inerrant Scripture. This is the one notable case in which there has been a recovery to orthodoxy following a turning away from it.

So we see that Dr. Davis's vision is limited only to those institutions which might not open their doors to disbelievers in inerrancy. But he has no concern for believers in inerrancy who are shut out even more tightly from open doors in institutions which at one time were evangelical but no longer are. His concern is misplaced unless first he sees to it that doors are opened to inerrantists in the great number of institutions where they are presently *persona non grata*.

Conclusion

I must regretfully conclude that the term *evangelical* has been so debased that it has lost its usefulness. Decades ago when the label *new evangelical* was coined its viability was based upon one positive and one negative aspect. On the positive side it took over without change the basic theological heritage of fundamentalism. By this I mean its commitment to historic orthodoxy as derived from the New Testament, and the Reformation, and expressed in the various creeds of Christendom since then. This theological heritage was acknowledged, accepted, and propagated by diverse groups, and yet allowance was made for differing interpretations such as Lutheran, Reformed, Arminian, and dispensational. On the negative side, it dispensed with the traditional fundamentalist sociology, i.e., fundamentalism's understanding of the relationship of the Christian to the world. Earlier fundamentalism tended to retreat from society beyond its own walled city with its own mores. Many fundamentalists demitted the major denominations that had turned from orthodoxy, building Bible churches, leaving behind groups of evangelical believers who still clung to their denominational attachments. The Bible school movement was the fundamentalist response to theological seminaries which had turned liberal, especially since fundamentalism tended to look upon theological education with grave suspicion. The *new evangelical* turned from fundamentalism's sociology to positive interaction with the world and engagement on the intellectual level with liberal theological education. This movement recovered the notion of the believer who is not *of* the world but who is sent back *into* the world for witness, and to challenge the powers of darkness as well as those of liberalism.

Forty years ago the term *evangelical* represented those who were theologically orthodox and who held to biblical inerrancy as one of the distinctives. The Evangelical Theological Society is one case in point. Fuller Seminary is another. Within a decade or so neoevangelicalism, that started so well and promised so much, was being assaulted from within by increasing skepticism with regard to biblical infallibility or inerrancy. For good or for ill this was the focal point around which today's

Maybe it would be better to accept the term *fundamentalist* with all of the pejoratives attached to it by its detractors, living has become the critical issue cannot be denied.

It was not long before the evangelical camp was divided into two parties—the one holding to theological orthodoxy with respect to matters of faith and practice as well as to inerrancy; the other limiting the trustworthiness of Scripture to matters of faith and practice, thus excluding other matters. It was at that point that the term *evangelical* took on different meanings to different people. Those who gave up on inerrancy while holding to biblical trustworthiness in matters of faith and practice continued to think of themselves as evangelicals. Thus one issue in the ensuing struggle was to center around the question whether such people are really evangelicals. All of this has led me to conclude that we should abandon the use of the term *evangelical* as a label for it no longer tells the world what historic evangelicals believe. There remains, then, the question what should be used in its place.

Some evangelicals have already decided to go back to the use of the term *fundamentalist*. It is true that this term is loaded and carries with it connotations which often do not express the true genius which lies behind the word, but it does have some distinct advantages. Liberals despise it. Current advocates of limited inerrancy never use it about themselves. Scholars like James Barr and much of academia look down their noses at it. Its theological dogmatism which includes intense opposition to syncretism, universalism, and the possibility that non-Christian religions are roads which lead to Paradise sharpens its image and establishes its uniqueness.

Moreover those who entertain these views are going to be labelled *fundamentalists* whether they like it or not. In the Missouri Synod battle the dissidents were not labelled what they really were—liberals—but were everywhere called "moderates" which they were not, while J. A. O Preus and his associates were everywhere called "fundamentalists." James Barr's attack on fundamentalism demonstrates that the academic world which hates the theology of orthodoxy will always label it fundamentalism. In its heyday neoorthodoxy also identified conservative Christianity by using the fundamentalist label.

struggle was to be centered. How all this happened is a story which has not yet been fully told. But the fact that inerrancy above its limitations and investing it with a better image by humility, compassion, and lovingkindness toward those with whom the so-called "divisive inerrantists" have major differences of opinion. When the quasi-liberals and academicians in Southern Baptist seminaries can label inerrantists "fundamentalists," thus repudiating a label so often applied to the people of the Southern Baptist Convention it can't be such a bad word as to render it nonviable. And when the Missouri Synod, standing without apology for historic orthodoxy, has been and now is being called fundamentalist we might as well take advantage of a term which, at the very least, lets everyone know they believe in a Bible that is free from error in the whole and in the part.

Believers in the view that Scripture and the Word of God are synonymous can always use an alternate label such as *Orthodox Protestant* which I have already surfaced in this chapter. But if neither the *fundamentalist* label nor the *Orthodox Protestant* one will do, someone can come up with a better name which will catch the public eye and serve to identify that group of people who hold to the fundamentals of the Christian faith including inerrancy. So far as I am concerned the term *evangelical* seems to be a confusing label and probably a lost cause.

NOTES

[1]Stephen T. Davis, *The Debate About the Bible* (Philadelphia: Westminster, 1977), pp. 130-31.
[2]James Barr, *Fundamentalism* (London: SCM Press, 1977), p. 287.
[3]Ibid., p. 247.
[4]John R. W. Stott, *The Authority of the Bible* (Downers Grove: Inter-Varsity Press, 1976), p. 11.
[5]Ibid., p. 26.
[6]Ibid., p. 34.
[7]Ibid., p. 33.
[8]Ibid., pp. 16, 17.
[9]Stephen T. Davis, pp. 130-31.
[10]Kurt E. Marquart, *Anatomy of an Explosion* (Fort Wayne: Concordia Press, 1977), p. 87.

9

Prospects for the Future: Bleak or Bright?

To begin the last chapter of this book by referring to Alexander Solzhenitsyn may appear to be a strange thing to do. Yet it has a bearing on what the prospects for the future may be with regard to the battle for the written Word of God.

Mr. Solzhenitsyn delivered the 1978 commencement address at Harvard University. This is North America's first college, founded in 1636 with a commitment to Christ and to truth. Jesus Christ has long since been removed from the Harvard motto leaving only *Veritas* (truth) behind. First established to train men for the Congregational ministry, Harvard has become a thoroughly secularized institution in whose hallowed halls God is either dead or irrelevant. What happened to Harvard is happening to the United States of America. It is the process of being thoroughly secularized, and in the religious realm, so-called evangelicals who have been moving recently from the theological right to the theological left, are assisting the process.

It seems unusual that Harvard University, presided over by a president who does not refer to Jesus Christ, and whose wife, Sisela Myrdal, is the daughter of nonreligious Swedish leftists, should have invited Mr. Solzhenitsyn in the first place, and a prophet at that. But no one need suppose that his visit will result in any reversal of Harvard University's stance. One newspaper said:

Prophets are not popular. They are not comfortable people to have around; they make poor house guests. Not only are they not honored in their own countries but sometimes not even in their own times. The greatest of them have been labelled as arrogant, self-righteous, presumptuous, ungrateful, unpatriotic. You would not

322

care to have Jeremiah to dinner, or Nathan ("Thou art the man!"), or Elijah or Haggai, or Habakkuk. . . . They look best to us at a safe distance of centuries, vouched for in the canon of Holy Scripture. There is something of the prophet in Alexander Solzhenitsyn. He comes on with his message just as authoritatively, uncompromisingly, tactlessly, not for the first time but never more intensely than in his recent Harvard commencement address. . . .

Mrs. (Olga) Carlisle, in only her second conversation with the writer in Moscow in April 1967, reports that he "emphatically declared that America's material well-being had corroded the fiber of her people. Spirituality had disappeared from America because of her excessive prosperity. . . . Such a view of America was commonplace in the Soviet Union." Some of what he has seen in America is what he expected to see. We see what we are looking for. Yet at peril would we pretend that much of what he sees is not real.[1]

Whether or not the disappearance of spirituality from America has been caused solely by affluence is beside the point. Whatever the cause, Mr. Solzhenitsyn has correctly diagnosed the condition. (And I might add that Harvard University shows no intention of doing anything to correct the disease in its educational programs.) What Alexander Solzhenitsyn could have said but did not say is that the spiritual plight of Western Europe is worse than that of the United States. He is also probably unaware of the declining situation in the American churches which can be accounted for by the departure from historic orthodoxy decades ago, a departure which is now being experienced by evangelicals whose spiritual forefathers resisted liberalism in the 1920s but whose children and grandchildren are squandering their heritage, repeating the errors of liberalism, and beginning to question the central affirmations of historic orthodoxy.

The documentation for this can be found in two sets of statistics—one having to do with church membership, the other with overseas missionary outreach. To them we now turn our attention.

The *Yearbook of American and Canadian Churches* comes as close to reporting vital church statistics reliably as does any other source.[2] The 1969 and the 1976 *Yearbook* statistics for major denominations provide the following information. For the most part the statistics in the 1969 edition are 1967 figures and those in the 1976 *Yearbook* are 1974 figures. This means that the two *Yearbooks* spanned a period of seven years. In that short space of time most of the major denominations suffered severe membership losses as follows:

United Methodist Church

1967	11,026,976	members
1973*	10,063,046	members
Net loss of	963,930	members

*The 1976 *Yearbook* figure for the United Methodist Church is for 1973. Thus the denomination lost almost one million members in six years.

United Presbyterian Church in the USA

1967	3,268,761	members
1974	2,723,565	members
Net loss of	545,196	members

The Christian Churches (Disciples of Christ)

1967	1,875,400	members
1974	1,312,326	members
Net loss of	563,074	members

The Protestant Episcopal Church

1966*	3,429,695	members
1974	2,907,293	members
Net loss of	522,402	members

*The figure for 1966 was given in the 1969 *Yearbook*. This means the time span was eight years.

The United Church of Christ

1967	2,052,857	members
1974	1,841,312	members
Net loss of	211,545	members

The Presbyterian Church in the U.S.

1967	960,776	members
1974	896,203	members
Net loss of	64,573	members

The American Baptist Convention

1967	1,454,965	members
1974	1,597,029	members
Net gain of	142,064	members

The missionary side of the picture is far grimmer. Evangelistic and foreign missionary outreach are the surest indices of the spiritual vitality of a denomination. Exceptional factors may account for declines, but when the mainline churches after fifty years of liberal infiltration present similar graph patterns it is hard to suppose that exceptional circumstancess account for the depressing picture. This is especially true when the statistics for the churches and agencies unrelated to the National Council of Churches are taken into account.

Not too many years ago the number of missionaries connected with the Division of Overseas Ministries of the National Council of the Churches of Christ.in the U.S.A. exceeded twelve thousand. In the 1976 report the number of missionaries had declined to 5010. This is only one half of the story. The number of missionaries supported by churches which are actually members of the National Council of Churches was 2776. There were 2234 missionaries connected with missionary agencies whose denominations are not members of the National Council of Churches. These missionary boards are listed under the title of "Affiliated Board." Of the 2234 missionaries in this category 1120 were from the Seventh-day Adventist denomination. The National Council claims a membership of forty million (a highly inflated figure) which means that it took more than 14,000 church members to support each overseas missionary.[3]

When these figures are compared with two evangelical agencies the remarkable difference will be seen. The Evangelical Foreign Missions Association (which is the arm of the National Association of Evangelicals) reported 7347 missionaries. The Interdenominational Foreign Mission Association reported 6101 missionaries. These two agencies reported more than 13,000 missionaries to the National Council's 5000.[4] These figures do not take into account the Southern Baptists, the Wycliffe Bible Translators, and agencies connected with other nonliberal groups. The conclusion is inescapable. The mainline denominations which have been penetrated by liberal theology are neither evangelistically inclined nor missionary inspired.

The denominational statistics tell their own story about the churches which were once overwhelmingly orthodox but which were "broadened" by liberalism in the early twentieth century. Wherever and whenever this happened evangelism and the missionary enterprise overseas were affected. Thus, before we can speak about the future, it is important first to take a look at the past. Today's declining situation must be understood within the context of that past.

David Hubbard, Fuller Seminary's president, said that "the battle between fundamentalist and liberals which characterized the American church in the first half of our century is more a matter of history than of living reality."[5] Later he added, in connection with the heroic battle fought by B. B. Warfield and William Henry Green: "I revere that battle, but I cannot fight it again."[6] In other words the fundamentalistliberal struggle is ancient history. Many don't think we should renew that controversy. The similarity, however, between the twenties and today are so obvious that it is worth making a comparison. But it must be made with certain facts in mind.

Today's struggle over theological orthodoxy is not a struggle involving the seminaries of the mainline denominations, excepting, of course, the Southern Baptist Convention and the Lutheran Church-Missouri Synod. Today's struggle is being waged in theological seminaries, Christian colleges, and in smaller denominations which have been clearly and unapologetically evangelical or orthodox or conservative. We shall see that what is happening to them is amazingly similar to what happened to comparable institutions in the early twentieth century. The difference is this: the institutions of the twenties were lost to historic orthodoxy and none of them has been recovered. The victory of liberalism over orthodoxy was overwhelming. And it appears that some evangelical or orthodox seminaries, colleges, and churches may well be irretrievably lost to orthodoxy in the decades ahead.

Ernest Gordon and *The Leaven of the Sadducees*

Anyone who read *The Battle for the Bible* or who reads this present volume should also read Ernest Gordon's *The Leaven of the Sadducees* published in 1926 (reprinted in paperback by the Church League of America, 422 N. Prospect, Wheaton, Ill. 60187). It traces the rise and fall of Christian institutions including colleges and seminaries, and marks the fall of Congregationalism into Unitarianism, all of which is being repeated before our eyes today. The record of yesteryear should be a warning signal to every evangelical who wishes to preserve and to perpetuate evangelical orthodoxy. The following case studies may help us see what happened in the past and to note how the past is being repeated in our generation.

Mt. Holyoke

Mary Lyon "made so much of Bible teaching" at Derry Academy "that the trustees objected."

> So she went with her green velvet collecting bag among the farmers of Western Massachusetts until she secured enough to found an institution (Mt. Holyoke) which should be "perpetually Christian." The output of useful women which followed through the century had no parallel. They were trained by her in the Scriptures and in Butler's *Analogy* and were followed to distant lands by her prayers, the tenderness of which was a tradition of the school.
>
> Prof. Laura H. Wild, who now teaches the Bible at Mt. Holyoke, has little of the old spirit in spite of her past as a Congregational preacher. Her views are "dynamic, not static." President Wooley introduces her to the public as "a re-interpreter of evangelical Christianity for the young men and women of the student classes who cannot be held to an outworn phraseology. . . ."
>
> "Shall we," she asks, "be followers of the interpretations of modern scholars or of interpretations evolved in the less enlightened days of Christianity?"[7]

Down went Mt. Holyoke!

Wellesley

Wellesley was founded by Harvard-trained lawyer Henry F. Durant who "was converted to Christ and became a lay preacher."

> A visit with D. L. Moody to Mt. Holyoke interested him in women's education. He presented that college with a library building and in 1871 laid the cornerstone of the new college at Wellesley. In that cornerstone they placed a Bible in which was written,
>
> "This building is humbly dedicated to our Heavenly Father with the hope and prayer that He may always be first in everything in this institution; that His Word may be faithfully taught here and

that He will use it as a means of leading precious souls to the Lord Jesus Christ. Except the Lord build the house they labor in vain that build." . . .

Miss Helen Gould founded a professorship in biblical history at Wellesley College. It is now filled by Prof. Eliza H. Kendrick, who . . . appeared at the 1917 convention of the Religious Education Association with a pupil who read a paper on the effect of the two years required Bible study at Wellesley. It describes an unenlightened girl coming to college "into a community where independence of thought is developed."

"She enters a class in biblical history. One by one she sees them go—the facts which to her were the very foundations of her religious life. She can no longer believe in the creation of the world as told in the Old Testament or in the story of Moses and the burning bush. As she goes on into the study of the New Testament higher criticism lays bare to her the fact that the story of Jesus' birth is not authenticated, that the feeding of the five thousand and Christ's walking on the sea cannot be taken literally and that possibly even her belief in the Resurrection is groundless. In fact all the mysterious and supernatural gifts of Jesus which had formed the core of her spiritual life now seem either based on unhistorical facts or disapproved by the workings of natural laws. . . . Her loss of faith in everything divine first stuns her but leaves her, at last, as she styles herself, 'a regretful agnostic.' "[8]

Down went Wellesley!

Smith College

A gift of $375,000 was left in the will of Sophia Smith to establish an "evangelically Christian college" for women at Northampton, Massachusetts. Her will included this statement:

Sensible of what the Christian religion has done for myself and believing that all education should be for the glory of God and the good of man, I direct that the Holy Scriptures be daily and systematically read and studied in said college and that all the discipline shall be pervaded by the spirit of evangelical Christian religion.

The usual dilution occurred. It reached the point where the Rev. Margaret B. Crook was made associate professor in biblical literature. She was a Unitarian woman preacher from England. Step by step Smith went the liberal route.[9]
Smith went down too!

Bryn Mawr

In the inaugural address at Bryn Mawr, President Rhoads spoke of the founding of the college through the instrumentality of Dr. Joseph Wright. This is what he said:

> "As in the case of almost all of our institutions of learning Bryn Mawr was founded in motives of Christian benevolence. Dr. Taylor desired that it should ever maintain and teach an evangelical and primitive Christianity as set forth in the New Testament and the trustees will endeavor to carry out this trust in the spirit in which it was imposed." A letter from an English Friend, Mr. J. Bevan Braithwaite, was also read at these exercises. "We well know," it ran, "that Dr. Taylor had especially at heart in its establishment an education hallowed and ennobled by the wisdom, the truth, and the love of God in Christ Jesus our Lord. . . . It was his prayer that Bryn Mawr should become in the highest and most blessed sense a school of Christ in which the students should learn of Him under the training and gracious discipline of His Holy Spirit the lessons of His truth and love. It was his joy to devote his property to the noble purpose of preparing Christian woman to take her just place of influence in the sin-stricken and self-seeking world. . . . He would have the college ever prove the presidency of the divine Master in a continual illustration of the world which seemed like a keynote of his humble and devoted life. 'God forbid that I should glory save in the Cross of our Lord Jesus Christ.' "[10]

Ernest Gordon made mention of Professor Leuba of his day who was on the faculty at Bryn Mawr. He was an atheist.[11] The college was moving steadily away from its moorings. In our times from 1969 to 1971 Bryn Mawr had Herbert Aptheker as a visiting lecturer on its faculty. He is the leading Marxist theoretician in the United States, a self-pronounced Communist, and father of a daughter who was one of the key leaders during the student rebellion days of the 60s when she was a student at the University of California at Berkeley.

Down went Bryn Mawr.

Andover Seminary

The Andover Seminary story cannot be understood without reference to Harvard College, which was established in 1636 to train men for the gospel ministry. Harvard was eventually subverted from its original purposes. The Unitarian defection in New England was intimately related to Harvard's downfall from historic Congregationalism to Unitarianism and now to secularism.

Ernest Gordon quoted a statement from Lyman Beecher's autobiography which helps to explain what happened at Harvard.

> Old foundations established by the Pilgrim Fathers for the perpetuation and teaching of their views in theology were seized upon and appropriated to the support of opposing views. A fund given for preaching an annual lecture on the Trinity was employed for preaching an annual attack upon it and the Hollis Professorship of Divinity at Cambridge was employed for the furnishing of a class of ministers whose sole distinctive idea was declared warfare with the ideas and intentions of the donor.[12]

The Hollis professorship at Harvard had been funded by money from Thomas Hollis, an English Calvinist Baptist who stipulated that the chair should be occupied by a man of "sound and orthodox principles." Additional funds were given in 1747 with the stipulation that the occupant of the chair should "profess and teach the principles of the Christian religion according to the well known confession of faith drawn up by the synod of the churches on New England."[13]

In 1805 Henry Ware, a known Unitarian, was seated in the Hollis chair at Harvard. From that day to this it has never been occupied by a teacher who was orthodox in the faith. By 1805 Harvard College had deserted its commitment to Christian orthodoxy. Once Harvard was on the way to Unitarianism the question was, "Where would men committed to orthodoxy secure their training for the ministry?" It turned out to be Andover Seminary which came into being in a strange way. Andover and Exeter academies had been founded by the Phillipses, and as far back as 1778 certain provisions were made for the theological education of their graduates at Andover Academy. Knowing that Harvard would block the granting of a charter for a new institution, Andover Seminary operated under the charter provisions of Andover Academy.[14] A statement of faith was constructed and every professor was obliged to subscribe to it publicly every five years; every conceivable precaution was employed to make certain that Andover would remain orthodox forever. Ernest Gordon noted that

> The seminary was still further strengthened by the institution of a
> Board of Visitors, similar to the Board of Overseers of Harvard
> and Bowdoin. It was to be a permanent institution, "to continue
> as the sun and moon forever." Election of professors required
> their ratification. They were supreme over the trustees, the repre-
> sentatives of the founders in the oversight of the seminary, in the
> protection of its funds, in the removal of professors for heterodoxy
> or neglect of duty. By the ninth article of the additional statute it
> was provided that "the Visitors should take the same pledge as
> the professors and should repeat it every five years."[15]

Before the twentieth century dawned Andover was on the
skids. Five professors "who broke down the old order were
charged with affirming that 'the Bible is not the only perfect
rule of faith and practice but is fallible and untrustworthy even
in some of its religious teachings: that Christ in the day of his
humiliation was merely a finite being limited in his attributes,
capacities and attainments' and fourteen other departures
from the creed." It is important to note that the five professors
were saying they did not believe in an infallible Bible in either
matters of faith and practice or other matters as well. It was the
same old story of subversion of confidence in the Bible as the
infallible Word of God.

The Board of Overseers tried to remedy the situation when it
decided that "E. C. Smith maintains and inculcates beliefs
inconsistent with and repugnant to the creed of said institution and contrary to the true intent of the founders and ad-
judged and decreed that he be removed from the office of
Brown Professor of Ecclesiastical History." The case went to
court and the decision was in favor of Professor Smith and
against the Board of Overseers.[16] From that point on the fate of
Andover was sealed and the institution was on the slide moving downward. There was one small ray of light in the progress of events. Two decades before the issue was sealed irretrievably Professor J. Henry Thayer resigned his chair at Andover and went to Harvard. He wrote about his decision in the
Congregationalist of June 14, 1882. He said:

> The statutes of the seminary require a rigid assent to the letter of
> the Creed on the part of all persons subscribing to it; the boards of
> administration, however, accept a general and approximate belief

to the doctrines of the Creed as the sufficient prerequisite to subscription. But the honesty of such general and approximate subscription has of late been publicly and extensively called into question; yet the trustees are disinclined publicly to acknowledge and vindicate it. To remain in my office, therefore, would be to remain constantly exposed to the charge or the suspicion of dishonesty without the prospect of open vindication and with the certainty that whatever I might say in my own defence would be largely neutralized. . . .

"But it is asked, 'Why do you not remain at your post and labor there to bring about a change?'

"I reply, 'Because my obligation to be and be known an honest man outweighs all other obligations to trustees or seminary. . . .'

"Yours truly,

J. Henry Thayer."[17]

In 1922 Andover Seminary was merged into the Harvard Divinity School. It brought with it property valued at more than a million dollars and a library of more than 70,000 volumes compared to Harvard Divinity School's 46,000 volumes. No Unitarian voice was raised to protest the theft of this institution. The deceitful charade was over. Andover was no more. Historic orthodoxy once more suffered a disastrous defeat at the hands of liberals.

Union Theological Seminary of New York

The grim story of Union of New York does not need repeating. It was covered in *The Battle for the Bible* in Chapter 10 titled "How the Infection Spreads." At one time, Union like Harvard and Andover, was orthodox. It was infiltrated by liberals and within a short time their efforts resulted in the subversion of the institution. In later years Union was to become the leading citadel of neoorthodoxy. It had on its faculty Paul Tillich whose personal life was a scandal and whose theology occasioned a remark by Nels Ferré that Paul Tillich was not a Christian and neither could anyone be a Christian who followed the theology of Paul Tillich.

Richard Quebedeaux

Is it too much to claim that the scenario set forth by Ernest Gordon relative to the loss of evangelical institutions to liberalism is still operative today? Or was what he said descriptive of a past age which represents a nonrepeatable experience? Here the remarks of Richard Quebedeaux, who has been a keen observer and analyst of the contemporary scene, may be of help. Apart from two of his books *The Young Evangelicals* and *The Worldly Evangelicals* his article in *Christianity and Crisis* sketches the current scene with remarkable accuracy even though he himself—at least at that time—did not profess to be a believer in the viewpoint of historical orthodoxy. This is what he wrote:

> Most people outside the evangelical community itself, however, are totally unaware of the profound changes that have occurred within evangelicalism during the last several years—in the movement's understanding of the inspiration and authority of Scripture, in its social concerns, cultural attitudes and ecumenical posture, and in the nature of its emerging leadership. . . .
>
> To be sure, the vanguard of what I have termed a "revolution in orthodoxy" is centered on a small, highly literate, zealous elite, many of whose spokespersons hammered out the Chicago Declaration of Evangelical Social Concern in 1973. . . .
>
> To begin, evangelical theologians have begun looking at the Bible with a scrutiny reflecting their widespread acceptance of the principles of historical and literary criticism (redaction criticism being the current favorite). Traditionally the "inerrancy" (or "infallibility") of Scripture, not only in its teaching concerning faith and conduct but also in its assertions about history and the cosmos (including biology and geology), has functioned—explicitly or implicitly—as the watershed of 20th-century American evangelicalism. . . .
>
> . . . the total inerrancy position has become increasingly difficult to maintain. . . . This position—affirming that Scripture is inerrant or infallible in its teaching on matters of faith and conduct but not necessarily in all of its assertions concerning history and the cosmos—is gradually becoming ascendant among the most highly respected evangelical theologians. They feel strongly that the doctrine of limited inerrancy both preserves the Bible's authority for the church and makes feasible the use of the historical-critical method in studying its contents. . . .
>
> A bombshell hit the evangelical community when Paul K. Jewett of Fuller Seminary published his positive theological treatment of feminism, *Man as Male and Female* (Eerdmans, 1975). . . . He challenges the limited inerrancy position (indirectly, at least) by stating that St. Paul, in his *teaching* about the subordination of women to men, was influenced both by his male-dominated culture and by rabbinic traditions representing a

time-bound authority not applicable to later Christians. In other words, St. Paul was wrong. Understandably, Jewett's hermeneutic has rocked the conservative evangelical establishment. . . .

. . . If Jewett can render as not binding the Pauline injunctions regarding the subordination of women to men—because of cultural conditioning—it is only one step away to do the same thing with St. Paul's admonitions against premarital intercourse and homosexual practice (in selected situations, at least). If this happens, we may discern the emergence of a "new morality" for evangelicals in which love becomes the only absolute ethical norm. . . .

In a word, all these new trends among the evangelicals are highly significant. They indicate that evangelical theology is becoming more centrist, more open to biblical criticism and more accepting of science and broad cultural analysis. One might even suggest that the new generation of evangelicals is closer to Bonhoeffer, Barth and Brunner than to Hodge and Warfield on the inspiration and authority of Scripture. Their evangelism looks more like a call to social justice and discipleship than the traditional call to conversion. One can even discern among them a subtle shift in the direction of belief in universal salvation. And some of the younger evangelicals, anyway, may be just about ready to celebrate the secular city. (There is scant reference to heaven or hell in their publications.) Only time will tell to what degree all of this will eventually become pervasive. But one thing is certain. Evangelicalism will never be the same.[18]

Dr. Quebedeaux's analysis happens to be quite accurate. What happened two generations or more ago can and is happening again in our generation. Evangelicals, or at least some who call themselves by that name, are moving away from their tradition and are headed in the direction of neoorthodoxy and liberalism almost irresistibly.

Hermeneutics and Methodology—Then and Now

Anyone who wishes to contrast the methodology and the hermeneutics of liberalism during the 1920s with that which prevails today will discover a remarkable similarity. Several things stand out sharply when this is done. First and foremost is the fact that the mainline denominations have a sizable group of unitarians in their theological institutions. This should come as no surprise. What happened at Harvard in the nineteenth century is catching up with the mainline denominations. The reason for this is simple. In both periods the Word of God yielded to the word of men who sit in judgment on Scripture, and who start with the presupposition that the Bible is not to be trusted in all its parts. However long it takes for the virus to work its way through an institution or a denomination it will do so, although at differing rates depending on secondary factors.

Moreover, the virus mentioned here is also at work in evangelical seminaries that use hermeneutical principles which, when not followed through to their logical conclusions, make it possible for faculty members to say they believe the Bible to be free from error. In this way they can have their cake and eat it too. They employ the same hermeneutics as liberals, and they do almost as much damage to the faith of their students as do the liberals. It is hidden, more sophisticated, and externally gives the appearance of solid orthodoxy. Of one thing we can be sure. Sooner or later many of their students will follow through on their principles, arrive at conclusions their mentors would not accept, and become theological shipwrecks as a consequence.

Mary Anne Pikrone, religion editor of *The Richmond News Leader*, got interested in surveying the religious scene after the debacle involving Robert Alley surfaced in Richmond, Virginia. The reader will recognize him as the Louisville graduate, teaching at the University of Richmond, ostensibly a Baptist-related institution, who publicly stated that Jesus is not God. Mary Pikrone interviewed "53 theologians, New Testament scholars, instructors and deans from eighteen divinity schools, seminaries, theological schools and colleges, ranging from liberal to conservative."[19] Anything and everything she said could have been found in the theological institutions in the 1920s. And they are to be found in the theological institutions today.

Burton and Goodspeed in their volume *A Guide to the Study* said: "The facts of history have shown that Paul was in error in his teaching about the coming of the Lord. . . . It is a palpable infidelity to truth to affirm that this teaching was true."[20] Of course liberals say the same sort of thing today.

H. W. Willett in *The Moral Leaders of Israel* wrote more than half a century ago: "The proofs of the origin of the Deuteronomic law in the days shortly preceding the great reformation of Josiah are so convincing that biblical scholarship increasingly holds the view."[21] And so do current professors at the Southern Baptist Seminary in Louisville as well as in other evangelical institutions.

Dr. Strickland in his book *Foundation of Christian Belief* said ages ago: "Just what the inscription on the cross over the head of Jesus really was we shall never know though all four evangelists state what it was. But each states it differently."[22] This has its parallel in redaction criticism today which does not regard the Gospels as straight history. Therefore they must get behind the Bible to find out what it really means. And numbers of evangelical New Testament scholars embrace redaction criticism concepts even while they try to hang on to biblical inerrancy. Somehow they fail to see that if they follow that road it will inevitably lead them straight into the liberal campgrounds.

Mary Pikrone wrote as follows:

> Jesus probably:
> *Did not make all those statements with the quotes around them in the New Testament.
> *Did not say he is God or call himself "Son of God" or "Messiah."
> *Did not predict his death and resurrection.
> *Did not perform all of those miracles.
> *Did not rise bodily—that is, his crucified corpse was not resuscitated—from the dead.
> This is the consensus among mainline Protestant and Roman Catholic New Testament scholars today, based on their modern, historical, critical interpretation of the Bible.[23]

Miss Pikrone stated that theologians from three conservative seminaries "said that some of Jesus' sayings were edited. But that does not change the basic meaning of truthfulness of what he said, they argued. They also said they use biblical criticism. However, they do not come to the same conclusions as mainline scholars, because they have different presuppositions, they said." It is of particular interest that Miss Pikrone endeavored to interview faculty members from the Southeastern Baptist Theological Seminary in Wake Forest, North Carolina. They "refused a *News Leader* request to be interviewed about what they are teaching about Jesus and his divinity." Rodney V. Byard, assistant to the president, said: "Such an interview could jeopardize our relationship with one of our very important feeder schools, the University of Richmond. Chronologically we feel we are too close to the recent theological controversy there. . . ." Byard also wrote: "We also feel that it would be extremely difficult to convey to our general public content matter of such highly technical nature. Academic pursuit of an understanding of Jesus could be easily misunderstood by persons without extensive theological background. . . ." Over the telephone he said: "It's a very technical thing and you know as well as I do that, particularly in the Southern Baptist Convention right now, there are a lot of people who are ready to jump down your throat one way or the other." Mr. Byard also said the decision not to interview the faculty members was approved by the president and was discussed at a faculty meeting.[24]

Anyone can see that the statements of Mr. Byard of Southeastern are ambiguous at best and damning at worse. One hardly needs extensive theological education to say whether or not Jesus is God. The phrase "academic pursuit of an understanding of Jesus" is nothing more than academic jargon indicating that either the users have doubts about what the church has believed through the ages, or they have reached the same conclusions as the liberals that Jesus "did not say he is God or call himself 'Son of God' or 'Messiah'." The Southeastern story needs to be told, but the project requires adequate study so that the conclusions can be documented beyond refutation.

There can be no doubt that the unitarianism of the New England stripe of the nineteenth century is now solidly entrenched in the mainline denominational seminaries and it has begun to infect evangelical schools as well. This supports the claim that today's battle which is being fought on every front is in substance the same battle fought during the Fundamentalist-Liberal struggle decades ago. Miss Pikrone quoted Dr. John Carter Diamond, Jr., Baptist clergyman and associate professor of theology and philosophy at the Interdenominational Theological Center in Atlanta, largest black seminary in the country. "Right, I don't make any bones about saying that Jesus is only man and not God," he said. "What God's will for Jesus was, was not to make him a God, but to make him the highest form of humanity known."[25] Miss Pikrone said that of the fifty-three scholars who were interviewed "only a handful denied the divinity of Jesus in language which would be clear to the layman. But many more hedged. Those at evangelical, conservative Roman Catholic, Lutheran and Southern Baptist institutions tended to be strongest in upholding the traditional belief. However, in the remaining mainline Protestant institutions, other theologians seemed to water down the traditional definition of Jesus' divinity in subtle ways. They showed discomfort at using traditional forms like 'divinity,' 'Nature,' 'Second Person of the Trinity,' and 'God' when talking about him. They defined him in ways which fell short of someone who is both God and man."[26]

Two things are clear from this discussion. The first is that liberals and equivocating evangelicals are using a hermeneutic which is destructive so far as accepting Scripture in any straightforward sense is concerned. Some are afraid of stating clearly and simply what their disbeliefs are. Some are clear enough in their denial of basic biblical truths. The second observation has to do with methodology. Many who deny important doctrines in their hearts use deceptive approaches in their teaching. Dr. J. Peter Schineller wrote that "The bare expressions 'Jesus is God' or 'Jesus is God and man' are very difficult to understand, and are not suitable or usable for simple tests of one's orthodoxy." "While popular lay belief interprets the Resurrection," said Miss Pikrone, "to mean that Jesus' corpse rose bodily from the dead, New Testament scholars say no, it wasn't that kind of 'resuscitation'."[27] In most cases scholars will say they believe in the Resurrection but in reality they mean something quite different from what the man in the pew thinks on the subject. The methodology is to lead the poor benighted laymen into the sacred conclusions of academia gradually. And it is the same methodology practiced by professors at Mt. Holyoke, Smith, Wellesley, Harvard, Andover, and Union decades ago.

The Present Situation

Evangelicalism, as has been shown in preceding chapters, has been infiltrated and deeply penetrated by those whose views are marginally evangelical. Their starting point is the denial of biblical trustworthiness in matters of fact, history, and science and the cosmos plus the use of the historical-critical method either deliberately or without an awareness of what its presuppositions are, how they undercut historic orthodoxy, or where they lead eventually. The extent and the depth of this antievangelical penetration is now well known and has been documented. Its existence and its successful track record can no longer be hidden or obscured. Whoever wishes to discover the facts for himself will find all the evidences he needs. The outward available evidence, however, is only part of the sad story. There are those who quietly and without publicizing their views in print are undermining and sapping the groups to which they are attached.

The question which must be faced is not whether there is a problem, but what to do about it. Several possibilities come to mind. The first one is to do nothing. This decision can be reached by several routes. To do nothing is consonant with complacent human nature. People like this convince themselves there is no problem or that it is of no great consequence. Or they hate a fight and do not wish to get involved. They profess a distaste for divisiveness while claiming to be proponents of peace. Some of them believe that the people working to change evangelicalism are the nicest persons with good intentions who would hardly want to destroy the foundations. I suspect that a large number of evangelicals prefer to sit on the sidelines and do nothing. But by doing nothing they help to guarantee the decline and downfall of orthodoxy in the groups to which they belong.

Second, there are those who for one reason or another are being used by those who are tearing away at the vitals of the old-time evangelical faith. Some are minorities on boards and agencies; they raise their objections when they vote but never command a majority. And in many instances they never will. Their presence on these boards and agencies makes it difficult for them to speak publicly about what they know is going on behind the scenes. To do so would give the appearance of treason even though truth may be on their side. Some of them hope to have a deterrent influence in the progression of the developing cancer. Some also hope there will be a reversal of the situation. Generally the influence of such people is neutralized, and their presence is an excellent political device for assuring the evangelical public that things are the opposite of what they really are.

Third, there are those who perceive the true nature of the situation and work to do something to correct it. They are willing to take a stand, face the consequences, and make unpopular decisions which will not endear them to many people. In the case of the Missouri Synod it meant the removal of John Tietjen from the presidency of Concordia Theological Seminary of St. Louis. It meant the departure of most of the faculty of the institution, for the cancer had developed and advanced to a dangerous stage. Action like this is costly, but the alternative is even more costly.

Multiplied millions of dollars given by orthodox believers to perpetuate orthodoxy have been diverted. Scores of institutions have been subverted and lost to the evangelical segment of the churches which brought them into being and nurtured them. Once they were lost it became necessary to start new colleges and seminaries. These institutions have come of age. Evangelicals have gained the attention of the media. And why not? Nonevangelicals are doing nothing significant in evangelism, church planting, church growth, or missionary outreach. Their major contribution has been and is negative. Whatever may have been the weaknesses of fundamentalism it stood for something. And so has evangelicalism. Liberalism, which cannot be understood apart from the historical-critical method, is known for what it is against. This needs to be understood, for orthodox believers are the truly positive proponents of the Christian faith; liberals are the opponents of that faith.

In the heyday of liberalism Harry Emerson Fosdick exemplified the negative mind set of liberalism. He rejected the virgin birth of the Lord Jesus, denied miracles, the blood atonement, the bodily resurrection, and a host of other Bible teachings. His entire ministry was based on denials of what the Bible teaches. The same thing is true of some men today. William Barclay, for example, in his autobiography denied Christ's deity, His virgin birth, His vicarious atonement, and the doctrine of eternal punishment, among other things. The British scholars who authored the book *The Myth of God Incar-*

nate (see *Christianity Today*, March 10, 1978) had for their major purpose the denial of the deity of Jesus Christ. They said that Jesus should only be admired, not worshipped. Against the affirmation of believers through the ages these scholars are engaged in denial, not in affirmation. They are known for what they do not believe rather than for what they do believe. James Barr in *Fundamentalism*, as shown by Carl Henry's three-part review of the Book in *Christianity Today*, denies many of the basic doctrines of the Christian faith. His is a proclamation of negation. Process theology denies God is the same yesterday, today, and forever. Redaction criticism denies that we have the actual words and deeds of Jesus truly reported in the Gospels.

Evangelicals such as Professor Berkouwer doubt the existence of hell, and do not believe Adam and Eve were our first ancestors. This is negative. Harry Boer doesn't believe the New Testament can be relied on for factual data. Paul Jewett denies what Paul taught about female subordination in the marital bond. Evangelical college professors deny the Bible teaching with respect to evolution. A number of evangelicals now deny that the Bible is trustworthy in all its parts. And thus they deny the teaching of Jesus and His lordship at the same time. Frank Stagg of Louisville denies the orthodox doctrine of the Trinity and the vicarious atonement. Dale Moody of the same institution denies the historicity of the first part of the Book of Genesis, including a literal snake and the Mosaic authorship of the Pentateuch as well as other points already mentioned.

The battle being fought in this generation on a hundred fronts turns on one issue: Do we or do we not believe the Bible in its entirety? It is as simple as that. It is the question Satan raised in Eden when he asked "Hath God said?" The true evangelical affirms that what Scripture says God says. The new evangelical is negative. He denies this proposition. He does not believe that what Scripture says God says. Those who limit truthfulness to matters of faith and practice fall into another negation. They deny that the Bible tells the truth in matters of fact, history, science, and the cosmos. If they affirm at the same time that what Scripture says God says, or that all of the Bible is the Word of God, they are saying that God did not tell us the truth in everything. They are denying the truthfulness of God which is a negation. They deny what true believers have always affirmed: God is truth. And if God lies, He is not truth.

There is still deeper negation intrinsic to the position of those who say the Bible cannot be trusted in all its parts. Such people deny that the Bible is the sole judge of all of men's opinions. In so doing they substitute that which becomes more authoritative than Scripture. One of these authorities is the historical-critical method which commences with its own negation—namely that Scripture and the Word of God are not synonymous.

Bernard Ramm is an example of this attitude when he does not accept Joshua's long day. He argues that the cosmic consequences of a long day are too mind-boggling for him to swallow. Therefore he denies the factuality of the biblical account. Thus the omnipotent God who created the cosmos no longer controls His creation. He is subject to it. Dr. Ramm lets science stand over Scripture and God. So the Bible is not normative. But at least he is willing to allow that God is great enough to create a fish which could house Jonah for three days and nights. James Barr in his antisupernaturalism does not even allow this as we have seen.

Stephen Davis sits in judgment both on Scripture and on God. He will not let the Bible sit in judgment on his own opinions. He says God cannot order the slayings of innocent women and children. Therefore He could not have commanded the Israelites to slay the Canaanite soldiers, woman, and children. Dr. Davis substitutes his own authority above the Word of God written. He signally fails to perceive that God commanded the extinction of these "innocent women and children" because they were not innocent. But Dr. Davis has ruled that they were innocent. So the Word of God does not tell us the truth at this point.

Scenario for the Future

I do not think the scenario for the immediate future is too bright. If the children of Israel could and did turn away from God in unbelief again and again, there is no reason to believe that those who now claim His name cannot or will not do the

same thing. The pages of church history are replete with instances of departure from orthodoxy.

The Reformation out of which Protestantism emerged is the
classic illustration of what I mean. According to the Reformers,
the Roman Catholic Church had ceased to be a true church.
The truths which it confessed were mingled with salvatory
errors which constituted denials of what the Bible affirmed.
The Roman Church denied that men are justified by faith alone
as Martin Luther perceived. And the Church did not change its
perception at this point. John Calvin correctly stated that the
sacrifice of the mass was blasphemous. According to Catholic
teaching, when the priest elevated the host, the bread and the
wine became the real body and blood of Jesus even though in
outward appearance it did not change. Thus, on a thousand
altars every day Jesus Christ was crucified afresh. John Calvin
argued from Scripture that Jesus died *once* for all as taught in
Hebrews. To sacrifice Christ a second time derogated from the
sufficiency and completeness of His first offering on Calvary's
cross.

A second illustration is the fundamentalist-liberal controversy earlier in this century. It was a struggle between two
different gospels. However unsatisfactory the theology of
Roman Catholicism may have been in the days of the Reformation, the theology of liberalism was infinitely worse. Indeed
the fundamentalists had far more in common theologically
with the Roman Catholic Church than they had with
liberalism. The fundamentalist-liberal struggle produced two
distinct but antithetical groups within the external or visible
church. And now history is repeating itself.

The great American denominations, whatever their super-
ficial differences in secondary matters, were theologically orthodox in their beginnings. They were overtaken from within
and emerged from the conflict as inclusivist churches compris-
ing people who were evangelical and those who were not.
Today the evangelical wing of these churches has been infected by the same virus which led to the fundamentalist-
liberal controversy. This infection is at work in a number of
places and in a number of ways.

The two great denominations which came through the
fundamentalist-liberal battle apparently unscathed have now

been infiltrated by the liberal virus. So have the smaller evangelical denominations which have been historically orthodox. So have the separatist groups such as the General Association of Regular Baptist Churches and the conservative Baptist Association of America. How many people realize that David Hubbard, one of the key leaders in the current struggle, was ordained by a Conservative Baptist church? Or that Daniel Payton Fuller was also. Or that Paul King Jewett came out of a General Association of Regular Baptist background? Or that George E. Ladd was at one time a member of and a supporter of the Conservative Baptist movement?

Some of the Bible institutes and Bible colleges have been infiltrated with the same virus. Christian colleges, particularly Southern Baptist ones and those of the Missouri Synod, have been under attack and either have capitulated or seem to be in the process of capitulating to nonevangelical penetration. Robert Alley and the University of Richmond is an example. Independent Christian colleges have felt the impact. David Hubbard and Ray Anderson both taught at Westmont College for a season. In some evangelical colleges, professors in the science division openly espouse theistic evolution.

The history of the Christian church teaches us that a little leaven leavens the whole lump. One bad apple will eventually infect other apples in the barrel. Peace without purity is a high price to pay for peace. Unfortunately there can be purity without peace, and this is scandalous. God wants both purity *and* peace for His church.

Apart from a great awakening there is little hope that the mainline denominations will return to the orthodoxy of their founding fathers. Nor will the once-Christian colleges become what they used to be—citadels of biblical faith based on a serious commitment to the Bible as the infallible Word of God. I do not see the mainline theological seminaries reversing their pattern. The observation of Gerald T. Sheppard of Union Seminary in New York is a sound one. He thinks the liberal institutions are moving leftward from neoorthodoxy to a liberalism which in my judgment is dangerously similar to the Unitarianism of Harvard, and of the once orthodox Congregational churches of New England—a unitarianism which will become more and more nontheistic. A good example of this trend can be seen in the strange pilgrimage of Harvey Cox of Harvard who thinks the "whole idea of faith in a belief system is ridiculous," that "in the very vigorous first two to four centuries of Christianity, there wasn't any New Testament. Oddly enough, just as it began to have a canon, its spirit began to decline."[28] He asked: "What is the source of evil or sin, and how does one get beyond it? There are no good answers to this." He spoke of a messianic *era* in which "not everyone would be worshipping Jehovah. Everybody would be worshipping their own god, but there would be concord among all the various peoples."[29] Professor Cox is opposed to capitalism and is interested in Marxism or collectivism. He was asked the question: "How do you reconcile your socialist ideals with teaching at Harvard, in view of Harvard's endowment with strongly capitalist investments in South Africa and so forth?" "I suppose," said Harvey Cox, "if you tried to live a completely uncontradictory socialist or even Christian life, maybe Thoreau's answer was the only one. I have been opposed to this aspect of Harvard ever since I've been here (thirteen years). One of the things that I almost got bounced for a few years ago was opposition to the construction of Rockefeller Hall at the Divinity School."[30] Harvey Cox's interview was conducted in his office and in his home, a home and study which are "filled with a mixture of Eastern and Western religious images—a cross next to a mandala, a picture of Buddha facing a Jewish star—yet all of these symbols seem unified in his presence with a simple spirit of brotherly love."[31] The interview was titled "Lost in Wonderland." And how true it is!

Who can foresee a reversal of the situation at Fuller Theological Seminary? One can predict that its powerful influence will be felt even among those who hold to inerrancy. The gifted and charismatic David Hubbard has set in motion forces which will move his institution to the left farther and faster than he himself ever intended or ever supposed was possible. His second-generation students will move farther to the left from where he is now, even as he, Daniel Fuller, Frederick Bush, and Ray Anderson, Fuller graduates, have moved to the left of the theological underpinning representative of the seminary when it was brought into being in 1947.

It is difficult to foresee any far-reaching and extensive reversal in the stance of the colleges connected with the Southern Baptist Convention. They appear to be too deeply infected with the virus which killed off the mainline denominational colleges long ago.

The Lutheran Church-Missouri Synod may be able to save some of its collegiate institutions (some are in good shape) but it is doubtful that schools like Valparaiso will be among them.

On the other hand God is at work and significant movements are gathering momentum. Jerry Falwell is building a college and seminary. He envisions a campus large enough to serve 50,000 students. Pat Robertson of the 700 Club is projecting a school of communications and has already begun a worldwide satellite communications network which has tremendous potential.

One of the most encouraging signs of evangelical vitality and outreach can be seen in theological seminary education. Most of the theologically orthodox seminaries have come into existence in recent decades. They are crowded with students, some are accredited by regional agencies or the Association of Theological Schools, and they are expanding rapidly.

These orthodox schools are formally committed for an inerrant Scripture. It would not be true to say they have no theological problems with respect to their faculty members. Some indeed do. But not all. It will probably always be true that orthodox schools will be infiltrated by those who either unconsciously or consciously are not in tune with the theological foundations of the schools to which they are attached. What is of primary importance is their commitment to orthodoxy including an inerrant Scripture. What is equally important is how they handle problems when they do arise. A failure to deal with any basic theological problem will lead to the unhappy departure from orthodoxy as has been demonstrated over the years.

Some of the institutions which are formally committed to an inerrant Scripture are: Asbury Theological Seminary, the Alliance School of Theology and Missions, the Assemblies of God Graduate School, the Baptist Bible School of Theology, Bethel Theological Seminary, Biblical Theological Seminary, Bob Jones, Capital Bible Seminary, Cincinnati Christian

Seminary, Columbia Graduate School of Bible and Missions, Concordia Theology Seminary of Fort Wayne and St. Louis, the Conservative Baptist Theological Seminary, Covenant Theological Seminary, Dallas Theological Seminary, the Evangelical School of Theology, Faith Evangelical Lutheran Seminary, Faith Theological Seminary, Gordon Conwell Theological Seminary, Grace Theological Seminary, the International Christian Graduate School of Theology, Liberty Baptist Seminary, Luther Rice Theological Seminary, Melodyland School of Theology, Mid-America Baptist Theological Seminary, Multnomah School of the Bible Graduate Division, Northwestern Lutheran Seminary, the Reformed Theological Seminary, Talbot Theological Seminary, Temple Baptist Theological Seminary, Trinity Evangelical Divinity School, Western Conservative Baptist Theological Seminary, Western Evangelical Seminary, Westminster Theological Seminary, and the Wisconsin Lutheran Seminary.

Bill Bright's Campus Crusade for Christ has projected a Christian University graduate school complex with the first unit, a theological seminary, already in existence. The Crusade staff of some six thousand members is evangelizing effectively around the world.

Billy Graham has brought into being the new graduate center at Wheaton College. It promises to be a strategic research, planning, and training center devoted to world evangelization. He is planning a Bible training center in North Carolina for which several thousand acres of land have already been acquired. The intention is to provide Bible training to equip lay people to become soul winners, personal workers, and lay evangelists in connection with their normal business and other pursuits.

The Greater Europe Mission has set up a network of theological educational institutions all over Europe. Hosts of young people are being trained in these schools to preach and teach and to evangelize Europe, which is one of the world's most needy mission fields.

The Interdenominational Foreign Mission Association and the Evangelical Foreign Missions Association together have more than twice as many missionaries as all of the churches connected with the missionary division of the National Council of Churches. While the mainline denominations are retreating in the number of overseas missionaries, these agencies are moving forward steadily, albeit more slowly than two decades ago.

All of the agencies in America and around the world who believe the Bible in its entirety are having to face the increasing secularization of western culture. The Hebrew-Christian tradition formerly acted as a cement which held society together. That tradition has lost its hold. The revolt against authority triggered by the Renaissance and exemplified by an antagonism to the Christian church and the Hebrew-Christian tradition has steadily gained strength among the nations. At this moment in history there is nothing in sight which suggests a serious or a large-scale movement away from human autonomy and back to the authority of God represented in the old Hebrew-Christian tradition. Quite the contrary, the world situation continues to deteriorate, and critics everywhere foresee the developing darkness which could well mark the end of western culture. Does this portend the end of the age and the consummation of history? It may well do so. Thus the eschatological note is the one on which to conclude.

God is sovereign. History moves inexorably toward its climax. The two strands of evil and good wax stronger. There will be apostate churches. But there also will be faithful churches and faithful people awaiting the coming of the Lord Jesus. There will be added to the body of Christ those who are to be saved. In the midst of the moving and the conflicting tides and currents which swirl around men everywhere, the people of God maintain their optimism as well as their confidence that God will be victorious, His kingdom will come, and His will will be done on earth as it is in heaven—even so, come quickly, Lord Jesus!

NOTES

[1] *The Wall Street Journal*, July 13, 1978, "The Wars of the Prophet" by Edmund Fuller.

[2] *Yearbook of American and Canadian Churches*. Constant H. Jacquet, Jr. editor (Nashville: Abingdon), 1969 and 1977 issues.

³*Mission Handbook,* 11th edition, Edward R. Dayton, editor (Monrovia: MARC, 1976), p. 382.

⁴Ibid., pp. 383-386.

⁵David A. Hubbard, *Reflections on Fuller's Theological Position and Role in the Church* (Pasadena: Fuller Seminary), p. 7.

⁶Ibid., p. 8.

⁷Ernest Gordon, *The Leaven of the Sadducees* (Chicago: Moody, 1926), pp. 111, 112.

⁸Ibid., pp. 114-16.

⁹Ibid., pp. 116, 117.

¹⁰Ibid., p. 117-18.

¹¹Ibid., p. 119.

¹²Ibid., p. 138.

¹³Ibid., p. 139.

¹⁴Ibid.

¹⁵Ibid., p. 142.

¹⁶Ibid., p. 144.

¹⁷Ibid., p. 145.

¹⁸Richard Quebedeaux, "The Evangelicals: New Trends and New Tensions," in *Christianity and Crisis,* September 20, 1976, pp. 197-202.

¹⁹*The Richmond News Leader,* July 17, 1978, p. 1.

²⁰Ernest Gordon, p. 217.

²¹Ibid., p. 219.

²²Ibid.

²³*The Richmond News Leader,* July 17, 1978, p. 1.

²⁴Ibid.

²⁵Ibid., July 18, 1978.

²⁶Ibid.

²⁷Ibid., July 20, 1978.

²⁸Sherman Goldman, "Lost in Wonderland: An Interview with Harvey Cox," in *East West,* May 1978, p. 33.

²⁹Ibid., p. 26.

³⁰Ibid., p. 23.

³¹Ibid., p. 22.

Appendices

Appendix 1
A Book Review
Article of
"The Battle For The Bible"

By Raymond F. Surburg

PRESIDENT McCALL'S REPLY TO LINDSELL'S BOOK

One of the chapters in Harold Lindsell's *The Battle for the Bible* concerned itself with the Southern Baptist Convention. Lindsell mentioned a number of individuals, members of influential Southern Baptist schools, who had questioned and rejected Biblical inerrancy and Biblical trustworthiness. Southern Baptist Theological Seminary, located at Louisville, Kentucky had once been a seat of orthodoxy with such men as John R. Sampey and A. T. Robertson staunch adherents of the inerrancy of the Bible and also opponents of radical types of Biblical criticism. At the same seminary today there are faculty members who have taken positions in opposition to Biblical inerrancy and promote the higher-critical method of Biblical interpretation.

President Duke McCall in the June, 1976 *Southern Baptist Seminary* came to the defense of his seminary and its professors and others who came under attack in Lindsell's book. In his critique of *The Battle for the Bible* McCall claims that the editor of *Christianity Today* "arouses too many snakes but kills none of them."

McCall does not come to real grips with the major issues raised by Lindsell but attempts to discredit the latter's book by claiming that Lindsell engages in "a silly game with words: human ideas, logic, or rhetoric do not make the Bible true. The Bible is true because of what the Holy Spirit has done, is doing, and will do with the Scriptures. When a fundamentalist[1] leaves the Holy Spirit out of the process by which

God causes men to know the truth of his revelation, a basic fundamental has been lost."

The issue to which Lindsell has addressed himself is this: how much of the Bible as God's Word is truthful, reliable and free from error? Did the Holy Spirit inspire all or only parts of the books of the Old Testament and the New? Is the Bible errant or inerrant? Lindsell does not define what he means by fundamentalism. Lindsell is accused of "fundamentalism" because of his effort, to quote McCall, "to aid the troops which fight under the flag of inerrancy, infallibility, and verbal inspiration." Because the editor of *Christianity Today* employs these words and insists that these are vocables which accurately and faithfully represent the characteristics of the Bible, he is said to be guilty of "stirring up snakes."

While McCall accuses Lindsell of engaging in a confusing war of words, the former himself does some word playing and confusing the facts. McCall understands perfectly what Lindsell means by the words "inerrancy," "infallibility," and trustworthiness, namely, that the Bible is free from error, a stance he does not accept as once understood even years ago at Southern Baptist Seminary.

However, since the autographs, which are said to be inerrant, are no longer in existence, it therefore according to the President of Southern Baptist Seminary, is inappropriate to speak of inerrancy, inasmuch as our transmitted manuscripts have errors in them. Since we have at length answered this same argument advanced by Pinnock it will not be answered here. (Cf. *Christian News,* November 22, 1976, p. 9) In dealing with the assertion of Lindsell that there are copyists' mistakes which, therefore, logically cannot be attributed to the autographs, McCall engages in the following specious type of argumentation: "But he assures his readers that this kind of error does not keep the Scriptures from being inerrant. Come now, even a master of imaginative rhetoric must know that you cannot say there are mistakes but there are no mistakes, there are errors, but there are no errors, fallible men have been infallible scholars." Lindsell argues that errors and mistakes are attributed to the copied manuscripts, but not to the original books as they left the pens of the Holy writers, whose writings are called "God-spirated," "Spirit-produced" (theopneustos). It appears that this essential difference McCall does not wish to recognize or even state that Lindsell is making it. How unfair therefore, McCall's statement: "That sort of statement only confuses the situation and proposes to divide Christendom in a battle over the meaning of words."

In opposition to President McCall one might cite the evaluation of another president, namely the remark of Dr. Harold J. Ockenga, president of Gordon-Conwell Theological Seminary of New England, who wrote: "There is a pressing need for Dr. Lindsell's book *The Battle for the Bible* in the burgeoning evangelical branch of Protestantism. If evangelicalism bids to take over the historic mainline leadership of nineteenth-century Protestantism, as Dr. Marty suggests, this question of biblical inerrancy must be settled. It is a time for an evangelical historian to set forth the problem . . . Dr. Lindsell has done the church, and especially the evangelical cause a great service in writing this book."[47]

McCall seems to imply that the meaning of a Biblical text may change from time to time. He confuses the nature of the Bible as the Word of God and the fact that the Holy Spirit uses the Word to convict people of sin, righteousness and judgment. Does this conviction occur because the Holy Spirit convinces a sinner on the basis of clearly understood words that he needs to repent of his sins, confess them and believe on the Lord Jesus as His Savior or does the Holy Spirit do this apart from the Word? McCall wrote: "The Bible is true because God inspired holy men of old to reveal the truth, and it is the continuing work of the Holy Spirit to guide men into all truth (John 16:13). The Holy Spirit can and does use any translation of the Holy Scriptures, and, beyond the dictionary meaning of words, he makes men perceive the eternal truth." We ask Dr. McCall: Did the Holy Spirit inspire men to write error, mistakes and write down erroneous theological notions? If the advocates of limited inerrancy are correct, then this is precisely what happened. Then men must sit in judgment over what the Holy Spirit has caused holy men to write down! They need to distinguish error from truth. No person will quarrel with McCall that the Holy Spirit can and does convert men through translations, but just what is this sentence supposed to communicate, namely, that the Holy Spirit makes men perceive the eternal truth beyond the dictionary meaning? Surely, false renderings of God's Word in the original cannot be an instrument for doing what the correct God-intended words were designed to accomplish.

This writer wonders what the readers of McCall's article: " 'Battle for the Bible' arouses too many snakes" understand when they read this sentence: "Incidentally, that business about 'words have specific meaning' is a very naïve understanding of the nature of human language. The fact is that words are symbols with varied nuanced meaning." McCall seems to imply that the reader of the Bible cannot be certain as to the exact intended sense of a Biblical author. He claims that Lindsell attempts to state in other words what the quotations of different scholars given in his book really mean. In trying to comprehend what the Bible says and teaches, McCall claims "I prefer the Holy Spirit as a guide into what the Scriptures say rather than Dr. Lindsell or any other human being." McCall seems to imply that the Holy Spirit, the true Author of Holy Writ, used language which is susceptible of different meanings and that the Holy Spirit is needed for a special communication to understand correctly the message of the Bible. If this is true, then the Bible is an unclear book and is not perspicuous. If the message of the Bible, couched in human language, written by men whom the Holy Spirit employed, cannot be comprehended as written, then the whole theological enterprise is in jeopardy of sinking in a quagmire of uncertainty. It has always been the belief of Christian theologians and Christian believers that the Bible was clear and that its message could be understood. McCall's understanding of the purpose of the science of Biblical hermeneutics is extremely faulty.

Appendix 2
The Right Battle
Gleason Archer

In a recent issue of *Action* (Winter, 1976) a spirited discussion appeared by Dr. Fred P. Thompson entitled "The Wrong War," dealing with the issues raised by Dr. Lindsell in his *The Battle for the Bible*. I must say that I appreciated Dr. Thompson's basic desire to avoid any needless cleavage in the ranks of American evangelicals in a day when our forces must be united against liberalism, Marxism, secularism, and all the rest. Nevertheless, I must register my conviction that *The Battle for the Bible* has put its finger upon the most urgent issue facing evangelicals today, and one which must be frankly and honestly faced by Christians everywhere. I believe that Francis Schaeffer was absolutely correct in describing this as "the watershed of the evangelical world," and that Harold Ockenga rightly insists that "this question of biblical inerrancy must be settled."

1. Objective authority demands an infallible Scripture. Because of the universal conviction on the part of all sane men everywhere that there is a difference between right and wrong, between the noble and the base, between justice and tyranny, we are driven to the conclusion that there must be such a thing as accountability before the moral order underlying the universe. But apart from divine revelation, we can never attain certainty as to the meaning and purpose of our existence. The Bible presents itself as that kind of "Thus saith the Lord" revelation. The distinction is clearly drawn in 1 Thessalonians 2:13: "When you received the word of God which you heard from us, you did not receive it as the word of men, but as it is in truth, the word of God." The Bible comes to us through human instrumentality, to be sure, but it presents us with a message that purports to be the word of God—a message incapable of human invention, and altogether repugnant to the wisdom of man, apart from the special enablement of divine grace.

But if this sacred Scripture is to attain any saving purpose, it must come to us as an infallible record of divine revelation. That is to say, it cannot contain any mistakes which would destroy its trustworthiness. It is doubtless true of all other books of religion or philosophy that they contain some truths, along with all their errors. But if the Hebrew-Christian Scriptures likewise contains errors, even in the smallest degree, they would not differ essentially from all the others; like them the Bible would be a mere mixture of truth and error, necessarily subject to human approval and verification before being accepted as authoritative and binding. Only if the human judge possessed in his own person the divine quality of infallibility could he reliably distinguish in each case between truth and error in the Bible.

If there were so much as a single mistake in Scripture, it would inevitably follow that the Bible is capable of mistake, and it would therefore require infallible human verification to certify it as valid. We would then be left to the mercy of mere opinion and conjecture, and we would have no genuine certainty as to the great issues of life and death. Only an infallible Bible can truly accomplish any saving purpose, or present a sure word of God to man.

2. Biblical infallibility is impossible without biblical inerrancy. If then the Bible is to be incapable of error or mistake in its disclosure of the will of God for our salvation, the question arises as to whether we must understand it as incapable of error even in "non-theological" or "peripheral" matters pertaining to mere history or science. Occasionally there are apparent discrepancies which emerge when we compare one scripture with another, and certainly there are records and statements in the Bible which conflict with modern scientific theory and historiography. How convenient it would be if we were at liberty to put all such difficulties out of contention simply by holding to the proposition that the Bible is infallible only in matters of doctrine and theology! It would be very convenient to evade the challenge altogether by demurring that such matters do not affect the theological trustworthiness of the Bible.

Yet notwithstanding the strategic advantages of settling for "infallibility" without inerrancy, this position suffers from at least three serious difficulties.

(a) In the first place, the Scripture itself does not appear to be aware of any such distinction between theological and non-theological truth. Quite clearly Psalm 105, for example, reaffirms the historicity of the 10 plagues upon the land of Egypt as recorded in Exodus; likewise the miraculous parting of the waters of the Red Sea and the sudden destruction of Dathan and Abiram are celebrated as historical occurrences in Psalm 106 and in several other Old Testament passages. These saving acts of God are related as factual episodes in the history of redemption. Christ clearly accepted the historicity of Jonah's experience with the whale (Matt. 12:40), the great flood and Noah's ark (Matt. 24:38-39), and implied the accuracy of the Exodus record of Moses conversing with God at the burning bush (Mark 12:26).

Episodes which are commonly rejected as fabulous or preposterous by modern skeptics (whether scientists or theologians) were certainly accepted as sober fact by the Psalmists, the Prophets, and Christ himself. In fact we may say that virtually all of biblical doctrine comes to us in a matrix of history and science. And if the Bible is not to be trusted as entirely accurate in such matters, it cannot possibly be authoritative in matters of doctrine either.

(b) The second difficulty with the view of infallibility without inerrancy quite obviously proceeds from the first. The New Testament stoutly affirms that Christ was and is God himself, the second person of the blessed Trinity. Now then, if Jesus was mistaken about the historicity of Adam and Eve, or if He believed incorrectly that Jonah was swallowed and preserved in the stomach of the whale, or the Flood carried off the entire human race except for the passengers on the ark, then it follows that God was mistaken. Or if, as some have suggested, Jesus was merely accommodating himself to the views of His own generation, even though He knew them to be historically and scientifically inaccurate, then He was deceptive and unworthy of credence in anything else He affirmed. What is at stake is nothing less than the integrity of God himself—and that is certainly a matter of theology!

(c) The third serious difficulty with affirming infallibility without holding to inerrancy is that it assumes a logical impossibility. That is to say, it suggests that even though Scripture may err in "factual" matters in its various parts, and make mistakes in matters of history or science which serve as the frame work or matrix of its theological teaching, nevertheless the Bible taken as a whole is without error. Thus we are given to understand that a concatenation of errors adds up to sublime, over-arching truth. This view is so seriously beset with self-contradiction that it lacks all power to maintain itself for very long. This is abundantly illustrated again and again in the history of American denominations and seminaries. There is a certain readiness to affirm the trustworthiness of Scripture in all matters of theology which it "teaches." Unhappily this is interpreted to mean that whatever affirmations of fact, whether historical, scientific, or even theological, which for any reason seem implausible or offensive to the theologian himself cannot really be taught by Scripture, even though they are contained in Scripture. Such has been the line of development in all the leading denominational seminaries that have surrendered the position of full inerrancy. Without exception they have shifted to a neo-orthodox or liberal stance towards Scripture, taking full advantage of the unfettered freedom allowed by that interpretation of "infallibility." And, once the concept of infallibility is abandoned, significant undermining takes place in the doctrinal structure as a whole. (This, of course, was one of the chief points made by Lindsell in *The Battle for the Bible,* which abounds in many other illustrations of this same progressive erosion.) This abandonment of the full authority of Scripture leads almost inevitably to the progressive undermining of the entire theological structure of any school or denomination that settles for a sub-scriptural human author. All the Reformers and all of their Roman Catholic opponents as well believed in the entire trustworthiness and inerrancy of Holy Scripture.

The real point at issue is whether we are going to adopt the view of Christ and His apostles concerning the inerrant trustworthiness of Scripture, or whether we are going to settle for some lower estimate of the reliability of the Bible. Every one of the "difficulties" of certain Scripture passages has been well known, carefully studied and thoroughly discussed for several hundreds of years by biblical scholars. Yet reconcile them we must, no matter how offensive this may seem to the hard- shelled rationalist who scoffs at every effort to harmonize the data of Scripture.

Again, to my mind, this doctrine of the objective authority of Holy Scripture is the most crucial issue we have to face in this century, and assumes as great an importance for us today as justification by faith assumed in Luther's time.

Dialogue must continue. The "battle for the Bible" clearly is the right battle.

Appendix 3
The Nature of Scripture

Biblical Authority, edited by Jack Rogers (Word, 1977, 196 pp., $6.95, $4.50pb) is reviewed by Norman L. Geisler, professor of philosophy of religion, Trinity Evangelical Divinity School, Deerfield, Illinois.

Seven scholars here respond to Harold Lindsell's *Battle for the Bible.* In the foreword, Paul Rees claims that what is at issue "is not evangelical commitment but evangelical comprehension." Many who defend the inerrancy of Scripture, he charges, "are hard put to show wherein their positions differ *practically* from the dictation formula they repudiate." With regard to Lindsell's claim of "total inerrancy that extends to the minutiae of chronology or geography or grammar" Rees gives a resounding "No." He feels that the discussion occasioned by Lindsell's book "threatens to create a serious cleavage in the evangelical community."

Jack Rogers of Fuller Seminary rethinks the history of Christianity and concludes that, apart from the unwholesome influence of Aristotelian-scholastic philosophy, which allegedly came into Protestantism via Turretin, there is no support for the classical doctrine of inerrancy. According to Rogers, even the great Christian thinker Augustine believed that "the Holy Spirit had 'permitted' one of the Scripture writers to compose something at variance from what another biblical author had written." And contrary to the claim of a scientifically errorless Bible, Rogers maintains that "for Augustine, Scripture was not a textbook of science." The great Reformer Luther did not accept the inerrancy of Scripture, says Rogers: "for him, Christ alone was without error and was the essential Word of God." It may also come as a surprise to many Calvin scholars to hear that this great Reformer neither believed in the inerrancy of every word of Scripture nor thought "that the Bible's teaching had to be harmonized with science." Not until what Rogers calls "post-Reformation scholasticism," especially Turretin, did the doctrine of inerrancy emerge. At this point some Protestants adopted a thomistic "natural theology" and the belief in "rationally demonstrable external evidence of the Bible's authority." Before this, according to Rogers, the internal testimony of the Spirit was the basis for belief in the authority of Scripture. Rogers agrees that Scripture is "not to be used as a source of information in the sciences." This post-Reformation scholastic doctrine of inerrancy with its concomitant rational and evidential apologetic was, according to Rogers, unfortunately adopted by the old Princeton theologians Hodge and Warfield. According to Rogers, Briggs, who opposed Warfield's belief in inerrancy, "was historically correct in claiming that the *Institutio* of François Turretin has become the textbook at Princeton and that the Westminster Divines were ignored." Rogers cites James Orr, Herman Bavinck, and Abraham Kuyper as men who did not hold to inerrancy. He quotes Bavinck as saying, "Historical, chronological and geographical data are never in themselves the object of the witness of the Holy Spirit."

The sharp edge of Rogers's sword is felt most in his conclusions. Of Lindsell he says, "It is historically irresponsible to claim that for two thousand years Christians have believed that the authority of the Bible entails a modern concept of inerrancy in scientific and historical details." He accuses John Gerstner of being "equally irresponsible" in saying "that the old Princeton theology of Alexander, Hodge, and Warfield is the only legitimate evangelical, or Reformed, theological tradition in America." Rogers chastises Francis Schaeffer for his demand for reasons prior to faith and for "a prior commitment to Aristotelian philosophy." Pleading against the use of the word "inerrancy," Rogers concludes, "We are called, not to argue Scripture's scientific accuracy but to accept its saving message." In the third chapter Clark Pinnock, an alleged believer in inerrancy, makes a passionate plea to avoid the extremes of liberalism, neoreformationalism, and the hyperfundamental "veneration for the divine authority of scripture." He claims it is an "overbelief" to "identify God's Word with the words of the Bible." Pinnock too repudiates the Warfieldian approach to inerrancy. In an apparent change of position, Pinnock no longer holds that inerrancy refers to the autographs. In view of his admission that the copies do have errors, it seems strange that Pinnock wishes to claim that the Bible is still "inerrant." Further, Pinnock claims that inerrancy is not a logical corollary of inspiration because "God uses fallible spokesmen all the time to deliver his word." Likewise, Pinnock repudiates the belief that inerrancy is the necessary foundation for epistemology, calling such a belief an example of the "fortress mentality." Likewise, Lindsell's claim that "biblical inerrancy is the only sure bulwark against apostasy" is rejected as a "gross overstatement." Neither is inerrancy theologically decisive for Pinnock. He claims, "Minute inerrancy may be a central issue for the telephone book but not for psalms, proverbs, apocalyptic, and parables." Pinnock implies that belief in inerrancy of detail is possible only for those, like Warfield, who do not take the difficulties of the Bible seriously. In short "the Warfieldian theory of perfect errorlessness" is not the "evangelical badge" Lindsell claimed, says Pinnock. Another noticeable shift to a more subjective and experiential apologetic emerges in his conclusion that "the moving of the Spirit accomplishes more on behalf of biblical authority than all the arguments of conservative evangelicals ever could." It is questionable whether such a disjunction of God and reason is legitimate.

Berkeley Mickelsen of Bethel Seminary attempts a survey of the Bible's view of its own authority. He argues that one *must* begin inductively with the text of Scripture and not abstractly with any definition of authority. "Doctrinal statements . . . cannot be final." Mickelsen claims that "*the authority* to which we go is still God and his Word, the Bible." This raises a perplexing question as to how one would get to God apart from his Word. Are there other sources of revelation for us today? According to Mickelsen, "the things revealed are found in the words of the law" (this is in apparent contrast to the view reflected in First Corinthians 2:13 that it is words themselves that are revealed by God). He claims that "revelation involves truths about God" (in apparent contrast to the view indicated in John 17:7 that verbal revelation *is* the truth about God). Mickelsen believes that attempts to reconcile some apparent contradictions (which utilize the law of non-contradiction) are a "form of rationalization." He believes that "instead of discussing what the Bible does not do (i.e., 'have any errors') we need to concentrate on the positive note. *The Bible teaches truth.*" One wonders what this will accomplish, for surely if the Bible teaches only truth, then it must be without error and we are right back to an inerrant Scripture—unless Mickelsen means to deny that the Bible teaches *only* truth. If the Bible teaches *some* error, then of course it is not errorless. Other ambiguous statements by Mickelsen are his claim that "biblical authority rises out of a unique series of relationships" and that "authority is felt and perceived in dialogue, by in-depth person-to-person communication." This all sounds very subjective and existential. In surveying the biblical data on authority Mickelsen concludes that "the highest view of authority in the Bible is obedience surrounded by love." The problem as he sees it with those on the other side of "the battle for the Bible" is a "printing press mentality" in which God's authority is identified with the written Word. Rather, when we look "at the contents of the Bible, we sense authority as we perceive *the interaction* of God with his chosen servants. . . . The various linguistic expressions and categories highlight this interaction." To my mind, this view is not perceptibly different from the neo-orthodox assertion that the Bible is not a propositional revelation but a record of the personal revelation of God with men.

Bernard Ramm's response to Lindsell is to attack the premise that his "doctrine of Scripture is the essence of Christianity." This claim is a theological oddity, says Ramm, because: (1) it reduces to a small group those who are true to Christianity; (2) it is contrary to the teaching of the Reformers; (3) God's acts in history preceded their being written; (4) one would have to conclude that some cults are orthodox since they hold this inerrant view of Scripture; (5) the *use* of Scripture is more important than the *theory* of Scripture; and (6) it emerges from a "Bible-only" mentality that makes "the record of revelation more primordial than the original revelation." Even if we overlook some questionable assumptions in Ramm's arguments, they seem to be directed against a straw man. What evangelical—surely not Lindsell—believes that the Bible is the "essence of Christianity"? Many hold the Reformers' view that "justification by faith alone" is the material principle of Christianity and that "the Scriptures alone" is the formal principle. But this is not to say that the Bible is the essence of Christianity. Ramm pleads for a broader view of revelation that includes the Bible as well as tradition, claiming that the "*sola scriptura* of the Reformers did not mean a total rejection of tradition." Ramm implies that some evangelicals use Scripture as the only test for truth in all areas in such a way that they idolize Scripture and make it what Emil Brunner called a "paper pope." However, by the same kind of argument would not Ramm have to conclude that one who uses the logical law of non-contradiction to assess all truth has made logic the essence of his faith? Does Ramm, like many existentialists, wish to give up this law of logic as a *sine qua non* of truth?

Earl Palmer in his chapter attempts to show how the Bible ought to function as an authority over experience, vision, and the like. With few exceptions the chapter seemed to fit better the other side of the "battle." He argues against basing one's faith on a "mystical Christ" apart from the concrete Christ of history. He warns against using visions as a source of our message and holds to the inspiration of the written Word. Palmer then offers a brief series of principles of interpretation to enable one to understand God's authoritative Word and apply it to our lives. One would question what he means when he says the Bible "receives its authority in borrowed fashion from its center, who is Jesus Christ." Does not the Bible *receive* its authority from the Spirit of God who inspired it? Was not Christ's role one of *confirming* this authority to us (e.g., Matt. 5:17) and *conveying* the Father to us (e.g., Luke 24:27, 44)?

In the last chapter David Hubbard, Fuller Seminary's president, offers "a way out" of the current "battle." In essence his solution is to reject the classical Hodge-Warfield view that all parts of Scripture are inspired. Hubbard praises Rogers's view of the history of biblical authority. Like others, Hubbard holds to an experiential test for truth based on "the inner witness of the Spirit as the chief evidence of the Bible's inspiration and authority." He finds it unnecessary "to try to harmonize all biblical statements with each other and with the result of scientific and archeological discovery." Hubbard seems to go much beyond the evidence when he claims that defending literal inerrancy "may lead to a collapse of trust in the gospel itself." Likewise, he wrongly blames the Lindsellian view of inerrancy for leading to neglect of major theological themes and for occasioning allegorical interpretations of Scripture. Hubbard denies that Genesis gives us an "academic account of our beginnings. They are a powerful sermon (almost a song) that celebrates God's power and glory." The Gospel must not be read as we read the newspaper (historically?), he says. Hubbard salutes but refuses to canonize Warfield's view of inerrancy: "we can seek a better approach to leave with our children."

Hubbard's "way out" of the problem is to go back to the Reformation view of the subjective "internal testimony of the spirit" to the "self-authenticating power of the Word." He does not tell us how we will maintain evangelical Christianity against the Mormon view of the self-authenticating witness of God for the Book of Mormon and other such fideistic claims.

Hubbard, Rogers, and Mickelsen have a distaste for evidential and rational apologetics, which they stereotype as "aristotelian," "scholastic," or "thomistic." At times their overreaction to these "systems" seems to lead them dangerously close to denying the very laws of logic common to all "systems," including their own. Hubbard at one point yields to the temptation warned against by his colleague, becomes very *a priori*, and legislates that "*error* theologically must mean that which leads us astray from the will of God or the knowledge of his truth."

Like others, Hubbard admits that the Bible may err on "minute details of chronology, geography, history, or cosmology," but nowhere does he prove there are such errors, nor are we told how to distinguish a minor error in history and science from a major one. Hubbard makes the errancy view even clearer when he says, "Scripture is not a collection of infallible rules. . . .; proverbs used for raising children in an ancient society are not automatically binding on Christian youth today. . . . Psalms may not always be reproduced in the lives of God's people."

Hubbard concludes with a plea for a fresh interpretation of Scripture, which he briefly attempts on some crucial texts. He admits that "Jesus and the Jews shared a high view of the divine character of the Old Testament" as shown in John 10:34-36 and Matthew 5:17, but he stangely concludes that "we seem to get no help from this passage for our basic question: the definition of inerrancy"! The same is true, in his opinion, of Second Timothy 3:16, 17 and Second Peter 1:20, 21. What Hubbard is certain about is that we must maintain an openness to this kind of "biblical scholarship along with fresh exegesis." His exhortation to be "aware today of the dangers of imposing a philosophy on the Scripture" is well spoken but not so well practiced, inasmuch as, in my opinion, at least, he himself has not avoided imposing critical and existential philosophies on his understanding of Scripture.

Overall the book is a helpful contribution to the task of clarifying essential differences on this crucial doctrine. It is a plea for continuing to use the term "evangelical" to include those who believe the Bible does contain "minor" factual errors and a plea not to divide Christians over this issue. The opponents are sure to ask: "Is this a plea for peace at any price—even the price of truth?" Some may agree with the late Edward John Carnell, "It is better to be divided by truth than to be united by error." At any rate, let us continue the discussion; the nature of Scripture is certainly a fundamental Christian doctrine.

Appendix 4
Biblical Authority

edited by Jack Rogers, Word Books, Waco, Texas, 1977

This book would not have been written were it not for Harold Lindsell's book, *The Battle for the Bible*, which dramatically exposed the liberal theology of many so-called Evangelicals concerning Biblical inspiration and inerrancy. Every writer of this symposium appears clearly threatened by Lindsell's expose, although a facade of scholarship and sophistication covers, albeit only superficially, their vulnerability. The discerning reader will readily discover that each of the authors has departed from the classical Protestant Biblical doctrine of inspiration and inerrancy, although he will want to use these venerable terms. Missouri Synod readers will find nothing new in the symposium: the arguments undermining, denying, and obfuscating the doctrine of Biblical inerrancy have all been employed in Missouri circles in the recent past, e.g., but the term "inerrancy" is unclear (Clark Pinnock), that it is a negative term (Berkeley Mickelsen), that we do not have the autographa (Rogers), that the doctrine of inerrancy should not be divisive (Pinnock), that the classical doctrine was inconsistent and self-contradictory (Bernard Ramm), that there has never been "one certain theory" (sic!) of inspiration" (Ramm), that Luther taught an existentialistic view of inerrancy (Rogers), that cults and sects representing persons of mediocre education and mind teach verbal inspiration (Ramm), that theologians with a low view of Scripture have written some good things (Ramm), that orthodox Christians have overreacted to liberal assaults against the Bible (David Hubbard), that the Reformed and Lutheran doctrine of inerrancy is rationalistic (Hubbard), that proponents of verbal inspiration have sometimes done bad exegesis (Hubbard), that the doctrine of inerrancy undermines the sufficiency of Scripture (Hubbard), that inerrancy is a secular concept (Hubbard), that the doctrine of Scripture is infallible rather than Scripture itself (Hubbard), that those who hold to the inerrancy of Scripture are really faulting Scripture by defending it (Hubbard). Hubbard seems to argue that every poor piece of exegesis by a fundamentalist or conservative is due to his belief in Biblical inerrancy. The ridiculous chiliasm and dispensationalist aberrations of some fundamentalists have even been laid at the foot of the doctrine of inerrancy.

The purpose of this symposium, apart from answering Lindsell's blasts, is apparently to alter radically the Protestant understanding of Biblical authority without letting the reader know what is happening.

And so the authors champion the *sola scriptura* principle, and they lay claim to such popular terms among Evangelicals as inspiration, infallibility, yes, and even inerrancy. We all really agree, they tell us, let us just rally around our consensus, Hubbard says. They want us to believe that they have changed nothing, and the differences between those who believe in inerrancy and those who do not are really not very important.

History is repeating itself. What happened at the St. Louis seminary prior to 1974 is happening at Fuller Seminary today. And it is happening elsewhere among those who call themselves Evangelicals. We can only hope and pray that lay people and pastors all over the country will recognize this and do something about it before it is too late.

Biblical Authority, edited by Jack Rogers, is a vindication of Harold Lindsell's book, *The Battle for the Bible.* Lindsell was right on target as he analyzed what is going on in evangelical circles today.

Reviewed by Robert Preus
May 25, 1978

Appendix 5
The Chicago Statement on Biblical Inerrancy

Preface

The authority of Scripture is a key issue for the Christian Church in this and every age. Those who profess faith in Jesus Christ as Lord and Savior are called to show the reality of their discipleship by humbly and faithfully obeying God's written Word. To stray from Scripture in faith or conduct is disloyalty to our Master. Recognition of the total truth and trustworthiness of Holy Scripture is essential to a full grasp and adequate confession of its authority.

The following Statement affirms this inerrancy of Scripture afresh, making clear our understanding of it and warning against its denial. We are persuaded that to deny it is to set aside the witness of Jesus Christ and of the Holy Spirit and to refuse that submission to the claims of God's own Word which marks true Christian faith. We see it as our timely duty to make this affirmation in the face of current lapses from the truth of inerrancy among our fellow Christians and misunderstanding of this doctrine in the world at large.

This Statement consists of three parts: a Summary Statement, Articles of Affirmation and Denial, and an accompanying Exposition.* It

*The Exposition is not printed here but can be obtained by writing us at the Oakland office.

has been prepared in the course of a three-day consultation in Chicago. Those who have signed the Summary Statement and the Articles wish to affirm their own conviction as to the inerrancy of Scripture and to encourage and challenge one another and all Christians to growing appreciation and understanding of this doctrine. We acknowledge the limitations of a document prepared in a brief, intensive conference and do not propose that this Statement be given creedal weight. Yet we rejoice in the deepening of our own convictions through our discussions together, and we pray that the Statement we have signed may be used to the glory of our God toward a new reformation of the Church in its faith, life, and mission.

We offer this Statement in a spirit, not of contention, but of humility and love, which we purpose by God's grace to maintain in any future dialogue arising out of what we have said. We gladly acknowledge that many who deny the innerrancy of Scripture do not display the consequences of this denial in the rest of their belief and behavior, and we are conscious that we who confess this doctrine often deny it in life by failing to bring out thoughts and deeds, our traditions and habits, into true subjection to the divine Word.

We invite response to this statement from any who see reason to amend its affirmations about Scripture by the light of Scripture itself, under whose infallible authority we stand as we speak. We claim no personal infallibility for the witness we bear, and for any help which enables us to strengthen this testimony to God's Word we shall be grateful.

A Short Statement

1. God, who is Himself Truth and speaks truth only, has inspired Holy Scripture in order thereby to reveal Himself to lost mankind through Jesus Christ as Creator and Lord, Redeemer and Judge. Holy Scripture is God's witness to Himself.

2. Holy Scripture, being God's own Word, written by men prepared and superintended by His Spirit, is of infallible divine authority in all matters upon which it touches: it is to be believed, as God's instruction, in all that it affirms; obeyed, as God's command, in all that it requires; embraced, as God's pledge, in all that it promises.

3. The Holy Spirit, Scripture's divine Author, both authenticates it to us by His inward witness and opens our minds to understand its meaning.

4. Being wholly and verbally God-given, Scripture is without error or fault in all its teaching, no less in what it states about God's acts in

creation, about the events of world history, and about its own literary origins under God than in its witness to God's saving grace in individual lives.

5. The authority of Scripture is inescapably impaired if this total divine inerrancy is in any way limited or disregarded, or made relative to a view of truth contrary to the Bible's own; and such lapses bring serious loss to both the individual and the Church.

Articles of Affirmation and Denial

Article I

We affirm that the Holy Scriptures are to be received as the authoritative Word of God.

We deny that the Scriptures receive their authority from the Church, tradition, or any other human source.

Article II

We affirm that the Scriptures are the supreme written norm by which God binds the conscience, and that the authority of the Church is subordinate to that of Scripture.

We deny that Church creeds, councils, or declarations have authority greater than or equal to the authority of the Bible.

Article III

We affirm that the written Word in its entirety is revelation given by God.

We deny that the Bible is merely a witness to revelation, or only becomes revelation in encounter, or depends on the responses of men for its validity.

Article IV

We affirm that God who made mankind in His image has used language as a means of revelation.

We deny that human language is so limited by our creatureliness that it is rendered inadequate as a vehicle for divine revelation. We further deny that the corruption of human culture and language through sin has thwarted God's work of inspiration.

Article V

We affirm that God's revelation in the Holy Scriptures was progessive.

We deny that later revelation, which may fulfill earlier revelation, ever corrects or contradicts it. We further deny that any normative revelation has been given since the completion of the New Testament writings.

Article VI

We affirm that the whole of Scripture and all its parts, down to the very words of the original, were given by divine inspiration.

We deny that the inspiration of Scripture can rightly be affirmed of the whole without the parts, or of some parts but not the whole.

Article VII

We affirm that inspiration was the work in which God by His Spirit, through human writers, gave us His Word. The origin of Scripture is divine. The mode of divine inspiration remains largely a mystery to us.

We deny that inspiration can be reduced to human insight, or to heightened states of consciousness of any kind.

Article VIII

We affirm that God in His Work of inspiration utilized the distinctive personalities and literary styles of the writers whom He had chosen and prepared.

We deny that God, in causing these writers to use the very words that He chose, overrode their personalities.

Article IX

We affirm that inspiration, though not conferring omniscience, guaranteed true and trustworthy utterance on all matters of which the Biblical authors were moved to speak and write.

We deny that the finitude or fallenness of these writers, by necessity or otherwise, introduced distortion or falsehood into God's Word.

Article X

We affirm that inspiration, strictly speaking, applies only to the autographic text of Scripture, which in the providence of God can be ascertained from available manuscripts with great accuracy. We further affirm that copies and translations of Scripture are the Word of God to the extent that they faithfully represent the original.

We deny that any essential element of the Christian faith is affected by the absence of the autographs. We further deny that this absence renders the assertion of Biblical inerrancy invalid or irrelevant.

Article XI

We affirm that Scripture, having been given by divine inspiration, is infallible, so that, far from misleading us, it is true and reliable in all the matters it addresses.

We deny that it is possible for the Bible to be at the same time infallible and errant in its assertions. Infallibility and inerrancy may be distinguished, but not separated.

Article XII

We affirm that Scripture in its entirety is inerrant, being free from all falsehood, fraud, or deceit.

We deny that Biblical infallibility and inerrancy are limited to spiritual, religious, or redemptive themes, exclusive of assertions in the fields of history and science. We further deny that scientific hypotheses about earth history may properly be used to overturn the teaching of Scripture on creation and the flood.

Article XIII

We affirm the propriety of using inerrancy as a theological term with reference to the complete truthfulness of Scripture.

We deny that it is proper to evaluate Scripture according to standards of truth and error that are alien to its usage or purpose. We further deny that inerrancy is negated by Biblical phenomena such as a lack of modern technical precision, irregularities of grammar or spelling, observational descriptions of nature, the reporting of falsehoods, the use of hyperbole and round numbers, the topical arrangement of material, variant selections of material in parallel accounts, and of the use of free citations.

Article XIV

We affirm the unity and internal consistency of Scripture.

We deny that alleged errors and discrepancies that have not yet been resolved vitiate the truth claims of the Bible.

Article XV

We affirm that the doctrine of inerrancy is grounded in the teaching of the Bible about inspiration.

We deny that Jesus' teaching about Scripture may be dismissed by appeals to accommodation or to any natural limitation of His humanity.

Article XVI

We affirm that the doctrine of inerrancy has been integral to the Church's faith throughout its history.

We deny that inerrancy is a doctrine invented by Scholastic Protestantism, or is a reactionary position postulated in response to negative higher criticism.

Article XVII

We affirm that the Holy Spirit bears witness to the Scriptures, assuring believers of the truthfulness of God's written Word.

We deny that this witness of the Holy Spirit operates in isolation from or against Scripture.

Article XVIII

We affirm that the text of Scripture is to be interpreted by grammatico-historical exegesis, taking account of its literary forms and devices, and that Scripture is to interpret Scripture.

We deny the legitimacy of any treatment of the text or quest for sources lying behind it that leads to relativizing, dehistoricizing, or discounting its teaching, or rejecting its claims to authorship.

Article XIX

We affirm that a confession of the full authority, infallibility, and inerrancy of Scripture is vital to a sound understanding of the whole of the Christian faith. We further affirm that such confession should lead to increasing conformity to the image of Christ.

We deny that such confession is necessary for salvation. However, we further deny that inerrancy can be rejected without grave consequences, both to the individual and to the Church.

International Council on Biblical Inerrancy, P. O. Box 13261, Oakland, CA 94661. (All gifts are tax deductible and receipts will be sent.)

Index

Index

375